D1478988

The Summer of '64

ALSO BY WILLIAM A. COOK

The 1919 World Series:
What Really Happened?
(McFarland, 2001)

The Summer of '64

A Pennant Lost

by WILLIAM A. COOK

McFarland & Company, Inc., Publishers
Jefferson, North Carolina, and London

Library of Congress Cataloguing-in-Publication Data

Cook, William A., 1944–
    The summer of '64 : a pennant lost / by William A. Cook.
        p.   cm.
    Includes bibliographical references and index.
    ISBN 0-7864-1216-X (softcover : 50# alkaline paper) ∞
    1. National League of Professional Baseball Clubs—His-
tory—20th century.   2. Nineteen sixty-four, A.D.   I. Title.
    GV875.A3 C66   2002
    796.357'64'097309046   2002002397

British Library cataloguing data are available

Manufactured in the United States of America

Cover photograph: Crosley Field, Cincinnati *(National Baseball Hall of
Fame Library, Cooperstown, N.Y.)*

McFarland & Company, Inc., Publishers
  Box 611, Jefferson, North Carolina 28640
    www.mcfarlandpub.com

In memory of my dearest wife, Sue

Contents

Introduction

Major league baseball in 1964 for the most part was still played the way it had been since the early 1900s. As a matter of fact, in the National League the game was still played in a lot of old ball parks built shortly after the turn of the century, such as Busch Stadium in St. Louis, Connie Mack Stadium in Philadelphia, Crosley Field in Cincinnati, Forbes Field in Pittsburgh, and Wrigley Field in Chicago. At Wrigley Field all games were still played in the sunshine, as the park had no lights.

Interleague play, division play, division playoffs, division championships and World Series games that ended long after midnight were still well in the future.

The players were without free agency and batting gloves too. Most rookies played for contracts of about $12,000 per year and there were only a few players who could command $100,000-a-year contracts. Agents—and player demands for such self-indulgent perks in their contracts as the availability of charter jets and offices at the home park where a staff could handle the marketing of their names—were more remote than the possibility of the Berlin Wall being torn down.

The designated-hitter rule utilized in the American League since 1973 and the rally caps of the 1983 Milwaukee Brewers would have seemed blasphemous to the National League in 1964. The players didn't wear earrings or gold chains, nor sport mustaches or beards. In fact, Major League baseball clubs and their owners closely monitored uniforms for irregularities in unlicensed logos and had strict dress codes for such things as how high the stirrups on the players' socks should be worn.

Old-fashioned baseball was still being played in 1964 and it was a tougher game than that of today. Pitchers regularly threw knockdown pitches and batters stood their ground at the plate without charging the mound very often. In the field, outfielders hustling after fly balls still slammed into unpadded concrete walls.

Most club revenues still came from attendance, and fans still mattered to the owners. In Chicago chewing-gum baron and Cubs owner Philip K. Wrigley withheld 5,000 general admission tickets for sale until the day of the game. The marketing philosophy of Mr. Wrigley was that if a man gets up in the morning and decides that he wants to attend a ball game, then it's his right to get a ticket.

In some ball parks like Cincinnati's Crosley Field you could still get a ticket for a seat in the bleachers for under a buck! In St. Louis at Busch Stadium a reserved ticket cost $2.25 and the cost of a general admission ticket was only $1.50.

However, as the decade of the 1960s progressed, change slowly began to transform the game into that which we would now recognize in the new millennium. The 1960s were the transition years for baseball: the years when the American and National Leagues would expand from the timeless tradition of eight-team leagues. By 1961 there were three teams on the West Coast as a result of franchise shifts in the late 1950s and expansion in the early 1960s. In 1961 the American League would expand to ten teams and in 1962 the National League did likewise.

By 1969 the National League had even become international by expanding into Montreal, Canada. In all, during the 1960s eight teams had been added to the Major Leagues through expansion.

In 1959 Major League Baseball had enacted a standardized stadium rule that mandated that any stadium built after that year must conform to having minimums of 325-foot foul lines from home plate to right and left field. During the 1960s, in nearly every National League city except Chicago, media people, politicians and fans were drawing up plans to build new stadiums. Still other expanding cities such as Atlanta were seeking Major League franchises and were building stadiums to house a team.

Still, in 1964 any fan who had not seen a Major League game in the past 20 years would have felt right at home in any Major League ball park. And the 1964 season just might have been the most remarkable season ever played in the National League.

The 1963 World Series had been little more than a fundamental exhibition in good pitching by the Los Angeles Dodgers' starters Don Drysdale, Sandy Koufax, and Johnny Podres and reliever Ron Perranoski. In the series the Dodgers swept the New York Yankees, four games to none, while limiting the Bronx Bombers to a meager total of four runs and 19 hits.

In the final game of the series at Dodger Stadium on October 6, 1963, fans who tuned into the national telecast on NBC were subjected to a weeping Mel Allen at the microphone, calling the game as Sandy Koufax mowed down his beloved Yankees, 2–1, to wrap up the World Championship.

Then suddenly and without warning, the nation was stunned with the brutal and senseless assassination of its beloved President John F. Kennedy in Dallas, Texas, on November 22, 1963. The grief of the nation led to a dreadful winter of despair. Slowly, however, it passed, and as the nation gradually began to heal the gaping wound in its psyche, an old friend emerged from the winter freeze. In April the 1964 baseball season began, and once again hope was in the air.

Most of the game's experts, and a great many fans alike, felt certain that the Los Angeles Dodgers would repeat their 1963 cake walk to the World Championship. No one really considered the Philadelphia Phillies as much of a threat to win the National League pennant, much less ever to be in a position to blow a 6–½ game lead in late September with ten games to go in the season. However, even fewer people would have gone out on a limb and predicted that the St. Louis Cardinals would even be in contention for the pennant, much less in the thick of the race in late September, after being down by 9–½ games on July 2.

Cincinnati—was it possible they would be in first place going into the last week of the season?

Along the way, during the 1964 season the National League would inaugurate a new home for the hapless Mets in New York at Shea Stadium, and then tear down a legendary ball park, the Polo Grounds.

Major League history would be made in unusual ways in the 1964 season. For example, in late April a Houston Colt pitcher would throw a no-hitter against the Cincinnati Reds and still lose the game.

The shining jewel of Queens, Shea Stadium, would be the site of several historic events in 1964. On the last day of May the longest doubleheader in Major League history would be played at Shea. Then on June 21 the first perfect game to be pitched in the National League since 1880 would happen there. On July 7 the National League would win the All-Star game at Shea Stadium, and so finally, after 31 years, the senior circuit would reach parity in games won with the younger American League.

Although by 1964 it had been 17 years since Jackie Robinson broke Major League baseball's color line in 1947, front offices and clubhouses alike were still unfortunately permeated with sporadic incidents of racism. In one such instance prior to the 1964, season the Cincinnati Reds' front office would even develop a scheme to prevent a young Pete Rose from hanging out with black players on the team. Then in August, a storm of controversy would surround the manager of the San Francisco Giants,

Alvin Dark, for allegedly making racial remarks to the press in regards to the mental capacity of the black players and Latin players on his team.

But by late September, as the Phillies painfully self-destructed, there would suddenly be four teams battling hard for the pennant. In the thick of the race would be the reeling Phillies and the powerful San Francisco Giants, who had gone head-to-head for first place most of the season. And in the middle of the fray were the Cincinnati Reds, attempting to win a pennant for their beloved and courageous cancer-stricken manager Fred Hutchinson, as they posted a nine-game winning streak in late September. And the St. Louis Cardinals, who in June had made one of the best player trades in baseball history with the Chicago Cubs, then proceeded to fight back from, being 11 games behind the league-leading Phillies on August 29 with 39 games remaining, into contention for the pennant in late September.

With three days remaining, there were four teams still in contention for the pennant and a four-way playoff scenario was developed by the National League office. Ultimately the pennant would be decided on the final day of the season, with the Reds, Cardinals and Phillies still in contention.

The year 1964 was probably the National League's greatest pennant race ever. It was as if all 810 games on the schedule seemed to have significant meaning. It was one of those seasons that caused fans to get the baseball scores the first thing in the morning before doing anything else, to see what had happened the night before. The daily suspense of the pennant race was simply mind-boggling.

In the words of *Cincinnati Enquirer* staff writer Bill Ford, in his column prior to the last game of season on October 4: "This, 1964, must be enshrined as 'The Year Nobody Wanted to Win the Pennant.'"

While it all happened nearly four decades ago, as you proceed through the following the pages you will have to ask yourself: why is all of this still so clear after all those years? Was the 1964 season a series of events so special that they are timeless?

I

Spring Training

Spring training is the time for baseball fans when the New Year officially begins. The Major League teams head south to renew themselves for the elusive pennant chase across summer skies into distant autumn winds, and there is something exhilarating to baseball fans after shoveling the winter snows, about turning on the radio and receiving a baseball broadcast from Sarasota, Tampa or Bradenton. With the touch of a dial summer has returned and high hopes prevail, and the ritual of predicting the outcome of the upcoming season suddenly takes center stage at dinner tables and in classrooms, offices, and barrooms alike across America.

In the spring of 1964, 15 Major League and 73 minor league teams called the state of Florida home for spring training. The Cincinnati Reds trained in Tampa, the Kansas City Athletics in Bradenton while Lakeland hosted the Detroit Tigers and Sarasota the Chicago White Sox. The Los Angeles Dodgers were at Vero Beach, Baltimore Orioles in Miami, New York Yankees at Ft. Lauderdale, Milwaukee Braves at West Palm Beach, Minnesota Twins at Orlando, Pittsburgh Pirates at Fort Myers, Washington Senators at Pompano Beach, and the Philadelphia Phillies in Clearwater.

Finally, for the 1964 season the Houston Colts had moved their training facility to Cocoa, Florida. The only teams not training in Florida were the San Francisco Giants, Cleveland Indians, Los Angeles Angels, Boston Red Sox, and Chicago Cubs.

This annual Major League mass exodus to Florida had been taking place since 1911, when a snow storm in Hot Springs, Arkansas the spring training camp of the Pittsburgh Pirates, caused the team to miss three days of practice. Consequently a Pirates fan, a Pittsburgh native living in St. Petersburg, began a campaign to promote Florida as an ideal training location for Major League teams. Subsequently, in the spring of 1914, the St. Louis Browns moved their training camp to St. Petersburg, and soon a flock of Major League teams followed the Browns to the Sunshine State. By 1964 the Florida Development Commission estimated that teams training in the state generated about $30 million in business annually.

In Vero Beach, Bud Holman, a director for the Los Angeles Dodgers and one of the city's leading citizens as well, usually sat next to the Dodger dugout during spring training exhibition games. When Peter O'Malley, the Dodgers' camp supervisor, learned that Holman actually had the wrong seat, he moved the dugout eight feet so that Holman would have his regular seat.

As spring training in 1964 got underway in Florida, as well as Arizona and California, the baseball experts—despite the dominance of the Dodgers in 1963—were predicting a free-for-all in the coming season in the National League race, with six teams potentially competing for the pennant: the Dodgers, Cardinals, Giants, Phillies, Reds and Braves.

Spring training in itself means different things to different persons in the game. To old-timers, it is a time to spin nostalgic tales of diamond heroes of the past. To rookies, it is the time to fulfill their dreams of making a big league roster.

Gene Mauch, manager of the Philadelphia Phillies in 1964, was against having his team take calisthenics in spring training. "I don't believe in calisthenics for baseball players. They may be good for other athletes but ballplayers' muscles must be loose and flexible. Calisthenics tend to tighten muscles and cause knots to form, especially in pitchers' shoulder muscles."[1]

On the other hand, established stars like Dodger pitcher Don Drysdale felt that Major League clubs didn't train long enough. "We've been down [in Florida] only six weeks and that isn't long enough. Strictly speaking for myself, I think pitchers need at least seven weeks in the warm weather to work in shape for the season. If we have another short training season next year, I'm going to come down a week early and work out on my own.

"As for the Dodgers, our power is pitching, not hitting."[2]

Still, on April 4, 1964, in Vero Beach, Florida, the Los Angeles Dodgers pulverized the Cincinnati Reds, 12–2, in a spring training exhibition game. In the fourth inning, 11 Dodgers went to bat as they broke open a scoreless game with a seven-run splurge. Don Drysdale went all the way for the Dodgers, giving up just seven hits to the Reds, although one was a home run by Frank Robinson with Bobby Klaus on base.

With opening day only nine days away and with wins of this magnitude, one would think that everything looked very good for the 1963 World Champions in the coming campaign. However, there was trouble brewing in Tinsel Town.

Sandy Koufax, for one, was not satisfied with his $70,000 contract and was not pitching particularly well in spring training. So far in his spring exhibition game mound appearances, Koufax had posted a 1–4 record, with a 3.10 ERA after 29 innings pitched.

Nonetheless Dodger skipper Walter Alston didn't seem to concerned about the lackluster performance of Koufax in Florida. "Sandy's been concentrating on conditioning," said Alston. "Whenever Koufax wants to put something extra on the ball, he can reach back and get it."[3]

Dodger pitching coach Joe Becker elaborated further on the status of Koufax. "Koufax has been hit hard a few times [in Florida], but he's like the Cardinals' Ray Sadecki and a lot of other pitchers who have to go through that stage—building up their arms.

"Our pitching has to stand up. I'm looking for 25 victories somewhere in addition to what we expect from Koufax, Drysdale, Johnny Podres and Ron Perranoski."[4]

At that time the only legitimate power hitter on the Dodgers team was Frank Howard, who first considered quitting professional baseball, then reported to spring training late, out of shape and grossly over his normal playing weight of 255 pounds. Furthermore, the Dodgers were without a regular starting third baseman. Ken McMullen, who had played the hot corner much of the 1963 season, was currently in the U. S. Air Force and was not expected to be out until sometime later in the month. If that wasn't enough, catcher John Roseboro had been sent back to Los Angeles for treatment of an ailing right knee.

So Walter Alston had some problems to work out before heading west to begin the 1964 season, but neither he nor General Manager Buzzy Bavasi was terribly worried. After all, they did have Koufax and Drysdale, and also the best relief pitcher in the game in Ron Perranoski. They had Doug Camilli to replace ailing first-string catcher Roseboro from time to time. Behind Koufax , Drysdale and Podres, Alston had several other first-class starting pitchers in Joe Moeller, Phil Ortega, Larry Sherry and Bob Miller. Tommy Davis had just won his second consecutive National League batting title in 1963; and the speedy Maury Wills, despite having an off year in 1963 as a result of a series of injuries, was still a constant threat on the base paths.

What's more, the Dodgers had some pretty classy rookies joining the 1964 roster in Jeff Torborg and Wes Parker. Torborg, a catcher, had batted .537 for Rutgers University in his senior year. Subsequently he was signed by a Dodgers scout to one of the largest bonuses in Dodger history. Alston anticipated that in the 1964 season Torborg would be the third-string catcher on club, behind John Roseboro and Doug Camilli.

In fact, Alston felt that the 1964 Dodgers could actually be a better club than the World Champs of '63. "Everyone knows that our club is short on power. For my club to be better, Willie Davis will have to hit like he did down the stretch last year. Frank Howard will have to have a big year, and one of the kids—Ken McMullen or pitcher Johnny Werhas— will have to come through."[5]

Alston was also counting on Wes Parker to add some punch to the lineup. "The kid is almost too good to be true. He plays the outfield and first base, and has been hitting the ball like mad and with power. But he could be a year away. We'll see."[6]

On April 4, Alston was optimistic: "But I think we can win again because we got the pitching. If anything, our pitching is better than it was a year ago and all it did was win for us. Speed and pitching will have to make up for the big punch."[7]

However, the next day on April 5 the Dodgers boarded their Electra team jet in Vero Beach and made the 25-minute flight to Tampa to play the Reds once again. While the Dodgers had another big inning in the game, scoring four runs in the top of the sixth inning, with two of them being back-to-back home runs off the bats of Jim Gilliam and Willie Davis, overall the Dodgers had hit only five home runs in the spring schedule so far and were not yet in championship form. They lost to the Reds, 7–6, as young Pete Rose delivered a bases-loaded infield single in the bottom of the ninth to score Chico Cardenas with the winning run.

Two days later, on April 7, the Dodgers were beaten by the Yankees for the second time in three spring tries as Don Drysdale, Nick Willhite and Jim Brewer yielded 12 hits to the Yanks. Soon after the game the Dodgers prepared to break camp in Florida and fly home to Los Angeles. Subsequently, they cut their roster down to 27 players by targeting 13 players for reassignment: pitchers Dick Calmus, Charles Bohling, Norm Koch, Bob Radovich, Ken Rowe, Bill Singer and Larry Stab; infielders Nate Oliver, Bart Shirley and Derrell Griffith; outfielders Al Ferrara, Bill Parlier and Roy Gleason.

For the Cincinnati Reds, the April 5 victory over the Los Angeles Dodgers was their first spring training victory over a National League team in ten games so far in 1964. The Reds in 1964 were a going to be a good team, but most baseball experts had their doubts if the team had the staying power to win the pennant.

The 1963 Reds had finished fifth, 13 games behind the Dodgers, with a record of 86–76. Their team leader Frank Robinson was coming off one of the worst years of his career in 1963, hitting just .259 with only 21 home runs.

The 1964 Reds team was a combination of holdover players from the 1961 National League pennant-winning team, such as Frank Robinson, Vada Pinson, Gordy Coleman, Johnny Edwards and pitchers Bob Purkey and Joey Jay, and the beginning seeds of the Big Red Machine of the 1970s, with Pete Rose already a starter. Later in the season Tony Perez would be called up from AAA ball in San Diego.

At shortstop they had the moody but highly efficient Chico Cardenas, who manager Fred Hutchinson proclaimed was the best shortstop in the National League. Better than Dick Groat, better than Maury Wills.

"Chico has wider range in covering either side and can throw from more positions with accuracy and speed," stated Hutchinson. "As opposed to Wills. I would have to say Chico has considerably more zing in his play now. Wills has slowed down a bit since setting a record for stolen bases in 1962, although there's no doubt he's still pretty good. But Cardenas is getting better every day. And whatta pair of hands, they look like Kentucky hams and Chico weighs only a scant 155 pounds."[8]

The Reds pitching staff was led by Jim Maloney, who in 1963 with his blazing fast ball had posted a record of 23–7 with six shutouts and 265 strikeouts. Along with Maloney, the Reds pitchers included Sammy Ellis and left-handers Jim O'Toole, 19-year-old reliever Billy McCool and veteran Joe Nuxhall.

Nuxhall, who has the distinction of being the youngest player ever to play in a Major League game, was in his third tour of duty with the Reds. In 1944 at the age of 15 he made a brief relief appearance in a game for the Reds against the Cardinals, even facing Stan "The Man" Musial. After his postpubescent mound appearance against the Cardinals, in which he was rocked for two hits and gave up five walks in just two-thirds of an inning, Nuxhall returned to the Reds' roster full-time in 1952 and won 84 games for the Reds in eight years.

But by 1960 he was doing poorly, and the fans at Crosley Field were booing his every appearance. Finally in mid-season the Reds sent Nuxhall, with a 1–8 record, down to the minors. The following January they traded him to the Kansas City Athletics for pitcher John Tsitouris and minor leaguer Johnny Briggs. Still Nuxhall, determined to be a starting pitcher in the Major Leagues again, fought his way back through stints with Kansas City and Los Angeles, and in the minors with the San Diego Padres, before being re-signed by the Reds in 1962.

Now down in Florida with the Reds for spring training in 1964, Nuxhall combined with relief pitchers Bill Henry and Al Worthington on April 10 to handcuff the Chicago White Sox, 5–2. Nuxhall pitched six strong innings, giving up just five hits and two runs.

Reds pitching coach Jim Turner heaped praise upon Nuxhall. "That fellow deserves a lot of credit the way he battled his way back from the minors. And he's such a great guy, you're happy for him. His control is uncanny. Do you realize he walked only 39 batters in 217 innings last year? That's fewer than two a game."[9]

However, most of the baseball experts felt that in order for the Reds to win the pennant, they would need a strong comeback year by team leader Frank Robinson and also better performances from pitchers Joey Jay (7–18) and Bob Purkey (6–10), who had very subpar seasons in 1963. Following the 1963 season, manager Fred Hutchinson, who was a heavy smoker, had been diagnosed with lung cancer. It was already being subtly suggested in some spring training quarters that a strong desire by the Reds to win for their cancer-stricken manager could prove most interesting.

In the case of Robinson, his potential contributions were in doubt at present. In fact, he wasn't even training with the Reds in Tampa, but rather was back in Cincinnati at Christ Hospital receiving treatment for an infection. Robinson had been pulled from an exhibition game against the Phillies after the fourth inning when he complained of a pain just below his waist in the thigh region. The diagnosis by team physician Dr. George Ballou was that the injury was the result of the infection.

As a team, however, going into the 1964 season the Reds really only had one position in the lineup in doubt: third base. Following the 1963 season the Reds had sent Gene Freese to the Pirates in a straight cash deal. Subsequently, they signed Steve Boros, who had brief stints with the Tigers and Cubs, as one hopeful candidate who could fill the void. To supplement Boros the Reds could play either Chico Ruiz or Tommy Harper at third as well.

Second baseman Pete Rose had been selected the 1963 National League Rookie of the Year after batting .270 with 170 hits. However, for Rose, the road to success on the field may have been easier than the road to success with his teammates.

When Rose joined the Reds in the spring of 1963, the second-base position was occupied by Don Blasingame. Blasingame was married to the beauty-queen daughter of former Cardinals star Walker Cooper and was very popular with the other Reds players. Also, with Rose's energetic style of play, such as running to first base on walks, some of the Reds players considered him a "hot dog" and felt that he was only on the roster as a result of having an uncle, Buddy Bloebaum, who was a scout for the Reds and had pulled strings for him.

But the fact of the matter is, Pete Rose had earned his way onto the

Reds' roster. In 1962 when Rose was playing with the Macon Peaches (Georgia) in the Sally League, opposing manager Ernie White of the Augusta club said of Rose: "He can get down to first base faster than anyone in our league. He is a Major League prospect, a fiery competitor who instills the desire to win in his teammates. He's an Eddie Stanky who can hit and field better than Stanky."[10]

Consequently, off the field most of the other Reds players ignored Rose. Nonetheless, he was befriended by black players on the team, such Frank Robinson and Vada Pinson.

Bill DeWitt (William O. DeWitt, Sr.), one-time office boy for Branch Rickey, had risen through the ranks and now with a group of business associates had controlling interest in the Cincinnati Reds. DeWitt, who also served as General Manager, took notice of Rose's fraternal habits with the black ballplayers on the Reds. One day during the middle of the 1963 season he summoned Rose to his office in the Central Trust Tower in downtown Cincinnati. At the meeting DeWitt asked Rose why he only hung out with the Negro ballplayers on the team. Rose replied that it was because of the players' allegiance to Blasingame. DeWitt, sensing that action was necessary to build team harmony, solved the problem when on July 1, 1963, he sold Blasingame to the Washington Senators.

It seems that every author who writes a book about Rose is always including a reference to the DeWitt–Rose fraternization confrontation as if it were some shocking revelation. However, Rose himself has been telling this story publicly during interviews for years. I first heard Rose speak about this matter during the summer of 1975 in an interview with Reds broadcaster Marty Brennaman on radio station WLW in Cincinnati.

In January 1963 the popular manager of the Reds, fiery-tempered Fred Hutchinson, had been diagnosed with lung cancer. Nonetheless he had arrived at spring training ready to go and proclaimed that his cancer was in remission. But on April 9, just a few days before the Reds' April 13 opener with Houston, it was announced that following the opening game Hutch would fly to Seattle, Washington, for a physical checkup and then rejoin the team when it arrived in Los Angeles on Thursday to begin a series with the Dodgers.

The Reds finished their games in spring training camp in Florida on April 9 by having a four-game winning streak snapped with an 8–1 loss to the Baltimore Orioles. The Reds now stood 12–12 for the spring schedule as they prepared to make their way north, playing a series along the way with the Chicago White Sox.

The burden of Fred Hutchinson's cancer was now beginning to take its toll on him. When the Reds finished their game on Saturday, April 11, with the White Sox in Charleston, West Virginia, Hutch planned to fly directly to Cincinnati. As the Reds and White Sox were then bound for Indianapolis to play the final exhibition game on their schedule, Hutchinson wanted to avoid the uncomfortable 100-mile bus ride from Indy to Cincy following the game.

The Milwaukee Braves were in high gear going into their exhibition game with Houston Colts on April 6, having the second best record (15–5) in the National League spring training standings behind San Francisco (21–5). While Houston starter Ken Johnson pitched perfect ball in six of the seven innings he faced the Braves, they had tagged him with four straight hits in the second inning and beat him 2–1. In the second inning Joe Torre, Gene Oliver, Frank Bolling and Roy McMillan stroked consecutive singles to account for the Braves' runs. Johnson then went on to retire 16 straight batters before leaving the game for a pinch hitter in the seventh. (Before the month of April was over in 1964, Ken Johnson would suffer another defeat pitching against the Reds that would be listed among the most unfortunate losses in Major League history.)

The Milwaukee Braves had been in a slow decline since winning the National League pennant and World Series in 1957, then repeating as National League champs in 1958. Bobby Bragan replaced Birdie Tebbetts as manager of the Braves following the 1962 season. In 1963 under Bragan the Braves finished sixth with a record of 84–78, 15 games behind the Dodgers, despite the fact that veteran Warren Spahn, pitching in his 19th season for the Braves, had a record of 23–7.

Nonetheless, the Braves decided that in order to be competitive in the 1964 season, they were going to need a fourth starting pitcher and more hitting. Therefore on December 3, 1963, they traded pitchers Bob Hendley and Bob Shaw, along with veteran catcher Del Crandell, to the San Francisco Giants for outfielder Felipe Alou, catcher Ed Bailey and pitcher Bill Hoeft.

The popular Crandell had played with the Braves for 13 seasons, appearing in eight All-Star Games and two World Series. The Braves brass determined that Del was expendable, since Bragan had begun using young Joe Torre regularly behind the plate in 1963, and Torre responded by hitting .293 with 14 home runs in 501 at bats.

In addition to the acquisition of Bailey, who at that point in time had hit 153 home runs in his career, including three in one game for Cincinnati in 1956 and 21 in the 1963 season for the Giants, Bragan could also use Gene Oliver behind the plate.

The key player in the deal, however, was outfielder Felipe Alou, brother of fellow Major League ballplayers Matty and Jesus Alou. Felipe had been the starting right fielder on the San Francisco Giants' 1962 pennant-winning team, while batting .316 with 25 home runs and 98 RBIs. However, Felipe was not getting along well with Giants manager Alvin Dark. Both Alou (a born-again Christian) and Dark (a Southern Baptist) were deeply committed to their religious beliefs, and some of the friction in their relationship stemmed from different interpretations of Christian scripture. Felipe alleged that he was having trouble communicating with Dark.

Then relations between the two completely broke down after Felipe's brother Matty injured a knee during the 1963 season. Dark approached Felipe and stated that they (the Giants management) were sending him down. First of all, Felipe resented the fact that Dark did not take personal responsibility for the demotion of his brother to the minors. However, he also felt that the Giants' action was inappropriate. Consequently, Felipe approached Dark and said, "Don't send him to the minors, send him to a doctor."[11]

Bobby Bragan was planning to use Alou as his lead-off hitter, batting Lee Maye second and slugger Hank Aaron third. This way Bragan reasoned that Aaron would always come up in the first inning and hopefully with men on base.

Following in the batting order, Bragan planned to have Eddie Mathews, Joe Torre and sometimes Bailey or Oliver, followed by weaker-hitting Roy McMillan and Don Bolling. But Bragan wasn't counting on McMillan or Bolling to get hits, he just wanted them to provide a tough defense up the middle of the infield.

Bragan was very enthusiastic about the addition of Felipe Alou. Over the winter he had been doing a weekly radio show in Milwaukee called "Hot Line to Bobby Bragan" in which he answered live questions on the air.

One woman called in to say, "Mr. Bragan, you talk too much about Alou and Bailey. How come you never say a kind word about Del Crandell, the man you sent away?" The lady began to cry. Bragan listened to her sobs for a brief time, then said, "Lady, I'd send away my own brother if I thought it would help this ball club."[12]

Bragan felt that in 1964 it was going to be a six-team pennant race and that the only clubs that were sure to be counted out of it were the Chicago Cubs, Houston Colts, Pittsburgh Pirates and New York Mets. "Chicago is out because they lost Ken Hubbs [who died in a plane crash] at second base. If they got to go out and get a second basemen, they weaken something else. Pittsburgh is still going through redevelopment of its infield, and the two new clubs [Houston and New York] aren't ready yet."[13]

However, for some reason he liked the chances of the Cincinnati Reds to upset the Dodgers in 1964: "Cincinnati ought to be in the race. All last year we kept waiting for the Reds to make their move. They never made it; had too many guys in a slump."[14]

By virtue of the trade with Milwaukee, the San Francisco Giants had added strength to their already fine pitching staff that included Juan Marichal, Gaylord Perry, Billy O'Dell, Ron Herbel and Jack Sanford. The Giants also had power to spare in the likes of Willie Mays, Orlando Cepeda and Willie McCovey. Also, one could not forget Harvey Kuenn, the 1959 American League batting champion, and also Matty Alou. In addition the Giants had a couple of extremely talented rookies in third baseman Jim Ray Hart and outfielder Jesus Alou.

However, regardless of their abundant talent, the Giants had failed to get the job done in 1963, finishing third with a record of 88–74, 11 games behind the Dodgers; and most sports writers were picking the Giants to finish second in 1964. The Giants still felt that they could enhance their chances in the 1964 campaign with the addition of a left-handed relief pitcher and a powerful left-handed pinch hitter, such as Duke Snider of the Mets. As a matter of fact, the Giants had already made an offer to the Mets for Snider in exchange for Matty Alou and cash.

The Philadelphia Phillies were having a mediocre spring. On April 7 they were tied with the Reds for seventh place in the National League spring training standings, with a record of 11–11 after suffering a 5–3 defeat the day before at the hands of the Reds. The Reds had jumped on Phillies' starter John Boozer for three runs in the first inning and then never looked back. Deron Johnson had homered for the Reds, and Gus Triandos and Cookie Rojas for the Phillies.

No one could deny the fact that the Philadelphia Phillies were really a solid ball club, and in 1963 they had finished fourth in the National League with a record of 87–75, a game ahead of the Reds and 12 games behind the first-place Dodgers. A lot of opinions in regards to the '64 Phillies were very typical of that expressed by second baseman Tony Taylor: "When we got to spring training in 1964, everybody knew we were going to win a lot of games."[15]

However, the criticism of the Phillies was that despite their strong pitching, with three potential 20-game winners in Chris Short, Art Mahaffey and Dennis Bennett, and their excellent starting lineup, they lacked depth. To that end the Phillies were casually seeking a right-handed-hitting outfielder; and to add some expertise in the bullpen they signed 36-year-old catcher Bob Oldis as their new bullpen coach.

But the Phillies had actually added depth to their pitching over the winter through a brilliant trade with the Detroit Tigers for All-Star Jim Bunning. On December 4, 1963, the Phillies sent outfielder Don Demeter and pitcher Jack Hamilton to the Tigers in exchange for Bunning and catcher Gus Triandos. Also coming north with the team was prized rookie third baseman Richie Allen to replace veteran Don Hoak, who had manned the hot corner for the Phillies in '63.

In 1963 Allen had led the International League in home runs with 33 and triples with 12. During his tenure in the minors he had played second base, shortstop and in the outfield. However, third base would be a new position for the rookie.

So in reality Gene Mauch had a dark horse, but still a pretty good Phillies team coming north. In fact one respected sportswriter, Arthur Daley of the *New York Times*, went out on a limb and picked the Philadelphia Phillies to win the 1964 National League Pennant in his Sunday column on April 12.

On April 12 the Phillies played their final spring training game of 1964 against the Pittsburgh Pirates in Asheville, North Carolina. Interestingly enough, the Pirates crushed the Phillies, 16–3, with 20 hits. It was Jim Bunning's first start against a National League team, and the Pirates included four home runs among their 20 hits off Bunning, Chris Short and Ryne Duren.

In the bottom of third inning a brouhaha occurred when Bunning low-bridged the Pirates' Don Clendenon with a pitch. This led to punches being exchanged between the Phillies' Tony Taylor and Clendenon, as both benches emptied and joined in the fracas.

As of April 7, with a week to go before their opener, the St. Louis Cardinals had the third-best record in National League playing in spring league games with a record of 14–7. However on Friday, April 10, they were rocked by the Houston Colts, 7–1, in an exhibition game that saw the Colts' Rusty Staub stroke a three-run pinch double to drive Cardinals ace Bob Gibson from the mound in the fourth inning.

The Cardinals had finished second in 1963 NL pennant race and the 1964 campaign would be their first without Stan Musial in 22 years. Bing Devine was starting his seventh season as the Redbirds general manager and he could boast that with Musial retired, there was now only one surviving member, Ken Boyer, from the team that he inherited from former GM Frank Lane.

The general feeling was that the Cardinals had the best infield in the league. As a matter of fact, the Cardinals infield had been the National League's starting infield in the 1963 All-Star game, with Bill White at first, Julian Javier at second, Dick Groat at shortstop and Ken Boyer at third base.

The Cardinals also had some real solid pitching with Ernie Broglio, Bob Gibson, Ray Sadecki and Curt Simmons, in addition to a fine young catcher in Tim McCarver. The Cardinals had hoped that Ray Washburn might hold down a spot on their 1964 pitching staff. However, as spring training came to a close, Washburn was hindered by a bad back and so was shipped to Jacksonville of the International League to allow him to get more work.

The Cardinals' weaknesses were perceived to be that they could use a good second-string catcher and a left-handed relief pitcher. Also, the experts looked at the Cardinals' outfield with skepticism and felt the players on the roster might be inadequate. In June general manager Bing Devine would take steps to correct that deficiency by consummating a couple of trades, one of which would ultimately be considered one of the best player trades of all time.

Trade winds would continue blow throughout all the teams' spring training camps right up until opening day—with the exception of the Los Angeles Dodgers. The Dodgers had decided to go against the grain of conventional wisdom and stand pat, something that is seldom done by a championship team attempting to repeat. Dodger manager Walter Alston rationalized the Dodger stance this way: "Unless you can make a trade that can help you, there's not much use in making it."[16]

In retrospect, when the 1964 season was concluded, Alston's decision to not trade some of his pitching for power would certainly be a reason for speculation as to why the Dodgers did not repeat as pennant winners.

The Chicago Cubs, devastated by the loss of second baseman Ken Hubbs in a plane crash on February 14, relentlessly kept attempting to pry away Dick Tracewski from the Dodgers but to no avail. When Tracewski proved unobtainable, the Cubs focused on trading for Chuck Hiller of the Giants. In the end the Cubs had to settle for Joey Amalfitano, whom they purchased from the Dodgers. In another nixed deal the Phillies offered shortstop Ruben Amaro to the Mets for outfielder Jim Hickman. As things turned out it looked fairly certain that rookie Jimmy Stewart was going to win the Cubs' second-base job in spring training.

But still there was one player that most clubs felt would be a strong addition if they could land him, and he just didn't seem to be available— pitcher Al Jackson of the Mets. Philadelphia and Milwaukee in particular coveted Jackson, who had won 21 of the 91 games that the New York Mets had won in their first two years in existence.

The Phillies even offered five players to the Mets for Jackson and outfielder Frank Thomas. The players the Phillies were willing to part with to get Jackson were pitchers John Boozer, Paul Brown and Dallas Green, rookie outfielder John Herrnstein and third baseman Don Hoak. The Braves wanted to land Jackson so badly that they were willing to part with shortstop Roy McMillan, center fielder Ty Cline and catcher Bob Uecker.

While the Mets declined the Braves' offer for Jackson, they announced that they would be willing to make the same deal for right-hander Jay Hook. In the end Jackson, whom manager Casey Stengel considered the ace of his meager pitching staff, stayed a New York Met and played a dramatic role in the pennant race on the final weekend of the 1964 season.

Pete Rose (Photofile)

As spring training concluded, the final standings in spring exhibition baseball for 1964 in the National League were the following.

Club	Won	Lost	Pct.
San Francisco	25	6	.806
Milwaukee	17	6	.739
Chicago	19	9	.679
St. Louis	17	9	.654
Pittsburgh	15	8	.652
Cincinnati	15	13	.536
Houston	11	11	.500
Philadelphia	12	13	.480
Los Angeles	9	14	.391
New York	10	17	.370

In polls the players seemed to favor San Francisco over Los Angeles in the upcoming pennant race. In the Associated Press annual poll, 294 sportswriters and broadcasters liked the Dodgers over the Giants and Cardinals in a tight three-way race. The writers and broadcasters also liked Milwaukee fourth, Cincinnati fifth, Philadelphia sixth; then rounding out the National League in order were Pittsburgh, Chicago, Houston and New York.

The general consensus was that the Dodgers' selection by the writers and broadcasters in the Associated Press poll was based on the deep respect that they had for the dominance of Sandy Koufax in the 1963 season, when he became a 20-game winner for the first time while pitching 11 shutouts, getting 306 strikeouts and posting a stingy ERA of 1.88. When they considered that Don Drysdale, one of Koufax's teammates, was also one of the most dominant pitchers in the game, it solidified their selection of the Dodgers.

On April 11 the Las Vegas professional oddsmakers issued their favorites for the 1964 Major League season and were in agreement with the sportswriters and broadcasters that the Los Angeles Dodgers would repeat as National League champions. However, a lot fans were skeptical of the oddsmakers, who had picked Sonny Liston a 7–1 favor over Cassius Clay (Muhammad Ali) in March for the heavyweight boxing crown.

The Probable Odds

National League		*American League*	
Los Angeles	6–5	New York	1–3
San Francisco	3–1	Minnesota	6–1
St. Louis	5–1	Chicago	6–1
Cincinnati	8–1	Detroit	10–1
Philadelphia	12–1	Baltimore	12–1
Milwaukee	15–1	Cleveland	20–1
Pittsburgh	25–1	Los Angeles	40–1
Chicago	75–1	Boston	40–1
Houston	150–1	Kansas City	100–1
New York	300–1	Washington	200–1

Therefore, with all the predictions in and the second-guessing already in progress, the stage was set for the 1964 National League pennant race to begin on Monday, April 13, 1964, with the traditional opening game at Cincinnati. The rest of the teams in the league would follow with opening games on Tuesday, April 14.

But as the new season was about to get underway, a large part of baseball history was disappearing right before everyone's eyes. In New York on April 10, the demolition of the Polo Grounds had begun. As construction on Shea Stadium, the Mets' new home park in Queens, was nearly complete for opening day, the old ball park at Coogan's Bluff was beginning to tumble down, girder by girder.

The Polo Grounds was probably better known for its short foul lines (279 feet down the left field line and a comfortable 251 feet down the right field line) than for the extreme depth to straightaway center field of 484 feet in the old ball park. Only three players had ever hit home runs into the cavernous center-field stands of the Polo Grounds. The first was Joe Adcock of the Milwaukee Braves, who hit a home run into the left-center-field bleachers in 1953, a drive of 483 feet. Then in 1962 both Hank Aaron of the Braves and Lou Brock of the Cubs hit home runs into the center-field stands.

The Polo Grounds had been rich in New York sports history. It was the sight of "Merkle's boner," where young Fred Merkle cost the New York Giants the pennant on the last day of the 1908 season when he failed to touch second base. Forty-three years later in 1951 at the Polo Grounds, "The Little Miracle of Coogan's Bluff" occurred when Bobby Thomson's home run, the "shot heard round the world," won the pennant for the Giants in a playoff series with the Brooklyn Dodgers. Willie Mays had made his dramatic back-to-the-plate catch of Vic Wertz's long drive in the 1954 World Series there. Jack Dempsey had knocked out Louis Firpo at the Polo Grounds, and Joe Louis rallied in the 13th round to knock out Billy Conn there.

"The Babe" (Ruth) had hit a lot of home runs there in 1920 and 1921, when it was the home of the Yankees. Later so did Mel Ott. Joe DiMaggio hit his last home run there in the 1951 World Series. John McGraw and Leo Durocher had managed there. Christy Mathewson pitched there. In the 1934 All-Star game there, Carl Hubbell struck out in succession Babe Ruth, Lou Gehrig, Jimmy Foxx, Al Simmons and Joe Cronin (all members of the Hall of Fame). Red Grange, Jim Thorpe, Sid Luckman and Sammy Baugh had played football there. The New York Jets played the last game there.

The Polo Grounds had been given a brief reprieve from the wrecker's ball as the home of the expansion Mets in 1962 and 1963, but its usefulness had come to an end with the near-completion of Shea Stadium. The old ball park was scheduled to be replaced with a low-rent housing project that would accommodate 1,614 families and include a school and community center. However, on its 17.5 acres that still included Coogan's Bluff, not one baseball diamond was planned to be built.

As a final tribute to the passing of the Polo Grounds into sports history, Howard Cosell had produced a documentary film, "Requiem for an Arena," that was to be shown by ABC on home television Wednesday, April 15, 1964. A few nights before its showing to the home audience, a private preview showing had been screened at Toots Shor's restaurant in Manhattan for a select few New York celebrities.[17]

II

Opening Day And Beyond

Beginning in the 1990s the cable television networks such as ESPN and Fox, by virtue of their megabucks contracts with Major League Baseball, started to dictate the scheduling of some Major League games. A good case in point is opening day. Tradition was set aside and totally ignored by ESPN and Fox as they decided when the Major League season schedule would begin, what day and at what time.

Later in the decade Major League Baseball itself, under the direction of Commissioner Bud Selig, upset the opening day apple cart further through attempts to attract an international audience by scheduling opening day games in Mexico. But it became even more ludicrous: to begin the 2000 season the New York Mets and Chicago Cubs played their season-opening games in Japan! This marketing wizardry by Selig meant that only the most supremely dedicated of Mets fans would rise in the morning and begin listening to a ball game at 5:30 A.M.

But in 1964 Major League Baseball was still bound to a couple of time-honored traditions for the opening of the season. The first was to have the Cincinnati Reds begin the season ahead of all other teams. This tradition was in deference to the fact that the forerunners of the Reds, the Cincinnati Red Stockings, had been the first organized baseball team with paid players in 1869. Therefore the Reds were recognized as the oldest professional baseball team and granted the honor of starting the Major League season.

Moments following the first pitch in Cincinnati, another time-honored event took place in Washington, D.C., as the President of the United States traditionally opened the American League season by throwing out the first ball in the Washington Senators' home opener. This presidential tradition was begun on April 14, 1910, when William Howard Taft became the first president to throw out the first ball at the Senators' opener with the Philadelphia Athletics.

On Monday, April 13, 1964, Major League Baseball was ready for a new season to begin and in Cincinnati, the Reds and the Houston Colts awaited the call of "Play ball!" The two-day celebration of openers, with ten games scheduled, was expected to draw about 330,000 fans through the turnstiles. Still millions of other fans who could not get the day off or get a ticket would be listening on the radio and watching the games on television.

Before there were chic sports bars with cable television broadcast over 36-inch screens with surround sound, or cookie-cutter restaurants decorated with ferns that served expensive cheeseburgers and were equipped with six televisions, there were neighborhood corner taverns and bowling alleys with draft beer, peanuts and 19-inch black and white television sets powered by tubes, and those places were packed to the hilt for the annual event. Opening day was a huge event, regardless of what city you lived in, and if possible, you wanted to be at the ball park. On opening day in 1964, the U.S. Mail arrived a little earlier and bankers with their early closing hours had it made. Some businesses closed on opening day and in most cities school kids with a ticket usually got excused early.

At Cincinnati, where they even had a parade each year on opening day, a crowd of 30,000 was expected at Crosley Field. It would be the 75th consecutive home opener for the Reds, a Major League record, and overall their 80th opening day.

The Reds were entering the 1964 season with a franchise record of 36 wins and 43 losses in openers and were seeking their second consecutive opening-day victory, having defeated the Pittsburgh Pirates in the 1963 opener, 5–2.

Among the Reds' avid fans in the Crosley Field stands on April 13, 1964, were William L. Clawson, 84, who was attending his 69th Reds opening game, and Ernie Bennett, who was attending his 60th.

As fans at Crosley Field passed through the turnstiles, they noticed that they were being greeted with higher concession prices for the 1964 season. Reds president Bill DeWitt, Sr., had permitted Sportservice, the concession contractor, to raise the price of hot dogs from 35 to 40 cents. However, the dogs were bigger, going from 1/10-pound to 1/8-pound per sandwich. Also bottle beer was up 5 cents to 40, and a 14-ounce draft beer would now cost thirsty fans 35 cents. Scorecards, however, would remain a dime.

The opening-day pitcher for the Reds was to be Jim Maloney, and for the Colts, Ken Johnson. In 1963 Maloney had a won-lost record of 23–7. He struck out 265 batters in 250 innings while setting a Cincinnati club record. Against Houston in 1963 Maloney had split four decisions.

Ken Johnson had posted an 11–17 record in 1963. Johnson had pitched for Cincinnati during their 1961 pennant-winning year. He had a record of one win and three losses against the Reds in 1963.

The Reds had been concerned about the late-spring-training hospitalization of their All-Star outfielder and team leader Frank Robinson with a groin infection. However, on Saturday, April 11, Robinson had been released from Cincinnati's Christ Hospital and would be ready for action in the opener.

The starting lineups for the opening game at Cincinnati were the following:

April 13, 1964, Crosley Field

Houston	Cincinnati
ss Ed Kasko	2b Pete Rose
2b Nellie Fox	3b Chico Ruiz
1b Pete Runnels	cf Vada Pinson
lf Walt Bond	rf Frank Robinson
rf Rusty Staub	1b Gordy Coleman
cf Jim Wynn	lf Bob Skinner
3b Bob Aspromonte	c John Edwards
c John Bateman	ss Leo Cardenas
P Ken Johnson	p Jim Maloney

Shortly before 2:30 P.M. a duet of brass bands, Smitty's Band and Col. Barney Rapp's Reds Rooters Band, played the national anthem as local television personality Marian Spellman sang and a color guard raised the flag on the center field pole. Then the Mayor of Cincinnati, Walton Bachrach, tossed the first pitch to City Manager William Wichman, while Ohio Governor James A. Rhodes, standing at the plate with a bat, waved at the pitch—and finally the 1964 season was underway.

The Reds were sporting new uniform shirts with the players' names on the backs, but when the game began the player who was dressed to kill was Houston center fielder Jimmy Wynn, a Cincinnati native who had a fine day playing before a hometown crowd that included his wife, mother and father.

Maloney and Johnson were locked in a scoreless duel through the first four innings. In the top of the fifth Maloney walked Bob Aspromonte and John Bateman. A force-out followed and an error then permitted Bateman to score the game's first run. Nellie Fox followed with a two-run single to give the Colts a 3–0 lead.

The Colts added three more runs off Maloney in the top of the sixth when Rusty Staub singled and Jimmy Wynn lined a Maloney change-up into the left-field screen for a home run. Bob Aspromonte and John Bateman followed with back-to-back singles, then Maloney's low throw on Ken Johnson's sacrifice bunt and Ed Kasko's fielder's choice gave the Colts a 6–0 lead. In the bottom of sixth inning Mel Queen pinch-hit for Maloney, and Wynn made a great one-handed catch of Queen's drive into far right-center, leaping to make the catch in a headlong dive.

Ken Johnson went to the mound in the bottom of the ninth, gunning for a shutout with a 6–0 lead, having permitted just two singles by the Reds in the first eight innings. However, singles by Vada Pinson and Frank Robinson, then a force-out of Robinson by Gordy Coleman, gave the Reds their first run. Bob Skinner followed with a two-run home run over the center-field fence to cut the Houston lead to 6–3. At that point Colts manager Harry Craft summoned reliever Hal Woodeshick from the bullpen, who quickly got Johnny Edwards for the final out.

As the 28,110 opening-day fans filed out of Crosley Field, many were wondering how Jimmy Wynn had gotten away from the Reds. Wynn had played high school baseball at Taft High School in Cincinnati's West End. In fact Wynn had been signed by the Reds, but in the winter of 1962 he had been drafted off the Reds' farm club roster for a paltry $8,000. When Wynn first joined the Colts during the summer of 1963, manager Harry Craft had planned to use him at shortstop. However, after observing Wynn go back into short left field for fly balls, Craft decided that he might make a pretty good outfielder.

Colts pitcher Ken Johnson dedicated the Houston win to pitcher Jim Umbricht, a teammate who had recently died of cancer. Johnson and Umbricht had been roommates on road trips during the 1963 season.

"There was a little extra reason for this one," said Johnson.

A Houston sportswriter asked, "You mean Jim?"

"I thought about him right before the game, all the fellows did," said Johnson.[1]

Immediately following the game Reds manager Fred Hutchinson, who was also battling cancer, left for Seattle to have a checkup. "I'm hoping to rejoin the team in time for the exhibition game with San Diego Wednesday night," said Hutchinson.[2]

In the American League opener at Washington, Lyndon Johnson continued the presidential tradition of throwing out the first ball. In fact LBJ threw out two first balls, then was seated with former St. Louis Cardinal star Stan Musial, his physical fitness chief; and Dave Powers, an aide to the late President Kennedy, was seated in front of him—equipped with a baseball glove. LBJ sat through the entire game along with 40,145 other fans. The President's box was surrounded with various political dignitaries, including Speaker of the House John McCormack of Massachusetts and members of the House, along with a number of Senators, including Senator Everett Dirksen of Illinois.

The game was won, 4–0, by the Los Angeles Angels, who were led by former National Leaguer Joe Adcock with three hits. Claude Osteen, who had started his career with the Reds, got the only Senators hit in the game when he doubled in the third inning off Angels pitcher Ken McBride, who went 6–⅓ innings before giving way to reliever John Navarro.

Prior to the game executives of the Los Angeles Angels told Anaheim, California, city officials that they were prepared to make a firm lease on the city's projected 50,000-seat stadium. Meanwhile, the Angels had a lease on Dodger Stadium through 1965.

The following day on April 14, while the Reds and Colts had the day off, the season opened full tilt in all the other Major League cities. In Los Angeles the World Champion Dodgers hosted the St. Louis Cardinals in their season opener and didn't disappoint the 50,451 fans in attendance for the night game.

Sandy Koufax was making the only Opening Day start of his career and it was to be a classy performance. Ernie Broglio was the starting pitcher for St. Louis. Koufax, shut out the Cardinals, 4–0, on six hits. Koufax struck out five and walked none. Koufax, who hadn't lost to St. Louis since September 21, 1962, extended his shutout string against the Cardinals to 24 innings in the game. In fact, it was Koufax's 10th consecutive victory, counting two over the New York Yankees in the 1963 World Series.

The only Cardinal even to reach second base against Koufax was Bill White, who had two of the Cardinals' six hits. In the fourth inning White singled, then took second on a wild pitch. For the Cardinals, Ernie Broglio went seven innings, giving up two runs on nine hits, while striking out four and walking two.

If the Dodgers were going to repeat as World Champions, they were going to need Frank Howard to provide some element of power hitting in an otherwise "Punch and Judy" hitters' lineup. In the bottom of eight inning Howard provided some hope to that end, when he hit a towering 420-foot home run off Cardinal reliever Ron Taylor that drove in two runs and gave the Dodgers a 4–0 lead.

The other Dodger runs were driven in by singles off the bats of Ron Fairly and Jim Gilliam. In the bottom of the sixth inning Willie Davis singled off Cardinal starter Ernie Broglio, then stole second, took third on an infield out, and rode home on Fairly's single. In the bottom of seventh inning John Roseboro reached base on a throwing error by Dick Groat. Koufax followed with a sacrifice bunt, sending Roseboro to third and then home with a run on the single by Willie Davis.

Meanwhile, up in San Francisco a record crowd of 42,894 fans at Candlestick Park gathered to see Juan Marichal (25–8) and Warren Spahn (23–7), two 20-game winners in the 1963 season, face off against each other. However, the Giants won their opening game over the Milwaukee Braves, 8–4, by doing just what the experts predicted they would do: slug their way to the pennant. In this opening victory the Giants hit five home runs, two by Willie Mays.

Milwaukee scored in the first inning off Giants starter Juan Marichal to take a 1–0 lead. However, in the bottom of the second inning Giant third baseman Jim Ray Hart hit a two-run homer off the Braves' starting pitcher, 42-year-old Warren Spahn, to give the Giants a 2–1 lead. In a post game interview Hart said his homer "came on one of Spahn's screwballs."

"Let Hart keep on thinking that way," Spahn rumbled. "It was a slider."[3]

The Braves came right back in the top of the third inning, scoring three runs to take a 4–2 lead as Ed Bailey, traded by the Giants to the Braves over the winter, knocked in two runs with a double off Marichal. But in the bottom of the third Willie Mays hit the first of his two home runs of the day, a two-run blast off Spahn to tie the game, 4–4.

The Giants pulled ahead to stay in the sixth when with one out Orlando Cepeda singled to left, Hart flied out and Spahn threw a wild pitch while facing Tom Haller. Cepeda took second on the wild pitch, then scored moments later on a single by Haller, giving the Giants a 5–4 lead.

Then in the bottom of eighth the roof fell in on the Braves. Willie Mays hit a 390-foot home run over the right-field fence, his second of the game, forcing Spahn to give way to reliever Hank Fischer. Fischer was then rudely greeted by Orlando Cepeda, who hit a home run, and then two hitters later Tom Haller swatted the Giants' fifth home run of the game, giving them an 8–4 lead. Marichal then closed out the Braves in the ninth, going the distance for the win while hurling a seven-hitter.

Back on the East Coast it was raining. As a matter of fact, over in the American League the New York Yankees had postponed their opener at Yankee Stadium against the Boston Red Sox. It was to be the managerial debut of Yogi Berra with the Yankees.

Nonetheless at historic Connie Mack Stadium in Philadelphia fans braved the threatening clouds to watch the Phillies defeat the New York Mets, 5–3, in an opening night game kicking off the 1964 campaign.

The Phillies jumped out ahead in the bottom of the first inning when Mets starter Al Jackson issued a pair of walks, then 37-year-old former American League All-Star Roy Sievers hit a home run, giving the Phillies a 3–0 lead. The Phillies scored again in the second inning as Clay Dalrymple singled, then took second on a wild pitch by Jackson, and scored on a single by Bobby Wine.

After spotting the Phillies a 4–0 lead, Jackson then settled down and retired the next 16 Phillies in a row. He left the game in the eighth inning, as rookie Richie Allen doubled in the Phillies' final run of the game.

In the fourth inning the Mets' Joe Christopher hit a home run into the left-field stands off Phillies starter Dennis Bennett. For the Mets it was their third opening game loss in as many years of their existence.

Rounding out the opening-day action, the Chicago Cubs spoiled the Pittsburgh Pirates' opener in front of 26,377 fans at Forbes Field with an 8–4 extra-inning win.

The Pirates had come back in the bottom of the ninth to tie the score, 4–4, on a double by Don Clendenon and a single by Bill Mazeroski. Then in the tenth-inning the Cubs scored four runs. The climax of the tenth-inning rally by the Cubs was Billy Williams' two-run homer off Pirate reliever Elroy Face, which carried into the upper deck of the right-field stands.

In the third inning Chicago had tagged Pittsburgh starter Bob Veale with pair of home runs by Andre Rodgers and Dick Bertell. Rodgers also had two doubles in the game.

Prior to the game the crowd observed a moment of silence in the memory of Ken Hubbs, the young Chicago second baseman who had lost his life on February 14 in a plane crash two months prior to the start of the season, and for Jim Umbricht, the Houston pitcher and former Pirate who had just died the week before of cancer.

So the 1964 season had begun, and after the opening games were played on April 13 and 14, the standings were the following.

National League Standings, April 15, 1964

Team	Won	Lost	Pct.	G.B.
Chicago	1	0	1.000	
Houston	1	0	1.000	
Los Angeles	1	0	1.000	
Philadelphia	1	0	1.000	
San Francisco	1	0	1.000	
New York	0	1	.000	1
Cincinnati	0	1	.000	1
Milwaukee	0	1	.000	1

Team	Won	Lost	Pct.	G.B.
Pittsburgh	0	1	.000	1
St. Louis	0	1	.000	1

Prior to their opening game in Philadelphia, the New York Mets announced that they had sold outfielder Duke Snider outright to the San Francisco Giants for $30,000, just slightly more than the waiver price of $25,000. Subsequently Snider, who learned of the deal just before the Mets were scheduled to leave for Philadelphia, instead left immediately to join the Giants on the West Coast.

A slugging legend during his 11 years playing with the Brooklyn Dodgers, Snider returned to the New York baseball scene when he was purchased by the Mets from the Los Angeles Dodgers on April 1, 1963. During his 1963 renaissance season in New York, Snider had appeared in 129 games for the Mets, hitting .243 with 14 home runs and 45 RBIs.

The Mets really never expected big offensive numbers out of Duke, though. They realized that his best days were behind him. However, they felt that the nostalgia generated by returning one of legendary threesome of 1950s center fielders that had played in New York—Willie (Mays), Mickey (Mantle) and the Duke (Snider)—would be good for the box office numbers.

In fact, on the evening of September 12, 1963, the Mets had honored him with a "Duke Snider Night" at the Polo Grounds. The Mets showered Duke with tons of gifts and even brought in several of his former teammates from his Brooklyn Dodger days to share his night with him.

Duke, who was now 37 years old, was raised on the West Coast, still lived in Fallbrook, California, and

Duke Snider. (PhotoFile)

had business and farming interests there. Recently he had been pressing the Mets to trade him to a West Coast team. He even stated publicly that he wanted to end his Major League career there.

Furthermore, Snider was unhappy that he was not playing for a contender in New York, didn't like the fact that he had taken a salary cut from $38,000 to $31,000 a year, and didn't appreciate that the Mets had declined his offer to become a player-coach.

"Just the opportunity to play with a contender again should add a couple of years to my career," explained Snider. "You'd be surprised how much younger you feel when you're playing with a contender."[4]

"I have been with a contender all my life except last year. It means a lot more when you go up to the plate for something more than individual achievement" he added.[5]

Today, however, nearly four decades later, the former "Duke of Flatbush" puts a different spin on his sale by the Mets in April 1964. Snider now relates unashamedly, tearing pages out of Jackie Robinson's biography, that when the Mets sold him to the San Francisco Giants, he seriously thought about quitting baseball rather than reporting to the hated Giants. His updated version of the transaction is that he only reconsidered because he was putting four kids through school and desperately needed the money; otherwise, he would have retired when the Mets sold him to the Giants.

Whatever. The Giants felt that the acquisition of Snider would give them a left-handed pinch hitter with power. According to manager Al Dark, with Snider on the Giants, opposing teams might not be so quick to switch to a right-handed pitcher.

The Mets probably broke even in the deal, reclaiming the dollars that they had spent to get Duke from the Dodgers. George Weiss, president of the Mets, said that he had hoped to get a player for Snider but couldn't, so he sold him.

Manager Casey Stengel felt that the sale of Snider was good for him as well as for the Mets. "Maybe he'll be more content on the coast and will help that club. But for us you've got to ask: How many games can he play? Can you cut young pitchers to make room for him; when he'd rather be nearer home, and then maybe he can play only part-time? What we need are young fellows who can play maybe eight or nine years."[6]

To fill the vacancy on the roster created by the departure of Snider, the Mets added rookie outfielder Larry Elliot, who had been working out with the team, although he was on the roster of Buffalo of the International League.

Meanwhile, on April 16 newspapers around the country ran a rather bizarre UPI photograph in their sports-page editions that made a lot of baseball purists and everyday fans alike do a double take. The photograph was of Duke Snider and Willie Mays standing side-by-side with bats on their shoulders, in uniforms that cried out with GIANTS printed across the breast. In 1987 Snider stated, "It was the most eeriest feeling in my life to look down at my uniform and see GIANTS. Oh no!"[7]

Club officials of the Los Angeles Dodgers didn't think the photograph was too amusing, either. When the Dodgers had sold Snider to the Mets, they were of the understanding that they were doing them a favor. In their first season in 1962 the Mets had lost 120 games, and during their encore season in 1963 they dumped 111 games.

Buzzy Bavasi, Dodgers general manager, said, "The Mets called me three or four times. They cried that they needed Snider for a gate attraction. They also said the deal would help the league and help their club.

"So what happens? They turn around and sell the guy to the Giants without even the courtesy of a phone call to me, asking if we want to buy him back."

When Bavasi was asked whether the Dodgers would have bought Snider back, he replied, "Before letting him go to the Giants? Yes."

Then Bavasi added: "Truthfully, I don't feel that Snider's going to the Giants will change the complexion of the pennant race, but I'm a little burned up in principle."[8]

However, Snider had some ill feelings towards the Dodgers' front office as well, and today at least he expresses them openly. According to Snider, "The saddest day of my life was when I was sold to the Mets for money. That's the time I realized that loyalty was no longer a part of the Dodgers' tradition."[9]

As events turned out, the Giants had no immediate need for Snider, winning their second game of the season in as many days. Willie Mays hit his third home run of the season, triggering a ten-run rally in the third inning that carried the Giants to a 10–8 victory over the Milwaukee Braves. The ten-run rally by the Giants was their biggest inning since they left New York for San Francisco after the 1957 season.

Back in Philadelphia, the Phillies kept pace with Giants, as they defeated the Mets for the second time in two days, 4–1, behind the seven-hit pitching of Jim Bunning. For Bunning, who had 11 strikeouts, it was his first victory in the National League. Bunning had been deadlocked in a 1–1 tie with Mets pitcher Tracy Stallard until the bottom of the eighth inning, when Tony Gonzalez hit a three-run homer to give the Phillies the edge.

At Los Angeles, the St. Louis Cardinals also had a big inning, scoring five runs in the eighth off Don Drysdale to beat the Dodgers, 6–2. Winning pitcher Bob Gibson started the Cardinal rally when he singled and moved over to second following an intentional walk to Bill White by Drysdale. Then Drysdale hit Charley James with a pitch, loading the bases. Ken Boyer followed with two-run single, breaking a 1–1 tie, and then Johnny Lewis, Curt Flood and Tim McCarver each followed with run-scoring singles. The Dodgers got one of the runs back in the bottom of the ninth, when Frank Howard hit his second home run in two days.

The next night, April 16, the Cincinnati Reds rolled into Los Angeles and downed the Dodgers, 5–2. The Reds were led by Vada Pinson, who had three singles, and rookie Chico Ruiz, who had a single, double and triple.

Vada Pinson was a player who everyone felt was destined for greatness. Fans, sportswriters, as well as other players, were always expecting bigger years from him. He would play for 18 years in the Major Leagues and wind up getting 2,757 hits, yet there remain even today critics who maintain that Pinson's career should have been the rival in stature to that of Willie Mays.

Vada Pinson was born in Memphis, Tennessee. However, his family eventually moved to South Carolina, where he grew up and went to the same high school as Frank Robinson and Curt Flood. When Pinson first arrived at the Reds' spring training camp, some of the Reds coaches, for some unknown reason, believed that he was a Latin ballplayer and assumed that he spoke Spanish.

In 1958 Pinson played 27 games for the Reds and then became a regular in the 1959 season. Despite the fact that, entering the 1964 season, Pinson had already collected 985 hits since joining the Reds, getting them faster than Stan Musial, Willie Mays or Hank Aaron did, everyone still expected more out of him. Pinson had led the National League in hits with 208 in 1961 and again with 204 in 1963. In 1959 and 1960 he led the league in doubles and in 1961 finished with .343 batting average, second only to Roberto Clemente's .351 for the National League batting crown. Going into the 1964 season Pinson had been up in the majors a little over five years and had hit 102 home runs and stolen 131 bases. But despite these outstanding achievements, he just never seemed to produce enough on the field to satisfy or silence his critics, and sometimes his fans, too.

Often criticism of Pinson was expressed in the idea that he did himself and the Reds team a disservice by not using his blazing speed to get more base hits by bunting. One such critic was *Cincinnati Post* sportswriter Earl Lawson. During the 1962 season Lawson had written a column for the paper, critical of Pinson's hustle, that resulted in Pinson's acting out his frustration by assaulting Lawson in the Reds' clubhouse. Then a second column written by Lawson in September 1963, entitled "Bunts Could Make Champ of Pinson," also got the ire of Vada. In the column Lawson stated that with Pinson trailing the Pirates' Dick Groat by only seven points for the National League batting title lead, he could help himself by using his speed and laying down an occasional bunt. After reading the column, once again Pinson assaulted Lawson in the Reds' clubhouse. However, this time Lawson signed a warrant for Pinson's arrest for assault and battery.

Another curious element of this incident is that also standing there, heaping verbal abuse upon Lawson during the fracas, was Reds star Frank Robinson. Lawson had befriended Robinson as a rookie in 1956 and also helped him gain legal assistance when Robinson was arrested a few years before on a concealed weapons charge.

Three weeks later Reds president Bill DeWitt intervened and met with Lawson, asking him to drop the charges against Pinson, citing potential adverse relations in the Cincinnati community as the expected result. DeWitt promised Lawson that no such further incidents would occur with Pinson. But Lawson demanded a public reprimand of Pinson by DeWitt, that would be approved by himself, then issued at court and released to the press.

When DeWitt refused to meet Lawson's demands, a legal hearing was held in October 1963, at which time Pinson's attorneys asked for a jury trial. Subsequently a trial date was set for December. The trial lasted two days and the jury of eight women and four men deliberated for two hours before returning with a stalemate. Judge Wood, who was presiding over the trial, declared a hung jury and set a new trial date for January 28, 1964.

Shortly before the new trial date Lawson dropped the charges. Pinson never did apologize to Lawson. Furthermore, following the 1963 incident, Pinson and Frank Robinson rarely spoke with Lawson again, about baseball or any other matter.

Also on April 16 at San Francisco, Curt Simmons, who was now with the St. Louis Cardinals but who had been one of the Philadelphia Phillies "Whiz Kids" pitchers on the famous 1950 pennant-winning team, began his 17th season in the Major Leagues by hurling a three-hit, 2–0 shutout over the Giants. The loss for the Giants was their first of the 1964 season, leaving them tied for second, one-half game behind the idle first-place Phillies, who were off to a 2–0 start and scheduled to begin a series Friday afternoon in Chicago.

The National League would see several new ball parks open during the 1960s. Candelstick Park had opened in San Francisco in 1960, and two years later the Dodgers moved into their new home in Chavez Ravine. Meanwhile a new ball park was under construction in St. Louis, and down in Houston they were building a new $31.6-million stadium with a plastic roof, that when completed would be dubbed the "Eighth Wonder of the World," the Astrodome.

Friday, April 17, 1964, was a special day for the New York Mets. It was to be the opening day for Shea Stadium, the Mets' $26-million, gleaming, new ball park in Flushing Meadow, Queens.

The Mets had lost 120 games in their first season in 1962 while playing home games at the Polo Grounds. Nonetheless they still had drawn 922,000 fans. They followed their inaugural season in the National League in 1963 with 111 loses while increasing home attendance to 1,080,000. In the 1964 season, when the Mets moved to Shea Stadium, they continued their losing ways with 109 loses on the season. Yet home attendance soared again to 1,732,000.

In the first three seasons Mets attendance for games with the former New York teams, the Dodgers and Giants, far surpassed the gate for any other National League teams, even if they were not high in the standings. This pattern at the gate would continue for years to come.

Loyal Brooklyn Dodgers and New York Giants fans continued to grieve for their former teams many years after they abandoned them for the West Coast. When the Mets began play in 1962, they were not viewed by mainstream fans as New York baseball. A lot of purists had fled to the Bronx and the domain of the Yankees, who had now monopolized the purists' feelings on what real New York baseball was.

As the ensuing seasons rolled by, despite the fact that the Mets had won World Championships in 1969 and 1986, and another National League Pennant in 1973, they were not perceived by New York baseball fans as the spiritual heirs of the Dodgers and Giants. In fact, the emotional bleeding over the loss of the Dodgers and Giants was really not cauterized until the "Subway Series" occurred between the Yankees and Mets in October 2000.

With the 2000 Subway Series, the Mets brought the lingering nostalgia for the golden era of New York baseball of the 1940s and 1950s to an end. The Mets had finally reached the soul of New York fans and thereby solidified their existence as being a legitimate entity in New York baseball lore. The Subway Series brought closure to the emotional void created by the loss of the Dodgers and Giants that had lingered, both consciously and unconsciously for 43 years, deep in the hearts of New York baseball fans.

But in April 1964, with just a few days to go before the opening of Shea Stadium, while concrete was still being poured by the dugouts and sod was being spread on the field, a union jurisdictional dispute between telephone and electrical workers arose over the installation of telephones in the stadium. However, work had been completed for installation of radio and television cables, so broadcast of the opening game was expected to take place. The dispute between Local 3 of the International Brotherhood of Electrical Workers and Local 106 of the Communications Workers of America, however, was not resolved in time for the Mets' opener with the Pittsburgh Pirates. Consequently there were no telephones or press box telegraph wires installed. In fact, there was only one telephone operable in the entire stadium, the one in the Mets' ticket office.

Less than a week before the opening game was scheduled, Mets officials had requested that the left- and right-field fences be set at 330 feet, and told the city to move the foul poles in. However, the city said it was impossible, that the poles were set and that the new sites would interfere with the movable stands, which were designed to shift for football games. The Mets then issued a communication from their spring training camp in St. Petersburg stating that, for the good of the game, they had decided to move the fence out to 341 feet—which was the original specification.

On Friday, April 17, the big stadium opened with 50,000-plus fans in attendance, and a carnival mood prevailed at Shea Stadium as the arriving fans marveled at the multicolored tiers of seats and escalators, while munching food available at the large number of concession stands. With the 1964 Worlds Fair occurring only a few blocks away from Shea Stadium, suddenly Flushing Meadows seemed liked the center of the universe to people arriving in the borough of Queens.

Prior to the game six members of Baseball's Hall of Fame were introduced: Zack Wheat, Frank Frisch, Luke Appling, Max Carey, Heinie Manush and Bill Terry. The scoreboard then flashed on their names and the total number of hits for each former player as they were introduced. However, a few of the names were misspelled. An apology was issued for the misspelling, with the explanation that it was caused by electrical shorts.

Then 73-year-old Mets manager Casey Stengel was placed in the center of a floral horseshoe at home plate and duly photographed for posterity. Prior to the game Casey held court with the press, sitting in the green-cushioned dugout.

"You could manage a club sitting right here," he said. "I used to use my glove to sit on. This park is an amazing thing for the spectators."[10]

The starting pitchers for this historic game were to be veteran right-hander Bob Friend for the Pirates and Jack Fisher for the Mets. Fisher's first pitch to Dick Schofield was a called strike and the assembled mass at Shea cheered wildly, then booed robustly as umpire Tom Gorman called the second pitch a ball. Then an explosion of cheers erupted again as Mets right fielder Larry Burright drifted into short center and hauled in Schofield's high pop fly for the first-ever out in Shea Stadium.

At the end of the game it would be Bob Friend who prevailed, spoiling the Mets opener at Shea by going all the way and pitching a seven-hitter to win a 4–3 victory. For Friend it was his tenth straight career win over the Mets without a loss. The Pirates' Willie Stargell had hit the first-ever home run in Shea Stadium, getting a total of four hits in the game while leading the Pirates' 16-hit attack against the Mets.

Box Score, April 17, 1964
(First game ever played at Shea Stadium)

Pittsburgh	AB	R	H	RBI	New York	AB	R	H	RBI
Schofield ss	4	0	0	0	Harkness 1b	5	0	1	0
Virdon cf	5	0	1	0	Altman rf	4	0	0	0
Clemente rf	5	2	3	0	Hunt 2b	4	1	1	0
Stargell lf	5	2	4	2	Gonder c	4	1	2	1
Clendenon 1b	5	0	3	1	Thomas lf	4	1	1	0
Bailey 3b	4	0	2	0	Hickman cf	0	0	0	0
Mazeroski 2b	5	0	2	1	Elliot cf	2	0	1	0
Pagliaroni c	2	0	0	0	Samuel ss	3	0	1	2
McFarlane c	3	0	1	0	a-Kranepool	1	0	0	0
Friend p	3	0	0	0	Moran ss	0	0	0	0
					Burright 2b	3	0	0	0
					b-Stephenson	1	0	0	0
					Fisher p	3	0	0	0
					Bauta p	0	0	0	0
					c-Taylor	1	0	0	0
Totals	41	4	16	4	Totals	35	3	7	3

a-Grounded out for Samuel in 8th; b-Struck out for Burright in 9th; c-Struck out for Bauta in 9th.

	1	2	3	4	5	6	7	8	9	R	H	E
Pittsburgh	0	1	0	0	1	0	1	0	1	4	16	1
New York	0	0	0	3	0	0	0	0	0	3	7	0

E-Mazeroski.   DP-Harkness, Burright and Harkness. LOB-Pittsburgh 12; New York 7.
2B-Hunt, Samuel, Stargell. HR-Stargell. S-Friend.

	IP	H	R	ER	BB	SO
Friend W 1–0	9	7	3	3	1	5
Fisher	6–⅓	11	3	3	1	4
Bauta L 0–1	2–⅔	5	1	1	1	1

In other National League games played on April 17, the first-place Philadelphia Phillies remained undefeated as they outslugged the Cubs at Wrigley Field, 10–8, while the Reds behind the pitching of Joey Jay defeated the Dodgers again, 7–3, to remain one game behind. Meanwhile the Giants kept pace as they edged the Cardinals, 5–4, in ten innings, and Milwaukee downed the Colts, 5–1, at Houston.

Following the Braves' game with the Colts, veteran pitcher Warren Spahn and the rookie catcher, 23-year-old Phil Roof, were involved in an early-morning incident in a Houston nightclub. Spahn and his roommate Roof were arrested, along with eight other patrons, during a raid of the club by Texas Liquor Control Board officers. Both Spahn and Roof were charged with consuming alcoholic beverages after the 1:00 A.M. closing time. After being taken into custody, both Spahn and Roof posted a $10 bond.

When notified of the incident, Braves skipper Bobby Bragan stated, "We have no curfew on this club, and I don't think we need one as long as the players don't bring embarrassment to me or the ball club." Bragan further stated that he planned no disciplinary action against the two players. "As I understand it, the incident occurred only ten minutes after closing time. I see no reason to fine either one."[11]

Furthermore, in regard to the 42-year-old Spahn, he stated, "He has never done one thing to discredit himself or his team. I've got to go along with a guy like that."[12]

A Braves spokesman in Milwaukee stated that Spahn and Roof had gone to the Houston nightclub with some close personal friends who had arrived late from San Antonio, Texas.

On Saturday, April 18, the Phillies lost their first game of the 1964 season to the Cubs when 35-year-old Bob Buhl shut them out, 7–0. Buhl was overwhelming in pitching a three-hitter. After he yielded a ten-foot single to lead-off hitter Tony Taylor in the first that just barely remained on the grass in front of the batter's box, Buhl did not yield another hit until Bobby Wine dropped a single in short center in the eighth inning. However, in the fourth inning one of Buhl's pitches had plunked Phillies hitter Tony Gonzalez in the head. Gonazlez was then hospitalized for observation. For the Cubs, Billy Williams hit his fourth home run of the season in the third.

Elsewhere in the National League, at Shea Stadium the Mets would have to wait further for their first win in their new stadium, as the Pirates with Bob Bailey leading the way with four hits downed them again, 9–5. Meanwhile the Cardinals edged the Giants, 3–2, at Candelstick. In the game Willie Mays hit his fifth home run in a season that was just five games old. The following day Willie Mays would hit his sixth home run of the season.

On Sunday at Los Angeles, Warren Spahn would make his first start since being busted during late-night barhopping in Houston. Spahn was relieved by Bob Tiefenauer, who got the win in the Braves' 3–2, 12-inning victory over the Dodgers.

Meanwhile in Rochester, Minnesota, Walter O'Malley, president of the Los Angeles Dodgers, was recuperating following surgery to correct a hernia condition. Reports were that O'Malley was doing well and was expected to be released from the hospital in about ten days.

As the second week of the 1964 season began on Monday, April 20, the fence-busting Willie Mays did not hit a home run. Nonetheless, Willie continued his torrid hitting by stroking two singles and a double off Bob Purkey as the Giants beat the Reds, 5–2. Also, in the bottom of the eighth inning, Mays raced home with the tie-breaking run for the Giants when Bob Skinner dropped a short fly ball hit by Tom Haller with two outs. Giants starting and winning pitcher Jack Sanford, who pitched a seven-hitter, also got support from a home run by Willie McCovey.

In Houston, Nellie Fox went on a tear of his own, driving in four runs with a single and triple as the Colts downed the Cardinals, 7–1. While the league-leading Philadelphia Phillies and New York Mets had their game at Shea Stadium rained out, the defending World Champion Los Angeles Dodgers fell to the cellar in the National League pennant chase, losing to the Milwaukee Braves, 7–1.

The Dodgers had now lost six in a row since Sandy Koufax shut out the Cardinals in the opening game of the season and were sitting at the bottom of the league standings with 1–6 record. The losing streak for the Dodgers was their worst in two years. So far the Dodgers had scored only 14 runs in seven games and produced just three in the last 35 innings. Collectively the team had only 41 hits in 213 at bats in the young season. The Dodgers' inability to score runs, demonstrated in April, would plague the club throughout the 1964 season.

Following the first eight days of the 1964 season, the standings were the following.

National League Standings, April 21, 1964

Team	Won	Lost	Pct.	G.B.
Philadelphia	4	1	.800	-
San Francisco	5	2	.714	-
Pittsburgh	3	2	.600	1
St. Louis	4	3	.571	1
Milwaukee	4	3	.571	1
Cincinnati	3	3	.500	1–½
Houston	3	3	.500	1–½
Chicago	2	3	.400	2
New York	1	4	.200	3
Los Angeles	1	6	.143	4

Finally on Monday, April 20, 1964, a sad note drifted through Major League club houses that Eddie Dyer, manager of the 1946 World Champion St. Louis Cardinals, had died at the age of 62. Dyer had suffered a stroke on January 2, 1963.

In Dyer's first year as manager in 1946, his Cardinals defeated the Boston Red Sox in the World Series. He quit baseball after the 1948 season when Fred Saigh, who then owned the Cardinals, only offered him a one-year contract. He then moved back to Houston and became successful in the insurance, oil and real estate businesses. Two former Cardinal stars, Howie Pollet and Jeff Cross, were business associates of Dyer's.

On Tuesday, April 21, the Phillies determined that they could use more relief pitching. So they acquired Ed Roebuck from the Washington Senators in a straight cash deal.

The reeling Dodgers were beginning to wonder about their pitching, too. On Wednesday, April 22, while beginning a series in St. Louis, Sandy Koufax, the Dodger starter, was forced out of the game after the first inning with a sore arm. Koufax returned to Los Angeles immediately for an examination and it was revealed that he was suffering from an elbow inflammation and a slight muscle tear.

Before leaving the game, Koufax had uncorked a wild third strike that eventually led to a three-run home run by Charley James. The Cardinals defeated the Dodgers, 7–6, handing them their seventh straight defeat. Koufax spoke with St. Louis team physician I. C. Middleman and told him that his arm had been hurting on and off since spring training. Middleman later remarked that Koufax hadn't bothered to report it, feeling that he could work it out.

Rain continued to plague the games on the East Coast and both the Pittsburgh-at-Philadelphia and the Chicago-at-New York games were halted. However, in other games played Wednesday, April 22, the Houston Colts blanked the Cincinnati Reds, 2–0, and San Francisco beat Milwaukee, 8–6, in a home-run slugfest between Willie McCovey and Joe Torre. While Willie Mays continued to swing a hot bat with a single and double, Willie McCovey—who entered the game hitting just .080—belted home runs in his first three plate appearances. McCovey's three round-trippers bested the Braves' Joe Torre, who hit two in the game.

The 1964 season was only ten days old when on Thursday, April 23, one of the most unusual games ever pitched in Major League history occurred. Ken Johnson of the Houston Colts became the first pitcher ever to throw a nine-inning no-hitter and lose. Pitching against the Cincinnati Reds he gave up no hits and lost the game 1–0.

Johnson had first appeared in the Major Leagues in 1959 with Kansas City. Shuttling between the minors and Athletics for three seasons, he was sold to the Reds on July 21, 1961. Now pitching for the Reds as they made their drive for the National League pennant, Johnson appeared in 15 games and had a 6–2 record, then threw two scoreless innings of relief in the 1961 World Series against the Yankees.

However, Johnson was left unprotected by the Reds in the 1962 expansion draft when the Colts and Mets were being stocked with players to enable them to be added to the League, and consequently Houston plucked him off the Reds' list of players.

Just a little over a week earlier, Johnson had beaten the Reds, 6–3, in the opening-day game at Cincinnati. On the night of April 23, 1964, Johnson was facing the Reds for the second time in the season and had been pitching a no-hitter through eight innings, while locked in a scoreless duel with veteran Cincinnati left-hander Joe Nuxhall.

Johnson, a 30-year-old knuckleball pitcher, was very aware of his no-hitter as the game progressed. After the seventh inning he confided in fellow Colt pitcher Don Nottebart, who had pitched the first no-hitter in the brief history of Houston Colts against the Philadelphia Phillies on May 17, 1963.

"How's a guy supposed to feel, Notty?" asked Johnson.

"Stay loose and keep going," replied Nottebart.[14]

In the top of the ninth inning, the Reds' Pete Rose laid down a bunt to the right of home plate toward the mound. Johnson fielded the ball and then threw wildly to Pete Runnels at first base, allowing the alert Rose to round first and pull up at second. Official scorer Dick Pebles immediately ruled an error on the play. Chico Ruiz then grounded out and Rose took third. This brought Vada Pinson to the plate and he hit a routine grounder to Nellie Fox. However, the veteran second baseman booted the ball, allowing Rose to score.

In the bottom of the ninth the Colts' Pete Runnels hit a ground ball and appeared to be thrown out at first. First base umpire Stan Landes called it that way. However, home plate umpire Augie Donatelli overruled Landes, saying that first baseman Deron Johnson never had full control of the ball.

The Reds immediately disagreed with Donatelli's call and announced that they were playing the game under protest. However, the Colts were not able to score off Joe Nuxhall and the left-hander finished the game, getting the win on a five-hit shutout.

After the game Ken Johnson wandered around the Colts' clubhouse with no trousers on and attired only in a warm-up jacket over his sweat-soaked uniform shirt. He had a grin on his face and appeared slightly bewildered by the fact that he had made history becoming the first pitcher to lose a nine-inning no-hitter.

"So I made history," he said. "Heckuva way to get into the books, isn't it?"[15]

All things considered, Johnson seemed to be taking the loss pretty well. "What else can I do?" he asked. "I've pitched the best game of my life. I can't feel bad because I lost it. Actually, I feel worse for the guys on the club. I guess that sounds funny, but it's true."[16]

Within the first few moments of entering the Colts' clubhouse, which was rather silent in mood, Johnson had gone over to veteran Nellie Fox, draped his arm around his shoulder and mumbled a few words. It had been Fox's error on Vada Pinson's grounder that permitted Pete Rose to score from third and that ultimately assured Johnson's place in baseball history.

"I just told Nellie it wasn't his fault," Johnson said. "It was mine. I put the guy [Rose] on base, and I have no one to blame but myself. I knew I had to make a quick throw. I grabbed the ball with three fingers and I threw a perfect sinker—low and away, and behind Pete [Runnels]."[17]

Johnson concluded his postgame remarks, shaking his head as he spoke, "I'll say this, though, when I came up throwing, I knew I had him. I can truthfully say that a good throw would have got him [Rose]."[18]

The error by Nellie Fox that permitted the winning run was certainly an enigma and uncharacteristic of Fox. He was in the Major Leagues for 19 years with the Philadelphia Athletics, Chicago White Sox, and Houston Colts/Astros, making only 209 errors in 2,367 games, finishing with a career fielding average of .984. The 1964 season would be the last one in Fox's brilliant career that saw him as a starting second baseman. Fox died in 1975 and was posthumously elected to the Baseball Hall of Fame. The following season in 1965, Fox was replaced as an everyday player at second base for Houston by another future Hall of Fame member, Joe Morgan.

The well-traveled Ken Johnson would wind up his big league career in 1970 with a record of 91–106, after pitching for the Kansas City Athletics, Cincinnati Reds, Houston Colts/Astros, Milwaukee/Atlanta Braves, New York Yankees, Chicago Cubs and Montreal Expos.

Box Score, April 23, 1964

Cincinnati	AB	R	H	RBI	Houston	AB	R	H	RBI
Rose 2b	4	1	0	0	Kasko ss	4	0	0	0
Ruiz 3b	4	0	0	0	Fox 2b	4	0	2	0
Pinson cf	3	0	0	0	Runnels 1b	3	0	1	0
a-Keough, cf	0	0	0	0	b-Lillis	0	0	0	0
Robinson rf	0	0	0	0	Weekly rf	4	0	0	0
D. Johnson 1b	3	0	0	0	Aspromonte 3b	3	0	1	0
Skinner lf	2	0	0	0	Wynn lf	3	0	1	0
Edwards c	3	0	0	0	Beauchamp c	3	0	0	0
Cardenas ss	3	0	0	0	Grote c	3	0	0	0
Nuxhall p	3	0	0	0	K. Johnson p	3	0	0	0
Totals	29	1	0	0	Totals	30	0	5	0

a-Ran for Pinson in 9th. b-Ran for Runnels in 9th.

	1	2	3	4	5	6	7	8	9	R	H	E
Cincinnati	0	0	0	0	0	0	0	0	1	1	0	2
Houston	0	0	0	0	0	0	0	0	0	0	5	2

Error-Cardenas, K. Johnson, Fox, D. Johnson. Double play-Cardenas and D. Johnson; Ruiz, Rose and D. Johnson; Cardenas, Ruiz and Cardenas. Left on base-Cincinnati 3, Houston 4. Double-Wynn.

	IP	H	R	ER	BB	SO
Nuxhall W 1–1	9	5	0	0	1	6
K. Johnson L 2–1	9	0	1	0	2	9

It is doubtful that it was any consolation for Ken Johnson, but he was not the only Major League player making history on April 23. Three hours after Johnson had completed his entry into the history books, over in the American League, Ken McBride of the Los Angeles Angels was also about to tie a Major League record. In the Angels game with the Indians, McBride had already hit two batters with pitches when in the ninth inning he plunked two more, forcing in Cleveland's winning run in a 3–2 victory, thereby equaling the Major League record of most hit batters in a game by a pitcher.

In other action on April 23, the Los Angeles Dodgers finally halted their losing streak and defeated the St. Louis Cardinals, 7–5. The winning hit was provided by rookie John Werhas, who stroked a two-run single in the eighth inning off Cardinal reliever Bobby Shantz, a hit that followed two walks and a safe bunt.

With San Francisco idle, the Phillies defeated the Pirates and moved into a deadlock for first place with the Giants. The Philadelphia victory was a come-from-behind affair against Pittsburgh on pinch hitter John Herrnstein's two-run double that climaxed a four-run ninth inning.

In New York the Mets regained sole possession of the National League cellar as they lost to the Cubs, 5–1. Ernie Banks and Andre Rodgers led the way for the Bruins with three hits each in a 15-hit attack.

On April 24 both Giants and Phillies won and the first place deadlock between the two teams continued. Once again the big stick for the Giants was none other than the "Say Hey Kid." In a 15–5 Giants romp over the Reds, in five at-bats Willie Mays hit his seventh home run of the season and two singles, walked twice, stole a base, drove in two runs and scored five. What else could you expect from the guy? Ironically, after he had raised his season average to .500, he was pulled in the ninth inning for a pinch hitter.

The Phillies kept pace with the Giants as Jim Bunning won his second game in his National League experience, shutting out the Cubs, 10–0, on six hits. Tony Gonzales led the hitting attack for Philadelphia with four runs batted in.

At Forbes Field in Pittsburgh, the Pirates defeated the Mets, 9–4, to keep in the race just a game and a half behind the Giants and Phillies. Bob Friend continued his dominance over the Mets, defeating them for the 11th time without a loss. Following the game, a rumble ensued in which hundreds of unruly teenagers spilled onto the field and fights broke out, sending four youths to jail and several others to the hospital.

At Milwaukee, Braves starter Hank Fischer gave up the fifth home run of the season to big Frank Howard, but it wasn't enough for the Dodgers as they returned to their losing ways, going down to the Braves, 6–3. In the game Ed Bailey had cracked a two-run home run for the Braves in the fifth.

As the month of April came to an end, a tight race for the National League pennant began to take shape. On April 30 the Phillies remained one-half game ahead of the Giants for the lead. However, four other clubs, Milwaukee, St. Louis, Pittsburgh and Cincinnati, were off the pace only by three games or less.

National League Standings, April 30, 1964

Team	Won	Lost	Pct.	G.B.
Philadelphia	8	2	.800	-
San Francisco	8	3	.727	½
Milwaukee	8	5	..615	1–½
St. Louis	8	6	.571	2
Pittsburgh	7	6	.538	2–½
Cincinnati	6	6	.500	3
Houston	6	9	.400	4–½
Los Angeles	6	9	.400	4–½
Chicago	4	7	.384	4–½
New York	2	10	.167	7

Actress Tallulah Bankhead is credited with saying, "There have been only two geniuses in the world. Willie Mays and Willie Shakespeare."[19] Well, Willie Mays was certainly showing his genius early in the 1964 season, leading the way for the Giants with the greatest start of his career.

Despite having great years statistically in 1962 (.304 average, 49 home runs, 141 RBIs) and also 1963 (.314 average, 38 home runs, 103 RBIs), Mays—who would be 33 years old on May 6—had not been extremely healthy the past two seasons. In September 1962 Mays had collapsed from indigestion and in September 1963 he left a game after suffering a dizzy spell. But after the first two weeks of the 1964 season, Mays was leading the National League in four categories besides his .488 batting average.

There was already talk about whether or not Mays could be the first .400 hitter in the National League in 34 years, since Bill Terry hit .401 in 1930, or even the Major Leagues since Ted Williams had last accomplished the feat in 1941 with .406 average.

San Francisco Giants manager Al Dark had said that today (1964) the odds were insurmountable for Mays to become the league's first .400 hitter since Bill Terry.

"Willie is just too brilliant an all-round player," said Dark. "When you play 162 games like Mays does—fielding like he does, running like he does—it is humanly impossible for him to hit .400.

"A .400 hitter has to concentrate on hitting. Willie concentrates on everything."[20]

As for Mays, he refused to discuss the possibility of hitting .400. "I'm not saying anything, but not anything," Mays commented. "Let other people talk. Me, I just play baseball and take my hits when I can get them."[21]

Most of the baseball soothsayers had predicted a tight race in 1964 between the Giants and Dodgers. What they didn't see in their preseason crystal balls was just how tough the Philadelphia Phillies were going to be in the pennant race. Thanks to Willie Mays, the Giants were keeping their end of the bargain up. However, as April turned into May, the Dodgers were struggling.

Losers in eight of their first ten games, nonetheless the Dodgers were starting to show some promise. On Sunday, April 26, Phil Ortega pitched a shutout for the Dodgers at Milwaukee. Then Don Drysdale, who was the last healthy member of the so-called Los Angeles Big Four, picked up where Ortega left off on Monday, shutting out the Colts, 6–0.

Encouraging news came out of Los Angeles on Sunday, too. Dr. Robert Kerlan reported that Sandy Koufax, who had been undergoing treatment for a muscle strain in his left arm, might be given permission to throw on the sidelines on the coming weekend.

Besides Koufax's coming down with a sore arm, the Dodger staff had been depleted by injuries to Johnny Podres and reliever Ron Perranoski. Furthermore, the Dodgers had been without the services of two-time National League batting champion Tommy Davis.

Regardless of the injuries, Dodger manager Walter Alston was not of a frame of mind to just assign the lackluster play of the Dodgers to injuries. "The injuries have hurt us," he said. "But the team was not playing up to par before anyone got hurt. Yes, we're crippled but that isn't all the reason for our troubles.

"What we've got to do is win as many as we can while we're crippled, then move when we get all the injured men back. There is nothing wrong with the morale of this team right now that a couple of good wins and some base hits won't cure."[22]

III

An Amazin' May

Throughout the month of May in 1964, the National League pennant race was a see-saw battle between the Philadelphia Phillies and San Francisco Giants. The Phillies entered the month on top of the standings, then suddenly dropped a couple of games with the Giants in hot pursuit.

Led by the hot hitting of Willie Mays and steady pitching of Juan Marichal, on May 3 the persistent Giants once again had moved into a tie with the Phillies for first place. San Francisco then took the lead but just could not shake loose from the ever-charging Phillies, who doggedly continued to challenge the Giants and finally moved past them again in mid-May into first place. Then the Giants would take the lead again. Subsequently, by May 26 the Phillies had regained the lead and would maintain their slim margin entering the month of June by a one-half game over the Giants. On the last day of the month the Giants and Mets would make a tired entry into the record books by playing in the longest doubleheader ever played.

But as this exciting month began on Friday, May 1, the league-leading Phillies opened a weekend series in Milwaukee. The Braves were only two games behind Philadelphia going into the series. In the Friday night opening game of the series the Phillies were led by rookie sensation Richie Allen, who hit his sixth home run and a double, lifting his average to .431. They beat the Braves, 5–3, for their 10th victory in 12 games.

Out on the West Coast, the second-place San Francisco Giants were opening a weekend series in Los Angeles just one game behind the Phillies. The Dodgers, who were entering the game 4–½ games behind the Phillies, had received some good news prior to the game. Sandy Koufax, who had been out with strained muscle in his left forearm since April 22, was given a clean bill of health by his doctors and pronounced fit to pitch. Also, Johnny Podres was declared ready for action again and listed as a possible starter in the Saturday night game.

Don Drysdale started for Los Angeles in the Friday night game played at Dodger Stadium before the largest crowd of the year so far, 52,733. The Dodgers defeated the Giants, 7–1, led by Tommy Davis, just recovered from a shoulder injury, who had four RBIs, and Drysdale, who pitched a five-hitter.

Despite the loss to the Dodgers, Willie Mays continued to swing an unbelievably hot bat, stroking his eighth home run of the season and also a single to raise his season average to .489. But most surprising was the fact that Mays wound up playing first base in the game for the first time in his brilliant 13-year Major League career at that point.

The reason that Mays, the perennial All-Star outfielder, suddenly became an infielder was that in the second inning he suffered a charley horse and was moved by manager Alvin Dark from his normal center-field position to first base. While playing first Mays did not make an error and handled several difficult chances.

On Saturday, May 2, the Phillies lost to the Braves, 11–2, as Bob Sadowski went the distance for Milwaukee, tossing a five-hitter. Meanwhile, out on the West Coast, the Giants beat the Dodgers, 5–4.

Then on Sunday the Giants once again fought their way back into a first-place tie with the Phillies by defeating the Dodgers, 6–3. Juan Marichal was the starting pitcher for the Giants, and he got off to a shaky start against Los Angeles before settling down and winning his 10th straight game since late in the 1963 season. Once again Willie Mays continued to pulverize the ball, socking his 10th home run and also getting a single, while raising his batting average to .490.

At Milwaukee, the Phillies lost to the Braves for the second day in a row. Hank Fischer pitched a masterful two-hit shutout, downing the Phillies, 1–0, and dropping them into a first-place tie with the Giants.

Another interesting development occurred on Sunday, May 3, at New York, as the fifth-place Reds were sweeping a doubleheader with the cellar-dwelling Mets. The Reds had taken the opening game, 6–5. However, a slumping Pete Rose went 0-for-4 in the opener and was benched by Reds manager Fred Hutchinson in the nightcap in favor of Billy Klaus, who went 0-for-3. The so-called "sophomore jinx" was beginning to descend upon Rose, the National League Rookie of the Year in 1963, and it would continue to dog him into the month of June.

Monday, May 4, was a wild night in the National League. The Phillies began a series in St. Louis and were beaten again, 9–2, for their third loss in row. Ken Boyer drove in four runs with a triple and two singles to lead the way for the Cardinals, while Curt Flood, Tim McCarver and Carl Warwick all hit home runs.

However, Cardinal-starter Bob Gibson, known throughout his career for moving hitters back in the box with tight inside pitchers, threw two fast balls in the third inning near the head of Phillies pitcher Dennis Bennett. Consequently he was slapped with an automatic $50 fine. Then in the fifth inning Gibson was ejected from the game by plate umpire Doug Harvey for throwing his bat at Phillies reliever Jack Baldschun after being hit by a pitch. As a result of the retaliatory pitch, Baldschun was also assessed a $50 fine. Roger Craig finished the game for the Cardinals and got the win.

Bob Gibson was an ultra-competitive player throughout his career, who was all business on the mound and in the clubhouse, too. He would often verbally chastise young Cardinal players for fraternization with opposing players around the batting cage. There is even one well-known incident where Gibson threw a ball at a fellow player's head who was in Gibby's conceptualization speaking too casually with an opposing player prior to a game. Tim McCarver called Gibson the most competitive player he ever played with.

Bob Gibson came up the hard way. Born in Omaha, Nebraska, on November 9, 1935, he was the youngest of seven children. His father had died three months before he was born and subsequently Gibson grew up in the tough public housing projects of Omaha. Conditions in the projects were so harsh that Gibson's ears bore scars from the nibbling of rats as an infant while he slept.

His oldest brother Leroy, nicknamed Josh for the great Negro League catcher Josh Gibson, was 15 years older than Bob. Leroy was a sports enthusiast and a coach at the local YMCA, and he steered the young Bob towards sports rather than mischief out on the streets.

Bob Gibson was an outstanding athlete by the time he had reached high school, but was known more for playing basketball than baseball. Nonetheless, after Gibson graduated from high school, he was offered a contract with the Kansas City Monarchs of Negro League. He turned down the offer and instead attended college by the way of a basketball scholarship at Creighton University. He was a standout basketball player in college and even received some honorable-mention nominations to All-American teams.

But Gibson also played college baseball at Creighton and was ultimately signed by the St. Louis Cardinals. After a few trials in the big leagues and trips back to the minors, Gibson came up to stay with the Cardinals in 1961, posting a 13–12 record with an ERA of 3.24. However, Bob Gibson would come into the national spotlight as one of the game's best pitchers in the 1964 season.

At Milwaukee tempers were flaring up as well, while the Braves beat the Mets, 2–1, before a sparse crowd of 7,368 to move into a tie for second place with the Phillies. Braves starter Denny Lemaster, who pitched a two-hitter, was tagged for a lead-off home run by Charlie Smith, then held the Mets hitless until the ninth inning when Ron Hunt stroked a one-out single. Frank Thomas then grounded out and on the play Hunt raced around third and tried to score. He was doubled up at home when Braves catcher Ed Bailey held on to the throw despite being bowled over by Hunt.

Bailey then got up and started to go after Hunt, but was restrained. Just then the Mets' Rod Kanehl, who wasn't even in the game, came charging out of the dugout and began tangling with Len Gabrielson and Gene Oliver, until order was restored by the umpires.

At San Francisco the Giants moved out one full game ahead of the Phillies and Braves by downing Houston, 3–2, in a 12-inning game. In the first inning Willie Mays hit his 10th home run of the year with a man on to give the Giants a 2–1 lead. In the sixth Walt Bond of the Colts tied the game up with a home run. Following Mays' first-inning blast, the Giants were unable to score off Houston pitchers Ken Johnson and Hal Woodeschick until the bottom of the twelfth inning, when Jay Alou singled and Chuck Hiller doubled.

The big news on the West Coast, though, was that Sandy Koufax was back. Koufax, making his first start since April 22 while nursing his ailing arm, beat the Chicago Cubs, 3–1. It was an impressive return by Koufax, who pitched a three-hitter while striking out 13. It was 52nd time in his career that Koufax had struck out 10 or more batters in a game, leaving him only two 10-strikeout performances behind Rube Wadell and Bob Feller, who were tied for the Major League record with 54.

The next night the Phillies continued to reel, as they dropped their fourth straight game. The Cardinals got to Phillies starter Jim Bunning in the fifth inning for two runs and that is all they would need in a 2–1 victory. In the fifth, Johnny Lewis led off with a double off Bunning, and then a single by Phil Gagliano drove home one run. Then singles by Curt Flood and Bill White sent the winning run home.

Ray Washburn, the winning pitcher for the Cardinals, pitched a seven-hitter, despite needing relief help in the ninth. Washburn had rejoined the Cardinals after spending some time in the minors in 1963 following a back injury. Prior to his injury he had been pitching spectacularly for the '63 Cardinals, winning five games against no defeats.

The loss by the Phillies suddenly dropped them into third place, two full games behind the Giants, who took a 2–1 decision over Houston, and one game behind the Braves. Thirty years after the 1964 season, Richie Allen would become philosophical about the September Phillies collapse, which had cost the club the pennant. In a 1994 interview he remarked that it all amounted to just one more win somewhere earlier in the season. Perhaps there was a Phillies win in this losing streak that Allen had in mind.

At San Francisco, Giants manager Alvin Dark decided to take no chances with a Willie Mays who was still ailing with the effects of the muscle spasm in his leg that he had suffered the previous Friday. With cold weather prevailing at Candlestick Park, Dark scratched Mays from the lineup and inserted Matty Alou in the outfield.

Matty Alou, one of two Alou brothers left on the Giants' roster following the winter trade of brother Felipe to the Braves, was feeling left out of things in San Francisco. While brother Jesus was a starting player, Matty had written to Giants owner Horace Stoneham and asked to be traded. "The Giants have too many outfielders and I want to play regularly," said Alou.[1]

Patrolling center field on May 5 in place of Mays, Matty Alou had three hits, while brother Jay (Jesus) got two hits. Collectively, the Alou brothers produced the winning run for the Giants in their 2–1 decision over the Colts, when in the fifth Jay singled, stole second and scored on Matty's single. Jack Sanford was the winning pitcher for the Giants with relief help from Bob Shaw.

At Milwaukee the Braves remained hot on the heels of the Giants, as Warren Spahn pitched the 63rd shutout of his career, defeating the Mets, 6–0, on a four-hitter. The game took just two hours and two minutes to complete and was played before yet another small crowd of 4,342 at County Stadium.

On Wednesday, May 6, the Phillies returned home to Connie Mack Stadium and finally got back on the winning track by defeating the Braves, 7–6. The Braves were leading the game, 6–5, in the eighth inning when rookie Richie Allen walked. Then two outs later Wes Covington hit a home run to give the Phillies the lead. In the first inning Allen had singled to start a four-run Philadelphia rally, and he also tripled and scored in the fifth. For the Braves Joe Torre homered.

With the win the Phillies pulled back to within one game of the league-leading Giants, who were defeated by the Cubs, 4–2, behind the five-hit pitching of Larry Jackson. Jackson retired the last 12 hitters to face him. Willie Mays, celebrating his 33rd birthday, contributed a double and a single to the Giants' losing efforts. Willie McCovey also stroked his sixth home run of the campaign.

Elsewhere, a bad week continued for the Cardinals' Bob Gibson. Following his $50 fine and ejection from Monday's game with Philadelphia, Gibson cost St. Louis a victory over Pittsburgh when he fired a peg over first base and let the winning run score. Consequently, the Cards lost the game to the Pirates, 1–0. The loss left the Cardinals 2–½ games behind the Giants.

Cincinnati remained deadlocked with St. Louis, also 2–½ games off the pace, as Sammy Ellis won his first Major League game and Frank Robinson and Chico Cardenas led the attack in a 12–4 romp over the Mets at Shea Stadium. Robinson produced three runs for the Reds with a home run and a single. Leo Cardenas went 4-for-5 in the game.

At Los Angeles, Don Drysdale finally broke a string of four straight losses to Houston pitcher Dick Farrell, hurling his third complete game in a 5–2 Dodger win over the Colts. John Roseboro went 3-for-3 in the game.

Also on May 6, over in the American League, Dave Nicholson hit what was believed to be the second-longest home run in baseball history when he homered over the left-field stands roof at Chicago's Comiskey Park, a drive of 573 feet. Babe Ruth had hit a home run in 1926 that measured at 600 feet. Helping the White Sox to win both ends of a double header with Kansas City, Nicholson had hit three home runs and struck out three times.

On May 8 the Milwaukee Braves traded veteran shortstop Roy McMillan to the New York Mets for $100,000 cash and pitcher Jay Hook and a minor league outfield prospect, Adrian Garrett.

Jay Hook, a graduate of Northwestern University, had originally been signed by Cincinnati and was a member of the Reds' 1961 pennant-winning team. Made available in the 1962 expansion draft, he was picked by the New York Mets. Hook then entered the Mets' record book when he became the first pitcher on the expansion club to be a winning pitcher in a game. After the team dropped their first nine games to start the 1962 season, Hook became the winning pitcher on April 23, 1962, in the Mets' first National League victory.

The following week the National League race continued at the same wide-open pace as the Giants kept trying to fight off the feisty Phillies, with the Braves and Cardinals hanging tough and never really losing any ground. Still, Cincinnati and Pittsburgh kept threatening to break through.

Willie Mays was still hot, hitting .471 through May 11. Young Pete Rose was starting to hit again, as his three-run homer provided the Reds with a winning margin in 7–6 victory at Pittsburgh. To say that the first month of the 1964 National League pennant race was anything less than terrific for the fans would be an understatement, with more than half the league challenging for the lead.

As the first month of play in the 1964 season came to an end, the standings on Thursday morning, May 12, were the following.

National League Standings, May 12, 1964

Team	Won	Lost	Pct.	G.B.
San Francisco	15	7	.682	
Philadelphia	14	8	.636	1
Milwaukee	14	10	.583	2
St. Louis	15	11	.577	2
Pittsburgh	13	12	.520	3–½
Cincinnati	13	12	.520	3–½
Chicago	9	11	.450	5
Houston	11	16	.407	6–½
Los Angeles	10	15	.400	6–½
New York	6	18	.250	10

In a night game played on May 12, the Giants' Willie Mays and Juan Marichal continued to be relentless as they ravaged the National League. In a 6–0 win over the Colts, Mays hit two home runs (12 & 13) and singled in five trips to the plate, driving in four runs and raising his average to an incredible .478, while extending his hitting streak to 19 games. Marichal won his sixth game, lowering his ERA to 1.73 with his second straight shutout.

In the last seven games that Marichal had started, Mays had gone 18-for-28 for an average of .643 with seven home runs and 16 RBIs. At this point, if Mays had suddenly gone into a slump he would have had to go hitless in his next 53 at-bats to lower his average to a paltry .301.

Marichal had won 25 games in 1963. With his sixth win of the 1964 season, he was now 12 days ahead of previous year's pace, when he didn't win his sixth game of the season until May 24.

Willie Mays was now riding high in May 1964, as the premier player in the National League, but he was still very aware of the rough start that he had breaking into the big leagues in May of 1951. Willie Mays had been purchased by the New York Giants from one of the old Negro League's teams for $15,000 in 1950 and was assigned to their affiliate in Trenton.

The next year Willie was in the AAA American Association with Minneapolis. After 35 games Mays was hitting .477, with 71 hits in 149 at-bats, when Leo Durocher summoned Mays from Minneapolis in May 1951 to play for the Giants.

Watching Mays' first workout with the Giants, owner Horace Stone-

The 1964 San Francisco Giants. Front Row: Mark Taylor, batboy; Jose Pagan, Jim Davenport, Jim Hart, Hal Lanier, Del Crandall, Randy Hundley, Tom Haller, Chuck Hiller, Ron Herbel. Second Row: Eddie Logan, equipment manager; Willie Mays, Matty Alou, Jim Duffalo, Whitey Lockman, coach; Harry Lavagetto, coach; Alvin Dark, manager; Herman Franks, coach; Larry Jansen coach; Orlando Cepeda, Jose Cardenal, Billy Pierce, Billy O'Dell, Frank Bowman, trainer. Third Row: Gaylord Perry, Bob Bolin, Harvey Kuenn, Cap Peterson, Willie McCovey, John Pregenzer, Dick Estelle, Duke Snider, Bob Shaw, Bob Hendley, Ken MacKenzie, Juan Marichal, Masanori Murakami. (© San Francisco Giants Archives)

ham asked Durocher what he thought of Willie. Durocher's reply was, "I'll marry him!"[2]

In Mays' first game in a Giants uniform he went 0-for-4 against Curt Simmons of the Phillies. Then the next day he went 0-for-5 against Robin Roberts. Then the Giants returned home to the Polo Grounds and got beat, 1–0. In the game Mays never hit the ball out of the infield. According to Durocher, following the game Giants coaches Herman Franks and Frank Shellenback came to him and said, "You better talk to your boy. He's crying in there."[3]

Mays was sitting at his locker sobbing and Leo sat down beside him and put his arm around Willie's shoulder. "Mr. Leo," Mays said, "I can't do it. They're too fast for me. You've gotta send me back to Minneapolis. I can't play here."[4]

Durocher then told Mays, "I'll tell you something, son, I brought you here to play center field and that's what you're gonna do. You're the best ballplayer I've ever looked at. Don't worry, even if you don't get a hit in 50 at-bats, you're still my center fielder. Go home and get a good night's sleep. You can't do anything about today's game any more."[5]

The next day, with Warren Spahn of the Braves pitching against the Giants, Mays hit the first pitch over the roof. According to Durocher, "From then on, he carried us on his back, literally carried us on his back."[6]

Mays finished the 1951 season with a .274 batting average, 20 home runs and 68 RBIs, playing in 121 games. Of course, he also got to play in his first World Series, too.

Willie Mays then went on to become a New York sports icon. In 1952, after just 34 games, he was drafted into the United States Army. However, when he returned to the Polo Grounds in 1954, he scorched the National League, hitting .345 with 41 home runs and 110 RBIs while leading the Giants to the pennant.

Of course, in the 1954 World Series he made "the catch" when he hauled in Vic Wertz's long drive to the deepest part of center field in the Polo Grounds, running full speed with his back to home plate. He continued to build the legend of the "Say Hey Kid" in New York following his 1954 heroics by belting 51 home runs in 1955 and also playing stick ball in the streets of Harlem.

The Major League folklore that has developed over the past 40-plus years is that Willie Mays had never won the hearts of fans in San Francisco to same extent that he had with the New York fans during the Giants' playing days there. However, the reason for San Francisco fans' being a little less in awe of the "Say Hey Kid" was simply because a lot of brilliant players besides Mays began joining the team in California than had recently played with the Giants in New York. The fans in San Francisco simply had more choices in designating their heroes.

It's a complete myth that San Francisco fans openly rejected Mays rather than have a New York baseball icon pushed down their throats. It is true that in New York between 1954 and when the Giants departed for the West Coast following the 1957 season, Willie Mays *was* the Giants, and as Leo Durocher said, he carried the team. However, when team arrived in California, talented players like Juan Marichal, Orlando Cepeda, Leon Wagner and Willie McCovey all joined the club and now shared center stage with Mays for the affection of San Francisco baseball fans.

The San Francisco fans were acutely aware of the value that Willie Mays brought to the Giants from day one, but the new stars that joined the team in its first years on the West Coast were exciting players, too. Willie Mays just no longer had a monopoly on Giants stardom.

In other games played on May 12, the Braves, behind the three-hit pitching of Hank Fischer, shut out the Mets, 2–0, and moved into a tie with Philadelphia for second place, two games behind the Giants. Fischer faced only 29 batters in the game and got all the runs he needed when Rico Carty hit his first Major League home run off Mets starter Alvin (Al) Jackson. Fischer had retired the first 12 batters that faced him before Frank Thomas doubled in the fifth inning.

At Philadelphia, Curt Simmons, with a little relief help from Roger

Craig, once again beat his old team for the 13th time in 15 decisions since being released in 1960, as the Cardinals downed the Phillies, 4–2. The following night the Phillies and Cardinals would be rained out.

The Reds-and-Pirates game at Pittsburgh was a rain-soaked affair, with delays that lasted four hours, before the Bucs prevailed over the Reds, 3–2. Prior to the rain delay, Cincinnati starter Jim Maloney had pitched four perfect innings.

In a day game at Chicago, the Cubs had defeated the Dodgers, 3–2, when Dick Tracewski fumbled pinch hitter Joe Amalfitano's grounder with two outs and the bases loaded in the bottom of the ninth inning.

On Thursday night, May 15, Houston pitcher Bob Bruce did something that no other pitcher in the National League had done since April 16: he held Willie Mays hitless in a game. The Colts behind the pitching of Bruce defeated the Giants, 4–3. Mays, going hitless for the first time in 21 games, saw his batting average dip to .449. Mays was completely handcuffed by Bruce, hitting into a fielder's choice with two men on in the first, lofting an easy fly in both the third and sixth innings, and fouling out to first in the eighth.

Meanwhile, the Phillies defeated the Cardinals, 3–2, to move within a half game of the Giants for the league lead. By May 19 the Phillies had taken the lead by just a few percentage points (18–10, .643) over the Giants (19–11, .633).

The night before, Jim Bunning had put a damper on a Houston Colts gimmick promotion game (Runs for Johnson), as he allowed the Colts just one hit in a 4–0 Philadelphia victory. The promotion was staged as an effort to score runs for Colts pitcher Ken Johnson, who had pitched a no-hitter on April 23 and currently had a 3–3 record, despite the fact that so far the Colts had only scored two runs for him. The gimmick was that all ladies who arrived at the ball park with runs in their nylons were admitted at a reduced rate. Of the 5,284 fans on hand, 186 were ladies with ruptured hose.

The result of the promotion was that the Colts could barely get a man on base off Bunning, much less score a run for Ken Johnson. Just two Colt batters reached base in the game. Nellie Fox was the first, when he was hit with a pitch in the first inning, and Jim Wynn lashed a ground single over third base leading off in the bottom of the fifth.

Bunning, now 5–1 on the young season, got the only run he needed in the fourth inning when Ken Johnson gave up singles to Wes Covington, John Herrnstein and Bobby Wine. The Phillies then added two more runs in the fifth when Richie Allen doubled, Johnny Callison singled and Tony Gonzalez doubled. In the seventh Gonzalez also doubled in another run after a single by Allen.

Hard-luck Johnson struck out nine Phillies and allowed nine hits before he was replaced in the eighth inning. However, Phillies manager Gene Mauch watched Bunning's stellar performance from the stands, having been fined $150 and suspended for two games as a result of a run-in with Umpire Lee Weyer in the previous Sunday's night game.

Meanwhile, Steve Blass won his first Major League start by pitching a seven-hitter as Pittsburgh defeated Los Angeles, 4–2, ending Don Drysdale's five-game winning streak,

The Giants were now in second place, ten percentage points behind the Phillies, after they were beaten by the Mets, 4–2. The big blow for the Mets came in the eighth when George Altman hit a three-run home run. In the game the Giants used Willie Mays as a defensive replacement in the eighth inning. Mays got to bat just once in the game and flied out. Mays' average had now sunk to .407.

Then matters worsened for the Giants, as suddenly Willie Mays went into a batting slump. On May 20, for the fifth straight game Mays went hitless as the Giants lost to the Phillies, 7–2. Also in the game Juan Marichal (6–1) had his 12-game string of victories snapped, a string that had extended back to August 30, 1963.

The loss tumbled the Giants into second place, eight percentage points behind the Phillies. Johnny Callison led the way for the Phillies, going 5-for-5 with a home run and four singles, while driving in three runs and scoring twice. The Phillies took the lead in the fifth inning and knocked Marichal out of the game when rookie Richie Allen hit a solo homer and Wes Covington also connected for a round-tripper.

The race was made even tighter as St. Louis, behind a four-hit, 12-strikeout performance by Bob Gibson, shut out the Cubs, 1–0. The win moved the Cardinals just one game behind the Phillies and Giants for the league lead.

By May 24 the National League pennant race was still nip-and-tuck, with only percentage points separating the Giants and Phillies for the lead.

The previous evening the Pirates had held the Giants in check as Bob Friend (4–3) pitched a five-hitter while Pittsburgh trounced San Francisco 9–2. In the game Friend had held slumping Willie Mays to a double in four at bats, slicing his average five points further to .400. Jerry Lynch and Roberto Clemente both homered for the Pirates off Giants starter Gaylord Perry.

Earlier in the day the Philadelphia Phillies had discovered that they had new landlords. Jerry Wolman and Earl Foreman, owners of the Philadelphia Eagles of the National Football League, announced the purchase of Connie Mack Stadium, home of the Phillies. Wolman and Foreman had purchased the stadium from J. A. Schlierfer Properties of New York, who had recently purchased the site from Milton Schwartz, a New York realtor.

Wolman told a gathering of the press, "Earl and I bought Connie Mack Stadium personally and strictly as a real estate investment, and it in no way is connected with our ownership of the Eagles. Also, we desire to assure the Phillies they have a home in Philadelphia as long as they wish."

Wolman reported that he and his partner paid $757,500 for the stadium. The Phillies had bought it for $1,675,000 in 1954 from Arnold Johnson, after he had bought the Athletics and moved them to Kansas City; then the Phillies sold the stadium in 1961 to Schwartz for $600,000.

On Tuesday, May 26, the Phillies headed for Pittsburgh after having pulled one-half game in front of the Giants and 1–½ games ahead of the Braves. The Cardinals were tied for third, with the Pirates only two games behind.

In the first game of the series, the Pirates crushed the Phillies, 13–4, as Vern Law won it by pitching a six-hitter, striking out seven and walking one. The Pirates scored 10 runs in the first two innings as their attack on Chris Short and Dallas Green was led by Manny Mota, who hit a solo homer, and Jim Pagliaroni, who hit a grand slam. For the Phillies, Cookie Rojas and Johnny Callison each homered.

The loss kept Philadelphia in first place by five percentage points over the Giants, who had their game at St. Louis postponed due to rain. Pittsburgh, with the win over Philadelphia, moved to within one game of the league leaders.

But the big news in baseball on May 26 was not in a game played between the league leaders, but rather one played between the two teams at the bottom of the heap at Wrigley Field in Chicago. The New York Mets were in last place with a record of 11–28, 12–½ games behind Philadelphia, when they suddenly slammed six Chicago pitchers in a 23-hit attack, downing the ninth-place Cubs, 19–1.

Mets manager Casey Stengel was ecstatic. "Well, I suppose most of the club owners will be trying to contact me now to get my players."[7]

First baseman Dick Smith became the first New York Met to ever get five hits in a game, going 5-for-6 with three singles, a double and a triple. The only home run in the game was a three-run shot hit by Charley Smith. Smith also added two singles and five RBIs to his totals for the day.

The Mets jumped on Cubs starting pitcher Bob Buhl for four runs in the first inning and completed their scoring for the day with six runs in the ninth. Jack Fischer (2–3) was the winning pitcher for New York, going the distance for the first time in 17 starts, eight of them so far in the 1964 season.

Milwaukee remained just one game out of first place after losing to Houston, 4–2. Dick Farrell, winning game for Houston, became the first seven-game winner in the majors, and Joe Torre of the Braves raised his average in the game to .376. Rounding out the day's action, Cincinnati, with Bob Purkey on the mound, beat Don Drysdale and Los Angeles, 6–2, and were now three games out of first place.

Earlier in the day, attorney John J. Raynolds of Chicago, who represented the National League Umpires Association, had issued an ultimatum to baseball that they intended to go on strike if the umpires did not receive a pension increase by July 3. Eighteen of the umpires had met with Raynolds in Chicago on Monday, May 25, and drafted a letter, which was then sent to National League president Warren Giles, and to each of the National League clubs. The letter read in part: "It is the position of the association that we have been courteous, patient and reasonable in attempting to negotiate an increase to the plan but have not been given an opportunity to negotiate on the increases.

"Therefore, we wish to advise that in the event we do not obtain the consent of the National League of Professional Baseball Clubs to the increase by 3 p.m. July 3, 1964, we will have no alternative but to take appropriate action."[8]

Baseball officials were stunned by the umpires' announcement. The Labor Relations movement in baseball had slowly been moving to the fore since 1953, when the Major League Baseball Players Association was founded. However, the owners had been successful in keeping an iron grip on the purse strings and little or no progress at all had been made by the inept and weak MLBPA. This, of course, would all change in 1966 when the players hired an experienced labor attorney, Marvin Miller, to head their association. Miller invoked Federal labor laws and forced the owners to bargain with the players.

At the National League office in Cincinnati, Warren Giles said that he had not heard about the strike threat. "I haven't heard from them directly yet and I don't want to comment on a news report."[9]

At the Commissioner's office in New York, Ford Frick said, "This is the first I've heard of any strike. I don't know anything about it, and I would have to say at this time that it's a league matter."[10]

While very little was ultimately accomplished by the umpires in 1964 and their strike never materialized, by the end of the decade of the 1960s, led by the progress made by the Major League Baseball Players Association, the umpires' association would also be formally recognized.

On Wednesday morning, May 27, when fans across America awoke and turned to the sports pages in their morning newspapers, what they found was a pennant race so tight in the National League that you couldn't get dental floss between the teams.

National League Standings, May 27, 1964

Team	Won	Lost	Pct.	G.B.
Philadelphia	21	14	.600	
San Francisco	22	15	.595	
St. Louis	22	17	.564	1
Pittsburgh	22	17	.564	1
Milwaukee	21	17	.553	1–½
Cincinnati	19	18	.514	3
Houston	20	22	.476	4–½
Los Angeles	19	22	.463	5–½
Chicago	14	21	.400	7
New York	12	28	.300	11–½

Later that evening at Crosley Field in Cincinnati in a battle of left-handers, the Reds' Joe Nuxhall would outduel the Dodgers' Sandy Koufax, 1–0. Koufax gave up just three hits but lost his fourth game in eight decisions. The veteran Nuxhall was superb in the game and did not walk a batter and allowed only two runners to reach second base.

In another shutout, Hank Fischer of the Braves outdueled Skinny Brown of the Colts, 2–0. Fischer gave up four hits in winning, while Brown gave up just two hits and was the losing pitcher.

In yet in a third shutout at Pittsburgh, the Phillies maintained a slim six-percentage-point lead over the Giants by downing the Pirates, 2–0. Art Mahaffey, completing his first game in eight starts, threw a four-hitter, allowing two doubles to Dick Schofield and singles to Donn Clendenon and Smokey Burgess. Doubles by Clay Dalrymple and Cookie Rojas and a single by Richie Allen in third inning gave Philadelphia all their runs off losing pitcher Bob Friend.

The Giants kept pace with the Phillies, edging the Cardinals, 2–1, behind the seven-hit pitching of Juan Marichal (7–1). Bob Gibson was the loosing pitcher for the Cardinals. In the game Marichal got out of tight situations three different times. He was staked to all the runs he would ultimately need in the first inning when Chuck Hiller and Duke Snider opened the game with consecutive home runs off of Gibson (4–1). In the battle for the bottom of the heap in the National League, the Cubs downed the Mets, 7–1. The Mets, coming off their 23-hit attack of the day before, could only muster seven hits off Chicago pitcher Dick Ellsworth. Mets pitcher Al Jackson (3–6) once again received absolutely no support from the Mets' bats. Jackson, who pitched 5–⅓ innings without the Mets' scoring for him in the game, had now pitched 36 consecutive innings without his teammates' scoring a run for him.

On May 28, the New York Mets announced that they would start to accept mail orders for reserved seats for the 1964 Major League All-Star Game at Shea Stadium on July 7. However, all general admission tickets would go on sale the day of the game at $2.10 each.

At Cincinnati on Thursday, May 28, it was a long night as the Reds and Dodgers battled to a 2–2, 17-inning tie. The game was halted by the National League curfew rule which mandated that an inning could not be started after 12:50 AM local time. Therefore the game, according to the rules, had to be replayed. Later in the 1964 season National League president Warren Giles would abolish the curfew rule.

The game was scoreless until the 12th, when the Dodgers scored two runs against Reds starter Jim Maloney on his throwing error and a run-producing single by Tommy Davis. The Reds came back to tie the score in the bottom of the 12th on run-scoring singles by Leo Cardenas and Johnny Edwards.

The Phillies had started the day leading the league six percentage points ahead of the Giants. But that evening Willie Mays hit his 18th home run of the season and San Francisco quickly climbed back into first place by one game after beating St. Louis, 2–1, while Philadelphia was losing to Pittsburgh, 6–5.

However, Phillies manager Gene Mauch protested the game, claiming that Pirates relief pitcher Elroy Face was in the space behind the scoreboard at Forbes Field, therefore being in a strategic position to steal signs. Face claimed that he was there, but only to use the restroom. Subsequently, the protest was sent for consideration to the National League Headquarters.

In other games played, a suicide squeeze bunt by Nellie Fox gave Houston a 4–2 victory over Milwaukee and Warren Spahn (4–4). Houston relief pitcher Hal Woodeschick, who hadn't been scored upon in his last ten relief appearances, preserved the win for Ken Johnson (5–4).

Also the Cubs downed the Mets, 2–0, on Billy Williams' 11th homer and the three-hit pitching of Larry Jackson (6–4).

On Friday, May 29, at Shea Stadium the cellar-dwelling New York Mets were making the San Francisco Giants miserable as they defeated them, 4–2. Down at Connie Mack Stadium in Philadelphia, the Phillies edged the Houston Colts, 7–6, thereby dropping the Giants a half game behind the Phillies.

Forbes Field, Pittsburgh. (National Baseball Hall of Fame Library, Cooperstown, N.Y.)

Then on Saturday afternoon, May 30, with 38,642 fans in attendance, the Mets beat the Giants again, 6–2, while later in a night game the league-leading Phillies would defeat the Colts, 5–1. Jack Fischer (3–3) was the winning pitcher for the Mets, going all the way in the game, pitching a six-hitter, walking one and striking out one.

"The Amazin" Willie Mays got the Giants off to a 1–0 lead in the first inning when he tripled and scored as Mets shortstop Roy McMillan dropped a throw from right fielder Joe Christopher to the infield. The Giants added their only other run of the game in the seventh as Jesus Alou singled and Jim Davenport doubled.

However, the "Amazin Mets" took the lead, 2–1, in the bottom of the first when Jessie Gonder singled with two outs, Frank Thomas was walked, then they both scored on a hit by Joe Christopher. In the fourth the Mets scored three more runs of Giants starter and losing pitcher Ron Herbel (2–1) when Frank Thomas doubled, then scored on a fly and an infield hit. Later in the inning, following a walk to Roy McMillan, Charlie Smith smashed a two-run homer. Joe Christopher produced the last New York run when he brought in Rod Kanehl with a sacrifice fly in the eight off reliever Bob Shaw.

The Mets and Giants were now poised to play on Sunday, May 31,

1964, at Shea Stadium one of the most infamous doubleheaders in baseball history. The starting pitchers announced for the epic twin bill were, for San Francisco, Juan Marichal (7–1) and Bobby Bolin (1–1) vs. New York, Al Jackson (3–6) and Bill Wakefield (0–1).

The largest crowd of the season in the Major Leagues so far in 1964 was on hand for the doubleheader at Shea Stadium, 57,037. There was nothing really unusual about the first game: it lasted two hours and 27 minutes and the Giants won 5–3 behind the pitching of Juan Marichal (8–1), who tossed an eight-hitter while striking out seven and issuing no walks.

For the Mets, Al Jackson (3–7) took the loss. However, the Mets broke a string of 37 scoreless innings without scoring a run for Jackson, when they pushed three runs across the plate for him off Marichal in the second inning.

In the bottom of the second, Joe Christopher and Ed Kranepool singled, and then Jim Hickman lined his third home run of the season into the left-field stands to give the Jackson a 3–0 lead over Marichal and the Giants.

The Giants scored a run in the top of the fourth and then broke loose to take the lead, scoring three runs in the sixth. Willie Mays walked, Jim Hart singled and Orlando Cepeda doubled to left, scoring Mays. Tom Sturdivant then relieved Al Jackson, and Jim Davenport greeted him with a long sacrifice fly to center to tie the score 3–3 as Hart scored and Cepeda went to third.

After one strike to Gil Garrido, Cepeda suddenly came streaking down the third base line as Sturdivant threw a low outside knuckle ball. Cepeda slid across the plate to steal home before Met-catcher Jessie Gonder could make the tag, and the Giants had a 4–3 lead. Garrido then followed with a single to left. From that point on the Giants never relinquished the lead, scoring again in the top of the ninth to expand the lead to 5–3.

Box Score, 1st Game Shea Stadium, May 31, 1964

San Francisco	ab	r	h	rbi	New York	ab	r	h	rbi
Kuenn, lf	5	0	3	1	Kanehl, 2b	4	0	1	0
d M. Alou, lf	0	0	0	0	McMillan, ss	4	0	0	0
Crandall, c	4	0	0	0	Gonder, c	4	0	0	0
Mays, cf	3	1	1	0	Thomas, lf	4	0	1	0
Hart, 3b	4	1	1	0	c R. Smith, lf	0	0	0	0
Cepeda, 1b	4	2	3	1	Christopher, rf	4	1	1	0
Miller, 2b	2	0	1	0	Kranepool, 1b	4	1	1	0

	San Francisco					New York			
	ab	r	h	rbi		ab	r	h	rbi
a Davenport, 2b	1	0	0	1	Hickman, cf	4	1	2	3
J. Alou, rf	4	1	2	1	C. Smith, 3b	3	0	2	0
Garrido, ss	3	0	1	0	Jackson, p	1	0	0	0
Marichal, p	4	0	0	0	Sturdivant, p	0	0	0	0
					b Altman	1	0	0	0
					Bearnarth, p	0	0	0	0
					e Stephenson	1	0	0	0
Total	34	5	12	4	Total	34	3	8	3

a Hit sacrifice for Miller in 6th, b Struck out for Sturdivant in 7th; c Ran for Thomas in 8th; d Ran for Kuenn in 9th; e Struck out for Bearnarth in 9th.

	1	2	3	4	5	6	7	8	9	R	H	E
San Francisco	0	0	0	1	0	3	0	0	1	5	12	1
New York	0	3	0	0	0	0	0	0	0	3	8	1

Errors—Hickman, Hart. Double play—Garrido, Davenport and Cepeda. LOB—San Francisco 8, New York 6.

Two base hit—Cepeda, C. Smith. Home Run—Hickman. Stolen base—Cepeda. Sacrifice—Davenport.

	IP	H	R	ER	BB	SO
Marichal (W 8–1)	9	8	3	3	0	7
x Jackson (L 3–7)	5	8	4	4	1	3
Sturdivant	2	2	0	0	0	0
Bearnarth	2	2	1	1	0	1

x—faced 3 batters in sixth.

HBP—By Marichal, C. Smith. Umpires—Burkhart, Sudol, Pryor, Secory. Time 2:27.

The second game of the doubleheader started at 4:02 P.M. and would take 23 innings to decide the winner, lasting seven hours and 23 minutes, before the Giants would prevail over the Mets, 8–6, and sweep the doubleheader. With the marathon second game, the Giants and Mets would play the most innings ever played by two big league teams in one day, 32, surpassing the 29 innings played by the Boston Red Sox and Philadelphia Athletics in a doubleheader on July 4, 1905.

The game was then the fourth-longest in baseball history. The record for a single game was set on May 1, 1920, when Brooklyn and Boston battled to a 24-inning, 1–1 tie. There had also been two 24-inning games previously played in the American League, one in 1906 when the Philadelphia Athletics defeated the Boston Red Sox, 4–1, and another between Detroit and Philadelphia that ended in a 1–1 tie. Still further on the books there had been a 23-inning tie between Brooklyn and Boston.

In the second game, the Giants had jumped on Mets starter Bill Wakefield for two runs in the top of the first. The Mets came right back to score in the bottom of the second, narrowing the Giants' lead to 2–1.

The Giants had been in a two-week-long batting slump, hitting as a team a paltry .173 when they got to Mets reliever Craig Anderson for four runs in the top of third, with singles by Jesus Alou, Orlando Cepeda, Tom Haller, Chuck Hiller, Jim Hart and Bobby Bolin. Now they seemingly had the game out of reach after giving starter Bobby Bolin a five-run cushion, taking a 6–1 lead in the game.

However, the Mets kept chipping away at the Giants' lead, scoring two runs in the bottom of the sixth, and they now trailed the Giants, 6–3. Then in the bottom of the seventh the Mets scored three runs to tie the game and send it into eventual extra innings. Roy McMillan and Frank Thomas singled off Bobby Bolin, then with a count of three balls and no strikes on Joe Christopher, the Mets' leading hitter with an average of .330, the Giants starter would come in with a fast ball which Christopher crushed for a three run home run that would tie the score at 6–6, where it would remain until 11:25 PM that evening.

Between the top of the eight inning and end of the game after 23 innings, the Giants' Gaylord Perry (3–1), the eventual winning pitcher, and the Mets' Galen Cisco (2–5), the eventual losing pitcher, would both pitch an entire game in relief, Perry going ten innings and Cisco nine. In some respects history was repeating itself. Just two weeks prior, in a 15-extra-inning game at San Francisco between the Giants and Mets, Perry had been the winner and Cisco the loser. Also the Mets' Larry Bearnarth worked seven scoreless innings of relief in the second game, after going two in the first.

In the top of the 14th inning the Mets pulled off a rare two-man triple play. Jesus Alou had singled and Willie Mays walked. Orlando Cepeda then smashed a line drive that Roy McMillan speared for the first out, then stepped on second base for the second out to get Alou, who was halfway to third, and finally fired a strike to Ed Kranepool at first to nail Mays for the third out.

This was the second triple play of the season for the Mets, having executed one previously against the Houston Colts. In the 15th inning and 17th inning, the Giants' Jim Davenport made brilliant tags at second base in starting double plays that snuffed out Mets rallies.

The lights had been on at Shea Stadium for nearly four hours with the score deadlocked at 6–6 when the Giants broke the 15-inning scoring drought in the top of the 23rd inning. Up until that point the Mets' pitchers had held the Giants scoreless for 19 innings.

Jim Davenport started the rally when he tripled into the right-field corner off Cisco. Cap Peterson was then given an intentional walk. Del Crandell was summoned from the bullpen to hit for Gaylord Perry, and he drove a whistler into the right-field corner that was ruled a ground-rule double, scoring Davenport. Jesus Alou then beat out a topper to the right of the mound and Peterson scored on the play, making it 8–6, Giants.

Bob Hendley then took over the mound duties for the Giants in the bottom of the 23rd and the Mets were set down in order with Chris Cannizzaro and John Stephenson striking out, then Amado Samuel flying out to right to end the marathon game at 11:25 P.M. with an estimated 8,000 die-hard fans of the original crowd of 57,000-plus still on hand.

The two teams' pitchers had set strikeout records in the doubleheader. In the second game, the 12 pitchers collectively had 36 strike outs. Also, the record for most strikeouts in one day was also achieved, with 47.

Although the Mets lost game two, they had 20 hits in the game and were the only Major League team so far in the 1964 season to have as many in a game. In fact, the Mets now had 20 or more hits twice in a game so far in the season, having done it for the second time in just six days.

Willie Mays, who for a time played shortstop in the historic game, went 1-for-10 at the plate after going 1-for-3 in the first game, and consequently saw his batting average drop 19 points during the doubleheader to .364.

By taking both games of the doubleheader the Giants remained just one-half game behind the league-leading Phillies.

A spokesman for the Mets' commissary contractor, Harry M. Stevens, Inc., said that the 57,037 fans consumed about two tons of frankfurters and hamburgers during the doubleheader. The Mets' attendance for the three day holiday weekend series with the Giants was 150,571. A club spokesman felt that the figure would possibly be topped the following weekend when the Los Angeles Dodgers came to Shea Stadium.

New York City television station WOR (channel 9) which televised the doubleheader had to send in a partial relief crew at 6 P.M. The original 14-man crew that was scheduled for the day's games began work at 9 A.M. Subsequently they worked an eight-hour day, with an hour for lunch. Then at 6 P.M. a seven-man crew went to Shea Stadium to relieve them. The crew members who remained were paid overtime by the station. As for the commercials aired by the station, the Mets had three sponsors who were spotted on the air for the entire length of the second game. The additional charge to the sponsors was just the overtime pay for the WOR television crew.

A popular Sunday evening television program at the time was "What's

My Line" with host John Daly. The show's format was that a panel of New York media types and thespians would attempt to guess the occupation of various guests on the show using a 20-questions type format. The show would also have celebrity guests on, who would disguise their voices, and the panel would don blindfolds and then attempt to reveal the guests' identity.

The show aired nationwide at 10:30 PM EST. When Daly came on the air, he told his audience that had been backstage watching "the most fantastic baseball game" he had ever seen. Immediately thousands of local viewers in the New York City metropolitan area switched channels to WOR. Consequently, Daly's remarks had hurt his own ratings.

Box Score, 2nd game Shea Stadium, May 31, 1964

San Francisco Giants	ab	r	h	rbi	New York Mets	ab	r	h	rbi
Kuenn, lf	5	1	0	0	Kanehl, 2b	1	0	0	0
Perry, p	3	0	0	0	c Gonder	1	0	0	0
J. Crandall	1	0	1	1	Samuel, 2b	7	0	2	0
Hendley, p	0	0	0	0	McMillan, ss	10	1	2	0
J. Alou, rf	10	1	4	2	Thomas, lf	10	1	2	0
Mays, cf, ss	10	1	1	1	Christopher, rf	10	2	4	3
Cepeda, 1b	9	1	3	0	Kranepool, 1b	10	1	3	1
Haller, c	10	1	4	1	Hickman, cf	10	1	2	0
Hiller, 2b	8	1	1	1	C. Smith, 3b	9	0	4	1
Hart, 3b	4	0	1	1	Cannizzaro, c	7	0	1	1
h M. Alou, cf, lf	6	0	0	0	Wakefield, p	0	0	0	0
Garrido, ss	3	0	0	0	a Altman	0	0	0	0
f McCovey	1	0	0	0	b Jackson	0	0	0	0
Davenport, ss, 3b	4	1	1	1	Anderson, p	0	0	0	0
Bolin, p	2	0	1	0	Sturdivant, p	0	0	0	0
MacKenzie, p	0	0	0	0	d D. Smith	1	0	0	0
Shaw, p	0	0	0	0	Lary, p	0	0	0	0
g Snider	1	0	0	0	e Taylor	1	0	0	0
Herbel, p	0	0	0	0	Bearnarth, p	3	0	0	0
i Peterson, 3b	4	1	0	0	Cisco, p	2	0	0	0
					k Stephenson	1	0	0	0
Total	81	8	17	8	Total	83	6	20	6

a Walked intentionally for Wakefield in 2nd; b ran for Altman in 2nd; c Flied out for Kanehl in 2nd; d Grounded out for Sturdivant in 5th; e Struck out for Lary in 7th; f Struck out for Garrido in 8th; g Grounded out for Shaw in 9th; h Grounded out for Hart in 10th; i Lined out for Herbel in 13th; j Doubled for Perry in 23rd; k Struck out for Cisco in 23rd.

	1	2	3	4	5	6	7	8	9	10	11	12	13	14	15	16	17	18	19	20	21	22	23	R	H	E
San Francisco	2	0	4	0	0	0	0	0	0	0	0	0	0	0	0	0	0	0	0	0	0	0	2	8	17	3

	1	2	3	4	5	6	7	8	9	10	11	12	13	14	15	16	17	18	19	20	21	22	23	R	H	E
New York	0	1	0	0	0	2	3	0	0	0	0	0	0	0	0	0	0	0	0	0	0	0	0	6	20	1

Errors—Garrido, Haller, Cepeda, Cisco. Putouts and assists—San Francisco 69–14, New York 69–31. Double plays—Perry, Davenport, Cepeda; Davenport, Cepeda; Christopher, Kranepool. Triple play—McMillan, Kranepool. Left on bases—San Francisco 16, New York 14.

Two base hits—J. Alou, Kranepool, Cepeda, Crandell. Three base hits—Kranepool, Haller, Davenport. Home run—Christopher. Sacrifices—Herbel, Hiller, C. Smith, Cisco.

	IP	H	R	ER	BB	SO
Bolin	6⅔	8	6	5	2	7
*MacKenzie	0	1	0	0	0	0
Shaw	1⅓	1	0	0	0	1
Herbel	4	3	0	0	0	3
Perry (W, 3–1)	10	7	0	0	1	9
Hendley	1	0	0	0	0	2
Wakefield	2	2	2	2	2	1
Anderson	⅓	4	4	4	0	0
Sturdivant	2⅔	3	0	0	1	2
Lary	2	0	0	0	0	2
Bearnarth	7	3	0	0	4	4
Cisco (L, 2–5)	9	5	2	2	2	5

*Faced 1 batter i 7th.

Hit by pitcher—By Shaw (Samuel); by Cisco (Cepeda). Passed ball—Cannizzaro. Umpires—Sudol, Pryor, Secory, Burkhart. Time 7:23. Attendance 57,037.

Of course, there were other games played on Sunday, May 31, in the tight National League race. At Philadelphia the Phillies topped the Colts, 4–1, to remain the league pacesetters at one-half game ahead of the Giants.

The win was powered by Richie Allen and Ruben Amaro, who both socked two-run homers to produce all the Philadelphia scoring. In fact, the Phillies needed only two pitches from Colts starter Jim Owens (1–4) to score in the bottom of the first. The hot-hitting Cookie Rojas singled on Owens' first pitch, then Richie Allen hit his second pitch high against the light standard atop the left-field stands at Connie Mack Stadium for this 10th home run of the year. Rojas was 2-for-3 in the game and raised his season average to .537.

Art Mahaffey (4–1), the starting pitcher for the Phillies, required relief help to nail down his fourth win against one defeat from Ed Roebuck. With one out in the seventh, after Mahaffey had walked the bases full, Roebuck was summoned from the bullpen. Al Spangler then got an infield hit off Roebuck that Ruben Amaro had knocked down, scoring the Colts' only run before Roebuck retired Walt Bond and Mike White on taps back to the mound to end the inning. The Colts had previously loaded the bases in the sixth with one out, but Mahaffey got Rusty Staub to fly out to short left and Dave Roberts to line out to right.

At St. Louis, with a crowd of 20,240 on hand, the Cardinals split a doubleheader with the Reds to remain just 2–½ games behind the Phillies. The Reds were now in fifth place, five games behind the Phillies.

In the first game, Bob Purkey (3–3) shut out the Cardinals, 6–0, with a six-hitter. Ray Washburn (2–2) took the loss. Cincinnati catcher Johnny Edwards drove in three of the Reds' six runs with a sacrifice fly in the first and singles in the third and eighth.

However, in the nightcap Bob Gibson (5–1) outdueled John Tsitouris (1–3) by pitching a six-hitter and defeating the Reds, 2–1. For St. Louis, it was sweet revenge against Tsitouris, who had shut the Cardinals down without scoring a run against him for the previous 29 innings over two seasons, until they scored twice in the eighth inning to provide Gibson with the decisive margin. The slumping Pete Rose went 1-for-8 in the twin bill.

The first game at St. Louis had been telecast on CBS with the team of Pee Wee Reese and Dizzy Dean at the microphones. Following the first game Reese drove to the airport and caught a plane for New York. Flying into Kennedy airport he saw the lights on at Shea Stadium. When he had deplaned at Kennedy he quickly took a cab to Shea Stadium and caught the last six innings of the Giants-Mets marathon 23-inning game.

At Chicago, Billy Williams' 13th home run of the season in the bottom of the 10th inning gave the Cubs a 4–3 win over the Braves. The loss dropped Milwaukee into a tie for fourth place with Pittsburgh, four games behind Philadelphia.

At Pittsburgh, the Pirates committed a couple of errors and were defeated by the Dodgers, 6–4. The Pirates had taken a 3–0 lead against Sandy Koufax in the first inning on a bases-loaded double by Gene Freese. The Dodgers took the lead in the third, with four runs on four singles and an error in center field by Manny Mota. However, the Pirates tied the game at 4–4 in the bottom of the third on a home run by Roberto Clemente. The Dodgers broke the 4–4 tie in the top of the eighth inning on successive singles by Jim Gilliam, Willie Davis, Tommy Davis and an error by Willie Stargell. Then Koufax (5–4) needed relief help from Ron Perranoski in the eighth to preserve the victory. With Pirate runners on second and third and one out, Perranoski got Bob Bailey to ground out, then walked Smokey Burgess to load the bases before getting Dick Schofield to bounce out.

As the month of May came to an end, the National League standings were almost a mirror image of what they had been at the beginning of the month, as the Phillies and Giants continued a tenacious battle for first place.

IV

A Perfect June

On Monday, June 1, 1964, the standings in the National League pennant race were the following.

Standings, National League, June 1, 1964

Team	Won	Lost	Pct.	G.B.
Philadelphia	25	15	.625	
San Francisco	26	17	.605	½
St. Louis	25	20	.556	2–½
Milwaukee	23	21	.523	4
Pittsburgh	23	21	.523	4
Cincinnati	21	21	.500	5
Los Angeles	21	23	.477	6
Chicago	19	22	.463	6–½
Houston	21	26	.447	7–½
New York	14	32	.304	14

On Tuesday, June 2, the Los Angeles Dodgers arrived in Philadelphia to begin a series with the league-leading Phillies. In the first game of the series the Phillies beat the Dodgers, 4–3.

The series would produce some classic pitching duels. In the game played on Wednesday night, June 3, the Phillies won, 1–0, for their fifth straight victory as the Dodgers left 15 runners on base.

Jim Bunning went head-to-head with Don Drysdale. The game went 11 innings and Bunning struck out 11 Dodgers before departing for a pinch hitter in the 10th.

In the bottom of the 11th inning, Drysdale gave up a double to the lead-off batter, the hot-hitting Cookie Rojas, then was relieved by Ron Perranoski. An intentional walk was then issued and followed by a force play at second, with Rojas taking third. He then scored the winning run when Jim Gilliam fumbled a ground ball hit by Tony Gonzalez and threw wild to first.

Don Drysdale (6–5) took the loss and Jack Baldshun (3–1) got the win in relief.

Walter Alston remarked after the game that "Gilliam's one man on our club who doesn't get excited in a tense situation, but he had to hurry his throw with Gonzalez the runner."[1] Alston also called Don Drysdale's losing effort "one of the greatest games he ever pitched," but said it was time to take Don out when he did.[2]

Cookie Rojas, who was placed in the lineup by Phillies manager Gene Mauch a little over a week before in Pittsburgh to give Tony Taylor a rest, was suddenly on a tear, now hitting at a .500 pace. Since replacing Taylor, he had gotten 16 hits in 24 at-bats, including four doubles, a triple and a home run, had been walked six times and had also fielded faultlessly.

Rojas, who barely weighed 160 pounds and wore thick horn-rimmed glasses, did not exactly look like the hero type. Despite his sudden starlight Rojas was humble in his reaction to all the media attention.

"I am only playing because Tony got a bad start and is tired," he said, following his eleventh-inning hit off Don Drysdale and scoring the winning run against L.A. "I like it, but soon Tony will be back. He's the greatest."[3]

When Gene Mauch was asked if he planned to keep Taylor in the lineup, he replied, "Bench a .500 hitter?"[4]

A few lockers down, Tony Taylor was listening. Taylor, who was currently hitting .228, entered the game as pinch runner, which was odd as that is the role that Rojas had been performing for the ball club before his sudden surge at the plate.

Rojas, a native of Cuba, was one of the many Cuban players signed by the Cincinnati Reds (Leo Cardenas, Mike Cuellar, Raul Sanchez, Tony Perez, Chico Ruiz, etc.) when they had a working agreement with the Havana AAA club, prior to Fidel Castro's revolutionary forces' taking over the island in 1959. He came up with Cincinnati in the 1962 season, then in November of that year was traded to the Phillies in exchange for pitcher Jim Owens.

Rojas played for 16 years in the major leagues with the Reds, Phillies, Cardinals and Royals, appearing in 1,822 games, finishing with a .263 lifetime average. Following his playing days he began a coaching career and in 1988 managed the California Angels to a fourth-place finish in the American League, more recently during the 2000 season Rojas was a coach on the National League Champion New York Mets team.

As for the hard-luck Drysdale, the Dodgers were just not scoring runs for him. Throughout the 1964 season the Dodgers would give horrible batting support to Big Don. Although Drysdale would start 40 games and finish with a record of 18–16 and have an ERA of 2.18 in the 1964 season, he would lose five games he pitched by scores of 1–0, 1–0, 1–0, 1–0, 2–0, including this 11-inning affair at Philadelphia.

Regardless of the hard luck Drysdale had with his Dodgers' offense, he had the supreme respect of hitters in the National League. A typical response from players in how they felt about facing Big Don was that offered by Cardinals shortstop Dick Groat. "Batting against Drysdale rates just behind going to the dentist."[5]

Dizzy Dean was a fan of Drysdale's and had told him that his chances of winning 30 games rested on picking up some victories in relief. However, with the strong relief pitching the Dodgers traditionally had year after year, the chances of seeing Drysdale in any relief appearance were remote. Following the 1–0 defeat at Philadelphia, Drysdale temporarily left the Dodgers to make a quick appearance in Washington, D.C., with coordinator Stan Musial in the Johnson Administration's national physical fitness program.

Elsewhere in the National League on June 3, the Giants beat the Pirates, 3–0. Rookie Ron Herbel (3–1) held the Pirates to just four hits in pitching the shutout. Herbel had hit Pirate starter Vernon Law in the elbow with a pitch in the sixth. Law had to leave the game, but was not expected to miss his next start.

Orlando Cepeda drove in all 3 runs for the Giants with a two-run homer and a sacrifice fly. In the game Willie Mays dropped a fly ball in center field for an error. This was the first such mistake made by the "Say Hey Kid" in ten years. The win kept the Giants 1–½ games behind the Phillies.

The Chicago Cubs' four-game winning streak was halted by the St. Louis Cardinals as Ray Sadecki (5–4), with a little relief help from Roger Craig, defeated the Cubs, 7–5. The two Cardinals pitchers held the Cubs' Billy Williams hitless in the game, thereby dropping his league-leading average ten points to .412. Ken Boyer had a three-run homer for the Cards. Bob Buhl (5–3), the Cubs' starter, took the loss. St. Louis now trailed the Phillies by 3–½ games.

At Milwaukee the Braves put a halt a four-game losing streak as Denny Lemaster (7–2) stopped the Reds on six hits while striking out ten in a 3–2 victory. Jim Maloney (3–6) took the loss for Cincinnati.

Houston playing at New York saw their game postponed by rain.

The following night, Thursday, June 4, at Philadelphia, Sandy Koufax pitched the third no-hitter in his brilliant career, beating the Phillies, 3–0. In holding the league leaders hitless in their home park, Koufax walked

only one batter and struck out 12. It was the 54th time in his career that
Koufax had struck out ten or more batters in a game, which tied him with
Bob Feller and Rube Waddell.

At that point in time Koufax had also tied Bob Feller for the most
no-hitters (3) in a career. Of course, 30 years later this record would
become the exclusive domain of Nolan Ryan, with seven career no-hitters.

Richie Allen was the only Philadelphia hitter to reach base in the
game as Koufax walked him on a 3-balls-and-2-strikes pitch in the fourth
inning on a low fast ball, thereby narrowly missing a perfect game. After
being walked, Allen was then thrown out attempting to steal second. So
Koufax faced the minimum 27 batters in the game, with 26 batters being
counted as official times at bat with the walk to Allen.

All three Los Angeles runs came in the seventh on a three-run homer
by Big Frank Howard off Phillies starter and losing pitcher Chris Short.
Howard's big blow came at the right time. Recently he had been under
heavy scrutiny by the L.A. fans and press alike as to how much he was
actually contributing to the Dodgers' dismal season so far, in light of the
fact that entering Thursday night's game he had only had one hit in the
last 33 official times at bat and was hitting just .216.

Buzzie Bavasi, being questioned on whether the Dodgers offered
Howard some sort of deal when he threatened to retire in spring training, replied. "Absolutely none. It's up to Walter Alston whether he plays
or doesn't. However, in my opinion, it is not fair to put the blame on
Howard for our problems. He's been doing what we expected. He's up
with the league leaders in home runs. He's hit 13 and batted in 29 runs.

"To me, the one I'm disappointed in is Tommy Davis. Tom is not a
.250 hitter. Tom has to produce, and Ron Fairly also, to get us started. If
those two begin to hit, things will pick up."[6]

In the locker room following the game, Koufax shocked the assembled media by revealing that in the first few innings he was attempting to
adjust his motion.

"I have been studying pictures in magazines of my form," said
Koufax. "Suddenly I realized that I had been stepping too far to the left
with the right foot across my body. So in the first few innings I concen-
trated on making an adjustment, stepping more to the right. It felt fine. I
had the old pitching rhythm back."[7]

As one sportswriter quipped, no one knew it was missing.

Koufax added, "As a matter of fact, by the fifth inning I forgot all
about it. Everything was natural again. I was throwing the way I wanted
to."[8]

Koufax then compared his control in the current no-hitter with two other previous gems he had thrown, in 1962 against the Mets and in 1963 against the Giants.

"This time I had my control. I felt I had better stuff here than I did in the other two. Thank goodness, it was the first time this season I've been able to put everything together."[9]

Bob Feller, who had become a successful insurance executive since leaving Major League Baseball, was attending the Cleveland Indians and Chicago White Sox game when he was informed of Koufax's no-hitter. Commenting on Koufax, Feller remarked, "Why, the way this guy is going, he has a good chance to pitch several more. Sandy has a wonderful future ahead of him, mainly because of his fast ball and his excellent control. Sandy has got a real good live fast ball that takes off."[10]

He felt that Koufax' fast ball had a good hop to it: "the kind that

Sandy Koufax (PhotoFile)

takes off when he lets it go."[11] Feller added, "The one thing that Koufax does different than I is that he concentrates more and works harder on his control. I got into a lot of difficulty walking too many batters."[12]

"Rapid Robert" concluded his remarks by stating that he felt Koufax was faster than Lefty Gomez. "Sandy is one of the best around today when he's right."[13]

Don Drysdale was doing temporary public relations work for Stan "The Man" Musial down in Washington, D.C., between starts, helping to hype the Johnson Administration's physical fitness program, when he heard of the no-hitter tossed by Koufax. "Did he win it?" Drysdale asked.[14]

Most baseball historians today seem to fall into a convenient trap, thinking that Drysdale's sarcasm in this matter was a dig at the nonsupport that the Dodgers' hitters had been showing for both Koufax and himself in the 1964 season so far by not scoring many runs when they took their turns on the mound. And, to a degree, that is true. However, it is much more likely that Drysdale was simply making reference to the unusual circumstances of Houston pitcher Ken Johnson, who had pitched the first no-hitter of the season back on April 23 against Cincinnati and yet lost the game, 1–0.

Box Score, June 4, 1964

	Los Angeles					Philadelphia			
	AB	R	H	RBI		AB	R	H	RBI
W. Davis, cf	4	0	0	0	Rojas, cf	3	0	0	0
Wills, ss	4	0	1	0	Callison, rf	3	0	0	0
Gilliam, 3b	4	1	1	0	Allen, 3b	2	0	0	0
T. Davis, lf	4	1	2	0	Cater, lf	3	0	0	0
Howard, rf	3	1	1	3	Triandos, c	3	0	0	0
Fairly, 1b	1	0	0	0	Sievers, 1b	3	0	0	0
McMullen, 1b	3	0	1	0	Taylor, 2b	3	0	0	0
Parker, rf	1	0	1	0	Amaro, ss	3	0	0	0
Camilli, c	4	0	0	0	Short, p	2	0	0	0
Tracewski, 2b	3	0	1	0	Roebuck, p	0	0	0	0
Koufax, p	3	0	1	0	Culp, p	0	0	0	0
					a Wine	1	0	0	0
Totals	34	3	9	3	Totals	26	0	0	0

a—Struck out for Culp in 9th.

	1	2	3	4	5	6	7	8	9	R	H	E
Los Angeles	0	0	0	0	0	0	3	0	0	3	9	0
Philadelphia	0	0	0	0	0	0	0	0	0	0	0	1

Error—Allen. Double play—Taylor, Amaro and Sievers. LOB—Los Angeles 4, Philadelphia 0.

Two base hit—Tracewski; Parker. Home Run—Howard.

		IP	*H*	*R*	*ER*	*BB*	*SO*
Koufax	W 8–4	9	0	0	0	1	12
Short	L 3–3	6–⅔	8	3	3	0	4
Roebuck		⅓	0	0	0	0	0
Culp		3	1	0	0	0	2

Umpires—Vargo, Forman, Jackowski, Crawford. Time—1:55 Attendance—29,706.

A little over a year later, on September 9, 1965, Sandy Koufax would pitch the fourth no-hitter of his career, a perfect game against the Chicago Cubs. Then, following the 1966 season and the Dodgers' loss in the World Series to the Baltimore Orioles, he would retire from baseball. Although Koufax had ultimately achieved greatness in his 12-year Major League career, he had been on the verge of quitting baseball following the 1960 season.

Born Sanford Braun in Brooklyn, New York, on December 30, 1935, when he was three years old he took the last name of his mother's second husband, who was an attorney. Koufax attended Lafayette High School in Brooklyn and played first base on the high school baseball team that included the New York Mets' future owner, Fred Wilpon, as a star left-handed pitcher. In addition to Koufax, Lafayette High School has produced several other Major League players that include Bob Aspromonte, Larry Yellen and John Franco.

Upon graduation from Lafayette High, Koufax attended the University of Cincinnati on a basketball scholarship. As freshman basketball coach Ed Jucker was also the baseball coach, Koufax tried his hand at baseball as a freshman, too. The rest is history and soon he was scouted by several Major League teams. A few years later Jucker would win national acclaim by winning back-to-back NCAA basketball championships at Cincinnati in 1961 and 1962.

In an interview conducted by the University of Cincinnati alumni magazine Horizons in 2000, Jucker said, "I didn't even know he could pitch. At the end of basketball season, he told me to come over to the gym to take a look at him. I was amazed. It was almost like the wonder man. It struck me in such a fashion. The way he could throw—the speed and the curve—you just didn't find that."[15]

In fact, Koufax threw so hard as a college freshman that only one fellow teammate, Danny Gilbert, would volunteer to catch him. "I would work with the pitchers," said Gilbert. "With Sandy, I held my mitt in the center of the plate and prayed that he could get it over or close. I will say this, though, when he got the ball over the plate, he was unhittable."[16]

Koufax's ability to throw a baseball 90 mph plus was his ticket to the big leagues. However, his penchant for wildness hampered him for several years. Koufax attended college for only one year, then was signed by the Brooklyn Dodgers in 1954 straight off of the University of Cincinnati campus to a bonus contract for $14,000.

It has been reported that while Gabe Paul, general manager of the Reds, had no interest whatsoever in signing Koufax, Branch Rickey of Pirates did and even offered him $5,000 more than the Dodgers. However, in the end Koufax felt a sense of loyalty to his hometown of Brooklyn and signed with the Dodgers.

Baseball rules at the time required Major League clubs to keep bonus players on their rosters for two years after signing them. Therefore Koufax had no minor league experience.

Walter Alston said in a 1964 interview by the Associated Press, "I've often thought back to the first time I saw Sandy. I can still see him pitching along the sidelines in Brooklyn. He looked like he had pretty good stuff and he was throwing the ball over the plate.

"The reason I remember this so well is the way he looked the next time I saw him, in spring training the year after. You wouldn't have believed it was the same kid. He was so wild he couldn't have thrown a strike if they let him pitch 15 feet away. I remember thinking to myself: What have we come up with now?"[17]

In 1955, his first year with the Dodgers, Koufax had a record of 2–2. Both victories were shutouts. Nonetheless, he walked nearly as many batters as he struck out. While he won 11 games in 1958, he also lost 11.

In 1959 the Dodgers won the National League Pennant and Koufax had a record of 8–6 with an ERA of 4.05. He started the fifth game of the 1959 World Series with the Dodgers on the verge of eliminating the White Sox, who were down three games to one.

The game was played before a record crowd on 92,706 fans at the L.A. Coliseum, and he lost the game 1–0, being relieved in the eighth by Stan Williams. Bob Shaw, the White Sox starter who went seven innings and was the winning pitcher, later said, "No human being ever threw harder than Koufax that day, and he didn't even need those white shirts."[18] (A reference to the crowd seated in center field.)

In 1960 Koufax was still struggling and had a record of 8–13 with an ERA of 3.91, and he walked 100 batters in 175 innings pitched. Consequently, he was seriously thinking about quitting baseball.

According to Alston, "Sandy is a perfectionist. He wants everything just so. Today he's not satisfied when one of his pitches misses by an inch. He was pretty disgusted a few years ago, before he had that first good season. I had the impression he was thinking of giving the whole thing up."[19]

Koufax stated in the same AP interview, "I was getting pretty close to it. I was beginning to wondering if it might not be better for me to get out while I was still young and go back to school."[20]

Then, as the story has it, one day during spring training in 1961, en route to a B exhibition game, Koufax had a discussion with Dodgers catcher Norm Sherry. Sherry had an idea that he wanted to expand on with Koufax.

"Look, let's try something different today. Forget all about trying to blow the ball by the hitters. Just concentrate on hitting my glove. Never mind how hard you're throwing."[21] Apparently Koufax tried the concentration method suggested by Sherry and pitched seven hitless innings in that exhibition game.

Subsequently during the 1961 season Koufax had a record of 18–13 with an ERA of 3.52 and led all National League pitchers in strikeouts with 269. He seemed finally to have gained control in the 1961 season, although some observers felt that it was more of a factor of his having more opportunity to pitch. Catcher John Roseboro put it another way: "It just seemed to come all at once."[22]

Of course Sandy Koufax is also famous for attempting to gain another kind of control off the mound, that is, economic control. Prior to the 1966 season Koufax, along with fellow Los Angeles pitcher Don Drysdale, didn't report for spring training and demanded that Dodgers owner Walter O'Malley cough up a million bucks to be split between the two hurlers over a three-year period. They also hired a lawyer to act as their agent in the contract talks. The strategy of Koufax and Drysdale was that they knew for certain that the Dodgers could not a win a pennant without them, hence they sought what they considered just compensation for their services.

When the smoke cleared Koufax and Drysdale did not get a multi-year deal out of O'Malley and had to settle for contracts of $125,000 and $110,000, respectively, for the 1966 season. However, they had opened up the issue of the validity of baseball's infamous reserve clause that prevented them from playing for another team—a rule that would be formally challenged in court in just a couple of more seasons by Curt Flood.

After retiring from Major League Baseball following the 1966 with a chronically arthritic elbow weak from too many cortisone shots, Koufax worked for a time as an NBC baseball broadcaster with Curt Gowdy and, by all accounts, was a pretty good color commentary guy. He was elected to the Baseball Hall of Fame in 1972.

For several years now Koufax has maintained a very private profile and avoided most public appearances and interviews. However, in

February 2000 Koufax, for the first time in 47 years since leaving school to play for the Dodgers, returned to where it all began at the University of Cincinnati campus.

The occasion was that Cincinnati was retiring the jersey of former baseball coach Ed Jucker. Koufax was there just to be part of it. He just wanted to be one of the guys. So, when the half-time ceremony at the Cincinnati basketball game occurred on February 13, 2000, Koufax, a three-time Cy Young award winner, simply strolled onto the court with his former University of Cincinnati Bearcat teammates to honor Coach Jucker. No interviews. No fanfare.

Shortly after being named to Major League Baseball's All-Century team in July, 1999, Koufax telephoned Jucker to inquire about his wife's health. It had been several years since the two last spoke. According to Jucker, "I asked him how things were going, and he said, I don't want to talk to you about that. I want to know how your wife is. I'll never forget that. It meant so much to me."[23]

The no-hitter pitched by Koufax on June 4 moved the Dodgers to within seven games of the league-leading Phillies. The Phillies' lead over the Giants remained at 1–½ games as Pittsburgh beat San Francisco, 4–2, behind rookie pitcher Steve Blass, who threw a five-hitter. The Pirates scored all four runs in the fourth inning.

Meanwhile the Cardinals remained 3–½ games off the lead after being edged by the Cubs, 2–1, in a pitchers' duel between Dick Ellsworth and Bob Gibson, who both tossed six-hitters. Ron Santo provided all the Cubs' runs with a two-run homer in the fourth, and Charley James provided the only run for the Cards with a home run.

At Milwaukee's County Stadium, the Reds beat the Braves, 6–3. Frank Robinson's second home run of the game, a three-run shot coming in the ninth inning, provided the winning margin for Cincinnati. However, in the second inning the Braves pulled off a triple play when Leo Cardenas lined to Mike de la Hoz with two Reds runners on base. De la Hoz, the second baseman, flipped the ball to shortstop Dennis Menke for the second out, who then threw the relay to first to get the third out.

The Braves' triple play was the second in the National League of the week—with the Mets previously pulling one off against the Giants in the 14th inning of Sunday's double-header marathon second game—a rarity in Major League Baseball and the third of the 1964 season.

Rounding out the National League action on June 4, Houston beat New York, 7–3, with the help of four Mets errors as Dick Farrell (8–1) won his eight game of the season against only one loss. Farrell's victory in the game was secured by 3–⅔ innings of ho-hit relief work by Don Larsen.

This is, of course, the same Don Larsen who had pitched the only perfect no-hit game in World Series history for the Yankees against the Brooklyn Dodgers in 1956.

Larson had started the 1964 season with San Francisco and was sent to Houston on May 20 in a straight cash deal. During the '64 campaign he would appear in 30 games for the Colts with a record of 4–8.

On Friday, June 5, following the no-hitter thrown against them by Sandy Koufax, the Phillies began to use their bats once again and got 10 hits against the Giants. However, it didn't do the job as San Francisco defeated the Phillies, 5–3, in 11 innings and moved to within one-half game of the league lead.

The Dodgers began their first-ever series in Shea Stadium on Friday night and were shut out, 8–0, by Galen Cisco (3–5). There were 54,790 fans on hand to see the Mets explode for seven runs in the third inning off Dodgers starting pitcher Joe Moeller (3–4).

The Los Angeles press making their first trip to Shea Stadium, gave it a mixed review:

"It [Shea Stadium] was designed by the same engineer, Emil Prager, who conceived Dodger Stadium. It is a beautiful ball park, but lacks the impact and feeling of awe one gets when first entering Taj O'Malley. With four decks, not counting a thin slice that comprises the press box row, it is much steeper than our park. The scoreboard and message board make Dodger Stadium's gizmos look bush by comparison. The board among other items, carries up-to-the-inning scores of games in both leagues, and it doesn't deign to run off plugs for every beer joint and bowling team within a 50-mile radius like they do at Dodger Stadium.

"Shea Stadium has seven escalators for the comfort of its fans, two elevators and 52 rest rooms. From Times Square, the heart of Manhattan, one can get to the ball park in 12 minutes for a paltry 15 cents.

"Dodger Stadium has one Stadium Club, Shea has three. It's quite a layout, yet leaves something to be desired in comparison to our plush apple orchard."[24]

In other games on Friday night, Cincinnati defeated St. Louis, 5–4, while Pittsburgh edged Houston, 4–3, and Chicago beat Milwaukee, 5–2.

The Cubs' Billy Williams, after going two-for-four in the game, was now leading the National League in batting with a .413 average. Roberto Clemente was second with a .363 average, followed by Willie Mays who was hitting .362. In fourth place was Joe Torre of the Braves with .347 average.

On Saturday, June 6, the lead in the National League pennant race once again changed hands. The Phillies, after maintaining a slim lead over the Giants for three weeks, suddenly found themselves in second place as they lost a head-to-head battle with San Francisco in the ninth inning, 4–2.

The game, played at Connie Mack Stadium, saw the Phillies take a 1–0 lead in the second when Wes Covington doubled off the right field wall, moved to third on Tony Gonzalez' bloop single, and then scored on a sacrifice fly by John Herrnstein.

The Giants then tied the score in the fourth off Phillies starter Dennis Bennett on a single by Orlando Cepeda and a triple by Jim Hart that hit the 405-foot mark in center field. In the seventh Jesus Alou hit his first Major League home run to give the Giants a 2–1 lead. Alou's shot landed on the left-field roof just inside the foul pole.

However, the Phillies came back to tie the score in the bottom of the eighth off Giants starter Jack Sanford in the bottom half of the inning, when Richie Allen singled and Cookie Rojas doubled. Sanford, who had held the Phillies without a hit from the third through the seventh, was then relieved by left-hander Billy O'Dell.

The two teams entered the ninth inning deadlocked at 2–2, when Jesus Alou singled and Tom Haller hit a home run to give the Giants a 4–2 lead.

For Billy O'Dell, it was his first victory of the year. For Phillies reliever Ed Roebuck, it was his first loss, giving up a run for the first time in the 1964 season after 37 innings pitched.

The loss dropped the Phillies a one-half game behind the Giants for the league lead. However, within a week the Phillies had once again moved a half game ahead of the Giants.

On Saturday, June 13, at Philadelphia, Jim Bunning (6–2) threw a five-hitter beating the Mets, 8–2, out-dueling former Detroit teammate Frank Lary (0–1). For the Phillies, Johnny Callison hit his fifth home run of the season.

The Giants were able to keep up the pressure on the Phillies, as they beat the Braves, 6–4, to remain one-half game behind. The Reds, meanwhile, were just one game behind the Giants as they won over the Colts, 6–1. Jim Maloney (4–7) went the distance for Cincinnati, pitching a six-hitter.

In a 23-hit slugfest a Wrigley Field, the Pirates beat the Cubs, 10–7. The decisive blow was a three-run homer by Smokey Burgess off Lew Burdette (2–1) in the 8th. Vern Law (4–5) got the win for the Bucs with relief help from Al McBean.

At St. Louis the Cardinals lost to L.A., 3–2, to drop below .500 (28–29) for the first time in the 1964 season since Opening Day. While the Cards were tied with the Cubs for 7th place, they were only five games behind the Phillies.

It was time for St. Louis to make some changes and they particularly needed help in the outfield. Earlier in the year they had passed on brining Duke Snider to St. Louis, as general manager Bing Devine wanted to concentrate on younger players. However, with the retirement of Stan Musial, the Cards were lacking a left-handed-hitting outfielder.

Curt Flood played regularly in center and was a steady performer, but the Redbirds were weak in both right field and left field. In order to stabilize their outfield and beef up their offense as well, on June 13 Devine traded minor league catcher Jim Saul along with a cash payment of $35,000 to the Reds for outfielder Bob Skinner.

Skinner, a journeyman outfielder who was going to be 33 years old in October, had been in the National League for ten years, primarily with Pittsburgh, 1954 – 1962, and then Cincinnati, 1963–1964. During his tenure with the Pirates he had batted over .300 three times. During his career he had achieved 1,017 hits with 92 home runs.

On Sunday, June 14, at Philadelphia a crowd of 21, 030 saw the Phillies come from behind in the first game, scoring three runs in the fifth and three runs in the seventh to defeat the Mets, 9–5, behind the relief pitching of Ray Culp (2–5) and the hitting of reserve outfielder John Briggs, who had three hits, and Richie Allen, who had two, including his 13th home run of the season. Briggs was making his first Major League start, playing in left field in place of injured Wes Covington. For the Mets, Ed Kranepool hit his second home run of the season and Galen Cisco (3–7) took the loss.

In the nightcap the Phillies downed the Mets, 4–2. Art Mahaffey (6–2) was the winner with relief help from Ed Roebuck. Al Jackson (3–9) took the loss. In the game Jim Hickman homered for the Mets and Johnny Callison for the Phillies.

The Giants once again kept pace with the Phillies, downing the Reds, 8–2. Ron Herbel (4–2) was the winning pitcher while Jim O'Toole (5–3), who lasted only two innings took the loss.

At Houston, the Cardinals continued to slide, losing to the Colts, 4–1, as Dick Farrell (10–1) became the first pitcher in the majors during the current season to win ten games. Bob Gibson (5–4) took the loss. Newly-acquired Bob Skinner started in left field for the Cardinals and went 0-for-3. The Cardinals had now lost four in a row and ten in their last 13 games.

On Monday, June 15, the National League office in Cincinnati announced that attendance in the 1964 season was up 16.1 percent over the 1963 season. In 1963 a record 11,382,277 paid admissions had turned out at National League ball parks.

However, to date in the 1964 season, 596,216 fans more than the record pace of the previous season had already gone through the turnstiles. The National League total for paid attendance through Sunday, June 14, was 4,282,267 compared with 3,686,051 for the same number of games the previous season.

Six clubs had shown an increase in attendance, while four clubs were running slightly below the previous year's pace. The largest gain in attendance was by the New York Mets, who so far had drawn 637,405 fans to their new Shea Stadium in just 23 dates, an increase of 233,302 over their first 23 dates the previous season at the Polo Grounds.

The Los Angeles Dodgers, despite their poor start in the 1964 season, were just shy of drawing one million fans for 30 dates. A total of 956,015 had already paid their way into Dodger Stadium, an increase of 106,358 over the 1963 championship-year pace.

The league-leading Philadelphia Phillies were 173,991 ahead of the previous season's paid total of 474,661 for the first 28 home games.

Other clubs that were ahead in attendance at that point in time were the Chicago Cubs, 256,841 for 24 games, an increase of 71,571; the Milwaukee Braves, 277,501 for 23 games, an increase of 102,913; and the St. Louis Cardinals, 293,828 for 23 games, an increase of 7,221.

The clubs that were showing a decrease included the Cincinnati Reds with 185,584 for 21 games, down 23,329; the Houston Colts, 346,669 for 37 games, down 32,472; the Pittsburgh Pirates, 245,878 for 23 games, down 36,759; and surprisingly, despite their constant challenge for the league lead, the San Francisco Giants, 607,825 for 30 games, down 6,430.

Standings, National League, June 15, 1964

Team	Won	Lost	Pct.	G.B.
Philadelphia	32	21	.604	
San Francisco	33	23	.589	½
Cincinnati	30	25	.545	3
Pittsburgh	29	27	.518	4–½
Milwaukee	30	28	.517	4–½
Chicago	27	27	.500	5–½
Los Angeles	28	30	.483	6–½
St. Louis	28	30	.483	6–½
Houston	27	32	.458	8
New York	19	40	.322	16

The season was now two months old and so far the race had been a constant seesaw between Philadelphia and San Francisco for the lead. Now suddenly Cincinnati had entered the picture, closing to within three games of the Phillies. Meanwhile, both Milwaukee and Pittsburgh had remained in the hunt throughout the first two months, but neither had yet mounted a serious drive for the top. Los Angeles following Opening Day was still having trouble getting above the .500 mark, while Houston and New York seemed destined to have a lock on ninth and tenth place in the league.

However, for St. Louis it was another matter, as the Cardinals were suddenly beginning to slip out of the pennant race. On May 27 the Cards were just one game behind the Phillies and on June 1 they were just 2–½ games behind the Phillies. Two weeks later they had fallen to 6–½ games behind. But then on June 15 the Cardinals made one of the most famous trades in baseball history.

The Chicago Cubs currently had several players—Ron Santo, Billy Williams and Larry Jackson—who were all having great years. Therefore, the Cubs' front office, led by general manager John Holland, surmised that they were perhaps just one starting pitcher away from competing for the pennant. On June 15 they were just 5–½ games behind the Phillies and very much in the chase. For some time the Cubs had coveted the Cardinals' 28-year-old right-hander Ernie Broglio, a former 20 game winner who had averaged 15 wins per year for the previous four years—and on June 15 they got him.

However, in order to get Broglio, the Cubs gave away future Hall of Fame member Lou Brock in the deal. Officially on June 15, 1964, at midday well before the Major League trading deadline, Cubs GM John Holland traded Lou Brock along with pitchers Jack Spring and Paul Toth to the Cardinals in exchange for Ernie Broglio, reliever Bobby Shantz and outfielder Doug Clemens. The Cardinals then sent Toth to the minors and called up from Jacksonville Mike Cuellar, who currently had a (6–1) record with 1.78 ERA.

Broglio apparently became expendable when the Cardinals acquired pitcher Glen Hobbie in an

Ernie Broglio (Photofile)

earlier trade with Cubs on June 2 in exchange for veteran pitcher Lou Burdette. Also, Broglio had recently aggravated manager Johnny Keane and general manager Bing Devine when he was recently sidelined for two weeks with a minor ailment.

Bing Devine said, in reference to the trade, "We need outfield help and some hitting, Brock adds youth, great running speed and is an improving ball player. It is always a gamble to give up starting pitcher. Fortunately, in the past whenever we've given up a starting pitcher, we've come up with someone who helped us. We've been after Brock since last winter. The trade itself actually has been in the works since Saturday."[25]

In Chicago, Cubs head coach Bob Kennedy (the Cubs used a rotating managerial system in 1964) stated, "We hate to lose Brock, and we think they are getting a mighty good player. But when you get a chance to fortify yourself in two places, you've got to go for it. We haven't had a left-handed reliever for some while. That's why we wanted Shantz. While Broglio will break right into the starting rotation."[26]

At St. Louis in 1960, Ernie Broglio had a season record of 21–9 with an ERA of 2.74, and in 1963 he was 18–8 with an ERA of 2.99. However, so far in the 1964 season, Broglio seemed to be slipping in his effectiveness and was 3–5 with a 3.53 ERA. As it turned out, nothing was left for Broglio in his career but hard times. Following the trade he would finish the 1964 season with a record of 4–7 for the Cubs, appearing in just 18 games. His combined record for the season was (7–12). He would then struggle for two seasons with the Cubs, achieving a (1–6) record in 1965 and a (2–6) record in 1966, before retiring from baseball after an eight-year career with a lifetime record of 77–74 and ERA of 3.74.

Another reason that the Cubs had decided to let go such a promising player as Brock was that they had called outfielder Billy Ott up from Salt Lake City where he had shown some steady improvement. But the maneuver turned out to be a total bust for the Cubs. Billy Ott would ultimately play in 20 games for the Cubs in 1964, hitting .179, and would never wear a Major League uniform again after that season, closing out a two-year trial with Cubs by appearing in just 32 games with a lifetime batting average of .169.

In 1964 Lou Brock was in his fourth season in the Major Leagues. In 1963 the speedy Brock had played in 148 games for the Cubs, hitting .258 with 24 stolen bases. At the time of the June 15th trade he was having a disappointing season, hitting .257 for Chicago with two home runs and 14 RBIs. However, Brock would ultimately wind up a 19-year Major League career in 1979, finishing with 3,023 hits, a lifetime batting average of .293 and 938 stolen bases. In 1975 he would be elected to Baseball's Hall of Fame.

Brock had played just one season in the minor leagues at St. Cloud in 1961 before being called up to the Cubs for a trial during the season, appearing in just four games. At St. Cloud he had showed great promise with 33 doubles, 14 home runs, 81 RBIs and a .361 batting average. Brock also was a good defensive ball player.

However, in Chicago Brock was an underachiever. The word on him was that he had a suspect glove and was capable of hitting for more average than he had. Suddenly he was known as "Brock like a rock."

Talking about his Chicago experience, Brock stated in an interview a few years ago, "My defense was pretty good, but that was playing mostly night ball games in the minors. No one told me Wrigley Field had sun."[27]

When Brock joined the Cardinals on June 16, manager Johnny Keane told him that he knew that he could play and that the Cards wanted him to steal bases. According to Brock, he didn't really see himself as base stealer in the same light as Maury Wills, Willie Mays or Vada Pinson. "I thought I was a power hitter," he said. "I wanted to play every day, the condition was I needed to steal bases."[28]

Subsequently Brock simply decided to acquiesce to Keane's demands and attempt to steal bases. He wound up with 43 stolen bases combined for the year in 1964 and would not steal less in any season for the next 13 years. "Nobody told you how or when to steal back then," Brock said. "It was pretty much up to me to figure it out."[29]

Lou Brock (PhotoFile)

Also, following the trade he would increase his batting average 64 points during the 1964 season and finish with a .315 average while scoring 111 runs.

Hardly one of Brock's Cardinals teammates really expected big things from him. In fact, pitcher Bob Gibson was forthright about Brock's prospects: "I thought it was a dumb trade. I didn't know how good Lou would be. No one knew. I didn't even remember facing him. I heard it and thought, for who? How could you trade Ernie Broglio for that?"[30]

The St. Louis Post-Dispatch was also skeptical of the deal. "The Ernie Broglio–Brock trade is expected to be X-rayed by fans and observers more than most of Bing Devine's trades. The first question raised by many is: Why didn't the Cardinals get more than Brock, a flashy outfielder who could become a star, for Broglio, an 18-game winner last season and still regarded as a top pitcher?"[31]

Prior to the Cardinals' acquiring Brock, they were under .500 with a 28–30 record, tied for eight place with Los Angeles. Following the arrival of Brock, the Cardinals would go 65–39 the rest of season and win the 1964 National League Pennant.

Lou Brock would go on to help the Cardinals win the National League Pennant again in 1967 and 1968, however his finest personal season would come ten years later in 1974. The Cardinals finished second to the Pirates in the National League eastern division.

While the Cardinals had just made one of the best trades in baseball history with Brock-Broglio deal, according to recently-retired $100,000-a-year Cardinal icon Stan Musial, bad trades had cost the Cardinals five pennants during his playing days. Musial, who was now a vice president in the Cardinal organization, notwithstanding his appointment by President Lyndon Johnson as the leader of the national fitness program, had some harsh words for previous deals made by the Redbirds.

Musial stated that the sale in 1941 of Johnny Mize by owner Sam Breadon and general manager Branch Rickey to the New York Giants for $50,000 and two players was "the worst mistake."[32] Mize, Musial said, was "one of the finest hitters I ever saw."[33]

Other bad deals by the Cardinals identified by Musial included the sale in 1946 of catcher of Walker Cooper by Breadon to the Giants for $175,000, and also, in 1949, the sale of pitcher Murray Dickson by owners Fred Saigh and Robert Hannegan to the Pittsburgh Pirates for $125,000.

"Among them, Breadon, Rickey, Saigh and Hannegan dealt the Cardinals, at a conservative estimate, out of four or five pennants," Musial said.[34]

The St. Louis Cardinals weren't the only club making changes on the June 15 trading deadline, as there were a couple of other minor moves, too. In an exchange of outfielders, the Houston Colts acquired Joe Gaines from the Baltimore Orioles in a deal for Johnny Weekly and cash. At Pittsburgh the Pirates took pitcher Don Cardwell off the disabled list and sent pitcher Fred Green to the minors. At San Francisco the Giants announced the signing of pitcher Dale Jansen, son of former Giants pitcher and current pitching coach Larry Jansen. The younger Jansen had been signed out of the University of Oregon and was assigned to Twin Falls, Idaho, of the Pioneer League.

With St. Louis fading quickly in the National League pennant race, Lou Brock and Jack Spring arrived, only hours after being traded by the Cubs on June 15, in the second inning of the Cardinals game at Houston and jumped into their new uniforms. Two innings later pitcher Mike Cuellar arrived.

Glenn Hobbie, the other recent acquisition by the Cardinals, was their starting pitcher against the Colts. When Brock and Spring arrived the Cardinals were leading the game 1–0 in the third.

In the seventh inning the Colts jolted Hobbie, scoring four runs to take a 4–3 lead, and Spring was called upon to enter the game. However, the 31-year-old left-hander was also ineffective, giving up four more runs to the Colts, who now had an 8–3 lead. In the top of the eighth Lou Brock, making his first appearance in a Cardinal uniform, pinch hit for Spring and struck out.

The Colts went on to a 9–3 victory, thereby dropping the Cardinals into a ninth-place tie with Houston, 7–½ games behind the Phillies. The defeat was the Cardinals' fifth straight and their 17th loss in the last 23 games.

For the Colts, Walt Bond drove in four runs with two singles, getting one each against Hobbie and Spring. Hobbie had also given up a two-run home run to Bob Aspromonte. Prior to the pasting that the Colts handed Glen Hobbie, he had been very effective in his first two starts as a Cardinal, allowing only two earned runs and eight hits in 16 innings.

According to back-up catcher Bob Uecker, the Cardinals actually had split for the night, as prior to the game Uecker had defeated the Colts' Nellie Fox in a cow-milking contest. However, prior to the contest, Uecker and Fox had agreed to split the $80 prize money.

In the only other game played in the National League on June 15, at San Francisco the Giants edged the Reds, 6–5, to pull even once again with the Phillies for the league lead. The loss dropped Cincinnati in second place to 3–½ games behind the leaders.

The Giants were trailing the Reds in the bottom of the eighth, 3–2, when they scored three runs on a pinch single by Cap Peterson to take a 5–3 lead. Then the Reds came back to tie the game in the top of the ninth, 5–5, with the help of an error by Jim Hart, a double by John Edwards which scored one run, and a sacrifice fly by Bobby Klaus which knocked in the other.

In the bottom of the ninth, Reds reliever Bill Henry walked Willie

McCovey. Ryne Duren then replaced Henry and Jim Hart greeted him with a single to drive in McCovey with the winning run.

The Giants' Willie Mays suddenly found himself in a power rut. Mays, the National League leader in home runs with 18, had now failed to connect for a home run in his last 17 games. Nonetheless, his 10 hits in his last 24 at bats had raised his average to .364, keeping him in second place ahead of the Pirates' Roberto Clemente with a .359 average, but still trailing league leader Billy Williams of the Cubs with a .382 average.

Also on June 15, the New York Yankees and New York Mets had scheduled a benefit exhibition game for sandlot baseball. However, the game was rained out and rescheduled to be played on Monday night, June 22.

On Tuesday, June 16, the topsy-turvy National League pennant race went upside down again as the Philadelphia Phillies beat the Chicago Cubs, 4–2, to regain first place, while the San Francisco Giants were defeated by the Cincinnati Reds, 9–4.

At Los Angeles, age seemed to be catching up with the 43-year-old Warren Spahn (5–5) as he failed to finish a game for the sixth straight time as the Dodgers beat the Braves, 5–1. Don Drysdale (9–5) was the winning pitcher, throwing a four-hitter.

At Colt Stadium in Houston, Curt Simmons (7–3) pitched a four-hitter, winning his first game in a month as the Cardinals beat the Colts, 7–1. The win put an end to the Cardinals' five-game losing streak. Lou Brock started his first game for the Cardinals and went 2-for-3 including a triple.

At Pittsburgh, the Pirates defeated the Mets, 3–1. Bob Veale, starting in place of ailing Bob Friend, had 12 strikeouts in the game, and for the second time in the season he tied the Pirate club mark for most strikeouts in a game.

On June 17 the Phillies, despite being pounded by the Cubs, 9–5, managed to hold on to first place by 7 percentage points over the Giants. Billy Williams (16 & 17) the leading hitter in the NL paced the Cubs with two home runs and single. Ron Santo (9) also homered as the Cubs exploded for 15 hits against four Philadelphia pitchers. Jim Bunning started the game but was unable to hold on to a 3–1 lead provided by a three-run homer by Bobby Wine in the second; Bunning was driven to the showers in the fifth following a two-run homer by Williams. The winning pitcher was Bob Buhl (8–3) and the loser Jack Baldshun (3–3).

At Candlestick Park the Giants' Bob Bolin (4–2) and Reds' Joe Nuxhall (6–4) had been locked in a pitching duel through eight innings with the Reds leading, 2–1. Then in the bottom of the ninth Willie McCovey

(10) hit a two-run pinch-hit home run to win the game for the Giants, 3–2. Willie Mays (19) broke his 20-game home run slump in the game with home run off Nuxhall in the first to give the Giants a 1–0 lead. However, Nuxhall (1) a better than average hitting pitcher, tied the game at 1–1 in the 5th with a home run. The Reds had taken a 2–1 lead in the 8th when Jim Davenport fumbled a grounder and Leo Cardenas singled to drive home Vada Pinson.

At Los Angeles, 41,868 fans had the pleasure of watching Sandy Koufax (9–4) shut out the Braves, 5–0, on a three-hitter, while striking out eight. In the game Koufax ran his string of scoreless innings to 22 while winning his 5th game in a row. Denny Lemaster (7–4) took the loss for the Braves.

At Houston, the Cardinals ended their disastrous road trip (5–11) with a win over the Colts, 2–1. Lou Brock took center stage in the victory as his single in the 8th scored Ray Washburn with what would prove to be the winning run. Ray Washburn (3–4) got the win and Ken Johnson (5–6) took the loss for the Colts.

At Pittsburgh, the Pirates beat the Mets, 3–2, to move into a third-place tie with the Reds, 3–½ games behind Philadelphia.

The New York Mets, aka "the Amazins," had a most colorful genesis as a legitimate Major League team. The stories of Casey Stengel's unique rhetoric and "Marvelous" Marv Throneberry's fielding blunders are timeless in baseball folklore. They are part and parcel of the legend of the Mets teams that lost 547 games in their first five years of play in the National League. You just never knew in those early days of the franchise when something unusual was going to happen on the field.

So it was that Saturday, June 20, 1964, was just such a bizarre day in Mets history. With the first-place Philadelphia Phillies playing at Shea Stadium, two players not known for their power hitting would take center stage. Outfielder Joe Christopher and Robert "Hawk" Taylor, a reserve catcher, would lead a bruising 16-hit assault on the Phillies in a 7–3 Mets victory, as both Taylor and Christopher would hit two home runs in the game.

There were 27,736 fans on hand at Shea Stadium (18,004 paying) when the game started, and Joe Christopher was the starting right fielder for the Mets. However, Hawk Taylor was sitting in the bull pen ready to warm up Mets relief pitchers as needed. But before two innings were completed, Taylor was in the game.

In the top of the second inning Mets catcher Chris Cannizzaro began arguing with home plate umpire Ken Burkhart over his calls on balls and strikes. Burkhart became extremely agitated as Cannizzaro kept up a steady diatribe over his calls—and then suddenly ejected him from the game. At that point Mets manager Casey Stengel summoned Taylor from the bullpen.

In the bottom of the third with no score in the game Joe Christopher slammed a home run off Phillies starter Dennis Bennett to give the Mets a 1–0 lead. Then, following a double by Charley Smith, Hawk Taylor teed off on Bennett and hit a home run to give the Mets a 3–0 lead over the Phillies.

Following Taylor's blast the Mets fans for the first time in their brief history began cheering an umpire. All at once the fans behind the plate started to chant, "We love you Burkhart!" Still later in the game this became "Burkhart's a Swell Guy."[35]

The Phillies came back to tie the score at 3–3 off Mets starter Jack Fisher before the Mets pulled ahead for good in the sixth. Hawk Taylor led off the bottom of the sixth with a single off Phillies reliever Dallas Green. When Amado Samuel singled to right, Taylor took off, chugging head down. He rounded second and was fortunate to make it to third as the throw from Johnny Callison in right had beat him to the bag. However, the ball bounced by Richie Allen, the Phillies third-sacker.

Apparently the Hawk must have thought that the ball bounced further and he took off for home. Unfortunately, Taylor was running out of luck on his dash around the bases. Allen had quickly retrieved the ball and threw to catcher Clay Dalrymple, who was patiently waiting at the plate to put the tag on the Hawk. While Hawk Taylor's dash for glory momentarily cost the Mets the go-ahead run, after "Fat Jack" Fisher struck out and Jim Hickman walked, Ed Kranepool singled in the go-ahead run.

In the bottom of seventh, lighting would strike twice as Christopher and Taylor once again connected for home runs, this time off Jack Baldshun, who pitched the seventh and eighth innings for the Phillies. Taylor's second home run came with Dick Smith aboard and landed about in the same place in left field as his first.

Jack Fisher got the win for the Mets with relief help from Al Jackson. The win was his fifth, making him top dog in victories on the Mets staff. Dallas Green took the loss for the Phillies.

Taylor, a former Milwaukee player who had been in and out of the Major Leagues consistently since 1957, wound up with four hits in the game. The Hawk's display of power was unusual though, considering he had only hit one home run in 111 career at bats prior to 1964. However, in 1962 playing with the Braves, a season in which Hawk had a total of 12 hits, he got five of them in one game against Houston.

Chirstopher, who came up with the Pirates, wasn't known as a "Sultan of Swat" either, having hit just eight home runs in 674 career at-bats prior to the 1964 season. However, he hit the longest home run of the day when his blast in the seventh sailed over the center-field fence.

Hawk Taylor would drift around the big leagues for five more seasons. On July 24, 1967, the Mets would send him along with Don Wallace and cash to the California Angels. He wound up his 11-year Major League career with the Kansas City Royals in 1970, having played in 318 games with 16 home runs and a career batting average of .218.

Joe Christopher would actually go on to have a decent season for the Mets in 1964; playing in 154 games, he hit for an average of .300 with 163 hits including 16 home runs. But he would play only one more season for the Mets in 1965 before winding up his eight-year career with a brief appearance with the Boston Red Sox in 1966. Christopher would leave the game with a lifetime batting average of .260 and 1,667 hits.

In other National League games played on June 20, the second-place San Francisco Giants routed the St. Louis Cardinals at Busch Stadium with a 20-hit attack, 14–3. For the Giants, Orlando Cepeda hit two home runs (his 9th & 10th), Harvey Kuenn had five hits including his 3rd home run of the season, and Willie Mays slugged his 21st home run of the season.

The Giants scored nine unearned runs in the game. In the top of sixth inning a wide throw by Cardinals shortstop Dick Groat on a grounder by Jose Pagan led to five runs. Bob Hendley (5–4), the Giants' starter and winning pitcher, held the Cardinals hitless in the four innings, but did yield a two-run home run to Phil Gagliano in the bottom of the eighth when the game was already out of reach, 13–3. Glen Hobbie (1–5) took the loss for St. Louis.

Newly acquired right fielder Lou Brock had two hits in the game and scored a run for the Cardinals as a crowd of 20,646 fans showed up at Busch Stadium to check out the new-look Redbirds.

Orlando Cepeda's first home run in the game was the 200th of his career. At that point in time only 60 previous Major League players out of nearly 10,000 had achieved that milestone in their careers.

However, in 1964 there were 15 other active Major League players with 200 or more career home runs. (National League: Hank Aaron, Ernie Banks, Ken Boyer, Willie Mays, Eddie Mathews, Frank Robinson, Duke Snider and Frank Thomas. American League: Joe Adcock, Rocky Colavito, Al Kaline, Harmon Kilebrew, Mickey Mantle, Roger Maris and Roy Sievers.)

Don Nottebart (3–7) scattered eight hits to defeat his former teammates as Houston downed Milwaukee, 3–2. Tony Cloninger, despite poor support from his teammates, went the distance for the Braves, allowing only four hits. The Colts scored a run in the third inning on a squeeze play, then scored two more in the seventh on sacrifice flies to give them the winning margin. Cloninger pitched his fifth complete game of the season but saw his record drop to 5–6. For the fading Milwaukee Braves playing before a sparse home crowd of only 6,619 fans, it was their fourth consecutive defeat.

The Pirates put a damper on Ernie Broglio's (0–1) (3–6 season) debut in a Cubs uniform as Joe Gibbon (4–2), with relief help from Al McBean with one out in the ninth, limited Chicago to just two hits while defeating them, 2–0. The game had been a scoreless pitchers' duel between Gibbon and Broglio until the bottom of the eighth when Gibbon's single drove in Bill Mazeroski who had tripled, then Gibbon scored on a triple by Dick Schofield. For Pittsburgh it was their fourth straight victory.

Prior to the game the Pirates had announced that they had exercised their option on pitcher Don Cardwell and sent him to the minors while recalling pitcher Tom Sisk. Cardwell had been bothered by a sore arm and had not pitched so far in the season.

At Crosley Field in Cincinnati, 24,559 fans were on hand to witness the surging Reds defeat the Dodgers, 6–4, with the help of three home runs and a bunt. In the second inning Drysdale hit Frank Robinson with a pitch, then catcher Johnny Edwards tagged Drysdale for a two-run home run to give Cincinnati a 2–0 lead.

Then the Dodgers came back to tie the game in the top of the fourth, 2–2. However, Vada Pinson led off the bottom of the fourth inning with a home run (his 10th) to once again give the Reds the lead 3–2.

The Dodgers counter-attacked by scoring two runs off Reds starting pitcher Jim O'Toole in the top of the fifth to take a 4–3 lead. Then Pinson connected for his second home run of the game (his 11th) to lead off the bottom of sixth and the game was tied again at 4–4.

In the bottom of seventh Leo Cardenas led off with a double and then went to third on a sacrifice bunt. Marty Keough pinch hit for O'Toole and walked. Pete Rose was then sent up to pinch hit for Bobby Klaus. Rose, who was mired in a batting slump and saw his batting average sink to .214, had recently been benched by Reds manager Fred Hutchinson. However, Rose came through as he laid down a squeeze bunt, sending Cardenas across the plate with the go-ahead run. Rose was thrown out at first on the play.

The Reds added an insurance run in the bottom of the eighth off Dodgers relief pitcher Ron Perranoski to make the winning margin, 6–4. Drysdale (9–6) took the loss, O'Toole (6–3) got the win with two perfect innings of relief help from Joe Nuxhall.

On the morning of Sunday, June 21, 1964, the leading hitters in the National League were the following.

National League Batting Leaders
June 21, 1964
(Based on 150 or more times at bat)

Player	Games	AB	Runs	Hits	Pct.
Williams, Chicago	58	227	43	84	.370
Mays, San Francisco	61	230	55	83	.361
Clemente, Pittsburgh	58	235	41	82	.349
Hunt, New York	60	219	30	73	.333
Stargell, Pittsburgh	41	161	25	52	.323
Torre, Milwaukee	58	217	34	68	.313
Santo, Chicago	57	212	41	66	.311
Boyer, St. Louis	64	243	33	75	.309

On June 21 at Shea Stadium in New York, the Mets would get no hitting heroics from Hawk Taylor or anyone else on the club for that matter, as Jim Bunning of the Phillies pitched the first perfect game in the National League in the Twentieth Century, retiring all 27 Mets hitters in a row. Bunning's no-hitter came in the first game of a doubleheader at Shea that saw the Phillies defeat the Mets, 6–0, as a large Father's Day crowd of 32,904 witnessed the historic event.

At that point in time, Bunning was the eighth pitcher in Major League history to hurl a perfect game. It had been 84 years since the last perfect game was pitched in the National League, and Bunning's gem was the first in the majors since Don Larsen of the New York Yankees pitched one against the Brooklyn Dodgers in the fifth game of the 1956 World Series.

Prior to Bunning's perfect game on June 21, 1964, the last pitcher in the National League to have pitched one was John M. Ward for Providence against Buffalo on June 17, 1880. Also, just five days prior to Ward's gem, John Lee Richmond of Worcester had pitched a perfect game against Cleveland (then in the National League).

Of course, there is only vague comparison in the perfect game of Bunning's and those pitched by Ward and Richmond, as the rules were vastly different in 1880 as opposed to those in effect in 1964. For one, the distance from the mound to plate in 1880 was only 45 feet, as opposed 60 feet 6 inches in 1964 and today. Also, in 1880 it took nine balls to gain a base on balls, and a batter was out if a foul ball was caught on the first bounce.

In addition, Bunning became the first pitcher in the modern era (since 1901) to pitch a no-hitter in both the American and National

Leagues. Bunning had previously pitched a no-hitter against the Boston
Red Sox on July 20, 1958, when he was with the Detroit Tigers. Lastly, Bunning's perfect game against the Mets was the first hurled during the regular season since Charlie Robertson of the Chicago White Sox pitched
one against the Detroit Tigers on April 30, 1922.

The Phillies had staked Bunning to a two-run lead, scoring in both
the first and second innings, and outside of two great defensive plays made
by his teammates, Bunning was never really in any kind of trouble on the
mound as he maintained in control throughout the game. Only three Mets
batters even came close to getting a hit.

In the bottom of the third inning shortstop Cookie Rojas made a
leaping catch of Amado Samuel's line drive, and in the bottom of the fifth
second baseman Tony Taylor made a fine diving stop of Jessie Gonder's
hard grounder toward right field and threw him out at first. Gonder hit
the ball half way between Taylor and first baseman John Herrnstein. Taylor made the play with a diving stab, slapping it to the ground, then quickly
recovered it and tossed to Herrnstein. The ball was hit so hard that when
Taylor knocked it down, Gonder had only reached about a third of the
way to first.

Phillies manager Gene Mauch said after the game that he had a hunch
that Bunning was working on something big, so early in the game he made
a defensive change. "I felt that Bunning himself sensed it early," Mauch
said. "By his attitude, the way he was moving his fielders around.

"I figured I'd try to make it easier for him, so I made a defensive
change in the fifth inning. I moved Cookie Rojas from shortstop to left
field in place of Wes Covington and sent Bobby Wine to short."[36]

The belief was that Mauch had been sensitized by the game that Bunning had pitched May 29 against Houston, when he had a perfect game
going with two outs in the seventh inning, when Mike White of the Colts
hit a soft liner to left field. Wes Covington got a late start on the ball and
it fell in for a single. Then the Colts scored five runs the next inning.

The moment was right for Mauch's legendary thinking and strategy,
even after the fact. However, more likely Mauch was not thinking about
a no-hitter, much less a perfect game, but was thinking about winning a
close game with the Giants nipping at the heels of league-leading Phillies.
When Mauch made the defensive change inserting Rojas in left field in
the bottom of the fifth inning, the score was Phillies 2, Mets 0, and it came
with full remembrance that less than 24 hours earlier the Mets had
pounded Phillies pitching for 16 hits in a 7–3 romp.

From the seventh inning on the usually partisan Mets fans were
behind Bunning as he blitzed along in the 91-degree heat. It took just two

hours and 19 minutes for Bunning to set down 27 straight Mets batters on only 86 pitches. Relying on his fast curve ball, a slider and three-quarter motion, Bunning had the Mets batters baffled and struck out ten along way to his perfect game.

Mets rookie John Stephenson was the 27th and last batter to face Bunning in the game and became his 10th strikeout victim. Then all at once his teammates rushed him as he returned to the Phillies dugout and the crowd began to chant, "We want Bunning, we want Bunning!"[37]

Shortly he returned to the field to be interviewed behind home plate by Mets television play-by-play announcer Ralph Kiner. The crowd, still standing, gave Bunning one of the biggest ovations yet heard in the Mets' new stadium.

"I was aware I was pitching a perfect game from the fifth inning on," said Bunning. "I even kidded about it on the bench and the boys kidded right back. Jinx? I don't believe in jinxes."[38]

In his postgame remarks Bunning then went on to acknowledge the diving lunge that Tony Taylor had made in preventing Jessie Gonder's fifth-inning liner from going through for a hit. "What a play that Taylor made!" Bunning said. "What a play."[39]

While Bunning was making his postgame television appearance, his wife Mary was at his side. Meanwhile, back at the Bunning summer household in Cherry Hill, New Jersey, where he had rented two adjacent four-room apartments to have his family with him for the season, six of their seven children, ranging in age from nine to two, were glued to the television set with their babysitter, Mary Fran Hoffman of Covington, Kentucky. The Bunnings' other child, 11-year-old daughter Barbara, was with the Bunnings in New York at Shea Stadium.

Son Jim, nine, was the only one of the Bunning children who watched the game, having viewed the last few innings. Subsequently, little Jim acted as the spokesperson for the Bunning children in an interview with Associated Press.

"Oh, I'm happy," he said. "I watched part of the game. When it was the last inning, I was yelling, 'He's gonna win.'[40] Baby sitter Mary Fran added, "My stomach is still jumping up and down. It was quite a nice Father's Day."[41]

While Bunning seemed to be cool, calm and collected after the game, he stated that his wife Mary, who had watched the game from behind the Phillies dugout with their 11-year-old daughter, Barbara, was all shook up.

"I was so excited I lost my sunglasses twice," said Mary Bunning.[42]

Gus Triandos, who came in the same trade with the Detroit Tigers that brought Bunning to the Phillies, was the catcher for the historic game.

However, it wasn't the first no-hitter that Triandos had caught in his career, having been behind the plate for the Orioles when Hoyt Wilhelm tossed a no-hitter against the New York Yankees on September 2, 1958.

When asked which no-hitter was more difficult to catch, Triandos replied, "Have you ever tried to catch Wilhelm's knuckler?

"No no-hitter is easy though," he added. "I had to be careful I didn't call for a wrong pitch. I was extra careful, too. He shook me off at least ten times.

"He didn't make a wrong pitch all afternoon. His curve has a habit of hanging in the late innings, but not today. He struck out the last hitter [John Stephenson] on three curve balls."[43]

In the ninth inning Bunning had called Triandos out to the mound. Triandos revealed that the strategy talk was simply that Bunning wanted a breather and told Gus that he should tell him a joke. "However, I couldn't think of any," remarked Triandos. "I just laughed at him."[44]

Box Score, June 21, 1964
(First Game)

Philadelphia	AB	R	H	RBI	New York	AB	R	H	RBI
Briggs, cf	4	1	0	0	Hickman, cf	3	0	0	0
Herrnstein, 1b	4	0	0	0	Hunt, 2b	3	0	0	0
Callison, rf	4	1	2	1	Kranepool, 1b	3	0	0	0
Allen, 3b	3	0	1	1	Christopher, rf	3	0	0	0
Covington, lf	2	0	0	0	Gonder, c	3	0	0	0
a-Wine, ss	1	1	0	0	R. Taylor, lf	3	0	0	0
T. Taylor, 2b	3	2	1	0	C. Smith, ss	3	0	0	0
Rojas, ss, lf	3	0	1	0	Samuel, 3b	2	0	0	0
Triandos, c	4	1	2	2	c-Altman	1	0	0	0
Bunning, p	4	0	1	2	Stallard, p	1	0	0	0
					Wakefield, p	0	0	0	0
					b-Kanehl	1	0	0	0
					Sturdivant	0	0	0	0
					d-Stephenson	1	0	0	0
Totals	32	6	8	6	Totals	27	0	0	0

a-Ran for Covington in 6th; b-Grounded out for Wakefield in 6th; c-Struck out for Samuel in 9th; d-Struck out for Sturdivant in 9th.

	1	2	3	4	5	6	7	8	9	R	H	E
Philadelphia	1	1	0	0	0	4	0	0	0	6	8	0
New York	0	0	0	0	0	0	0	0	0	0	0	0

Errors-None. LOB-Philadelphia 5, New York 0.

Two base hit-Triandos, Bunning; Home Run-Callison; Sacrifce-Herrnstein, Rojas.

	IP	H	R	ER	BB	SO
Bunning W (7–2)	9	0	0	0	0	10
Stallard L (4–9)	5–⅔	7	6	6	4	3
Wakefield	⅓	0	0	0	0	0
Sturdivant	3	1	0	0	0	3

Wild Pitch-Stallard. Time-2:19. Umpires-Sudol, Pryor, Secory, Burkhart. Attendance-32,036.

Inning-By-Inning Account of Jim Bunning's Perfect Game

1st inning: Jim Hickman was called out on strikes. Tony Taylor threw out Ron Hunt. Ed Kranepool popped out to shortstop Cookie Rojas.

2nd inning: Joe Christopher flied out to John Briggs in center. Jesse Gonder fouled out to Gus Triandos. Bob Taylor flied to Johnny Callison in right.

3rd inning: Charlie Smith struck out. Amado Samuel lined to Rojas. Tracy Stallard flied to Wes Covington.

4th inning: Jim Hickman struck out. Ron Hunt struck out. Ed Kranepool popped to Gus Triandos.

5th inning: Joe Christopher popped to Rojas. Gonder grounded to Tony Taylor, who made a diving stop and threw him out. Bob Taylor grounded out.

6th inning: Smith flied out to Briggs. Samuel popped to short. Rod Kanehl batted for relief pitcher Bill Wakefield and grounded out to short.

7th inning: Hickman struck out. Hunt grounded to third. Kranepool struck out.

8th inning: Christopher struck out. Gonder grounded to second. Bob Taylor struck out.

9th inning: Smith popped to short. George Altman batted for Samuel and struck out. John Stephenson batted for relief pitcher Tom Sturdivant and struck out.

James Paul David Bunning was born on October 23, 1931, in Southgate, Kentucky. Southgate was a working-class suburb of Cincinnati, located just south of Newport on the Kentucky side of the Ohio River, an area that could be referred to geographically as the southside of Cincinnati.

Newport, just north of Southgate, was a bawdy area that had a notorious reputation for gambling and prostitution. The gambling element was legal in Kentucky until the late 1950s. The prostitution industry was not but nonetheless flourished throughout the area and to a lesser degree remains active even today as a side industry to the many strip clubs in the community.

The wide-open action during the 1940s and 1950s in Northern Kentucky ranged from poker parlors in back rooms of corner saloons to elaborate casinos such as the Flamingo and Lookout House, complete with floor shows and headliner acts.

Then when Las Vegas began to blossom as the gaming capital of America in the early 1950s, Newport and its surrounding areas began to crack down on the seamy elements operating in its community. Reform groups such as "The Committee of 500," led by former Cleveland Browns back-up quarterback George Ratterman, tried in vain to rid the vice from the Northern Kentucky communities along the Ohio.

Then in the early 1960s the "coup de grace" came with the intervention of United States Attorney General Robert F. Kennedy in a nationwide crackdown on organized crime, and the last vestiges of hardcore Newport nightlife fled to Las Vegas to set up shop.

Jim Bunning, despite growing up within a stone's throw of the unsavory elements that surrounded his boyhood home, took a different, more positive direction in life. He had been a smoker, but gave it up sometime around 1963 and only enjoyed an occasional social drink in the off-season.

Bunning, a devout Catholic, regularly attended Sunday masses on road trips in the Major Leagues, and also spoke to Holy Name groups whenever possible.

He met his future wife, Mary Theis, in the sixth grade. He went to high school at St. Xavier High School, a private Jesuit school that was located in downtown Cincinnati at Seventh and Sycamore Streets until its demolition in 1960 and subsequent relocation to the Cincinnati suburbs.

He always played baseball in his formative years in amateur leagues, knothole leagues and at more sophisticated levels of competition such as American Legion leagues. All along the way Bunning excelled at that game. However his parents would not let him sign a Major League contract after he had finished high school, but rather insisted that he attend Xavier University in Cincinnati on a basketball scholarship.

He graduated from Xavier in 1953, finishing his degree in business administration in just 3–½ years, then without receiving a bonus, signed a contract with the Detroit Tigers. During college he and Mary had gotten married and started a family with the birth of daughter Barbara, the first of the Bunnings' seven children.

Bunning then pitched in the minor leagues for a few years at Richmond, Davenport, Williamsport, Buffalo and Little Rock, learning along the way that he would need to develop a breaking ball to complement his sharp fast ball.

Jim Bunning (PhotoFile)

He came up to the Major Leagues with Detroit in 1955 and pitched in 15 games, finishing with a 3–5 record and 6.35 ERA. However, within two years he would have the only 20-game-win season in his brilliant career, when in 1957 he went 20–8 with an ERA of 2.69. The following season on July 20, 1958, he pitched a no-hitter against the Boston Red Sox as Detroit beat Boston, 3–0.

In nine seasons with Detroit, Bunning had a record of 118–87. During the 1963 season he began to have some differences with Tigers manager Chuck Dressen. Therefore on December 4, 1963, he was traded along with catcher Gus Triandos to the Phillies for outfielder Don Demeter and pitcher Jack Hamilton.

But Jim Bunning seemed to have a record of dissention with managers. He has also at various times in retrospective interviews referred to Gene Mauch as having been arrogant.

In the ensuing seven years between 1964 and 1971, pitching for Philadelphia, Pittsburgh, Los Angeles and a second stint back at Philadelphia, Bunning would win another 106 games to finish his career with 224–184 record for 17 years, becoming the first pitcher in the modern era to win 100 games in both the American and National Leagues. He was also the first pitcher in the modern era to have 1,000 strikeouts in both leagues and of course he pitched a no-hitter in both leagues—a feat since duplicated by Nolan Ryan and Hideo Nomo. At the time of his retirement in 1971, Bunning was second in career strikeouts 2,855 behind Walter "Big Train" Johnson. In fact, Bunning was the only pitcher to have struck out Hall of Famer Ted Williams three times in one game.

Despite having a terrible season in 1968 at Pittsburgh (4–14) while pitching for a Pirates team that nearly played .500 ball—and despite the fact that he was not a "Rookie of the Year," never was selected as an MVP, never won a Cy Young Award or even won just one Gold Glove in his entire Major League career—Bunning's credentials were still good enough to land him in Cooperstown. In 1996 Bunning was elected to the National Baseball Hall of Fame by the Committee on Baseball Veterans, i.e., the veterans committee.

During his playing days Bunning invested his baseball earnings wisely and in 1964, he and Mary owned a $55,000, nine-room colonial home in Fort Thomas, Kentucky, just up the road from his boyhood home of Southgate. The family traveled around northern Kentucky in a Plymouth station wagon, although the Bunnings also owned a Cadillac.

At this point of his career in 1964, during the off-season he worked as a stock broker. Bunning had previously tried selling insurance, but didn't care for it much. However, when his playing days were through following the 1971 season, he spent five years managing in the Phillies minor league system and tried his hand at being a player agent and an investment broker for athletes. He is also considered to be a dominant figure in the founding of the players' union (MLBPA) and had a significant role in establishing the players' pension fund.

But soon he broke into another field of endeavor; politics. In 1977 Bunning, a Republican, won election to the Fort Thomas, Kentucky, City Council. In 1979 he was elected to the Kentucky State Senate and served until 1983. He also tried a run at becoming Governor of Kentucky, but fell short.

Then in 1986 he was elected to United States House of Representatives from Kentucky and served until 1998, when he was elected to the United States Senate. Upon being sworn into the Senate in January, 1999, one of his first duties was to serve as a juror in the impeachment trial of President Bill Clinton.

Currently Bunning serves on three Senate committees, including the Special Committee on Aging, Energy and Natural Resources and the Committee on Banking, Housing and Urban Affairs. While Jim Bunning is the first and only member of the National Baseball Hall of Fame to serve in the United States Congress, it is fair to say that based on his weak legislative record to date, he will never equal the fame he had on the pitcher's mound in Congress.

However, in Philadelphia Jim Bunning is still a hero. On Opening Day in April 2001 the Philadelphia Phillies retired his Number 14 jersey. Bunning's jersey was the fifth to be retired by Phillies, joining Richie

Asburn (1), Robin Roberts (36), Steve Carlton (32) and Mike Schmidt (20).

There was also a second game at Shea Stadium on June 21 and the Phillies won that, too. Rookie Rick Wise (1–0) with relief help from veteran Johnny Klipstein, defeated the Mets in the nightcap of the Father's Day twin bill, 8–2.

It was the first Major League victory for Wise, who was still 18 years old and would go on to pitch 18 years in the Major Leagues and finish with a record of 188–181, including a no-hitter against Cincinnati on June 23, 1971.

Former Detroit Tiger Ace Frank Lary (0–2) started for New York and took the loss. For Philadelphia, Johnny Callison, who had homered in the first game, also hit his second home run of the day and 10th of season in the second game. John Briggs also homered for the Phillies.

While Philadelphia was winning a doubleheader at Shea Stadium and making history to boot, San Francisco was pounding out a 7–3 win over St. Louis with 13 hits. Hal Lanier, son of former Major League pitcher Max Lanier led the way for the Giants with four hits including his first Major League home run. Willie Mays also hit his 22nd home run of the season. The win kept the second-place Giants just two games behind the Phillies.

All three Cardinals runs were driven in by newly acquired Bob Skinner and Lou Brock. Skinner doubled home two runs in the first and Brock (3) hit a solo home run in the third. Jack Stanford (5–7) was the winning pitcher and Curt Simmons (7–6) the loser.

At Cincinnati, the Reds, who were starting to move on the Phillies, split a twin bill with the Dodgers before a packed house of 29,183. The doubleheader was made necessary by the 17-inning game with the Dodgers that had been called on June 21 due to the National League curfew.

In the first game the Dodgers beat the Reds, 6–2, as Sandy Koufax (10–4) won his 10th game of the year supported by Big Frank Howard, who drove in two runs with a single and his 15th home run. Bob Purkey (3–4) took the loss for Cincinnati. Koufax was unable to go further than the 6th inning, however, due to the incredibly hot temperature prevailing in Cincinnati. Robert Miller pitched the last three inning for the Dodgers.

In the second game the Reds prevailed, downing the Dodgers, 2–1. Cincinnati scored all their runs off losing pitcher Larry Miller (0–1) in the first inning when Vada Pinson doubled and Deron Johnson homered. Joey Jay (4–2) went the distance and was the winning pitcher for the Reds. The doubleheader split kept third-place Cincinnati 4½ games behind Philadelphia.

As it was a day for doubleheaders in the National League with four scheduled, Chicago swept their twin bill with Pittsburgh, 2–1 and 7–2.

In the opening game it was the Larry Jackson (9–5) show. Jackson pitched a three-hitter for the Cubs as he retired the last 22 batters to face him and also knocked in both runs. On the day Jackson went 3 for 4, all singles.

In the second game Cubs veteran Lou Burdette (3–1) went seven innings allowing only five hits, before giving way to relief help from Lindy McDaniel. Steve Blass (3–4) took the loss for the Pirates.

Rounding out the action on June 21, Houston swept a doubleheader from Milwaukee, 5–2 and 5–4, to drop the reeling Braves into ninth place 9–½ games behind the Phillies. The Braves had dropped the entire four-game weekend series to the Colts and now had run their losing streak to six.

For the Colts Rusty Staub had the big stick in the opener, pounding Warren Spahn and two Milwaukee relievers for four hits including a pair of home runs. In the nightcap home runs by pitcher Ken Johnson and Joe Gaines did the trick.

National League Won and Lost Records
June 22, 1964

	Phil	SF	Cin	Pitt	Chi	St L	Hou	LA	Mil	NY	Won
Philadelphia	–	1	4	4	6	1	6	4	3	9	38
San Francisco	5	–	6	2	2	6	3	4	4	5	37
Cincinnati	1	2	–	2	5	4	4	10	2	4	34
Pittsburgh	3	5	2	–	4	3	3	3	2	8	33
Chicago	3	1	3	5	–	3	4	1	5	5	30
St. Louis	4	6	3	2	3	–	4	2	4	4	32
Houston	1	3	3	3	2	5	–	2	9	4	32
Los Angeles	2	2	2	5	3	5	4	–	3	5	31
Milwaukee	2	2	3	4	2	4	4	6	–	3	30
New York	2	4	2	2	3	2	2	1	2	–	20
Lost	23	26	28	29	30	33	34	33	34	47	–

On June 22, the Mayor's Trophy game between the Mets and Yankees was postponed for a second time. A rainstorm had forced the postponement of the June 15 game. Now the game was forced to be rescheduled again due to a rainstorm in Chicago.

The Yankees were rained out of a game in Chicago on Friday, June 19, and had to make it up on June 22.

However Philadelphia did not remain in the lead very long as the seesaw battle continued and by the end of June the Giants had once again moved back into first place.

On Tuesday, June 30, at Candlestick Park the Giants defeated the Mets, 5–0, to remain one-half game ahead of the Phillies entering the month of July. Gaylord Perry (6–3) pitched a three-hit shutout, and Orlando Cepeda and Tom Haller homered for the Giants in a game that saw Perry and losing pitcher Galen Cisco (3–10) of the Mets engage in a duel of knockdown pitches.

It all started in the first inning when Willie Mays came to bat with runners on first and second and no outs. At that point, one of Cisco's pitches was close inside and sent Mays sprawling on the ground at the plate. The Giants took it personally and immediately determined that Cisco was throwing at their captain.

Mays didn't charge the mound and hardly made any fuss about the brush-back pitch at all. Rather he smashed a ball back toward the mound that caromed off Cisco to the shortstop and became a Mets double play. However, on the play Hal Lanier scored from third, giving the Giants a 1–0 lead in the game.

When Cisco came to bat in the top of the third, Perry retaliated and grazed Cisco's batting helmet with a pitch. Then when Perry led off the bottom of the third, Cisco aimed his pitches at Perry's legs while striking him out. The next batter was Hal Lanier and Cisco knocked him down with a pitch. This brought swift action from plate umpire Tom Gorman, who sternly made it known that enough was enough, and at all once the war of dusters was ceased between Cisco and Perry.

Willie Mays went on to have a highly productive game while doing nothing more than hitting grounders off of fielders gloves, yet still scoring two runs and accounting for another. In the fourth Mays led off by beating out a grounder to deep short and when Cepeda followed, bouncing one wide of third, Mays was heading full steam on a hit and run. He rounded second while John Stephenson was throwing Cepeda out and slid into third well ahead of Ed Kranepool's return throw from first. Kranepool's high throw got past Stephenson and Willie dashed home across the plate with the Giants' second run of the game.

In the sixth Mays singled off Ron Hunt's glove, then Cepeda followed with his 13th home run. One out later Haller hit his 7th home run.

Prior to the game the Mets had formally concluded the acquisition of Frank Lary from the Detroit Tigers with a payment of $40,000. Lary had been a 30-day conditional purchase.

Philadelphia kept pace with the Giants by downing Houston, 8–1. Jim Bunning (8–3) went all the way for the Phillies, pitching a five-hitter. Ken Johnson (6–7) was losing pitcher for the Colts. However, Johnson was the victim of three errors committed by his outfielders in the first inning. The three errors committed by Walt Bond and Joe Gaines, coupled with three hits and two walks, accounted for five Phillies runs in the first inning.

At Wrigley Field the Cubs beat the Reds, 1–0, as Larry Jackson (10–5) pitched a one-hitter. Jackson had a perfect game for six innings until Pete Rose, back in the lineup following his monumental batting slump earlier in June, led off the seventh with a single. Joey Jay (4–4), who went the route for the Reds, pitched a two-hitter and took the loss.

The game was fastest played so far in the 1964 season in the National League, just one hour and 40 minutes. Larry Jackson threw only 85 pitches in the game, walked none, had five strike outs and only faced 28 batters.

The only two Chicago hits in the game yielded by Jay came off the bat of rookie shortstop Jim Stewart. Stewart doubled in the first and then singled in the sixth inning, driving in Dick Bertell who had walked, then reached third on a sacrifice by Jackson. Jackson was also safe at first when Jay dropped the ball for an error. Bertell had been the first man to reach base following 14 consecutive batters that had been set down by Jay. The loss dropped the Reds into fourth place, 6–½ games behind the Giants.

In the only other game played on June 30, Milwaukee defeated St. Louis, 5–4. The loss dropped the Cardinals to seventh place, 9–½ games behind the Giants.

V

July, Part One

National League Standings, July 1, 1964

Team	Won	Lost	Pct.	G.B.
San Francisco	45	28	.616	—
Philadelphia	43	27	.614	½
Pittsburgh	38	32	.543	5–½
Cincinnati	38	34	.528	6–½
Chicago	35	34	.507	8
Milwaukee	36	37	.493	9
St. Louis	36	38	.486	9–½
Los Angeles	34	38	.472	10–½
Houston	35	40	.467	11
New York	22	54	.289	24–½

In the 1963 season Sandy Koufax had won 25 games and lost five, prompting Yogi Berra of the New York Yankees to say following the 1963 World Series, "I can see how he won twenty-five games. What I can't see is how he lost five."[1]

While Juan Marichal was not getting the same respect from the game's elders as Sandy Koufax, the record showed nonetheless that he too had won 25 games in 1963 (25–8).

Juan Marichal had been an instant success in his National League debut in 1960, throwing a one-hit shutout against the Phillies; then in his second start against the Pirates he tossed a four-hitter.

Born in Laguna Verde, Dominican Republic, on October 20, 1937, Marichal became known as the "The Dominican Dandy" as he mesmerized hitters with his high leg kick and jerky motion, no-wind-up delivery for 16 Major League seasons between 1960 and 1975, establishing a career record of 243–142. Between 1963 and 1969 he won 20 or more games six out of seven seasons.

On June 15, 1963, Marichal threw a 1–0 no-hitter against Houston.

He also pitched in eight All-Star games and was the winning pitcher in two, 1962 and 1964.

In 1965 he won the prestigious Arch Ward Trophy as the Game's Most Valuable Player. However, despite all of Marichal's achievements, he never won a Cy Young Award or was ever selected as the National League MVP. The Giants weren't winning pennants and consequently the accolades he so deserved went to his contemporaries, such as Sandy Koufax and Bob Gibson, whose teams were.

Despite his achievements on the mound, Marichal's image as a player is forever imbedded in the memories of fans for an incident that occurred while he was at bat. In late 1965 the Giants and Dodgers were in a heated battle for the pennant. On August 22 in a game with the Dodgers, Marichal had thrown a couple of knockdown pitches at Los Angeles hitters.

Consequently, when his turn at bat came, Los Angeles catcher John Roseboro called for Sandy Koufax to retaliate with a knockdown pitch. Marichal accepted the subsequent duster thrown by Koufax as the opposing pitcher's just taking care of business. However, he became enraged by Roseboro's return throw to the mound, which whistled by his ear. All at once Marichal hammered Roseboro over the head with his bat, opening up a nasty gash, and then it took the umpires and several players from both teams to wrestle the bat away from Marichal, who had gone bonkers and wanted to inflict further blows upon Roseboro's bleeding cranium.

For his actions the National League fined Marichal $1,750 and suspended him for nine days. However, the impact of the incident on fans' collective psyche never went away. It's possible that a lot of baseball writers never forgot the Marichal–Roseboro incident, either, and passed him by when they had the chance to vote for various postseason awards.

If there was ever a bit of irony in nonrecognition of the greatness of Juan Marichal, it is epitomized by his performance in-between the 1966 season, when he had a record of 25–6 and was passed over for the Cy Young Award in favor of Sandy Koufax, and the 1968 season, when he had a record of 26–9 and was passed over for the Cy Young Award in favor of Bob Gibson. Strange as it may seem, in 1967, the year Marichal had his only subpar season in the decade of the Sixties with a record of 14–10, his teammate Mike McCormick was given the Cy Young Award with a record of 22–10.

Recognition of "The Dominican Dandy" finally came in 1983 when he was enshrined at Cooperstown, having been selected to the National Baseball Hall of Fame. Nonetheless, Marichal did not win election to the Hall in his first two years of eligibility.

Now at this point in July 1964, Koufax and Marichal seemed to be in race to win the most games again as both got their 11th wins of the season on July 1. Koufax gave up five hits in beating Philadelphia, 3–2, at Dodger Stadium, while Marichal gave up eight hits in beating Pittsburgh, 2–1, at Candlestick Park to move the first-place Giants out in front of the Phillies by 1–½ games in the National League pennant race.

At L.A. in the fourth inning the Phillies had taken the lead in the game, 2–0, after Johnny Callison had homered off Koufax following a triple by Cookie Rojas. However, Philadelphia starter Dennis Bennett could not hold the lead. Despite the gopher ball to Callison, Koufax struck out ten in the game, thereby allowing him to reach the lifetime total of 1,600 strikeouts.

Marichal was given quick support by his teammates as Willie Mays (23) homered in the first and then the Giants scored again in the second off Pirate starter Bob Veale with consecutive doubles by Del Crandall and Jose Pagan.

In a game under the lights at Crosley Field in Cincinnati on July 1 with 7,642 fans on hand, a two-out home run by Pete Rose in the bottom of the tenth sunk the Cubs, 6–5, moving the Reds into a third-place tie with the Pirates, 6–½ games behind the Giants. The round-tripper was the second of the season for Rose, who connected off Chicago starter Dick Ellsworth, hitting ball into the right-field bleachers.

Ellsworth (10–7) was also gunning for his 11th win but came up short. Ellsworth entered the bottom of the ninth with 5–1 lead before errors by himself and Andre Rodgers led to a four-run rally by the Reds to tie the game.

Steve Boros reached first when his grounder went through Rodgers, went to second on a single by Rose and then scored when Ellsworth threw the ball wildly on a grounder by Tommy Harper. Vada Pinson then followed with an infield hit that filled the bases. Frank Robinson followed with a sacrifice fly, narrowing the Cubs' lead to 5–3. That brought Deron Johnson to the plate, who promptly tied the game with a triple, scoring two.

Ron Santo had touched Reds starter Bob Purkey for a pair of bases-empty home runs in the second (14th) and fourth (15th). Billy Williams also connected for a solo shot in the sixth (19th), as Chicago had built a 5–1 lead going into the ninth inning against the Reds. The Reds used four pitchers in the game: Purkey, Ryne Duren, Sammy Ellis and Bill Henry, who got the win (2–1).

Likewise, Houston's Dick Farrell (10–2), who had not won a game since June 14, was going after his 11th win of the season but was hit hard by the New York Mets. However, Farrell escaped the loss, departing after

2–⅔ innings as the Mets pounded the Colts, 8–6. For the "Amazins" it was another feast-or-famine game, this time getting 16 hits off four Colt pitchers. For the losing Colts, Walt Bond stroked two home runs (12 &13) and for the Mets, Bob Aspromonte (9) and Larry Elliot (2) homered. Elliot also had two singles in the game, while Ed Kranepool collected a single, a double and a triple, and John Stephenson added three singles. Earlier in the day the Mets had made it official on former Detroit Tigers pitcher Frank Lary by parting with $40,000 to wrap up the his 30-day conditional purchase.

Rounding out the NL action on July 1, Curt Simmons got his ninth win (9–6) as St. Louis defeated, Milwaukee 6–1. Julian Javier had the big stick for St. Louis as he singled in the first run in the Cardinals' three-run rally in the second and then hit a three-run home run in the third.

On Friday, July 3, National League teams began the weekend of play before the three-day All-Star Game break.

At San Francisco the Giants and Phillies were matched up in a head-to-head battle for first place. The Phillies prevailed in the first game of the series, 5–1, behind the six-hit pitching of Ray Culp (5–6). Richie Allen hit his 16th home run of the season in the game.

At Cincinnati the Reds beat the Cardinals, 4–1. John Tsitouris (5–5) went the distance for the Reds while Vada Pinson provided the run support, getting three RBIs with three hits, including a triple. Bob Gibson (6–6) took the loss for St. Louis.

At Los Angeles, with a big crowd of 42,616 on hand, the Dodgers beat the Mets, 6–2, behind Don Drysdale (11–7). Jessie Gonder homered for the Mets, his 4th, while Jack Fisher (5–7) took the loss. Drysdale had nine strikeouts in the game.

Pittsburgh continued to hang in the race, defeating Houston, 2–1. Vern Law (7–6) went 8–⅔ innings for the win, being relieved in the 9th by Al McBean. The only Colts run came as a result of a home run by Joe Gaines, his third. Jim Owens (3–6) took the loss.

At Milwaukee slugger Eddie Mathews, batting in the lead-off position for the Braves, hit his 9th home run of the season as they downed the Cubs, 8–2. Lee Maye, batting in the clean-up spot for Milwaukee, went 3-for-4 including a home run, his 7th.

Tony Cloninger (7–7), the winning pitcher for the Braves, gave up nine hits, but also struck out nine batters. Former Brave Bob Buhl (9–4) took the loss for the Cubs.

Now with the All-Star Game just a few days away, the individual leaders in various categories in the National League were the following.

National League Leaders
Saturday, July 4, 1964
Batting

Individual Batting		Hits		Home		RBIs	
Mays, S.F.	.347	Clemente, Pitt.	99	Mays, S.F.	23	Mays, S.F.	55
Clemente, Pitt.	.345	Mays, S.F.	95	Howard, L.A.	19	Boyer, St. L.	54
Williams, Chi.	.335	Williams, Chi.	95	Williams, Chi.	19	Santo, Chi.	49
Rojas, Phil.	.326	Flood, St. L.	92	Allen, Phil.	16	Stargell, Pitt.	48
Carty, Mil.	.321	Groat, Pitt.	91	Santo, Chi.	15	Pinson, Cin.	47
Hunt, N.Y.	.316	Aaron, Mil.	89	Cepeda, S.F.	14	3 tied with	45
				Robinson, Cin.	14		

Pitching

Wins		ERA		Strike Outs		Innings Pitched	
Drysdale, L.A.	11	Short, Phil.	1.58	Koufax, L.A.	126	Drysdale, L.A.	162
Koufax, L.A.	11	Perry, S.F.	1.65	Drysdale, L.A.	121	Ellsworth, Chi.	145
Marichal, S.F.	11	R. Miller, L.A.	1.83	Maloney, Cin.	109	Marichal, S.F.	144
Ellsworth, Chi.	10	Koufax, L.A.	1.84	Veale, Pitt.	106	Koufax, L.A.	132
Farrell, Hou.	10	Drysdale, L.A.	2.06	Marichal, S.F.	104	L. Jackson, Chi.	127
L. Jackson, Chi.	10	Herbel, S.F.	2.15	Bunning, Phil.	99	Bunning, Phl.	125

Team Batting

	AB	R	H	HR	RBI	Pct.
Pittsburgh	2502	305	665	50	291	.266
St. Louis	2621	295	684	52	280	.261
Milwaukee	2559	338	657	77	319	.257
Philadelphia	2437	302	619	58	287	.254
Cincinnati	2595	317	648	62	292	.250
Chicago	2476	296	620	76	279	.250
Los Angeles	2571	272	631	38	.249	.245
New York	2709	263	657	45	245	.243
San Francisco	2591	315	619	74	294	.239
Houston	2538	258	586	41	229	.231

After the dust had settled on the National League action that took place Saturday, July 4th, suddenly the Cincinnati Reds were in sole possession of third place, just five games behind the Phillies, after they whipped the Cardinals, 3–2, before a big holiday crowd of 21,320 at Crosley Field. The loss dropped St. Louis 10 games out of first and their prospects for the season began to look bleak.

The Reds took a 3–1 lead into the ninth, with starter Jim O'Toole on the mound. Then Ken Boyer doubled off O'Toole and he was relieved by lefty rookie Billy McCool.

McCool, who was just ten days shy of his 20th birthday on July 4th, proceeded to strike out Bill White and Charlie James, but then Boyer scored when shortstop Leo Cardenas threw wild on Julian Javier's grounder. McCool then fanned Tim McCarver to strike out the side and preserve the victory for O'Toole (8–4).

Despite the throwing error by Cardenas, he had driven in the first two Cincinnati runs with a bases-loaded single in the first off Cardinals starter Mike Cueller (0–2), who had walked the bases full. The winning run by the Reds was scored in the fifth when Tommy Harper walked and was advanced by an infield out and then raced home from second on an infield hit by Frank Robinson.

Lou Brock had two hits in the game for the Cardinals. Since coming to St. Louis on June 15 he had raised his batting average by 22 points in 19 days, from .257 to .279.

Out in San Francisco before 30,529 fans on Saturday, July 4, the Phillies once again regained the National League lead by one-half game after they beat the Giants, 5–3, for the second straight day in the scheduled three-game series.

Richie Allen, who entered the game hitting .303, led the way for the Phillies in the victory by driving in the winning run in the top of the 11th inning with a triple. Wes Covington (8) then followed with a home run. Earlier Allen had driven in a run in the first inning with a double and scored another after walking, thereby figuring in four of the five Phillies runs in the game. The hot-hitting Allen had now hammered Giants pitching for five hits in ten plate appearances in the first two games of the series.

For Philadelphia, Jim Bunning (9–2) pitched scoreless ball after giving up two runs in the first on a home run by Duke Snider (4). He allowed just six hits in the game and retired 17 out of the last 18 batters he faced before being replaced by Jack Baldschun in the 11th.

Gaylord Perry (6–4) took the loss for the Giants. Perry had taken over for Jack Sanford in the sixth and extended his scoreless streak of innings to 18 before the Phillies scored off him in the top of the 11th.

On Sunday, July 5, the Phillies completed the three-game sweep of the power-laden Giants with a 2–1 victory. In the game Dennis Bennett (9–5) and Jack Baldschun combined pitching efforts on a six-hitter for the Phillies, enabling them to beat Juan Marichal (11–4). Richie Allen, whose fielding talents would be brought into question following the season as one of the primary reasons for the Phillies' collapse, was nothing short of brilliant in the Phillies' Sunday victory over the Giants before 38,461 fans at Candlestick Park.

The key play in the game occurred in the bottom of seventh when the Giants' Jim Ray Hart (10) hit a lead-off homer against Bennett over the left-field wall. Orlando Cepeda then reached first via a wild-pitch third strike by Bennett. Jesus Alou followed by singling Cepeda to third.

Bennett then got veteran catcher Del Crandell to hit a grounder to Richie Allen at third. Allen caught Cepeda in a rundown between third and home and tagged him out. On the play Alou had come all the way around to third and then quickly broke for home when Allen threw to second, attempting to get Crandell, who was sliding into the bag. Subsequently Alou was caught in a rundown between third and home.

Bennett was relieved after Gene Mauch sent Cap Peterson up to hit following a lead-off single in the top of the eight. Jack Baldschun finished up the game for the Phillies, retiring the Giants in order in the eight and ninth, striking out Willie Mays for the final out with the tying run on base.

So in the National League pennant race at the 1964 All-Star break, it certainly appeared that "Fightin'" Phillies had more than a fighting chance for the pennant. Following their three-game series sweep of Giants, the Phillies arrived at the 1964 All-Star Game break in first place in the National League with a 1–½ game lead over San Francisco and a comfortable six-game lead over third-place Cincinnati.

Meanwhile, at Crosley Field in Cincinnati on July 5, the hard-charging Reds and fading St. Louis Cardinals had been locked in a 1–1 tie through six innings with Roger Craig of the Cards battling Joey Jay of Reds on the mound, before a modest crowd of 11,854 fans. Ultimately the Cardinals prevailed in the game, winning 3–1.

The Cardinals scored in the first inning when Jay walked Lou Brock, who then stole second, went to third on a wild pitch and then trotted home on a single by Dick Groat. The Reds answered the Cards by scoring in the bottom of the second as Leo Cardenas led off with double into the St. Louis bullpen. Cardenas then went to second on a fielder's choice and was driven home on a single by Deron Johnson.

The Cardinals scored the winning tallies in the seventh when Bill White doubled off Jay and then raced home on a single by Bob Skinner, starting a two-run rally. Tim McCarver followed with a single to drive in Skinner. Despite the fact that Cardinals starter Roger Craig (5–4) gave up ten hits, he went the distance for the win.

Cincinnati starter Joey Jay (4–5) pitched a six-hitter and lost. The defeat left the Reds in third place, six games behind the Phillies at the All-Star break. The St. Louis Cardinals at the break were now a distant ten games off the pace.

Meanwhile, the Pittsburgh Pirates remained in the hunt with a 7–1 victory over the Houston Colts, powered by home runs off the bats of Jerry Lynch (7) and Manny Mota (3), leaving the Bucs in fourth place, seven games out of first place at the break. Lynch (sometimes referred to as "Lynch in the pinch") hit his 16th career pinch-hit home run to start the Pirates' winning rally.

At the All-Star Game break, the standings of the Major League clubs were the following.

Major League Standings
July 6, 1964

National League	W	L	Pct.	G.B.	American League	W	L	Pct.	G.B
Philadelphia	47	28	.627	—	Baltimore	48	28	.632	—
San Francisco	47	31	.603	1½	Chicago	44	30	.595	3
Cincinnati	42	35	.545	6	New York	45	31	.592	3
Pittsburgh	40	35	.533	7	Minnesota	43	37	.538	7
St. Louis	39	40	.533	10	Detroit	38	39	.494	10½
Los Angeles	38	39	.494	10	Boston	38	41	.481	11½
Milwaukee	38	40	.486	10½	Los Angeles	37	44	.457	13½
Chicago	36	38	.486	10½	Cleveland	34	42	.447	14
Houston	37	43	.463	12½	Kansas City	31	47	.397	18
New York	23	58	.284	27	Washington	32	51	.386	19½

As the players who had been selected for the American and National League All-Star teams assembled to meet in the mid-summer classic at New York, rumors were running rampant in the baseball community at large that the Milwaukee Braves were going to move to Atlanta starting in the 1965 season.

Braves chairman of the board William Bartholomay vehemently dismissed the rumors of the franchise's moving, stating that "during the past few days the Braves have again been subject to unsubstantiated rumors concerning the relocation of our franchise."[2] Bartholomay reaffirmed the Braves' commitment to Milwaukee, saying that he felt there was "tangible evidence that we are dedicated to rebuilding interest in Milwaukee."[3]

There had not been a franchise relocation in the National League for 50 years, from 1903 to 1953, when the Boston Braves began an exodus of Major League teams during the Fifties from unprofitable markets to fields of schemes in other cities that would uproot team traditions and leave hundreds of thousands of loyal fans empty-handed.

There was never was a doubt in any Boston fan's mind where their primary allegiance had always been—Bean Town was Red Sox territory.

From 1901 through 1952 the Braves had won only two pennants and had finished in the second division 40 times. In the 1952 season they had only drawn 281,000 fans through the turnstiles in Boston. After leaving Boston and moving to Milwaukee for the 1953 season, the Braves drew an incredible 1,820,000 fans at home.

Seeing the overwhelming success of the Braves' move, several greedy baseball owners immediately determined that a franchise move could solve both a club's cash flow problems and their inability as baseball executives to field a competitive team in their current city.

Subsequently in 1954 the hapless St. Louis Browns headed east to Baltimore. Then in 1955 the Philadelphia Athletics simply ignored the fact that Connie Mack ever existed, packed up and headed west to Kansas City. Their cross-continental odyssey would eventually land them in Oakland in 1968, where they have never seemed to be satisfied, despite winning several pennants and a string of World Championships in the 1970s.

Following the New York Giants' sweep of the Cleveland Indians in the 1954 World Series, the Giants teams began a free fall in the standings for the next few years, finishing third in 1955, then dropping to sixth place in 1956, 26 games behind the pennant-winning Brooklyn Dodgers.

Consequently, attendance hit rock bottom at the Polo Grounds and Giants owner Horace Stoneham began to look for greener pastures. For a while it looked as if the Giants were headed to Minneapolis.

In 1956 the three New York teams, the Dodgers, Giants and Yankees, had a combined gate of 3,300,000. However, this attendance figure was considered subpar, due to the romantic notion of the club owners that the competitiveness of the 1950s baseball era in New York deserved over-whelming fan support. The Giants' and Dodgers' owners were also concerned about the deteriorating condition of the neighborhoods where the Polo Grounds and Ebbets Field were located, and also the large amount of "white flight" to the suburbs of Long Island and New Jersey, which they considered to be eroding their primary fan base.

Dodgers owner Walter O'Malley also was cognizant of how the Braves had suddenly gone from being a franchise of poor fan support and eco-nomic desperation in Boston to one now making money hand-over-fist, drawing two million fans a year in Milwaukee. O'Malley publicly stated, "At this rate, no team will be able to match the Braves in the bidding for talented young ballplayers. They will have an advantage so overwhelming that none of the other clubs in the league will be able to match them."[4]

When negotiations broke down with Mayor Robert Wagner and the City of New York to build a new ball park for Dodgers, Walter O'Malley began secret negotiations on the West Coast with the Mayor of Los Angeles, Norris Poulson.

At the same time, San Francisco Mayor George Christopher contacted Giants owner Horace Stoneham and the rest is history. "There's gold in them thar' hills!"

By 1961 the Washington Senators would metamorphose into the Minnesota Twins and tightfisted owner Calvin Griffith would begin living the good life off big fan revenues just outside Minneapolis in Bloomington.

With these franchise moves the average fan was now for the first time confronted with the reality that baseball was as much a business as a sport. What would have seemed like some sort of heresy a few years earlier—to move a club from its traditional municipal surrounding and civic identification—was suddenly becoming a common modus operandi.

In 1964 columnist Arthur Daley stated in an article in the *New York Times*, "Baseball was once a game involving sportsmen who gloried in their profitable years and suffered through their bad ones. But they stayed where they were. They had roots that were deeply embedded in the loyalties of their fans. Such is the case no longer. The Great American Game has become as commercial as General Motors."[5]

Daley went on to say, "Just the other day, a radio broadcaster summed up the imminent departure of the Braves in priceless verbiage. 'They have milked dry the goose that laid the golden egg,' he said, 'in a soaring flight of rhetoric that has not been matched since Shakespeare's day.'"[6]

Braves attendance had hit a high of 2.25 million in Milwaukee in the late 1950s, but the honeymoon didn't last, as it had now shrunk to an average of 750,000 a year. Subsequently, in 1965 the Braves played another season in the sunlight of Milwaukee's County Stadium, then took "a midnight train to Georgia" to set up shop for the 1966 season in Atlanta.

VI

The 1964 All-Star Game

The 1964 All-Star game was to be the 35th in the classic series which began in 1933 (two All-Star Games were played annually from 1959 through 1962). The 1964 game was scheduled to be played at the New York Mets' shining new stadium in Queens starting at 1:00 P.M. on July 7. While New York had previously been host to five All-Star Games, this would be the first to be played in the Borough of Queens.

Playing the 1964 All-Star Game at Shea Stadium meant a lot to rejuvenating the National League's presence in New York City. For a lot of New York fans, the abandonment by the Brooklyn Dodgers and New York Giants to the West Coast following the 1957 season was still painfully engraved in their memories. While the National League had attempted to make amends through a reestablished presence in New York with the start-up of an expansion team in 1962, the Mets in 1964 were still at most laughable, playing .287 ball at the All-Star Game break, 27 games out of first place.

Also the New York fans were still endeared to Willie Mays. The New York press still referred to Mays as "The Wonder," "The Amazing" and "The Incomparable." For die-hard New York National League fans, having a legitimate reason to root for the "Say Hey Kid" again, if only for one brief afternoon in the New York sunshine, was more than just nostalgic, it was what New York baseball tradition had been and symbolic of what they were rebuilding—excellence in the game.

A huge crowd of 55,000-plus was anticipated to pass through the turnstiles at Shea Stadium for the midsummer classic and 300 ushers were scheduled to be on hand, three times the normal stadium staffing. However, two days before the game only 40,000 tickets had been sold. Ticket prices for the game were $4.20 for the upper grandstand, $6.30 for other reserved locations, and $8.40 for box seats. On the day of the game the last seats would go on sale as general admission for $2.10 each.

The Rosters for the 1964 All-Star Game

American League

Bob Allison—Minnesota Twins
Louis Aparicio—Baltimore Orioles
Eddie Bressoud—Boston Redsox
Dean Chance—Los Angeles Angels
Rocky Colavito—Kansas City Athletics
Whitey Ford—New York Yankees
Bill Freehan—Detroit Tigers
Jim Fergosi—Los Angeles Angels
Jimmie Hall—Minnesota Twins
Chuck Hinton—Washington Senators
Elston Howard—New York Yankees
Al Kaline—Detroit Tigers
Harmon Killebrew—Minnesota Twins
Jack Kralick—Cleveland Indians
Jerry Lumpe—Detroit Tigers
Frank Malzone—Boston Red Sox
Mickey Mantle—New York Yankees
Tony Oliva—Minnesota Twins
Camilo Pascual—Minnesota Twins
Joe Pepitone—New York Yankees
Garry Peters—Chicago White Sox
Juan Pizarro—Chicago White Sox
Dick Radatz—Boston Red Sox
Bobby Richardson—New York Yankees
Brooks Robinson—Baltimore Orioles
Norm Siebern—Baltimore Orioles
John Wyatt—Kansas City Athletics

National League

Hank Aaron—Milwaukee Braves
Ken Boyer—St. Louis Cardinals
Jim Bunning—Philadelphia Phillies
Smoky Burgess—Pittsburgh Pirates
Johnny Callison—Philadelphia Phillies
Leo Cardenas—Cincinnati Reds
Orlando Cepeda—San Francisco Giants
Roberto Clemente—Pittsburgh Pirates
Don Drysdale—Los Angeles Dodgers
Johnny Edwards—Cincinnati Reds
Dick Ellsworth—Chicago Cubs
Turk Farrell—Houston Colts
Curt Flood—St. Louis Cardinals
Dick Groat—St. Louis Cardinals
Ron Hunt—New York Mets
Sandy Koufax—Los Angeles Dodgers
Juan Marichal—San Francisco Giants
Willie Mays—San Francisco Giants
Bill Mazeroski—Pittsburgh Pirates
Ron Santo—Chicago Cubs
Chris Short—Philadelphia Phillies
Willie Stargell—Pittsburgh Pirates
Joe Torre—Milwaukee Braves
Bill White—St. Louis Cardinals
Billy Williams—Chicago Cubs

The managers for the 1964 All-Star Game were Walter Alston of the Los Angeles Dodgers for the National League and Al Lopez of the Chicago White Sox for the American League. Lopez, who had led the White Sox to a second-place finish in the 1963 AL campaign, was chosen to replace Ralph Houk, who after piloting the 1963 New York Yankees to a pennant was promoted to General Manager for the 1964 season and replaced as manager by Yogi Berra. To assist him in the All-Star game Lopez named a two-man coaching staff that consisted of Washington Senators manager Gil Hodges and Tony Cuccinello, who was one of Lopez's coaches on the White Sox.

The 1964 All-Star game was to be the first game since 1943 in which Stan Musial would not be a member of the National League team, having retired after the 1963 season.

The All-Star vote had been lifted from the fans in the late 1950s after Cincinnati Reds fans began the practice of stuffing the ballot box and twice nearly elected an all-Reds starting All-Star lineup. In fact, in the 1957 game

Stan Musial of the Cardinals was the only non-Cincinnati Red elected to the starting lineup by the fans, who had stuffed the ballot box, electing Reds to seven of the eight starting positions (the starting pitcher is selected by the manager). The year before in 1956 Reds fans had elected five of their hometown players to the All-Star starting lineup.

However, in 1964 the Major League players selected the starting lineups for the game. Mickey Mantle would be making his 15th All-Star appearance and Willie Mays his 14th. However, the players' selections for the starting lineup certainly raised a few eyebrows, too. The players had left both of the 1963 batting champions, Carl Yastrzemski of the Boston Redsox and Tommy Davis of the Los Angeles Dodgers, off the starting lineups. Furthermore, they had not selected any of the 1963 World Champion Los Angeles Dodgers to the lineup nor any of the red-hot National League-leading Philadelphia Phillies.

Al Kaline of the Detroit Tigers, who had been selected to the American League squad, suffered a severely bruised ankle in the Tigers game on Saturday, July 4th. Consequently, he was being replaced on the AL roster by Rocky Colavito of the Kansas City Athletics.

Ron Hunt of the New York Mets, the starting second baseman for the National League, was the first-ever Met elected as an All-Star and in 1964 the only member of the team on the squad.

The starting lineups for the game were the following.

American	National
Fergosi ss	Clemente rf
Oliva rf	Groat ss
Mantle cf	Williams lf
Killebrew lf	Mays cf
Allison 1b	Cepeda 1b
Robinson 3b	Boyer 3b
Richardson 2b	Torre c
Howard c	Hunt 2b
Chance p	Drysdale p

Mets manager Casey Stengel had been chosen by NL manager Walter Alston as a coach. Prior to the game Stengel was noticed to be fixated as he gazed at the lineup card that had been taped to the wall of the National League dugout.

"It's the damndest lineup card that's ever been on that wall." Stengel was making reference to the fact that previously the only the lineup card which had hung in that position was that of the hapless Mets. "Look at them extry men, Aaron, White, Koufax, Bunning."[1]

Willie Mays and Don Drysdale. (Photofile)

While volunteering Mets pitchers Al Jackson and Carl Willey pitched batting practice for the National League team, Sandy Koufax was assigned the duty of guarding the baseball bags during batting practice for the NL. Just as odd was the fact that Whitey Ford was given this casual duty during the American League batting practice.

It was doubtful that Whitey Ford was going to pitch in the All-Star game, though. Ford, who had such an unbelievably successful record in World Series action, being the all-time leader in eight pitching categories including a string of 33 scoreless innings in a row, had been roughed-up pretty good by National League hitters in his previous All-Star appearances. In 12 previous innings of All-Star Game work, Ford had a won-lost record of 0–2 and an ERA of 8.25.

The World Champion Dodgers were trailing the league-leading Phillies by 10 games at the break, tied with St. Louis for fifth place, and it was unlikely that Walter Alston was going to use Sandy Koufax in the All-Star game if he could avoid it. Koufax had just pitched a brilliant six-hit shutout on Sunday prior to the All-Star Game as the Dodgers defeated the Mets, 5–0. For Koufax, now 12–4 on the season, it was his eighth victory in a row. During the streak Koufax had allowed only six runs in 69 innings.

With the largest All-Star Game crowd on hand at New York's new Shea Stadium (50,850) since the 1959 second game played at the Los Angeles Coliseum (55,105), the game was scheduled to begin at 1 P.M. with two Los Angeles pitchers, Dean Chance of the Angels and Don Drysdale of the Dodgers, facing each other.

Don Drysdale would be starting an All-Star Game for the fourth time, having started in both games in 1959 at Pittsburgh and Los Angeles, then starting the first game in Washington in 1962. (Drysdale would also start the 1968 game in Houston.)

The selection of the starting pitchers was made difficult for both Alston and Lopez as, with the exception of Drysdale, the Phillies' Chris Short and reliever Dick Radatz of the Red Sox, all of the other 15 picked pitchers had worked in games over the weekend.

It was presumed that Alston chose the right-handed Drysdale over the left-handed Short to start the game because the American League lineup was predominately a right-handed-hitting one.

The practice of using All-Star pitchers so near to the day of the game prompted Mets manager Casey Stengel to offer the solution that baseball pass a rule that would prohibit the use of any All-Star pitcher the Sunday before the game was played.

July 7, 1964, at Shea Stadium, New York

	1	2	3	4	5	6	7	8	9	R	H	E
American	1	0	0	0	0	2	1	0	0	4	9	1
National	0	0	0	2	1	0	0	0	4	7	8	0

The American League sprinted to an early lead as they scored an unearned run in the first off National League starter Don Drysdale. Jim Fergosi of the Angels led off the game with a ground single between third and short, then took second base on a passed ball by NL catcher Joe Torre. With two out Fergosi scored on a long single to left by Harmon Killebrew. Following the first Drysdale did not allow another base runner in his three innings of work.

Likewise, Dean Chance was equally impressive in his three innings of work, allowing only two singles while throwing 37 pitches to 11 batters, with only seven pitches being called as balls.

In the top of the fourth inning Jim Bunning of the Phillies replaced Don Drysdale as the NL pitcher and immediately made All-Star history. By taking the mound Bunning became the first player ever to pitch for both leagues in All-Star Game competition. Previously Bunning, playing with the Detroit Tigers, had pitched in six All-Star Games as a member of the American League squad in 1957, 1959, 1961 (twice), 1962 and 1963. Two American League batters reached base off Bunning in the fourth, Harmon Killebrew with an infield hit and Brooks Robinson with a line single to right, before the side was retired.

In the bottom of the fourth inning the Kansas City Athletics' John Wyatt replaced Chance on the mound for the AL, and the National League took the lead on a pair of solo home runs by Billy Williams of the Cubs and the Cardinals' Ken Boyer.

Williams hit the first pitch by Wyatt over the fence in right center. Willie Mays then fouled out. Orlando Cepeda of the Giants followed by hitting a line drive off Wyatt's shin. However, Wyatt recovered the ball in time to throw Cepeda out at first. Ken Boyer then hit a home run into the left-field bullpen, giving the National League a 2–1 lead.

Williams and Boyer were asked after the game what type of pitches they had hit.

"Mine was a slider," said Williams. "It was the first pitch he threw, but I didn't figure to get a better one."

"Mine was a fastball," said Boyer.[2]

Boyer didn't know it at the time, but his home run was to be the first leg of a little Major League history in the making for him. That history would be concluded in the fall of 1964 when, in the top of fifth inning of the fourth game of the 1964 World Series, he would hit a grand slam home run, thus becoming the sixth player in Major League history to hit a home run in the All-Star Game and World Series in the same year.

Bunning had no trouble holding the American League scoreless in the top of the fifth and concluded his history-making, two-inning stint by allowing two hits while striking out four.

The National League added another run in the bottom of fifth against Camilio Pascual of the Twins to move out to a 3–1 lead. With two outs Roberto Clemente of the Pirates bounced a hit off second base. Then Dick Groat of the Cardinals followed by lining a double out of the reach of Harmon Killebrew in left field, scoring Clemente.

Chris Short followed Phillies teammate Jim Bunning to the mound in the top of the sixth, and the American League came back and scored two runs to tie the game at 3–3. Short, the only left-handed pitcher to appear in the 1964 All-Star Game, was suffering from a pulled muscle on his side, but the injury was felt not serious enough to prevent him from playing.

Short struck out the first batter to face him, the hot-hitting Tony Oliva of the Twins, who at the All-Star break was batting .335, second highest average in the AL to league-leading teammate Bob Allison's .336.

However, Mickey Mantle and Harmon Killebrew followed with singles. Short then got Bob Allison to fly out to Mays for the second out. Then Brooks Robinson of the Orioles hit the ball deep to the wall in right center as Willie Mays tumbled in a desperate attempt to chase the ball down on the fly. Robinson wound up at third with a triple, scoring Mantle and Killebrew to tie the game. The American League rally came to abrupt halt as the next batter, Bobby Richardson of the Yankees, tapped the ball back to Short on the mound for the third out.

Short remarked about his All-Star mound appearance following the game.

"I felt good out there, but I could feel this in my side and I was sort of afraid to throw hard. I threw my breaking stuff hard but I didn't let go on my fast ball. I told Alston after the inning I wasn't right, and he took me out. In a way I'm glad it happened. It's better to find out now than it would have been in a Phillies game."[3]

The game remained tied at 3–3 as Pascual held the National League scoreless in the bottom of the sixth. In the top of seventh Dick Farrell of the Colts replaced Short on the mound for the National League. Farrell proceeded to hit the first the batter he faced, as he plunked the Yankees' Elston Howard in the shoulder with a pitch.

Now, most baseball strategists would agree that at this point, it would make sense to bunt and attempt to sacrifice the go-ahead run into scoring position. However AL manager Al Lopez sent Rocky Colavito of the Athletics up to the plate to hit for Pascual. In fact the National League players on the field didn't even consider setting up a defense for the bunt. Subsequently it came as no surprise to anyone when Colavito hit the ball hard to left center, out of the reach of Mays for a double, with Howard stopping at third. Jim Fergosi then followed with a sacrifice fly to Mays in center, scoring Howard to give the American League a 4–3 lead in the game.

The new pitcher for the AL in the bottom of seventh was Dick Radatz of the Red Sox and he handled the National League batters with ease. In the top of eight Dick Farrell allowed a walk and a single, but was saved from giving up another run when Willie Mays made a brilliant running catch of a long drive to left center off the bat of Elston Howard for the final out in the inning.

Once again Radatz held the NL scoreless in the bottom of the eighth. In the two innings he had worked so far he had struck out four of the six batters that faced him. So when Bobby Richardson made a terrific play to end the inning and prevent Willie Mays from coming to bat with a man on, the American League appeared to be in command of the game with a 4–3 lead.

Juan Marichal of the Giants took over the mound duties for the National League in the top of the ninth and retired the three batters that faced him in order. In the bottom of the ninth Dick Radatz took the mound for the American League with confidence as he faced lead-off hitter Willie Mays. His first pitch to Mays was a strike, then Willie fouled off the second. Mays then fouled off five more pitches from Radatz before drawing a walk.

Orlando Cepeda was next up and Mays wasted no time in stealing second. On Radatz's second pitch he broke for second and beat Elston Howard's throw to Bobby Richardson to the bag easily.

Cepeda, who had swung at both pitches and missed, swung at Radatz's third pitch too, hitting it on the handle of the bat on a high arch into short right field. Rocky Colavito playing in right could not quite get to the ball and it fell safely for a bloop single. Mays had remained standing at second until he saw the ball hit the ground, then ran for third. Colavito made a good throw from right to the plate but the ball bounced about ten feet in front of the plate and skipped over catcher Howard's glove as he barely deflected it.

Meanwhile, Radatz had been slow in leaving the mound to back up the play at the plate. Also, he seemed momentarily confused as to whether he should back up the play at third or home. Consequently, when Colavito's throw to the plate bounced over Howard, Radatz was more towards the third base side of the plate instead of directly behind Howard. Therefore, as Radatz had to run toward the play and attempt to scoop up the ball, Mays seized the moment when the ball passed Howard and raced for home, making it easily, while Cepeda took second.

Ken Boyer, whose home run in the fourth inning had given the National League a 2–1, lead was next up, but Radatz got him to pop up to Brooks Robinson near the plate. Johnny Edwards, the left-hand-hitting catcher of the Reds, was the next batter and he drew an intentional walk to set up the possible double play with Cepeda still on second.

Ron Hunt, the only Met on the National League team, was due up next. However, rather than give Hunt the opportunity for All-Star glory in front of his hometown fans at Shea Stadium, NL manager Walter Alston called on Hank Aaron to pinch hit for Hunt. However, Aaron became the second out as Radatz struck him out on four pitches.

That brought the Phillies' Johnny Callison to bat. Callison had entered the game as a pinch hitter for Jim Bunning in the fifth and popped up against Camilo Pascual. He stayed in the game to play right field and faced Radatz previously with two out in the seventh, when he hit the first pitch deep to Mickey Mantle in center, almost 400 feet to the wall.

Again Callison swung at the first pitch from Radatz and this time drove the ball into the right-field upper grandstand, just a few rows from the auxiliary scoreboard. His home run brought Cepeda and Edwards home ahead of him on the grand tour of the bases and gave the National League a 7–4 triumph! Meanwhile, the National League players had jumped up out of the dugout and were waiting at the plate to pound Callison on the back as they laughed and cheered.

Johnny Callison was certainly an unlikely hero of the All-Star Game. At the All-Star break he was not among the National League leaders in average, home runs or RBI's. He had not finished first or second in the players' balloting for the right field position and was just one of three extra men chosen by Walter Alston to round out the NL All-Star squad.

In his postgame remarks Walter Alston said in regard to his choice of Callison on the National League squad, "He beat us enough. I figured he owed us something."[4]

Alston was referring to a recent series in Los Angeles where Callison had hit two home runs in a game against the Dodgers. Whatever. But here was Callison, suddenly the toast of New York and recipient of the Arch Ward Memorial Award as the Most Valuable Player of the 1964 All-Star Game. He would continue to play in the Major Leagues until 1973, when he wrapped up a 16-year career with the Yankees. After leaving baseball he would work at jobs as a bartender and car salesman.

Ironically, Callison had come up to the majors with the Chicago White Sox and it was American League skipper Al Lopez who had traded Callison in December 1959 to the Phillies for Gene Freese.

"No I don't regret it" said Lopez. "I was aware that Callison had great

Johnny Callison is mobbed after hitting his decisive home run in the 1964 All-Star Game. (© Bettmann/CORBIS)

potential, but he was just a green kid then with a beautiful swing. We had won the American League pennant in 1959 and we were out to win again in 1960. I needed more experienced players. And to think that before the game I shook hands with Johnny and wished him good luck."[5]

Nonetheless, a lot of baseball historians and fans alike consider the trading of Callison by Lopez a major blunder and one that could have cost the White Sox a couple of pennants in the middle 1960s.

Although it had been widely known that Callison was hurt personally when the White Sox traded him, rather than inject controversy in the event, he stated that he did not get any particular pleasure or feeling of revenge in beating Lopez.

"I never faulted Lopez for trading me. I felt then the deal was good for me because I would have more of an opportunity to play with Philadelphia."[6]

And in the summer of 1964, to Johnny Callison the National League All-Star victory meant: "This looks like the Phillies' year. It's gotta be, it's gotta be."[7]

Despite the fact that Willie Mays went hitless in the game, his seven putouts in center field tied an All-Star Game record that was set by Chet Laabs of the St. Louis Browns in 1943 All-Star game, and his walk off

Radatz in the 9th inning and stolen base eventually led to the tying run. However, to Mays the All-Star Game victory meant one thing: "We're even."[8]

The National League by virtue of its victory had finally erased the deficit in losses that had existed since the game's inception in 1933 and tied the series at 17 games each, with one tie.

The press had other ideas though about the contributions of Willie Mays to the National League's victory. In the postgame ramblings of the press it was said the other players considered Mays as "the star of stars."[9]

Playing down his stolen base off Radatz and his dash to the plate on Orlando Cepeda's short fly into right field, Mays said, "I tell you, I was lucky. I got a good jump and I went. No, I didn't get a signal from Alston [NL manager Walter Alston]. He told me if I got on base—run. Go talk to those other guys, Callison and Marichal. They won the game. Why do want to talk to a man who didn't get a hit?"[10]

Mays insisted, "Go get Callison, go get Callison, I'm no hero."[11]

The *New York Times* summarized the National League victory this way:

"Johnny Callison of the Phils put the issue out of reach with a three-run homer in the ninth. But it was the incomparable Willie (The Wonder) Mays who put it within reach. Willie made no hits yesterday and he normally hits like crazy in these midsummer festivals. However, he was a wizard afield and a marvel in his only visit to the base paths.

"And now the two leagues are even in this series. The surge of the Nationals from nowhere to a 17–17 tie coincides with the arrival of Mays in the National League squad. Willie the Wonder is all of that."[12]

For American League skipper Al Lopez, it was his fourth All-Star Game loss as manager. Lopez did receive some criticism for bringing in John Wyatt of the Athletics to replace Dean Chance on the mound in the fourth inning when he was promptly greeted with home runs by Billy Williams and Ken Boyer. But the fact of the matter is that Wyatt was having very good year with a very bad Kansas City team and in fact at the time of the All-Star Game he had the 9th-lowest ERA in the American League (2.44).

Also, while at least one player from 19 of the 20 Major League teams appeared in the game, no Cleveland Indian played in the game.

However, when all aspects of the 1964 All-Star Game are considered, one has to acknowledge the courage of Fred Hutchinson. Hutchinson, the Reds' manager, had been chosen by National League skipper Walter Alston as one of his coaches and, despite his failing body, wracked with excruciating pain from cancer, Hutchinson assumed his appointed duties every inning at third base in the game, while also being jovial with fans and American League players all day long, as if there were absolutely nothing wrong with him.

Box Score 1964 All-Star Game

American	ab	r	h	rbi	National	ab	r	h	rbi
Fergosi, ss	4	1	1	1	Clemente, rf	3	1	1	0
Oliva, rf	4	0	0	0	Short, p	0	0	0	0
Radatz, p	1	0	0	0	Farrell, p	0	0	0	0
Mantle, cf	4	1	1	0	g White	1	0	0	0
Hall, cf	0	0	0	0	Marichal, p	0	0	0	0
Killebrew, lf	4	1	3	1	Groat, ss	3	0	1	1
Hinton, lf	0	0	0	0	d Cardenas, ss	1	0	0	0
Allison, 1b	3	0	0	0	Williams, lf	4	1	1	1
f Pepitone, 1b	0	0	0	0	Mays, cf	3	1	0	0
Robinson, 3b	4	0	2	2	Cepeda, 1b	4	0	1	0
Richardson, 2b	4	0	1	0	h Flood	0	1	0	0
Howard, c	3	1	0	0	Boyer, 3b	4	1	2	1
Chance, p	1	0	0	0	Torre, c	2	0	0	0
Wyatt, p	0	0	0	0	Edwards, c	1	1	0	0
b Siebern	1	0	0	0	Hunt, 2b	3	0	1	0
Pascual, p	0	0	0	0	j Aaron	1	0	0	0
e Colavito, rf	2	0	1	0	Drysdale, p	0	0	0	0
					a Stargell	1	0	0	0
					Bunning, p	0	0	0	0
					c Callison, rf	3	1	1	3
Totals	35	4	9	4		34	7	8	6

a Grounded out for Drysdale in 3rd; b Flied out for Wyatt in 5th; c Popped out for Bunning in 5th; d Ran for Groat in 5th; e Doubled for Pascual in 7th; f Ran for Allison in 8th; g Struck out for Farrell in 8th; h Ran for Cepeda in 9th; j Struck out for Hunt in 9th.

Error-Pepitone, Left on bases-American 7, National 3,

Two-base hits-Groat, Colavito, Three-base Hit-Robinson, Home Runs-Williams, Boyer, Callison, Stolen base-Mays, Sacrifice fly-Fergosi.

	IP	H	R	ER	BB	SO	HBP	WP	Balks
American									
Chance	3	2	0	0	0	2	0	0	0
Wyatt	1	2	2	2	0	0	0	0	0
Pascual	2	2	1	1	0	1	0	0	0
Radatz	2–⅔	2	4	4	2	5	0	0	0
National									
Drysdale	3	2	1	0	0	3	0	1	0
Bunning	2	2	0	0	0	4	0	0	0
Short	1	3	2	2	0	1	0	0	0

	IP	H	R	ER	BB	SO	HBP	WP	Balks
Farrell	2	2	1	1	1	1	1	0	0
Marichal	1	0	0	0	0	1	0	0	0

Winning Pitcher-Marichal, Losing Pitcher-Radatz. Time of Game-2:27. Attendance-50,850.

Umpires-Sudol (N) plate, Paparella (A) first base, Secory (N) second base, Chylak (A) third base, Harvey
(N) left field, Salerno (A) right field.

VII

July, Part Two

As usual during the All-Star Game break, the teams attempt to make some strategic player moves in order to strengthen themselves for what is considered symbolically rather than mathematically the second half of the season, despite the fact that less than half of the season's scheduled games have actually been played. However, in 1964 during the break, while there were very few such player moves made, one deal would be significant in the long run.

On July 7, the St. Louis Cardinals sold right-handed-hitting first baseman and outfielder Jeff Long to the Chicago White Sox after the other National League teams failed to claim him on waivers. Then the Cardinals replaced Long on the roster by recalling infielder Mike Shannon from their Jacksonville, Florida, farm club. At the time of the recall Shannon, 25, was hitting .279 with 11 home runs.

The recall of Shannon combined with the addition of Lou Brock, who had been acquired in a trade with the Chicago Cubs three weeks earlier on June 15, would prove to be vital to the Cardinals' turn-around and eventual winning of the pennant.

Cards manager Johnny Keane said of the decision to bring Shannon up: "If he can cut the mustard we'll have the best defensive outfield we've had in years. With Curt Flood and Lou Brock also in the outfield, we have three who can go get the ball and throw it after they get it."[1]

Immediately following the All-Star Game, play resumed in the National League. On Wednesday, July 8, at Wrigley Field the Giants split a twin bill with the Cubs, losing the opener, 2–0, then rebounding to take the night cap, 7–2.

Bob Buhl (10–4) pitched a four-hit shutout for the Cubs in the opener, ending the Giants' longest winning streak of the year so far at four games. It was Buhl's third shutout of the season and he became the third Cubs pitcher to reach ten or more victories in the 1964 season. Billy

Williams had three hits for the Cubs in the game including his 20th home run.

With Larry Jackson (11–5) and Dick Ellsworth (10–8) and Buhl (10–3) each having ten wins at the halfway point in the season, it began to fuel speculation as to whether the Cubs could finish the season with three 20-game winners on their pitching staff, as at this point Jackson, Ellsworth and Buhl had accounted for 31 of the Cubs' 37 victories.

This feat had not been accomplished in the National League since 1923 when the Cincinnati Reds produced three 20-game winners on their pitching staff. Adolfo Luque won 27, Pete Donohue, 21, and Eppa Rixey, 27. Of course, in the American League it had only been eight years since a club had three 20-game winners—the Cleveland Indians of 1956, with Bob Lemon, Early Wynn and Herb Score each winning 20.

Interestingly, neither the Reds nor the Indians won a pennant with their three 20-game winners as both clubs finished second. However the Indians had just missed having three 20-game winners in their 1954 pennant-winning year, as Lemon and Wynn both won 23 and Mike Garcia won 19.

Despite the fact that the Cubs had three pitchers with 31 victories between them, the remainder of the staff had only produced six wins. This void in the pitching rotation was supposed to be filled by the acquisition of Ernie Broglio from the Cardinals in mid-June. However, so far Broglio had not won a game in a Cubs uniform. He started the second game of the July 8 twin bill at Wrigley Field and was hammered by the Giants for his fourth straight loss.

Willie Mays hit his 24th home run of the season in leading the Giants to a 7–2 victory in the game that was called after seven innings of play because of darkness in Wrigley Field, which still at the time was without stadium lights.

Ernie Broglio (3–9) for the fourth straight start failed to win his first game as a Cub. Ron Herbel (7–4) got the win.

The twin bill split ended the Giants' four-game losing streak and left them 1½ games behind the Phillies, who had their game with the Cardinals postponed due to rain. The Cardinals vs. Phillies game was to be a makeup game for the rain-out on May 13. However, with another wash-out the game was rescheduled for Thursday, September 10.

In the only other game scheduled, home runs by Manny Mota (4) and Willie Stargell (12) powered the Pirates over the Reds, 9–1, to move them into third place, one percentage point ahead of Cincinnati. In fact, Mota and Stargell, along Roberto Clemente, had each driven in three runs in the game. In addition Clemente raised his league-leading batting average to .350. Bob Veale (8–6) got the win; Jim Maloney (7–9) took the loss.

The Los Angeles Dodgers, having a break in the action on July 8, played an exhibition game at Santa Barbara with their Class A farm club there. The Dodgers won, 5–3, as Ron Fairly hit a two-run homer and both Doug Camilli and Wes Parker connected for solo shots. Outfielder Willie Crawford, recently signed by the Dodgers for $100,000 and assigned to Santa Barbara, singled his first time at bat, then struck out the last three times.

National League Standings, July 9, 1964

Team	Won	Lost	Pct.	G.B.
Philadelphia	47	28	.627	—
San Francisco	48	32	.600	1½
Pittsburgh	41	35	.539	6½
Cincinnati	42	38	.538	6½
Los Angeles	38	39	.494	10
St. Louis	39	40	.494	10
Chicago	37	39	.487	10½
Milwaukee	38	40	.487	10½
Houston	37	43	.463	12½
New York	23	58	.284	27

The next day, Thursday, July 9, at Wrigley Field the Giants would pound the Cubs with 16 hits in 9–4 victory. For the Giants, Willie Mays would hit his 25th home run, Willie McCovey would add a two-run shot in the sixth, and Jim Hart would have four hits. San Francisco starter Jack Sanford was forced out of the game in the second inning when the Cubs lined two balls off his pitching arm.

The Braves followed the Reds into Forbes Field and whipped the Pirates, 11–6. Although the Braves provided starting pitcher Warren Spahn with nine runs in the first three innings, he failed to finish the game, being replaced in the sixth. It was 11th time since May 19 that Spahn (6–8) had been unable to pitch a complete game. Suddenly the sad reality of time was beginning to catch up with the 43-year-old Spahn.

Warren Spahn had made his first appearance with the Boston Braves toward the end of the 1942 season, after winning 17 games with Hartford of the Eastern League, when he appeared in four games without a decision.

"Spahnie," as he was called by his teammates, was then drafted into the U.S. Army for service in World War II and didn't return to play for the Braves until July 1946, when he went 8–5. However, in 1947 he became a starter in the Braves' rotation and achieved the first of his 13 career 20-game win seasons by going 21–10.

While he won only 15 games in the 1948 season, the Braves won the National League Pennant, racing home 6½ games ahead of the second-place Cardinals. The 1948 season was one that lives in baseball folklore, with Spahn joining Braves right-hander Johnny Sain, who won 24 games, leading to the popular jingle of Braves fans at that time: "Spahn and Sain, and pray for rain."

Between 1949 and 1963 Spahn would win 20 or more games 12 times, missing winning 20 games only in 1952 (14–19), 1955 (17–14) and 1962 (18–14).

During his career Spahn went through an evolution in his pitching style, going from being a power pitcher earlier in his career to one of location and finesse in the later years. Regardless of however he pitched, some National League clubs like the Cincinnati Reds were hardly ever able to beat him. The popular saying was that all Spahnie had to do in order to beat Cincinnati was throw his glove on the mound. More than 70 of his 363 career victories came at the expense of the Reds.

On September 16, 1960, Spahn at the age of 39 would throw the first no-hitter of his career against the Philadelphia Phillies, 4–0. The following season at the age of 40 on April 28, 1961, he would pitch a second no-hitter against the San Francisco Giants, 1–0.

Now in 1964 Spahn was having trouble. He insisted that it was something wrong with his motion, but all the signs were very clear that his seemingly endless brilliant career was finally at an end. He would not win another a game in the 1964 season, finishing 6–13.

Years later, reflecting on the 1964 season, Hank Aaron remarked in regard to the decline of Spahn's pitching skills that season, that it all happened suddenly and that despite the fact that Spahn was now 43 years old, the Braves didn't really ever see Warren Spahn as doing anything else but continuing to win games. Aaron felt that if Spahn had been anything like the pitcher that they had always known, the Braves might have won the pennant in 1964, as Spahn went from 23–7 in 1963 to 6–13 in 1964. In fact the Braves would finish 5th, just five games behind the Cardinals, with young pitchers like Tony Cloninger and Denny Lemaster leading the way.

Following the 1964 season on November 23 the Braves sold Spahnie to the New York Mets. In 1965 Spahn, now 44 years old, would pitch in 20 games for the Mets, achieving a record of 4–12, before finishing up the season in San Francisco, pitching in 16 games with a record of 3–4. He had a combined record of 7–16 with an ERA of 4.01, completing 8 games in 30 starts. There were no contract offers for another season in 1966.

Warren Spahn finished with a career record of 363–245. He is fourth on the all-time career list for wins and number one for wins by a left-hander. In 1973 Spahn was elected to the National Baseball Hall of Fame.

Spahn, like many of his contemporaries in the late 1980s and early 1990s, made the rounds for cash, signing autographs at the baseball card and memorabilia shows across the land. Spahn delights in telling about one youthful baseball card collector who approached him at one of the shows. He states that he confronted the boy with the fact that he could not possibly have seen him pitch due to his young age. The youth agreed, but stated that his father had told him that getting Spahnie's autograph was a good investment, because a lot of the guys like him aren't going to be around much longer.

In other post-All-Star Game action, Houston came from behind, scoring four runs in the ninth to beat Don Drysdale and the Dodgers, 8–5. The ninth-inning rally was capped by a two-run single by Nellie Fox.

At New York on July 9, following all the All-Star Game hoopla, a sparse crowd of 13,804 turned out at Shea Stadium as the Mets beat the Cardinals, 4–3. Al Jackson (5–10) went all the way for the Mets and Curt Simmons (9–7) took the loss for the Cards. Simmons took a 3–2 lead into the bottom of the ninth, then Frank Thomas was sent up to pinch hit for Roy McMillan with one on and two out. Thomas, who hadn't played since May 31, when he came up to bat against Simmons promptly hit a home run to win the game. The loss dropped St. Louis into sixth place, six percentage points behind Milwaukee and 11 games behind the front-running Philadelphia Phillies.

On July 9 the league-leading Phillies would entertain the fourth-place Reds as All-Star Game hero Johnny Callison threw out the potential tying run at the plate, allowing the Phillies to beat the Reds, 4–3. While Callison did not get a hit in the game, he did score the go-ahead run for the Phillies in the seventh inning.

On Friday evening the Reds came back and beat the Phillies, 5–1, behind the pitching of Jim O'Toole (9–4), who went all the way, allowing the Phillies eight hits. For the Reds, Deron Johnson (8) and Frank Robinson (15) homered. Dennis Bennett (9–6), who lasted just three innings, would take the loss for the Phillies.

On Saturday, July 11, at Connie Mack Stadium the Reds would again beat the Phillies, 3–1, while the Giants were shutting out the Cubs, 7–0, at Wrigley Field. Once again the Giants moved into first place, one-half game ahead of the Phillies. The Reds beat Jim Bunning (9–4) when they scored all three runs in the sixth inning. Veteran lefty Joe Nuxhall (7–4) and Sammy Ellis held the Phillies to just five hits.

In stifling 90-degree-plus temperatures Bunning and Nuxhall had been locked up in a scoreless duel until the top of the sixth, when the Reds scored on singles by Frank Robinson, Vada Pinson, and John Edwards and a double by Leo Cardenas to right field. For Jim Bunning, it was his first loss since pitching a perfect game against the Mets on June 21.

Surging San Francisco once again defeated Chicago (for the fourth straight time) as Willie McCovey and Jesus Alou both drove in two runs. The 7–0 shutout was pitched by Bob Bolin (3–3) who gave up seven hits in the game while striking out 12. Sterling Slaughter (2–3), pitching in the only Major League season of his career, took the loss for the Cubs.

Then on Sunday, July 12, the Reds moved on up the East Coast to Shea Stadium in New York for a doubleheader with the Mets, and the Braves moved into Connie Mack Stadium for a twin bill with the Phillies. As it all turned out, July 12 was a day of underdog victories in the National League.

The Reds were swept in their doubleheader by the Mets, 1–0 and 5–2, while the Braves won both ends of their twin bill at Philadelphia, 4–3 and 6–2. Later down at Houston the Colts beat the front-running Giants in a night game, 5–4. Elsewhere around the league, Chicago and Los Angeles split a doubleheader, and the doubleheader scheduled between St. Louis and Pittsburgh was rained out.

In the first game at New York the Mets' Galen Cisco and the Reds' Joey Jay hooked up in a scoreless duel until the bottom of the ninth, when Joe Christopher doubled home George Altman to beat the Reds, 1–0. In the second game Frank Lary went all the way for the Mets to beat the Reds, 5–1. Deron Johnson hit his 9th home run of the season for the Reds in the game.

It was the first doubleheader sweep for the Mets in over a year, having last taken a twin bill on June 23, 1963, when they defeated the Phillies at the Polo Grounds, 5–0 and 4–1.

With Phillies losing a doubleheader, the Giants getting beat and Pittsburgh being rained out, the Reds lost only an additional one-half game in the standings to slip into a tie for third place with the Pirates, 6½ games behind the Giants.

In the first game at Philadelphia, won by the Braves, 4–3, Wade Blasingame (2–1) held the Phillies to just five hits in seven innings. In the game Johnny Callison hit his 13th home run of the season. Chris Short (7–5) took the loss for Philadelphia.

In the second game, also won by Milwaukee, 6–2, the Phillies had jumped out to a 2–0 lead through three innings. Then in the fourth Hank Aaron doubled and scored on Ed Bailey's single to narrow the score to

2–1, Philadelphia. The Braves then took the lead in the fifth, scoring twice to make it a 3–2 ball game.

Then in the seventh the Braves added two more runs. One of the runs occurred when Hank Aaron knocked in Eddie Mathews with a single. The single was the 2,000th career hit for Aaron. The Braves added an insurance run in the ninth to make the score 6–2. Also for the Braves, Frank Bolling would hit his 5th home run and Eddie Mathews his 11th.

Hank Fischer had started the game for Milwaukee but was replaced by Billy Hoeft (3–0) in the third after the Phillies had scored two runs on five hits in the first two innings. Hoeft then held the Phillies scoreless from the third on and hitless until the eighth. Art Mahaffey (7–4) took the loss for Philadelphia.

While Hank Aaron had collected his 2,000th hit in the game, he would finish his career in 1976 with 3,771 hits, third on the all-time list behind Pete Rose and Ty Cobb. Of course, in career home runs Aaron is second to no one. His 755 career home runs are the most ever hit by anyone in the Major Leagues and make him the undisputed home run king. Aaron also won National League batting titles in 1956 (.328) and 1959 (.355) and finished his 23-year Major League career with .305 lifetime batting average.

Despite Hank Aaron's monumental career achievements, he never received the celebrity that his contemporaries such as Willie Mays, Mickey Mantle and Roberto Clemente received. Some would argue that in the public's failure to recognize his greatness, "Hammerin' Hank" was a victim of racial prejudice. There certainly is a huge case for that when one considers the death threats and volumes of hateful mail he received in 1973 and 1974 while closing in on what had been baseball's most sacred and pious record, Babe Ruth's 714 career home runs.

But there's more to it than the simplistic notion of racism. Others would argue that Aaron's lack of recognition was simply a result of location. Aaron played his entire career in Milwaukee and Atlanta, which were not media centers at that time, like New York, Chicago and Los Angeles. Perhaps if Aaron had played in Atlanta at the time cable television arrived there in the presence of Ted Turner's giant CNN, maybe his star would have shone a little brighter throughout the baseball world through wider media exposure of his playing abilities.

However, Aaron doesn't agree. He always felt that playing in Milwaukee was right for him. He felt that if he had played in New York, he would have felt lost. Aaron also had a love affair with the Milwaukee fans and felt that they were most loyal fans that any player could ever ask for. In reality, this is probably the reason that Aaron returned to Milwaukee in 1975 to wind up his career with the Brewers.

Hank Aaron (PhotoFile)

Nonetheless, Aaron said in a 1974 interview that he changed his style of hitting when the Braves moved from Milwaukee to Atlanta in order to win over new friends in the Braves' newest home in Georgia: "I came down here the first year [Atlanta] with intentions of winning the home run crown. So when we moved to Atlanta I changed from being a contact hitter to a pull hitter. I felt that I could win the fans over quicker by hitting home runs than singles, and I did. That was the easiest way to make new friends and save my legs, too."[2]

The reality is that there are a lot of factors involved in assessing the failure of baseball fans, the press and Major League Baseball itself to recognize the greatness of Hank Aaron, but one other factor needs to be included in the equation, too: Hank Aaron himself.

Hank Aaron the player did not seek celebrity and constantly shunned the limelight throughout his career. So it probably really didn't matter in what city Hank Aaron played during his career. Hank Aaron was and still is in most respects a very private person. Today he rarely makes public appearances on popular television sports talk shows, doesn't answer fan mail, and hardly ever has permitted himself to be paraded as a spectacle at memorabilia and baseball card signing shows.

Early in his career Aaron was asked how he wanted to be remembered as a Major League ball player and his response was typical of those throughout his career. "I don't want to be anything special or anyone special," he said. "I just want to be remembered as plain Henry Aaron."[3]

In the doubleheader at Chicago, the Cubs defeated the Dodgers, 6–3, in the first game on Billy Williams' (21) three-run homer in the ninth off Ron Perranoski with two outs. Bob Buhl (11–4) was the winning pitcher, and Robert Miller (3–5) took the loss.

In the second game it seemed as though Ernie Broglio might get his first win as a Cub when he entered the top of the ninth with a 2–0 lead, having limited the Dodgers to just four hits through the first eight innings. However, after pinch hitter Jim Gilliam led off the ninth with a single and Derrell Griffith followed with a single, Dick Ellsworth replaced Broglio on the mound. The Dodgers then proceeded to score six runs in the inning. Tommy Davis got the rally going, driving in two runs with a bases-loaded single to tie the game, 2–2. Then Ron Fairly scored the lead run on an infield out by Frank Howard.

Also on Sunday, July 12, in New York the twice-cancelled Mayor's Trophy game between the Mets and Yankees was rescheduled for the third time to be played on August 24 at Shea Stadium.

National League Leaders
Monday, July 13, 1964
Batting

Individual Batting		Hits		Home Runs		RBIs	
Clemente, Pitt.	.348	Williams, Chi.	109	Mays, S.F.	27	Mays, S.F.	62
Williams, Chi.	.344	Clemente, Pitt.	108	Williams, Chi.	21	Santo, Chi.	57
Mays, S.F.	.338	Mays, S.F.	104	Howard, L.A.	19	Boyer, St.L.	55
Torre, Mil.	.318	Aaron, Mil.	102	Santo, Chi.	16	Aaron, Mil.	52
Cepeda, S.F.	.318	Allen, Phil.	96	Allen, Phil.	16	Stargell, Pitt.	51
Aaron, Mil.	.312	Torre, Mil.	95				
Santo, Chi.	.311	Santo, Chi.	93				
Hunt, N.Y.	.309	Hunt, N.Y.	93				
Allen, Phil.	.307						
Roseboro, L.A.	.305						

Pitching
(based on 8 or more decisions)

	Won	Lost
Koufax, L.A.	13	4
Marichal, S.F.	12	4
Buhl, Chi.	11	4
Bunning, Phil.	9	3
Gibbon, Pitt.	6	3

The hand-to-hand combat for the National League lead saw no change on Monday, July 13, as the Giants retained a one-game lead over the Phillies by defeating the Colts, 5–3, and the Phillies topped the Braves, 3–2.

Tom Haller (8) and Jim Hart (12) hit home runs to power San Francisco over the Colts. Bob Aspromonte (10) clouted a four-bagger for Houston. The Giants' Billy O'Dell (3–1) pitched four innings of relief and got the win, while Don Larsen (0–3) took the loss for the Colts.

For the second night in a row Colts manager Harry Craft was ejected from the game. Craft's most recent banishment came in the ninth inning when he disputed a call by umpire Tony Venzon.

The Phillies broke a four-game losing streak to left-handers with their victory over Warren Spahn (6–9) of the Braves. While Spahn took the loss, he went the distance for the first time in 12 games, yielding six hits.

Richie Allen was the hitting star for the Phillies in the game with a triple and double while scoring two runs. The Phillies' deciding run was scored by Wes Covington, who came home on a triple by Bobby Wine.

Ray Culp (7–6) started for the Phillies but was relieved in the ninth with a 3–2 lead by Jim Bunning after Ed Bailey led off with a single and Rico Carty followed with a hit. Bunning came on to pitch to Ty Cline, who sacrificed, moving Bailey to third and Carty to second. Gene Oliver then popped up. Bunning then issued an intentional walk to Ed Mathews to fill the bases. Merritt Ranew was then sent up to pinch hit for Frank Bolling and grounded out.

Although he had primarily pitched in relief during his first season in the majors with Detroit in 1955, from that point on it was a rare relief appearance for Jim Bunning. In his 17-year career Bunning had a record in relief of 9–4 with 16 saves.

Cincinnati was rained out at New York, thereby losing one-half game in the standings to remain in third place, seven games behind the Giants.

At Pittsburgh the Pirates dropped a twilight doubleheader to the Cardinals, 5–4 and 12–5, to fall into fourth place, eight games behind the Giants.

The first game was a 12-inning affair that saw the Red Birds prevail on Julian Javier's run-scoring single. Lou Brock had seven hits in the doubleheader for St. Louis. In the first game he had a single, double and home run (4). Then in the second game Brock had four hits including two singles, a triple and home run (5). Bill White (8 & 9) also homered in both games for the Cardinals.

Roberto Clemente, who entered the evening as the National League's leading hitter, went 1-for-10 in the doubleheader to drop seven points to a .341 average.

The Cardinals were suddenly surging, having in five days climbed from 10 to 7½ games out of first. Rounding-out the National League action on July 13, the Cubs downed the Dodgers, 10–4.

On Tuesday, July 14, both San Francisco and Philadelphia lost, so at the top of the National League standings there was no change, with the Phillies remaining a game behind the Giants.

At Milwaukee the Giants were defeated by the Braves, 8–7, as rookie Rico Carty and veteran Eddie Mathews (12) hit home runs. Mathews' homer was the 434th of his career and broke a tie with Willie Mays for eighth place on the all-time list at that point in time. The victory was 12th in the last 17 games for the Braves. Juan Marichal (12–5) took the loss for the Giants.

At Pittsburgh the Pirates rebounded from their twin bill defeat the previous night to whip the Phillies, 4–3. The Pirates entered the fifth leading 2–0, then scored two runs on an infield hit by Manny Mota with the bases loaded, and a grounder by Roberto Clemente that drove in a run. Bob Veale (9–6), the Pirates starter, was the winning pitcher.

Dennis Bennett had been scheduled to start for the Phillies but was scratched for Cal McLish, who had been on the disabled list. However, McLish was unable to survive the first inning.

Calvin Coolidge Julius Caesar Tuskahoma (Buster) McLish was making one of the final two appearances of his 15-year major league career in the game. McLish, part Cherokee Indian, had been born in Anadarko, Oklahoma, on December 1, 1925. He came up to the majors at the age of 18 during World War II in 1944 with the Brooklyn Dodgers and had a 3–10 record during that season.

On May 3, 1947, he was traded by the Dodgers, along with Gene Mauch, Kirby Higbee, Hank Behrman and Dixie Walker, for Al Gionfriddo and $100,000. Gionfriddo, of course, would make one of the greatest catches in World Series history in the sixth game of the series on October 5, 1947, when his seemingly impossible one-handed catch of Joe DiMaggio's smash near the 415-foot marker in Yankee Stadium near the left-field bullpen saved the game for the Dodgers in an 8–6 victory over the Yankees.

Dixie Walker, traded with McLish, was of course sent out of Brooklyn due to the fact that he abhorred the thought of having a Negro teammate, as Branch Rickey had recently brought Jackie Robinson up to the majors, breaking baseball's color line. Gene Mauch was now in 1964 McLish's manager on the Phillies.

McLish was in the Pirates organization a few years without success and then was shipped to the Chicago Cubs in late 1948, where he was shuttled back and forth to minors for several years before landing in the Pacific Coast League for an extended stay. However, McLish had established himself as one of the best pitchers in the Pacific Coast League, winning 16 games at Los Angeles in 1953; then he won 13 in 1954 and 17 in 1955. This was his ticket back to the majors.

Coming back to the majors in 1956 with the Cleveland Indians, McLish had a record of 9–7. Then in 1958 he went 16–8 and in 1959 led the Tribe's hurlers with a record of 19–8 and even pitched two scoreless innings of relief for the American League in the second All-Star Game that year played at Los Angeles.

Then on December 15, 1959, he was traded by the Indians along with Billy Martin and Gordy Coleman to Cincinnati for All-Star second baseman Johnny Temple.

The trade, engineered by Reds general manager Gabe Paul, was very unpopular with the Reds fans. In 1959 the Reds had finished sixth with a team that produced the highest batting average in the league (.274) and the second-highest ERA (4.31) Therefore Paul reasoned that the Reds could improve with a solid starter such as Cal McLish.

Johnny Temple, however, was popular with Reds fans and batted .311 in the 1959 season, an average equal to team leader Frank Robinson's batting average. Temple was well known around town in Cincinnati, too; he made television commercials and even had a ghost-written column in the *Cincinnati Post & Times Star.*

When McLish failed to live up to his billing in 1960, the Crosley Field boo birds made him their number one target for abuse. He finished the 1960 season with a 4–14 record and was traded over the winter to the Chicago White Sox along with Juan Pizzaro for Gene Freese. Ironically, the acquisition of Freese by the Reds was considered instrumental in helping them to win the 1961 National League Pennant.

McLish would finish his 15-year Major League career in 1964 with the Phillies, appearing in just two games with a record of 0–1. For his career he was 92–92.

Meanwhile, on July 14, 1964, the Cincinnati Reds had returned to the friendly confines of Crosley Field and swept a twilight doubleheader from the Houston Colts, 6–5 and 10–3. Suddenly the Reds were right back in the pennant race, 5½ games behind the Giants and 4½ games behind the Phillies.

In the first game the Reds scored three runs on wild pitches by Colts pitchers, two on consecutive tosses by Larry Yellen and the third on a wild heave by Hal Woodeshick in the bottom of the 11th. However, in the second game the Reds pounded out 16 hits.

St. Louis continued to rise in the standings, defeating Sandy Koufax and the Dodgers, 8–7. With the victory the Cardinals had now climbed back into fifth place, seven games behind the Giants.

Led by John Roseboro, who drove in three runs with three singles, the Dodgers had built a 5–0 lead and it looked as if Koufax was well on his way to winning his 10th straight game and 14th of the season. But home runs by Mike Shannon and Bill White, followed by two runs in the bottom of the eighth, sent Koufax to the showers as Ron Perranowski came on in relief to snuff out the rally. Then Perranowski, with a 7–4 lead, let the game get away in the bottom of the ninth as a two-run pinch single by Bob Skinner capped a four-run St. Louis rally to win the game.

At New York the Cubs downed the Mets, 4–2, as Dick Ellsworth won his 11th game. On July 15, Milwaukee beat San Francisco again, 6–2, and Pittsburgh downed Philadelphia, 3–0. Consequently, the pennant race tightened a little more.

The hard-charging Braves won their 13th in the last 18 games as Hank Aaron's run-scoring single and a two run double by Lee Maye in the seventh inning gave Milwaukee the victory. Hank Aaron's three singles in the game broke the Braves all-time club record for career hits of 2002 set by Fred Tenney in 1911. Aaron now had 2005 career hits.

At Pittsburgh, Bob Friend (8–8) tossed a seven-hit shutout as the Pirates beat the Phillies, 3–0. Jim Bunning (9–4) took the loss for Philadelphia, giving up four hits in seven innings of work. In the fourth off Bunning, after Manny Mota had singled and Roberto Clemente reached base on an error, pinch hitter supreme Jerry Lynch (8), playing left field for the Bucs, hit a 440-foot home run over the left-field wall at Forbes Field.

In Cincinnati the Reds moved to within 4½ games of the Giants after defeating Houston, 2–1. Marty Keough (5) provided the winning margin for the Reds with a two-run home run in the sixth. Jim O'Toole (10–4) was the winning pitcher and Dick Farrell (10–5) took the loss. For Farrell it was his seventh attempt at his 11th victory since getting his 10th win back on June 14.

Prior to the game the Reds had given Johnny Temple his unconditional release as a player. Following the 1963 season the Houston Colts had released Temple and subsequently the Reds reacquired Temple as a player-coach during the winter of 1963, at the insistence of manager Fred Hutchinson. Hutchinson reasoned that Temple, being a good contact hitter, could serve the club well as a pinch hitter.

Hutch also had a subterfuge reason for wanting Temple to return to the Reds. Remembering the isolation that Pete Rose had been subjected to by his fellow players during his rookie year in 1963, Hutch wanted to have Temple on the team to serve as a sort of mentor for him. That way on the road Pete would have someone to go to dinner with and a role model who could assist him with developing his social skills.

There is, however, another more blighted version of Fred Hutchinson's reasoning behind wanting to establish a personal relationship between Pete Rose and Johnny Temple. Hutchinson was concerned that Rose might not have been able to take care of himself off the field. And when Rose came up to the Reds, Hutch had given his word to Pete's father, Harry Rose, that he would look after him.

Hutchinson also shared the concern of general manager Bill DeWitt that Rose was spending too much time socializing with the black players on the Reds. In order to intercede in the friendships that Rose had cultivated with Frank Robinson and Vada Pinson, that for some reason were an embarrassment to the Reds' front office, Hutchinson reasoned that by assigning Temple to look after Rose, he would adopt more of a white man's cultural approach to being a member of a big league team.

Johnny Temple had cultivated a certain quiet dignity about himself; he dressed well and was a regular at Toots Shor's restaurant when the team was in New York; and he fit in magnificently with the newsmen, celebrities and other high-profile ballplayers that frequented the establishment.

While Temple was released from the playing part of his duties on the Reds on July 15, he remained as a coach on the Reds. Temple's removal from the roster was necessary to make room for catcher Don Pavletich, who was being brought up from the Reds' San Diego farm club in the Pacific Coast League. The addition of Pavletich was made necessary after All-Star catcher Johnny Edwards was sidelined with a sore arm. Reds officials said Temple would work with the players prior to games but would not be allowed to be in uniform on the bench during actual play.

In other games played on July 15, the Cubs defeated the Mets, 3–2, and the Dodgers whipped the Cardinals, 13–3.

So at the mid-point of July, the National League standings were the following.

National League Standings July 16, 1964

Team	Won	Lost	Pct.	G.B.
San Francisco	52	35	.598	—
Philadelphia	49	34	.590	1
Cincinnati	47	39	.547	4½
Pittsburgh	44	39	.530	6
St. Louis	44	42	.512	7½
Milwaukee	44	42	.512	7½
Los Angeles	42	43	.494	9
Chicago	41	43	.488	9½
Houston	39	49	.443	13½
New York	26	62	.295	26½

On July 16 the Phillies regained the National League lead by four percentage points (.595 to .591) after defeating the Pirates, 7–5, while the Giants were shut out by the Braves, 6–0, for their third straight loss.

For the Phillies, Cookie Rojas led the way with two doubles and a single while starting two rallies. In the second Clay Dalrymple smashed a two-run double. Then Rojas singled to start a two-run rally in the third, and later in the fifth his double ignited a three-run outburst. Art Mahaffey (8–4) got the win for Philadelphia with three innings of two-hit relief pitching from Jack Baldschun. Joe Gibbon (6–3) took the loss for the Pirates.

The victory, while only the second for the Phillies in the last eight games, was enough to send them back to the top of the standings as Hank Fischer (7–5) pitched a four-hit shutout in leading Milwaukee over San Francisco, 6–0. In fact, Fischer had a no-hitter going until Duke Snider led off the sixth with a double. Fischer also helped his own cause by doubling home two runs in the Braves' eighth. Gaylord Perry (7–6) was the losing pitcher, giving up three runs and seven hits in seven innings of work.

Cincinnati continued to rise in the standings with a 3–2 victory over Houston, moving the Reds to within 3½ games of the league lead. The winning margin for the Reds occurred in the third inning, when the speedy Marty Keough beat out a hit to deep short, then raced all the way home from first base following a single by Deron Johnson to right center to break up a 2–2 tie. Bob Purkey (4–6) got the win in relief of Joe Nuxhall and Don Nottebart (3–8) took the loss for the Colts.

Also on July 16, after seven starts Ernie Broglio (4–9) finally won a game with the Cubs, going all the way with a nifty ten-hitter to defeat the Mets, 11–1, at Wrigley Field before 9,078 happy fans. The Cubs pounded out 16 hits in the game off five Mets hurlers. Tracy Stallard (5–12), the Mets' starter, took the loss.

At St. Louis the Dodgers defeated the Cardinals, 10–2. Joe Moeller (5–7) was the winning pitcher for the Dodgers, while Ray Sadecki (10–7) took the loss for the Cards. Ron Fairly drove in four runs for L.A. with three hits including a home run (6).

On Friday, July 17, the San Francisco Giants playing at home suffered their fourth straight defeat, losing to the Houston Colts, 5–2. Meanwhile the Philadelphia Phillies now had sole possession of first place after they defeated the Reds, 5–4, while playing on the road in Cincinnati.

On Saturday, July 18, Pete Rose entered the game batting .265 after getting three hits in a losing effort to the Phillies the night before. However, in the Saturday game Rose (3) drove in six runs with four hits including a grand slam homer, the first of his career, as the Reds blasted the Phillies, 14–4, in Cincinnati. Rose started a four-run rally in the first when he drew a walk off Phillies starter Ray Culp. Then in the second he drove in a run with a double, singled in another in the third, and belted his grand slam in the fifth off Philadelphia reliever Dallas Green, after a walk and singles by Steve Boros and pitcher John Tsitouris. Finally Rose added a single in the seventh, going four-for-four in the game.

Also in the Reds' 17-hit assault on Philadelphia pitching, Deron Johnson (10) and Don Pavletich (1) hit home runs, while Vada Pinson had three hits, a double and two singles.

For Philadelphia, Coston Shockley (1) and Clay Dalrymple (4) hit home runs. Shockley's home run was number one in a career total of three that he would hit in two Major League seasons split between the Philadelphia Phillies and California Angels.

In the first inning Phillies left fielder Wes Covington was hit in the head by a John Tsitouris pitch. Covington had to be carried from the field and was taken to Cincinnati's Christ Hospital for X-rays. He was reported not to be seriously hurt and in fair condition.

Tsitouris (6–6) went all the way for the Reds, allowing nine hits, while Ray Culp (7–7) took the loss for the Phillies. The victory kept the Reds 3½ games behind the league-leading Phillies.

Meanwhile, San Francisco dropped its fifth straight game, losing to Houston again, 2–1. Despite the losing streak, the Giants were still in second place and only one game behind the Phillies.

On Sunday, July 19, five doubleheaders made up the National League schedule, and by the end of the day Philadelphia was still holding on to first place by four percentage points over San Francisco.

At Cincinnati a big Sunday near-sell-out crowd of 27,245 on hand saw the Reds and Phillies split a twin bill. In the first game Pete Rose's hot hitting was finally held in check as he went 0-for-4. Nonetheless the Reds, using five pitchers—Jim Maloney, Bob Purkey, Bill Henry, Billy McCool and Sammy Ellis—overcame a 4–0 deficit through the fifth to eventually beat the Phillies, 7–4.

Jim Bunning started the first game for Philadelphia and had a 4–0 lead until the sixth, when he gave up two unearned runs. He was replaced by Chris Short in the seventh after three singles by the Reds cut the lead to 4–3.

Jack Baldshun (3–4) came on to pitch the eighth and lasted one-third of an inning as the Reds teed off on him and Ed Roebuck for four more runs to make the score 7–4. The big blow for the Reds was an eighth-inning two-run home run by Don Pavletich (2). Billy McCool (3–0), the fourth Reds pitcher who came on in the eighth, got the win. Jack Baldshun (3–4) took the loss.

Richie Allen hit his 17th home run of the season in the first game, tying the Philadelphia Phillies' record for home runs by a rookie player. The record was shared by Del Ennis (1946), Harry Anderson (1957) and Ed Bochee (1957).

In the second game it was the Phillies who came from behind to beat the Reds, 4–3, on Johnny Callison's (15) three-run ninth-inning homer. Callison, a left-handed batter, stroked his homer off southpaw Bill Henry, who had replaced Ryne Duren (0–2) with one out in the ninth after a single by Clay Dalrymple and a walk to Cookie Rojas.

John Boozer (1–0), just recalled from the minors by the Phillies, got the win. Marty Keough had three hits for the Reds, including his 6th home run of the season.

Out in San Francisco, the Giants swept a pair of games from the Colts, 4–2 and 1–0. The doubleheader sweep moved the Giants back within four percentage points of the Phillies, as the seesaw battle that had been going on between the two clubs since opening day continued.

Meanwhile, Milwaukee kept up its torrid pace, knocking off Pittsburgh twice, 6–2 and 5–4. The Braves were now in 4th place, six games behind the Phillies. The following day Pirates infielder Bob Bailey would be suspended for two games by National League president Warren Giles for what he termed a bumping incident with umpire Ed Vargo.

Out at Dodger Stadium, Chicago downed Los Angeles, 8–2 and 9–1.

At St. Louis the Cardinals split their doubleheader with the Mets, losing the first game, 3–2, then rebounding to take the nightcap, 7–6. Prior to the game the Mets had obtained infielder Bobby Klaus from the Reds for cash.

On Monday night, July 20, the Reds and Phillies concluded their five-game series, with the Reds winning, 6–1. Joe Nuxhall (8–4) got the win with relief help from Billy McCool. Dennis Bennett (9–7) took the loss. The 36-year-old Nuxhall looked like he was about to pitch a complete game until being tossed out by umpire Mel Steiner in the 8th after questioning a call on the first pitch, a ball to Bobby Wine.

Prior to the game, friends of Jim Bunning's from Northern Kentucky and Cincinnati showered him with gifts to celebrate his perfect game against the Mets on June 21. Bunning received such gifts as a barometer clock and 127 T-bone steaks, one for each game that he had won in the majors up to that point in time; and the Wiedemann Brewing Company informed Jim that they were not only giving each of his seven children a U.S. Savings Bond, but were also going to deliver a case of their beer to his home each week for the remainder of the year. Among other things, Bunning was also informed that a park in Campbell County, Kentucky, near his boyhood home, would be named in his honor.

With Chicago beating the Giants, 6–4, on a 9th-inning three-run homer by Ron Santo (18), the Reds moved to within 2½ games of the lead, with the Phillies and Giants only separated by percentage points.

Gene Mauch said before the game that he really didn't know who was the team to beat for the pennant right now. "I'm not dodging the question, but I really don't know. This league is so evenly matched that any one of six clubs could win. I'm not counting the Dodgers out of the running. I know they're running eighth at this time. But it's the same club that won the pennant by seven games last year and then went on to knock off the Yankees in four straight games. With some 70 games left to play you can't say that kind of club doesn't have a chance."[4]

On Tuesday, July 21, the Phillies increased their lead over the Giants to a full game after defeating Milwaukee, while the Giants were beaten by the Cubs.

Third-place Cincinnati lost to the Mets, 4–2, and dropped 3½ games back of the Phillies. The Reds all at once seemed to be having a tough time with the Mets, losing their fourth straight and fifth in nine games with the perennial cellar dwellers.

Reds manager Fred Hutchinson was dumb-founded by the play of the Mets against his team. "Unbelievable. I read about all the beating the Mets take, then I see them and they play like champs."[5]

The following evening, on July 22, the Mets made it five straight over Cincinnati, beating them 4–3 in 10 innings. With two out in the 10th, pinch hitter Jim Hickman doubled home Ron Hunt with what would be the winning run off reliever Billy McCool (3–1) to drop the Reds 4½ games behind the Phillies, who for the second night in a row beat Milwaukee.

Willard Hunter, a sidearm left-hander and the third Mets pitcher in the game, was the winning pitcher. For Hunter it was his first victory in the majors since 1962. He would be out of the Major Leagues for good following 1964, finishing with a career record of (4–9).

Prior to the game the Mets' Frank Thomas attempted to assault Jack Lang, a reporter for the *Long Island Press*, as the two conversed around the batting cage. Thomas was still smarting over not being awarded a hit during the previous night's game by the official scorer. Lang was not the scorer, but was attempting to explain the official scorer's judgment to Thomas when all at once he threw a punch at him.

"He merely grazed me," said Lang. "Right here"—pointing to the left side of the neck, just beneath the ear.[6] For the record, Frank Thomas was 6'3" and weighed 200 pounds. Jack Lang was 5'6" and weighed 200 pounds.

Philadelphia had beaten the Braves, 4–1, to stay ahead of the Giants by a full game. The game had been tied, 1–1, in the 7th when Bobby Wine hit a bases-empty homer off Warren Spahn to put the Phillies ahead.

At San Francisco, the Giants snapped a four-game losing streak, beating the Cubs, 7–3.

On Thursday, July 23, the Cincinnati Reds finally ended the hex that they seemed to have on them while playing the Mets with 5–4 victory. Jim Maloney (9–9) started and had nine strikeouts in six innings, before having to leave the game with a strained muscle in his back with the Reds leading, 5–3.

The Phillies, meanwhile, picked up a full game on San Francisco as they won at Milwaukee, 13–10, while the Giants were being beaten by the Chicago, 13–4.

On Friday, July 24, the Reds called up a pair of players from San Diego of the Pacific Coast League, third baseman Chico Ruiz and future Hall of Famer first baseman Tony Perez.

On Monday, July 27, in a game played at Milwaukee, Perez would get the first of his 2,732 Major League hits, a line-drive double over short in the second inning off Braves starter Denny LeMaster (10–7). Perez would get two hits in the game and the Reds would go on to win the game, 11–2, behind Jim Maloney (10–9), who held the Braves to six hits and had seven strikeouts in the game.

On July 28, with the Braves in 6th place, manager Bobby Bragan took Warren Spahn out of the Braves' starting rotation and assigned him to the bullpen. Spahn, who had failed to finish 11 out of his last 12 starts, said of the demotion, "I don't relish the idea of going to the bullpen, but if I can help the club there I'll try to do the job."

Also on July 28 at Philadelphia, the Phillies beat the Giants, 4–0, to increase their lead over them by 1½ games. As July came to an end, the Phillies and Giants were still struggling for the league lead. Neither seemed capable of pulling away and neither team gave any indication of folding.

On Wednesday, July 29, in another head-to-head battle at Connie Mack Stadium, San Francisco turned the tables on the Phillies and defeated them, 6–3, in ten innings in a game that included a 30-minute rain delay, to once again pull within one-half game of the Phillies for the lead.

Juan Marichal (15–5) won his 15th game of the season, allowing the Phillies just four hits. However, two of the hits Marichal yielded were home runs to Richie Allen (18) and Ruben Amaro (2). Nonetheless, Marichal's performance was strong as he didn't allow a hit after the fourth and retired the last 19 men he faced.

Jim Ray Hart (16 & 17) hit two solo home runs for the Giants. Earlier in the game the Giants' All-Star first baseman Orlando Cepeda wrenched his shoulder swinging the bat while striking out against Phillies starting pitcher Dennis Bennett. Consequently, Giants manager Alvin Dark sent in Willie McCovey to replace Cepeda.

McCovey had been struggling recently and his batting average at game time was a paltry .203. Subsequently he struck out his first time at bat. However, in the eighth he doubled to score Willie Mays with the tying run, and then in the tenth inning he hit a two-run single to provide the winning margin for the Giants. The towering ball hit by McCovey traveled to the 447-foot mark in center field.

Alvin Dark's response to McCovey's sudden resurgence following the game was simply, "You never know about this game."

Later it was discovered that despite Juan Marichal's strong performance in the game, he had injured his back. He would spend a week in the hospital and it would be more than a month before he would attempt to pitch again.

In a Ladies Day game at Milwaukee with 9,109 fans watching, the Braves continued to flirt with being a contender as they beat Cincinnati, 6–2. The Braves jumped all over Reds starter Joe Nuxhall (8–6) for five runs in the first inning, then starter Tony Cloninger (10–9) coasted to his 10th victory. Despite the loss the Reds remained in third place, four games behind the Phillies.

The Pirates were still threatening to break out and challenge for the lead as well. On July 29 they defeated the Colts, 5–2, and were in fourth place, 4½ games out of first.

In the game the Colts' Dick Farrell (10–7) failed once again to win his 11th game. Farrell had not won a game now in his last ten starts since June 14.

For the Pirates, Bob Friend (9–10) threw a complete game and got the win as Roberto Clemente with two hits raised his league-leading average to .345 with two hits while driving in a pair of runs.

On July 1, St. Louis had been in 7th place, 9½ games behind the Giants. Now on July 30 they were tied with Milwaukee for fifth place after they defeated Chicago, 9–1, for their fifth straight victory.

In the seventh the Cardinals sent 12 batters to the plate in a seven-run scoring splurge. Ironically, the runs were all yielded by former Cardinals pitchers Lew Burdette, Bobby Shantz and Lindy McDaniel. Curt Simmons won his 11th game of year for the Cardinals and didn't allow a run for 5⅓ innings.

At New York the last-place Mets, 26½ games out of first place, had taken a 3–0 lead over the Dodgers before a steady summer rain forced the postponement of the game.

Now as the four-month-old dog fight for the league lead between the Phillies and Giants continued, the dog days of August lay straight ahead. Interestingly enough, an oddity existed in the National League: with the season more than half over, not one manager had been fired yet. In fact, the only rumor that was flying around the league at the end of July was that in St. Louis, manager Johnny Keane's job could be in jeopardy if the Cardinals did not start playing winning ball soon. Meanwhile, former Cardinals all-time favorite Red Schoendiest was waiting in the wings for the call to pilot the club, should Keane continue to falter in the job.

VIII

Trials and Tribulations of the Dog Days

As the pennant race entered August, the Philadelphia Phillies began to believe in themselves that they were legitimate contenders. People on the streets of Philadelphia believed in the Phillies, too, and were making them the topic of daily conversation.

Manager Gene Mauch had a ball club that was showing poise and the ability to win games in the late innings. At this point, they were even in the season series played with the powerful San Francisco Giants (6–6), and the only club that had given the Phillies much trouble so far was the St. Louis Cardinals (4–9).

But what did that matter? No one at this point saw St. Louis as a serious threat. They had some ground to make up, and on August 1 the Cards were in fifth place, seven games behind the Phillies.

Nonetheless, the Cardinals were starting to play ball and in July they had achieved a winning percentage of .647 (17–11). This was quite a turn-around for St. Louis, when it is considered that in June the Cardinals for the month had an undistinguished winning percentage of .379 (11–18).

One could argue the degree of influence that the Lou Brock trade may have had on the Cardinals' winning percentage. The record shows that on June 15, prior to the Brock-Broglio trade, the Cardinals had a losing record of 28–31, and following the trade through games of July 31, a winning record of 25–18.

But as August began, the Cardinals made it known that they intended to make a run at the pennant. To that end on Friday, July 31, the Cards called up infielders Dal Maxvill from Indianapolis of the Pacific Coast League and Ed Spiezio from Tulsa. Maxvill was batting .285 with 51 hits in 179 at bats for Indy. Also the Redbirds added strength to their bullpen by calling up knuckballer Barney Schultz from Jacksonville in the International League. Schultz at 38 years old would be the oldest player on the Cardinals, a place that had until this season been reserved for retired outfielder Stan Musial at 43 years old. To make room for Schultz on the roster, the Cardinals sold pitcher Glenn Hobbie (1–5) outright to Jacksonville. Hobbie had come to St. Louis on June 2 in a deal that sent pitcher Lou Burdette to the Cubs.

The Cincinnati Reds, Pittsburgh Pirates and Milwaukee Braves would continue to threaten at a run for the top, then each of the teams would quickly drop a few key games. All season long so far, the Reds, Pirates and Braves seemed to be more in contention with each other, having a private race for third place, rather than challenging for the league lead with the Phillies and Giants. Also, the Reds seemed to be having enormous trouble beating the Giants, behind so far in the season series, 3–9.

There was also growing concern in Cincinnati and the baseball community at large for the failing health of manager Fred Hutchinson. The worsening condition of Hutchinson had to have some psychological effect of stress on the Reds team daily.

Hutch, withering away from his cancer, now had to ingest painkillers daily to deal with the agony of the disease. During July he stopped making road trips with team and began to transition coach Dick Sisler into the manager's role. The eventual demise of Fred Hutchinson was now apparent to everyone around him.

As August began, Hutchinson was confined to Cincinnati's Christ Hospital for a checkup. He was allowed no visitors other than family and members of the Reds team. However, he was permitted to listen to the Reds games on radio with the play-by-play of legendary broadcaster Waite Hoyt.

Commenting on Hutchinson's hospitalization, team physician Dr. George Ballou said, "There's nothing definite about his release, but there's still a chance he may be out this weekend. Nothing will be made public on the results of the tests."[1]

In August, sports columnist Murray Olderman wrote, "Between you'n'me, hounding Fred Hutchinson about the Cincinnati manager's state of health has become a ghoulish exercise in journalistic bad taste."[2]

Pete Rose told author Roger Kahn, "We saw Hutch go from 220 pounds to 140 pounds with the cancer and he never once complained. Tough. Really tough. More than baseball tough. He was a man. He had this cough and he was getting skinnier every day, but Hutch was a fighter. He'd come into the clubhouse to conduct the meetings and after a while, looking at Hutch was like looking at a skeleton. But I'll tell you this. That skeleton was in charge."[3]

Fred Hutchinson, 1964. (The Sporting News)

As for the struggling 1963 World Champion Los Angeles Dodgers, going into the month of August, despite the strong performances by starting pitchers Sandy Koufax and Don Drysdale, it was apparent to everyone that they were through for the season and would not repeat in as the pennant winners in 1964. The Dodgers didn't score many runs and their bullpen, namely Ron Perranoski, was having trouble getting batters out. Furthermore, the Dodgers were personally looking like the Giants' personal patsies, behind in the season series with their West Coast rivals, 3–10.

The Chicago Cubs were also struggling to stay ahead of the Houston Colts. They also had trouble winning against the West Coast teams for some reason. Billy Williams and Ron Santo were having great years and Larry Jackson was on his way to a 20-game-win season. Ernie Banks was still a solid everyday player, too. But the Ernie Broglio deal was already considered a bust; and Dick Ellsworth, a 22-game winner for the Cubs in 1963, and Bob Buhl didn't seem to have the magic on the mound that each had earlier in the season.

The Houston Colts had demonstrated improvement so far in 1964, but the only thing certain for the club was that they were not going to finish in the cellar. The Colts, while getting some valuable playing experience for younger players like Rusty Staub and Jimmy Wynn, continued to use a lot of aging veterans in their lineup and were more likely already thinking about playing in their air-conditioned domed stadium, scheduled to open in 1965.

The New York Mets, on August 1, were mired in last place 29 games behind first-place Philadelphia. It was already certain for Casey Stengel's crew that another season with 100 or more losses was imminent. Nonetheless, the fans in Queens loved the team and the Mets were challenging the contending clubs for the league lead in home attendance.

On August 1 to most observers it did indeed look like 1964 was going to be a Phillies' year, as Johnny Callison had stated following the All-Star Game in early July. The Philadelphia Phillies had been in contention from Opening Day on and now were on solid footing with excellent starting pitching coming from Dennis Bennett, Jim Bunning and Chris Short, as well as Jack Baldshun out of the bullpen.

Clay Dalrymple, despite being a little weak at the plate with the bat, had proven to be solid receiver behind it and was handling the Phillies' pitchers with extreme skill. The bulk of the run production was being provided by Johnny Callison and rookie Richie Allen. In fact, at this point in the season Allen was looking like a shoo-in for National League Rookie of the Year.

"We have a ball club that has a will to win," remarked Allen. "We have no long ball hitters like the Giants and Braves, but we have a scrappy team. "I'm just grateful for the chance to make the club and it was through Gene Mauch that I got the chance."[4]

In the same midseason interview Jim Bunning also expressed his confidence in regards to the Phillies' being a legitimate pennant contender: "I thought all along in spring training that we had a chance to win the pennant, we had a good ball club. Then once around the league, I was more convinced than ever that we can win the pennant."[5]

In fact Bunning, the off-season stock broker who was looking more like a 20-game winner with each passing day, was already contemplating his contract talks with Phillies general manager John Quinn for the 1965 season. "I think about this winter and how happy I'm going to be dealing with Mr. Quinn on my contract," remarked Bunning.[6]

With a good young ball club that was still developing and one that so far had been in serious contention for the pennant all the way through the 1964 season, Phillies manager Gene Mauch was asked if he was beginning to look forward to 1965.

"No," remarked Mauch. "You can't have a master plan for a ball club as far as having the ballplayers coming to you and playing your game. You have to adapt to the players you have."[7]

This prophetic philosophy of Mauch's would become apparent in the selection of his infamous pitching rotation coming down the stretch in late September.

On Friday, July 31, the Los Angeles Dodgers followed San Francisco into Philadelphia for a weekend series. Meanwhile the Giants, hot in pursuit of the Phillies for the lead, turned westward and headed to Pittsburgh for their weekend games.

In the bottom of the first inning at Philadelphia, Johnny Callison homered and Richie Allen singled off Dodgers starter Joe Moeller. Then Moeller bore down and handcuffed the Phillies' batters, proceeding to retire 17 straight batters. Nonetheless, the Phillies erupted for three runs in the eighth to wrap it up. In the top of the eighth Jack Baldshun had replaced Chris Short (10–5) and worked out of a bases-loaded jam.

But the Giants kept pace as they downed the Pirates, 8–6. Once again Willie Mays led the way by stroking three singles, scoring three runs and driving in a run. However, the Giants were given some assistance by five Pirates errors—three by second baseman Bill Mazeroski, considered to be one of the best-fielding second basemen in the National League, and two by third baseman Bob Bailey.

The Reds were still well within striking distance, staying close behind the Phillies and Giants in third place. On Friday night, July 31, they defeated the Cardinals, 7–6, bringing a halt to the Cards' winning streak at six games. A crowd of 22,000-plus had come out to Bush Stadium to welcome the Cardinals back home.

Cincinnati had scored five unearned runs in the second inning following two St. Louis errors. However, the decisive blow in the game was a two-run single by Vada Pinson in the fifth. The hit was surprising to the Cardinals, as Pinson had entered the game having gotten only two hits in his last 33 at bats. In the ninth inning St. Louis shortstop Dick Groat suffered a bloody nose when he collided with umpire Ed Sudol at first base.

In a day game at Wrigley Field in Chicago, the Braves pounded the Cubs, 13–3. In a classic display of the Braves power, Hank Aaron hit a three-run homer, while Dennis Menke and Joe Torre also hit round-trippers and a triple each, to hand the Cubs their fourth straight defeat.

In a twi-night doubleheader battle for the basement in the National League on July 31, the Mets swept the Colts, 3–0 and 6–2. Frank Lary, a 33-year-old American League cast-off, tossed a two hit shutout for the Mets in the opening game. In the nightcap the Mets' Jack Fisher scattered seven hits and Ed Kranepool hit a two-run homer.

National League Standings, August 1, 1964

Team	Won	Lost	Pct.	G.B.
Philadelphia	59	41	.590	—
San Francisco	59	44	.573	1½
Cincinnati	56	47	.544	5
Pittsburgh	53	45	.541	5
Milwaukee	53	48	.525	6½
St. Louis	53	49	.520	7
Los Angeles	50	50	.500	9
Chicago	48	52	.485	11
Houston	45	60	.429	16½
New York	32	72	.308	29

The Phillies expanded their lead to 2½ games on Saturday, August 1, by whipping the Dodgers, 10–6, while the Pirates downed the Giants, 6–1.

Tony Gonzalez and John Herrnstein led a 14-hit Philadelphia assault on Don Drysdale and three other L.A. pitchers. Gonazalez had two singles and a double, scored two runs and drove in another. Herrenstein added two singles and a home run (5), while driving in two runs.

Meanwhile at Pittsburgh, the Pirates beat the Giants as former bonus baby Bob Bailey redeemed himself after his two errors the previous night's game and had a big day, scoring three runs and hitting a two-run homer. Joe Gibbon (8–4) won his eighth game, pitching an eight-hitter, and was never in any serious trouble throughout the game.

The Pirates started the scoring against Giants starter Ron Herbel (7–6) in the third when Bailey reached first base on an error, went to second on an infield hit and then scored on a double by Roberto Clemente.

Then in the fourth inning, following a walk to Dick Schofield, Bailey hit his 6th home run of the season that touched off a four-run Pirates rally. Bill Virdon and Clemente followed with singles to send Herbel to the showers.

Former White Sox pitching ace Billy Pierce relieved Herbel and was greeted with a two-run triple by Jerry Lynch. In the sixth Pittsburgh got its last run of the game when Bailey walked and scored on another single by Clemente. The Giants' lone run of the game off Gibbon came in the ninth when Jim Hart tripled and scored on an infield hit by Jose Pagan.

In a Ladies Day game at St. Louis, Cincinnati moved to within two games of second place after they had defeated the Cardinals, 6–5. The Cardinals entered the top of the seventh with starter Bob Gibson (8–9) cruising along with a 3–1 lead. Then pinch hitter Mel Queen, who was hitting .171, smashed a three-run homer off Gibson to start a five-run Reds rally. The Reds tagged Gibson for five straight hits in the inning, including a double by Don Pavletich and pinch-hit single by Marty Keough.

In the bottom of half of the seventh the Cards fought back against Billy McCool, who had came in to replace Reds starter Joey Jay (6–8), with three successive singles by Tim McCarver, Charley James and Curt Flood. Then McCool walked Lou Brock to score a run.

Sammy Ellis replaced McCool on the mound and stopped the Cardinals' two-run rally with the bases loaded. After Ellis walked Dick Groat, scoring the second Cardinal run of the inning, he then proceeded to strike out the meat of the Cards' order in the presence of Ken Boyer and Bill White to preserve the victory for Jay.

Light-hitting Mel Queen, who led the Reds' comeback in the game, was the son of former Major League pitcher Mel Queen (27–40) who played for eight years between 1942 and 1952 with the New York Yankees and Pittsburgh Pirates. Queen, 23 years old, was a bonus player whom the Reds had brought up to their Major League roster for 1964 because he had no options left.

Mel Queen the younger would wind up the 1964 season with the Reds playing in 48 games, 20 in the outfield, while batting .200 with two home runs. The following year he would play in only five games with the Reds while going hitless.

Then in 1966 the Reds began to convert Queen into a pitcher. In the 1967 season he started 24 games for the Reds and had a respectable record of 14–8 with an ERA of 2.76. Queen was also popular with the Cincinnati's younger fans, as he often socialized with them in the trendy bistros located in the neighborhood of Mt. Adams and the college taverns around the University of Cincinnati campus.

However, the Reds ultimately threw in the towel on the Mel Queen experiment without giving him much more of a chance to prove himself.

The 1964 St. Louis Cardinals infield: Ken Boyer, Dick Groat, Julian Javier, Bill White. (PhotoFile)

On October 24, 1969, Queen was sold by the Reds to the California Angels, where he finished up his Major League career in 1972 after spending parts of nine years in the big leagues with a pitching record of 20–17 and a surprising ERA of 3.14.

Queen's career batting average turned out to be not much higher than that when he hit the last Major League home run of his career off Bob Gibson, August 1, 1964, as he finished with a .179 average with 49 hits and two home runs.

The irony in the Mel Queen saga is that he is one of the hundreds of marginal ballplayers that just had the misfortune to play in the era before free agency, out-of-control salaries and half-thought-out league expansion. In the baseball market of today's game, Queen would undoubtedly be a multimillionaire and laughing all the way to the bank with his lifetime .179 batting average.

In Chicago the Cubs lost their fifth straight game, losing to the Braves, 8–4. For the Braves it was their fourth victory in a row.

In the eighth inning, Hank Aaron (17) greeted Cubs relief pitcher and former Milwaukee teammate Lou Burdette with a home run on his first pitch. Aaron's blast broke up a 4–4 tie; then the Braves added two more runs on a double by Rico Carty, a Cubs error and a sacrifice fly. The Braves added two more runs in the ninth.

The Cubs had pulled even at 4–4 in the seventh with three runs off starter Denny Lemaster and reliever Warren Spahn. Spahn would make 13 relief appearances in 1964 with credit for four saves. Eddie Mathews had homered for the Braves in the first inning.

Rounding out the action in the Saturday, August 1, games the Mets again downed the Colts by a score of 3–2.

Bob "Hawk" Taylor, another one of those marginal Major Leaguers born too soon to be a millionaire like Mel Queen, had another big day for the Mets. In the fifth Taylor (4) hit a two-run homer off Houston pitcher Gordon Jones (0–1). Then he scored the Mets' winning run in the seventh after he doubled, then went to third on an infield hit by Roy McMillan off of Jones' glove, and dashed home on a wild throw to first.

McMillan's smash had caromed off Jones' glove and bounced toward second, where Nellie Fox fielded it and attempted to throw him out at first. However, Fox threw the ball low and it skipped away from first baseman Walt Bond. However, Bobby Klaus followed with a single off Jones, thus turning the run scored by Taylor into an earned run, since the clean hit would have scored Taylor from third. Al Jackson (6–11) got the win for New York.

On Sunday, August 2, just as it looked like the Phillies might start to pull away from the Giants, the National League race tightened up instead.

Los Angeles whipped the Phillies, 6–1, behind the pitching of rookie Larry Miller (2–2) who stopped Philadelphia on seven hits and the key play of veteran Maury Wills. Wills contributed to the LA cause a double and a single, stole two bases, and started two double plays in the field. Dennis Bennett (9–9) took the loss for Philadelphia.

Meanwhile, San Francisco beat Pittsburgh, 2–1, thereby moving back to 1½ games behind the Phillies for the league lead. The Giants' Bob Hendley (10–6) and the Pirates' Bob Friend (9–11) had been locked in a

1–1 duel into the eighth when Jose Pagan led off with a single off Friend. Two outs later Duke Snider delivered a game-winning single, driving home Pagan.

Third-place Cincinnati failed to advance on Philadelphia, as they dropped a 5–4 decision to the Cardinals at St. Louis with 14,010 fans on hand. Jim Maloney, the Cincinnati starter who had won six out of his last seven decisions, was knocked out of the game in the third inning, giving up seven hits and four runs.

Curt Flood led off the game with his fourth home run of the year, drilling a 1–1 pitch from Maloney into the left-field stands. The Reds squandered a pair of home runs by Deron Johnson (13th and 14th) as the Cardinals snapped a 4–4 tie in the eighth on Carl Warwick's sacrifice fly with the bases loaded off reliever Billy McCool.

Prior to the game at Busch Stadium, the Cardinals had signed Lennie Boyer to a Major League contract calling for a $25,000 bonus. Lennie, a shortstop and brother of the Cardinals' Ken Boyer and the Yankees' Clete Boyer, was assigned to the Cardinals' farm club in Bruck Hill, South Carolina. Another Boyer brother who made it to the big leagues was Cloyd, a pitcher with the Cardinals, 1949–1952, and Kansas City Athletics, 1955. However, Lennie Boyer, unlike his famous brothers, never made it to the big leagues.

Chicago broke its five-game losing streak, defeating Milwaukee, 5–1, behind a strong performance by Ernie Broglio. Billy Cowan homered for the Cubs.

The Mets and Colts were wrapping up a five-game weekend series at Shea Stadium with their second doubleheader in three days.

Houston prevailed in the opening game, 9–7, with a ninth-inning rally capped by a two-run homer by center fielder Carroll Hardy (1). Don Notterbart (4–8), the third Houston pitcher in the game, got the win. Jack Fisher (7–13) took the loss for New York. Walt Bond (15) had also homered in the game for the Colts and Larry Elliot (8) and Ed Kranepool (5) homered for the Mets.

In the nightcap, New York snapped a 2–2 tie in the seventh inning with Charlie Smith's 13th homer to win the game, 4–2. Bob Locke (1–1) was winning pitcher for New York and Don Larsen (1–5) took the loss for Houston.

On Monday morning, August 3, there was still a tight pennant race in the National League with the Philadelphia Phillies in the lead by 1½ games over second-place San Francisco Giants. Cincinnati was still holding down third place, 4½ games behind.

The Phillies had an off day on Tuesday, August 4, as they waited to

begin a series at home with Houston commencing with a twi-night doubleheader on Wednesday.

However, up in New York the Mets and Giants were once again
engaged in a marathon game. Back on May 31 the Mets and Giants had
played the second game of a twin bill that lasted 23 innings, or seven hours
and 23 minutes, before San Francisco won the game.

Now on August 4, the Giants battled the Mets for 14 innings before
they beat them, 4–3, on a single by Jim Davenport that scored Jose Pagan
from first base with the winning run. San Francisco had taken a 3–1 lead
in the 11th inning on a two-run single by Orlando Cepeda, but the Mets
came back to tie the score in the bottom half on a pinch single by Jim Hickman. A huge crowd of 53,498 turned-out at Shea Stadium for the game
that saw the Giants pull back within 1½ games of the league-leading
Phillies.

At Crosley Field in Cincinnati, 16,285 watched as the Reds gained a
full game on Philadelphia after they took a doubleheader from Milwaukee, 5–2 and 4–2.

Bob Purkey (5–6) was winning pitcher in the opener for the Reds with
relief help from Sammy Ellis in the ninth inning. Tony Cloninger (10–10)
took the loss. Deron Johnson (15) hit his third home run in the last two
games in the first inning with two on.

The first game included three rain delays: one for 43 minutes that
delayed the start of the game, another for 27 minutes in 3rd and finally a
43-minute delay in the 7th.

In the second game Jim O'Toole (12–4) pitched a complete game for
the victory, outdueling Braves starter Bob Sadowski (5–7). Frank Robinson
(18) hit a solo shot homer into the left-field screen in the fourth to give the
Reds a 2–0 lead. The Braves came back to tie the score in the 6th, but in the
bottom half of the inning the Reds scored two runs to regain the lead.

Reds manager Fred Hutchinson had been released from Cincinnati's
Christ Hospital on Monday and was in uniform in the first game to manage the Reds for the first seven innings. Then he dressed in his street clothes
and watched the second game from Reds president Bill DeWitt's private
box alongside the press the box up on the roof of Crosley Field.

In another twin bill at Forbes Field in Pittsburgh, the Pirates went
belly-up, losing both ends to the Dodgers, 5–1 and 10–7.

In the first game Sandy Koufax became the first pitcher in the 1964
season to win 16 games as he allowed the Pirates just six hits, struck out
six and walked five before giving way to Bob Miller in the ninth with the
bases loaded. Miller then got Bob Bailey to line into a game-ending double play.

In the doubleheader sweep Willie Davis had three stolen bases and scored each time for the Dodgers. Also, Derrell Griffith hit a three-run homer in the nightcap and Tommy Davis hit safely in both games, running his consecutive-game hitting streak to 16.

At St. Louis the Cubs blanked the Cardinals, 4–0. Lou Burdette pitched his first shutout in more than a year to get his eighth win of the season, and Billy Williams hit his 25th home run of the season.

It was Family Night at Busch Stadium. Members of the Cardinals and their families were introduced prior to the game by the Cards' radio announcer Harry Caray. For the event the Cardinals reduced ticket prices. The head of the family was admitted to the park for $2.25, the full price of a reserved seat ticket, and each dependent paid only $1.25. On general admission the ticket price reductions were similar: the family head paid the $1.50 full price for the ticket and each dependent paid just 50 cents.

National League Standings, August 5, 1964

Team	Won	Lost	Pct.	G.B.
Philadelphia	60	42	.588	—
San Francisco	61	46	.570	1½
Cincinnati	59	48	.551	3½
Pittsburgh	55	48	.534	5½
Milwaukee	54	51	.514	7½
St. Louis	54	51	.514	7½
Los Angeles	53	51	.510	8
Chicago	50	53	.485	10½
Houston	46	62	.426	17
New York	34	74	.315	29

Here it was early August, the San Francisco Giants were battling hard for the pennant only 1½ games behind the Philadelphia Phillies, and suddenly their manager Alvin Dark found himself in very hot water involving a storm of controversy that had erupted over public remarks that he made against minority ballplayers on the Giants team in a *Newsday* article written by sports columnist Stan Isaacs.

In the article Dark had been quoted by Isaacs as saying, "We have trouble because we have so many Negro and Spanish-speaking players on the team. They're just not able to perform up to the white players when it comes to mental alertness. You couldn't name three colored players in our league who are always alert to take advantage of situations."[8]

Following the Giants' 14-inning game with the Mets on August 4, Dark held a news conference at Shea Stadium in an attempt to sort out his remarks. "No racial problem was involved," Dark said of his talk with

Stan Isaacs. "I think there is a misunderstanding and the reporter made the wrong interpretation."[9]

Dark was now saying that he criticized the team in general to Isaacs and hadn't picked out individuals. "I never try to run a club except on the basis of ability," Dark said. "Race, color, religion, make no difference. I'm interested only in performance."[10]

Dark remarked that Stan Isaacs had visited with him in Philadelphia when the Giants played there the week before and had apologized for the way his column appeared, saying it did not come out as he had intended.

Isaacs, who had arrived late at Shea Stadium for Dark's news conference, said he had apologized for the trouble he had caused Dark personally, but still insisted that the quotes he used in his article were accurate.

Regardless of whatever Dark intended to say or did say, the end result was that his ramblings put an even greater strain on his already-strained relationship with Giants owner Horace Stoneham. Following the Giants' August 4 game in New York, the Associated Press was told by an unnamed club official that Alvin Dark would not be back as manager of the San Francisco Giants next year.

The source went on to say that Dark's firing might even be announced before the end of August. However, the source also said that Dark's dismissal would not be due to public statements attributed to him construed as being prejudicial remarks about Negroes and Latin Americans. The AP source concluded his remarks by stating that strained relations existing between Dark and Giants owner Horace Stoneham had worsened in recent weeks to a point where Stoneham reportedly had decided a change in his manager was necessary.

Dark's relationship with Stoneham had indeed been strained and he was confiding to a friend that he had enough with San Francisco, no matter where the Giants finished in the 1964 season. Furthermore, the reasons for Dark's wanting out of San Francisco were more about Horace Stoneham than about the flak he was taking from his recent racial interview.

For one thing, Dark refused to socialize with Horace Stoneham. Stoneham, by the way, had been referred to in the press as a "little Howard Hughes-ish" in his habits.[11]

Then Stoneham allegedly did not like the way Dark was platooning some of his positions. Furthermore, Stoneham objected to Dark's leaving pitcher Billy O'Dell in a game for seven innings to take a 12-run pounding the same day he returned from Hawaii.

Alvin Dark was also having problems with his married home life and there were rumors of the pious Southern Baptist having an extramarital affair with an airline stewardess, which didn't sit well with Stoneham.

Lastly, it was reported that Dark had talked to Houston officials about the manager's job there without first clearing it with the Giants' front office.

Today one can't consider the Alvin Dark affair of 1964 without conjuring up memories of the unfortunate interview with former Los Angeles Dodgers general manager Al Campanis on ABC's *Nightline* in 1987.

When *Nightline* host Ted Koppel asked Campanis about the scarcity of Black managers in the Major Leagues, he remarked, "Blacks may not have some of the necessities to be, let's say, a field manager or general manager."

Horace Stoneham. (© San Francisco Giants Archives.)

What followed was a virtual storm of protest directed at both ABC and the Dodgers. Consequently Al Campanis was promptly fired by the Dodgers.

In today's highly charged, politically correct environment, Alvin Dark of course would have been toast following the press release of his remarks.

It was precisely this "zero tolerance" for racial remarks environment in existence today that caused Marge Schott to lose ownership of the Cincinnati Reds following derogatory racial remarks she had made in private about Reds players Eric Davis and Dave Parker in 1992.

Furthermore, the politically correct environment of today, taken to its extreme, is epitomized by Baseball Commissioner Bud Selig's arbitrarily arriving at the conclusion that he had the authority to fine Atlanta Braves reliever John Rocker $50,000 following a diatribe he launched against various racial and ethnic groups in the New York City area in an interview published by *Sports Illustrated* early in 2000. Later, Rocker's fine was reduced to $500 and the incident opened up a serious debate on the freedom of speech issue and athletes.

But in 1964, even though Dark's insensitive racial remarks enraged minority players on the team, the Giants' management essentially looked the other way, and Willie Mays talked the dissenters out of demanding that his head be taken by the Giants' front office. At least at that point in time, Dark had survived the controversy.

Alvin Dark. (© San Francisco Giants Archives)

Alvin Dark, who was nick-named "Blackie" because of his jet-black hair, had been a football star in the early 1940s at Louisiana State University (LSU). He had in fact been drafted by the Philadelphia Eagles, but instead signed a con-tract with the Boston Braves for a $50,000 bonus.

He had a cup of coffee with the Braves in 1946, playing in just 15 games. Then in 1948 he returned and had a stellar season, hitting .322 while playing in 137 games, helping the Braves to their first pennant in 34 years and being named Rookie of the Year. How-ever, Dark only hit .167 in the 1948 World Series as the Cleveland Indi-ans defeated Boston, 4 games to 2.

Following the 1949 season, Dark and Eddie "the Brat" Stanky were traded by the Braves to the New York Giants in exchange for Sid Gordon, Buddy Kerr, Willard Marshall and Red Webb.

Subsequently Dark, playing in the third game of the 1951 National League playoffs for the Giants, started the rally in the ninth inning that eventually led to Bobby Thompson's famous pennant-winning home run off Brooklyn's Ralph Branca.

In the 1951 World Series, Dark hit .417 against the Yankees, and three years later in the 1954 World Series against the Cleveland Indians, Dark got his revenge for the 1948 loss as he hit .412 against the Tribe.

Author Roger Kahn stated in his book, *The Boys of Summer*, that dur-ing the early 1950s young boys would have arguments on the streets of New York as to which local team had the best shortstop, Alvin Dark of the Giants, Phil Rizzuto of the Yankees or Pee Wee Reese of the Dodgers.

In June 1956, the Giants packaged Dark into a blockbuster nine-player trade with the St. Louis Cardinals. The Giants sent Dark, Ray Katt, Don Liddle and Whitey Lockman to the Cardinals in exchange for Jackie Brandt, Red Schoendienst, Bobby Stephenson, Dick Littlefield and Bill Sarni.

However, the deal proved to have a zero net effect on the finish of both clubs as the Giants finished the 1956 pennant race in 6th place, 26 games behind the Dodgers, and the Cardinals finished in 4th place, 17 games behind.

Alvin Dark would make a few more stops in Chicago, Philadelphia and Milwaukee before winding up his playing career in 1960. In all he played for 14 years in the National League and finished with a career batting average of .289 with 2,089 hits.

Dark was, however, to be involved in one more trade. On October 31, 1960, the San Francisco Giants sent Andre Rodgers to Milwaukee to acquire the rights to Dark. However, the Giants didn't want Dark as a player, but rather as a manager.

Author Bruce Chadwick does not enter into an analysis of Dark's troubles resulting from his racial interview in 1964, but rather elects to make remarks about the promise for the Giants that followed Dark's being appointed manager.

"Alvin Dark, a no-nonsense player who became a no-nonsense manager, was named the new skipper, and players and fans realized right away that this was a new ball club. Dark did not hobnob with writers the way [Bill] Rigney had, or [Leo] Durocher before him. He wanted his own operation, too, and in spring training he released Lefty O'Doul, the San Francisco hero and spring training volunteer batting coach whom fans venerated. Dark stuck up for his players and entered dozens of fierce disputes with umpires in order to back up their plays. Within weeks the new manager had built a new spirit on the team."[12]

Under Dark's first year of leadership the Giants finished 3rd in 1961, then they won the pennant in 1962 and eventually lost the World Series to the New York Yankees in a hard-fought, seven-game series.

Alvin Dark would ultimately manage in the Major Leagues for 13 years. After being terminated by the San Francisco Giants at the end of the 1964 season, Dark would resurface as manager of the Kansas City Athletics in 1966, spending two stormy years at the KC helm under the oversight and second-guessing of owner Charles O. Finley.

After being fired by Finley after the 1967 season, Dark was signed to manager the Cleveland Indians, where he toiled until 1971. Then in 1974 he was reunited with Charlie Finley as manager of the twice-transplanted Philadelphia, Kansas City, now Oakland "As."

In his first year at the Oakland helm, Dark not only won the American League Pennant but also the World Series, defeating the Los Angeles Dodgers, 4 games to 1.

In 1975, Dark's Oakland "As" again finished first in the American League Western Division, but lost in the league playoffs series to the Boston

Red Sox, and then he was fired by Finley for a second time. Returning to manage in the 1977 season after taking over from John McNamara after 48 games, he piloted the San Diego Padres to a 5th-place finish in the National League Western Division and then never managed in the Major Leagues again.

While Alvin Dark's career statistics in all batting and fielding categories are higher or nearly equal to those of his contemporaries, Pee Wee Reese and Phil Rizzuto, unlike them he is not in the National Baseball Hall of Fame.

Both Reese (1984) and Rizzuto (1994) were elected to the Hall via the New Veterans Committee, and to most observers their selections are ones that represent more of a ballot-box-stuffing, sentimental notion by the Veterans Committee for the Golden Days of New York baseball in the 1950s, rather than an attempt to categorize them as great players.

The next evening on Wednesday, August 5, the embattled Giants took the field against the Mets in New York with another packed house of 45,642 on hand at Shea Stadium and were victorious, 4–1. Ron Herbel (8–6) went the distance for San Francisco and Jack Fisher (7–14) took the loss for New York.

Two of the black players on the Giants led the way to victory, as Willie Mays (30 & 31) hit two home runs and Willie McCovey (15) added a solo shot. Willie Mays had showed up at Shea Stadium prior to the game with a heavy cold. When Alvin Dark had made up the lineup card, Mays was not on it.

Nonetheless, five minutes before game time Mays decided to play. "I shouldn't be playing," said Mays. "I'm doing it only to help the manager."

"These guys are trying to get Dark fired," Mays said. "I've got to help the man. All this should not have happened. What are they trying to do?"[13]

Prior to the game, Dark had met with the Giants' players and attempted to assure them he had never held any prejudice against non-white members of his team.

However, the Giants' victory did not help them in their pursuit of the Phillies. In fact, the Giants lost one-half game in the standings as Philadelphia swept its twi-night doubleheader with the Colts, 4–1 and 2–1. The Phillies now had a full two-game lead over the Giants and a five-game lead over the Reds.

Milwaukee came from behind to score five runs in the 8th inning and beat Cincinnati 6–3. John Tsitouris (7–4) had been locked in a pitching duel with Denny Lemaster (11–7) until the Braves' five-run outburst in the 8th. The Braves sent nine batters to the plate in their 8th-inning rally, which began when former Red Ed Bailey pinch hit for Lemaster and hit a single. Eddie Mathews then followed with his 15th home run of the year, driving the ball into the right-field bleachers. After getting Lee Maye on a fly ball to left, Tsitouris gave up singles to Hank Aaron and Rico Carty. Joe Torre also singled, then Vada Pinson threw the ball high and wide past third base as two runs scored. Ryne Duren then replaced Tsitouris and gave up a single to Felipe Alou that scored another run.

For the Reds, Don Pavletich (4) and Leo Cardenas (8) hit solo home runs.

In other National League games played on August 5, St. Louis defeated Chicago, 4–2, and Pittsburgh downed Los Angeles, 4–3.

Also, on August 5 it was reported that Baseball Commissioner Ford Frick had decided to retire. Frick had been commissioner since September 20, 1951, when he succeeded A.B. "Happy" Chandler. Although Frick's contract was not due to expire until September 21, 1965, he stated that he was ready to step aside just as soon as the baseball club owners could elect his successor.

Frick remarked, "I'll stay on as long as they want me to—that is, until the end of my term. If they want me to stay around and work with the new commissioner for awhile, I'll be happy to do that, too." Ford Frick would wind up serving the entire length of his term as commissioner and eventually be succeeded by General William Eckert on November 17, 1965.

Shea Stadium was indeed an interesting place to be on the evening of August 5. While visiting club manager Alvin Dark was having his own difficulties in the Giants' dugout, over in the Mets' dugout Casey Stengel was fuming over reports coming in from the Associated Press that he was going to be dumped as manager by the Mets following the 1964 season.

Prior to the Wednesday night game with the San Francisco Giants, the Mets issued an official statement through club President George Weiss that said:

"Casey has always insisted on being free to decide on the following year at the end of the season and the same procedure will be followed this year."

Speaking in the Mets' dugout prior to the game, Stengel was livid in his comments about the AP story. "The AP is not running my life and Reichler [AP writer Joe Reichler] is not running my club."[14]

On the morning of Thursday, August 6, 1964, it was reported by the Associated Press in New York that the Mets' owner, Mrs. Charles S.M. Payson, and Donald M. Grant, chairman of the board of directors, were going to give Mets manager Casey Stengel his walking papers at the end of the 1964 season.

It was not clear to the press on the morning of August 6 whether or not Mrs. Payson and Mr. Grant had given notice to Mr. Stengel. However, one thing was clear to all observers, that Casey Stengel had served his purpose well as the inaugural manager of the New York Mets franchise in publicity-bringing, promotional and image-building services.

"They feel [Payson and Grant] the club after three years of existence, all in the National League basement, has reached a stage in its young life where it must be developed on the field, as well as at the box office. And they agree, too, that a younger man is needed for the job—a man closer to the age of the Mets players," AP reported.

There had been recent rumors that Alvin Dark could be Stengel's successor, but those rumors were now being touted as premature.

"Several names have been suggested to and by us," an unidentified source told the Associated Press. "But no one has been given serious, or even semi-serious consideration. The only thing I can tell you with some degree of definiteness is that Casey will not be back with us in 1965.

"He has served his purpose. He has done everything we wanted of him—and more. He has done a wonderful job in every way you can imagine.

"I cannot tell you adequately enough how grateful we all are to him. I assure you it will be eternal. We would have liked to have kept him longer. But there comes a time for every man—even for Casey.

"We believe he should no longer be forced to endure the hardships of the daily grind of being in the dugout and on the field."[15]

But Casey Stengel did return to the helm of the Mets for the 1965 season. However, he lasted only 95 games before being replaced by coach Wes Westrum. The New York Mets also continued their losing ways in 1965 and also the management habit of bringing established players at the end of their careers to play for the club.

In 1965 Warren Spahn joined the Mets. Casey Stengel had been Spahn's first big league manager with the Boston Braves in 1942. Upon joining the Mets, Spahn remarked, "I'm probably the only guy who has worked for Stengel before and after he was a genius."[16]

On August 6, Houston's Dick Farrell finally won his 11th game. Farrell had been the majors' first 10-game winner in the 1964 season back on June 14. Since then he had made 12 attempts at gaining his 10th win of the season.

However, Farrell's victory, despite needing a little relief help to accomplish it, was a big one, as the Colts beat the league-leading Philadelphia Phillies, 2–1.

Farrell had pitched a shutout through eight innings, allowing the

Phillies just three hits. However, Hal Woodeschick came on in relief of Farrell in the ninth after Wes Covington doubled. Woodeschick proceeded to yield a run-scoring single to Gus Triandos, then was replaced on the hill by Jim Owens who preserved the long-sought-after victory for Farrell.

The Colts had scored both their runs in the fourth inning as Al Spangler tripled and was knocked in by Nellie Fox's double. Then Fox scored after a single by Walt Bond and a sacrifice fly by Bob Aspromonte.

The Phillies' loss cut their lead to 1½ games over second-place San Francisco, who were not scheduled and were heading to Cincinnati to begin a weekend series.

Meanwhile at Cincinnati the Reds played a doubleheader with 7,228 fans on hand. In the first game the Reds' fathers played their sons in the annual "Fathers & Sons" exhibition game. National League umpire Paul Pryor officiated and as usual the sons beat the dads.

Then in the main attraction the Reds walloped the Braves, 9–3. In the game Deron Johnson and Frank Robinson duplicated their efforts at the plate, as each hammered out a triple, double and single, while Vada Pinson (15) hit a home run. In all the Reds blasted five Milwaukee pitchers for 15 hits. Hank Aaron homered (18) for the Braves.

The victory allowed the Reds to pick up a full game in the standings, now being four games behind first-place Philadelphia and just 2½ games behind the Giants, who were on route to Crosley Field for a head-to-head battle.

Prior to the game Milwaukee manager Bobby Bragan was praising the skills of his All-Star catcher-first baseman, Joe Torre. "Joe Torre is the hottest property in baseball today," said Bragan. "I'm not kidding. I wouldn't trade Torre for Willie Mays or anybody else you can name. If I did trade him for Mays, I'd be giving away 10 years."[17]

Meanwhile the controversy surrounding San Francisco Giants manager Alvin Dark continued to swirl. However, Giants owner Horace Stoneham denied published reports that he planned to fire Dark.

Stoneham said that he felt Alvin Dark's reply to the New York newspaper story, quoting the manager as downgrading the ability and intelligence of Negro and Latin American players, had been very generally accepted. Stoneham called the story "exaggerated and distorted."

"Alvin was misquoted in some cases, and in some cases the writer elaborated on what he [Dark] did say," Stoneham stated.[18]

"Personally, I find his reply completely satisfactory and want to take this occasion to deny all reports that a managerial change is contemplated. It is evident that all our players support Dark strongly. Their responses pleases me greatly, and I believe that in that spirit they can go on to win the pennant."[19]

Stoneham, asked why he waited two days to deny reports that Dark would be fired, said in a telephone conference call to baseball writers traveling with the Giants en route to Cincinnati: "I wanted to wait until you got away from New York and that atmosphere."[20]

In other National League games played on August 6, at Pittsburgh Bill Mazeroski drove in three runs for the Pirates with a double and a single as the Bucs beat the Dodgers 4–1. Bob Friend scattered nine hits to get the win. However, L.A.'s Tommy Davis got three of them, all singles, to extend his consecutive game hitting streak to 18 games.

At Busch Stadium, Bob Gibson evened his season record at 9–9 with his first victory since July 19 as St. Louis beat Chicago, 5–3. Bill White and Dick Groat each drove in two runs in support of Gibson. The victory left the Cardinals seven games behind the first-place Phillies with 55 games left to play on the 1964 season schedule.

On Friday, August 7, the Phillies were scheduled to begin a weekend series at home with the Mets at Connie Mack Stadium. Prior to the series' start, the Phillies made a strategic player acquisition with the Mets to strengthen their club against left-handed pitching.

The Phillies obtained veteran right-handed power hitter Frank Thomas from the Mets in exchange for minor league outfielder-infielder Wayne Graham. Also, at the time of the trade the terms called for the Phillies to deliver two other players at later dates on August 12 and October 31. However, for the record, only one other player was later delivered by the Phillies, rookie pitcher Gary Kroll, and the other compensation was settled in cash.

Frank Thomas was an 11-year veteran in the National League who prior to the 1964 season had hit 272 home runs playing for Pittsburgh, Cincinnati, Chicago, Milwaukee and New York.

Thomas had come up with the Pittsburgh Pirates in 1951. In 1953 he hit 30 home runs for a hapless, cellar-dwelling Pirates team that finished 55 games behind the first-place Brooklyn Dodgers with a dismal season record of 50–154. In 1958 he hit 35 home runs, second-best in the National League, for a vastly improved and experienced Pirates team that finished second with a record of 84–70, eight games behind the Milwaukee Braves.

Then on January 30, 1959, Frank Thomas was involved in one of the worst trades in Major League Baseball history. Thomas, along with Whammy Douglas, Jim Pendelton and Johnny Powers, were dealt by the Pirates to the Cincinnati Reds in exchange for Smoky Burgess, Harvey Haddix and Don Hoak.

The results were that the Reds had just provided the Pirates with the strategic plugs that they needed to fill voids in various positions and subsequently, after a 4th-place finish in 1959, the Pirates in 1960 won the National League Pennant and ultimately the World Series, with Burgess, Haddix and Hoak each playing key roles.

At Cincinnati, Frank Thomas was a disaster. For the Reds in 1959 he had one of the worst seasons in his career, hitting just .225 with 12 home runs, his lowest production since becoming an everyday player in 1953.

The Cincinnati fans felt duped in the trade and took out their frustration on Thomas verbally. Reds general manager Gabe Paul, feeling the heat, decided to implement a fire sale on Thomas and on December 6, 1959, shipped him to the Chicago Cubs in exchange for Bill Henry, Lou Jackson and Lee Walls.

The change of scenery at Wrigley Field didn't do much for Thomas and he suffered through another agonizing year in 1960, hitting .238 with 21 home runs. Then in 1961, after playing just 15 games with Chicago, Thomas once again packed his bags, this time for Milwaukee.

In 1962 Frank Thomas had the distinction of being one of the original New York Mets and once again playing on a dismal club that finished last with a record of 40–120, 60½ games behind the Giants. However, the agony of defeat for Thomas was made more tolerable by the friendly left-field fence of the Polo Grounds, and he socked 34 home runs for the Mets.

Now in August 1964, Frank Thomas was coming to Philadelphia with a shot at finally playing on a pennant-winning club.

The Phillies were predominately a left-handed-hitting club with Johnny Callison, Wes Covington, Ton Gonzalez, Clay Dalrymple and John Herrnstein all swinging from the left side of the plate. Therefore, Phillies manager Gene Mauch expected that with the acquisition of Thomas the club would no longer be such an easy target for opposing teams' southpaws and that he would also provide some additional power.

As for the players that the Mets picked up in the Frank Thomas deal, Wayne Graham was at the time hitting .305 with the Phillies' Arkansas team in the Pacific Coast League, with 11 home runs and 56 RBIs. Graham would play in 20 games for the Mets in 1964, hitting .094 and would not return to play in the Major Leagues again.

To make room for Thomas on the Phillies' roster, the club placed rookie pitcher Gary Kroll (0–0) on waivers, who then became part of the Thomas deal as one of the players named later. In 1965 Kroll pitching for the Mets would go 6–6. Then he would appear in 10 games for Houston in 1966 and later in 19 games for Cleveland in 1969 without a decision, finishing his big league career with a record of 6–7 and an ERA of 4.24.

Frank Thomas actually arrived in Philadelphia on Friday, August 7, with the New York Mets and then signed a new contract and dressed for the game as a Phillies player.

Nonetheless, his press reviews were not exactly sterling upon his arrival in the City of Brotherly Love. A typical press report in regard to the arrival of Thomas in Philadelphia read, "Frank Thomas is a slow-footed, 35-year-old Met cast-off with a future as rosy as his new red pinstripes."

Regardless, in his first game as a member of the Philadelphia Phillies, Frank Thomas played a key role in a victory. Only hours after the Phillies acquired him, Thomas, playing first base, drove in two runs with a double and single, then started a double play from first base as Philadelphia beat New York, 9–4.

Al Jackson had started the game for the Mets but lasted only one-third of an inning as the Phillies pounded him for five hits and three runs. Ed Roebuck (4–2), pitching in relief of starter Art Mahaffey, got the win, and Bill Wakefield (3–4) took the loss in relief after he followed Carl Willey to the mound in the fourth.

Frank Thomas wasted no time in making the deal for him look good. His first two times up he hit safely, doubling home the second run off Al Jackson in the first and then driving in Richie Allen, who tripled in the third.

The Mets fought back in the fourth for a 4–4 tie on Roy McMillan's two-run single and a two-run home run by Joe Christopher (13). However, in the seventh the Phillies broke the game open with a four-run rally to wrap it up.

With the victory the Phillies once again increased their National League lead to 2½ games over the Giants, who lost to the Reds, 5–3, at Crosley Field in Cincinnati.

The San Francisco Giants were always a big draw for some reason at Crosley Field and Friday, August 8, was no exception as 19,965 fans attended the game.

Cincinnati pitchers Jim Maloney and Bill McCool stifled the Giants at the plate as they combined for 15 strikeouts. Maloney at one point had struck out six Giants in a row and had fanned 12 Giants in just six innings before being forced from the game due to his arm's tightening up. Billy McCool came on to finish up and proceeded to whiff three more Giants, but also gave up two runs including a home run to Jim Hart (18). The home run that McCool gave up to Hart was the first gopher ball he had tossed in his brief Major League career.

Frank Robinson (19) led the Reds' attack with a home run, a run-scoring double and single. Orlando Cepeda had singled, doubled and homered for the Giants. Jim Maloney (11–9) got the win and Bob Hendley (9–7) took the loss.

While the victory was 6th for the Reds in their last eight games, it was only their 4th victory against the Giants in 13 games so far in the season.

In other games played on August 7, St. Louis defeated Houston, 4–0, and Chicago swept a doubleheader from Pittsburgh, 7–4 and 4–3.

On Saturday, August 8, at Milwaukee, Sandy Koufax won his 17th game of the season as the Dodgers beat the Braves, 5–4. En route to his victory Koufax reached 200 strikeouts for the season and set a National League record for that point in time of striking out 200 or more batters for the fourth straight season. It was also the 12th victory for Koufax in the last 13 games, having lost only one game since June 4.

Braves starter Tony Cloninger was the losing pitcher. He had taken a 2–1 lead into the fifth when the Dodgers jumped on him for four hits including a bases-loaded triple by Ron Fairly, that sent him to the showers.

Koufax had begun the rally with a single, then Maury Wills also singled, moving Koufax over to second base. As Koufax took a lead off second Cloninger wheeled and attempted to pick him off second. Koufax dived back into second and landed on his left elbow. It all seemed so inconsequential at the time, but Koufax had injured his elbow and ultimately it would prove to be a season-ending injury in just a few more days' time.

Willie Davis then walked and Ron Fairly followed with his second triple of the game, clearing the bases and giving the Dodgers a 4–2 lead. Tommy Davis then added another run with a single to extend his hitting streak to 20 games.

Davis' 20-game hitting streak had previously been accomplished twice before in the 1964 season by Willie Mays of San Francisco in the National League and Ed Bressoud of Boston in the American League. In the eighth the Braves trimmed the Dodgers' lead to 5–4 when Dennis Menke (8) homered.

A crowd on 17,647 was on hand for the game at County Stadium, thereby raising the Braves' home attendance for the 1964 season to 676,989, a gain of 206,663 over the 1963 season.

The next morning on Sunday, August 9, Sandy Koufax awoke in his room at the Schroeder Hotel in Milwaukee with a stiff and inflamed elbow. Nonetheless, during the ensuing week he would pitch again and win his 18th game of the season.

That afternoon, playing before a sparse home crowd of 7,687, the

National League-leading Philadelphia Phillies pounded the New York Mets' pitching for 14 hits en route to a 12–5 victory. However, the Phillies' Frank Thomas went 0–4. The Phillies' victory gave them an 11–2 edge in the 1964 season series against the Mets at that point.

That evening at Cincinnati, 30,669 fans turned out to see the Reds battle the Giants. The bulging crowd in the tight confinements of Crosley Field was the largest to attend a game since August 17, 1962.

However, the overflow crowd did not see the hometown Reds prevail as the Giants won the game, 1–0. The only run of the game occurred in the Giants' half of the sixth when Reds starter Joe Nuxhall (8–7) gave up a single to Willie McCovey followed by a triple to Willie Mays to drive home McCovey. Gaylord Perry went all the way for the Giants, allowing the Reds only two hits.

The following day on Sunday, August 9, another overflow crowd of 26,733 packed into Crosley Field for the finale of the three-game series with the Giants bringing the unusually large gate for the three games to a total of 77,367.

The Giants' domination over the Reds continued as they won the game, 7–5, to give them an 11–4 edge in the season series. In the game Willie Mays (32) and Willie McCovey (16) homered for the Giants and Frank Robinson (20) hit a round-tripper for the Reds. Billy O'Dell (4–5) despite a sore arm got the win in relief of starter Bob Bolin. John Tsitouris (7–9), the Reds' starter, took the loss.

On August 13 cancer-stricken Cincinnati manager Fred Hutchinson took a leave of absence and turned the Reds over to interim manager Dick Sisler. Hutchinson had remarked to *Cincinnati Post* sportswriter Earl Lawson, "Damnit, Earl, I'm so skinny it hurts just sitting down."[21]

On Friday, August 14, at Houston the Colts toppled the Reds, 3–2, as Walt Bond (17) hit a solo home run in the 7th inning off Bob Purkey (6–7), pitching in relief, to break a 2–2 tie. Jim Owens (5–7) got the win.

Out on the West Coast the San Francisco Giants used their power to defeat the Milwaukee Braves, 3–0. All the Giants' runs came on home runs by Willie McCovey (17), Orlando Cepeda (21) and Willie Mays (35). Bob Bolin (4–4) got the win and Denny Lemaster (12–8) took the loss.

Also on August 14, the Philadelphia Phillies swept a doubleheader with the New York Mets, 6–1 and 6–4, behind the pitching of veteran Jim Bunning and 19-year-old rookie Rick Wise. Recently acquired Frank Thomas led the attack for Philadelphia, driving in five runs in the doubleheader, including a two-run homer in the nightcap.

On Saturday, August 15, the Phillies again defeated the Mets, 8–1, for their third victory over the New Yorkers in 24 hours.

At San Francisco a pinch-hit single by Duke Snider in the 8th knocked in the winning run as the Giants defeated the Braves, 8–7. Snider's hit followed a triple by Jim Hart. The Giants had been leading, 6–2, in the fourth when the Braves scored five runs led by a pair of two-run home runs by Eddie Mathews (17) and Hank Aaron (21).

Orlando Cepeda had a big day for the Giants. In a five-run Giants uprising in the 2nd, Cepeda had a three-run double, and in the fifth Cepeda (22) homered. Billy O'Dell (5–5) got victory in relief. For Milwaukee Bob Sadowski took the loss in relief.

For the second night in a row the 9th-place Houston Colts defeated the Cincinnati Reds, this time by a score of 7–4. The Colts, who before coming to Cincy had lost 13 times in the last 16 games, roughed up five Reds pitchers (Nuxhall, Tsitouris, Duren, McCool, Ellis) for 13 hits in the game. Al Spangler was 3-for-4 and Bob Aspromonte was 4-for-5.

For the Reds, Vada Pinson (16 & 17) had two home runs. Don Nottebart (6–8) got the win for the Colts and John Tsitouris (7–10) took the loss in relief.

Rounding out the action on Saturday, August 15, the L.A. Dodgers beat the St. Louis Cardinals, 4–3. The Dodgers scored what proved to be the winning run in the 7th when Bob Gibson attempted to pick off Dick Tracewski at first and Nate Oliver scored from third when Tracewski ended up in a rundown. For the Cardinals' Bob Gibson (10–10), it was his tenth loss of the season. For the Dodgers, Joe Moeller got his 7th victory of the season.

At Chicago in the 9th inning Bob Bailey scored from third on an infield hit by Don Clendenon to give the Pirates a 5–4 win over the Cubs.

As the 1964 National League pennant race arrived at mid-August, the Philadelphia Phillies were beginning to show signs of pulling away from the pack.

However, some observers were beginning to advance the theory that the success that the Phillies were experiencing was based on an ageless two-prong strategy: win as many games as possible with the hapless clubs in the league and break even with the serious contenders. This midsummer's theory of Phillies success was starting to look like it had some credibility as against 9th-place Houston and 10th-place New York, Philadelphia had won 24 and lost 16, while against 2nd-place San Francisco, 3rd-place Cincinnati and 4th-place Pittsburgh, they had a record of 18–17.

On August 16 the Phillies, now four games ahead of the second-place San Francisco Giants, were scheduled to play an afternoon game with the Mets in New York. The day before it had been announced that the Phillies had obtained veteran left-hander Bobby Shantz from the Chicago Cubs for cash.

Phillies general manager John Quinn reasoned that by acquiring Shantz, who would be 39 years old on September 26, the team had added depth to its bullpen staff to help out in the final weeks' drive for the pennant. For Shantz, it was the second time within two months that he had involuntarily changed team jerseys, having been traded by the Cardinals to the Cubs along with Ernie Broglio in the Lou Brock deal back on June 15.

As the Phillies began to move towards the stretch drive, their one-two run-scoring punch of Richie Allen and Johnny Callison was leading the charge. As a matter of fact, Allen was even being speculated on heavily to be named National League Rookie of the Year. His name was also being circulated in MVP talks. If Allen took both awards, he would be the first Major Leaguer ever to do so.

Just the same, Johnny Callison was also being mentioned as an MVP candidate. As of August 15, Allen and Callison were tied for the club lead in home runs with 20 each. Callison led in RBIs with 70 to Allen's 61.

On the other hand, Richie Allen had been making errors at third base. But Allen was quick to point out that he was making errors at third base because that was in reality a change of position for him. In the minors he had played shortstop and in the outfield.

When asked what he thought of the fans' getting on him for booting balls at third, he replied, "Fans have a right to boo or say anything they want to after they pay their way into the ball park. No one intentionally lets a ball go through their legs, though."[22]

In Houston, with the Colts 22 games out of first place, they were talking about special grass instead. Special grass had been designed to thrive on the playing field of Houston's new $30-million domed stadium that was scheduled to open the following season.

The special grass, known as Turfway 419, was being grown south of Wharton where a nursery area had been set aside. It had been developed in Georgia for stadiums, golf courses and lawns. Turfway 419 was selected after testing by Texas A & M University showed it was the variety that grew best in the shape which was foremost in consideration for Houston's new domed stadium. Hermon Lloyd, one of the stadium architects, said, "The grass will be rolled up in Wharton like a carpet and then rolled down over the field."[23]

In 1965, Turfway 419 made its debut in the new air-conditioned Harris County Domed Stadium in Houston and was a complete bust, as it died. To find a solution, the Houston management came up with a bright green plastic substitute they dubbed "AstroTurf," that was held together with zippers.

A lot of players were skeptical of "AstroTruf." When left-hander Tug McGraw was asked if he liked artificial grass, he replied that he didn't know; he'd never smoked it. "If the horses won't eat it," the Phillies' Richie Allen said, "I won't play on it."[24]

Although AstroTurf was not immediately accepted by the players, by the 1970s it or similar artificial turf would be the playing surface in ten Major League parks.

Also the Houston club was now selling private clubrooms in the new stadium. For $18,000 a year a fan could get one of 40 private clubrooms being built in the stadium, each of which seated 30. Each clubroom was going to be elegantly furnished with closed-circuit television, lounge and bar. Admission to the private clubrooms came with a key.

Another unique feature being constructed into Houston's new domed stadium was dugouts that would be 120 feet in length, twice the size of those in existing parks of the time. Bullpen crews would occupy the far end. As many fans now and then desired seats behind the dugout, the Houston club's management reasoned that they would be able to accommodate twice amount of fans with the extended-length dugouts.

As it turned out this new behind-the-dugout seating arrangement was not exactly like what one would expect with such a coveted seat at Wrigley Field, as a lot of fans in this new arrangement would actually be seated in the outfield areas.

National League Standings, August 16, 1964

Team	Won	Lost	Pct.	G.B.
Philadelphia	70	44	.614	—
San Francisco	67	49	.578	4
Pittsburgh	62	52	.544	8
Cincinnati	63	54	.538	8½
St. Louis	61	54	.530	9½
Milwaukee	58	56	.509	12
Los Angeles	57	57	.500	13
Chicago	54	61	.470	16½
Houston	50	68	.424	22
New York	35	82	.299	36½

On Sunday, August 16, the Phillies didn't exactly look like league leaders, as they were pounded by the Mets, 12–4. Recently acquired second baseman Bobby Klaus led the 17-hit New York attack by stroking four singles, scoring three runs and driving in one. In fact, everyone in the Mets' lineup hit safely with the exception of pitcher Galen Cisco. Also, the Phillies helped the Mets' cause by committing five errors.

Klaus led off in the first inning with a single off Phillies starter Art Mahaffey (10–6). Singles followed by Ed Kranepool and Joe Christopher to score the Mets' first run before a wild throw by Phillies first baseman Frank Thomas let in the second.

The Mets nearly scored a third run in the first when with the bases loaded, Chris Cannizzaro grounded to Richie Allen at third, who then threw home to catcher Clay Dalrymple to force Joe Christopher.

Mahaffey lasted just one-third of an inning, yielding three hits and two runs. He was then followed on the mound by Ed Roebuck, Bobby Shantz and Ray Culp, who gave up a total of 14 hits and 10 runs in relief. For New York, Galen Cisco (5–13) went all the way, pitching a nine-hitter. However, two of those hits were home runs by the Phillies' Richie Allen (20) and John Herrnstein (6).

Despite the loss to the Mets, the Phillies actually gained one-half game in the standings as the Giants dropped both games of a doubleheader to Milwaukee, 5–4 and 10–2, at Candlestick Park with 40,713 fans on hand.

The Braves won the opening game on a three-run homer in the seventh by Eddie Mathews (18), despite four home runs' being hit by the Giants. The Giants scored all four of their runs in the first game on solo home runs, two by Willie Mays (36 & 37), and one each by Willie McCovey (18) and Orlando Cepeda (23). Frank Larry (3–3), who had been acquired by the Braves from the Mets on August 8 for Dennis Ribant and cash, was the winning pitcher and Gaylord Perry (8–9) took the loss.

In the nightcap, the Braves put the game away in the third with a four-run rally capped by Gene Oliver's (9) three-run homer. Braves starter Tony Cloninger (12–11) went the distance yielding seven hits.

At Cincinnati, the Reds finally defeated the Colts, 8–3, to salvage the last game in the three-game series and move within one percentage point of a tie with the Pirates for third place, 7½ games behind the Phillies, but only three games behind the second-place Giants.

For the Reds, Frank Robinson (22) hit a two-run home run and drove in three as Joey Jay (9–8) tossed a six-hitter. Working in the humid 90-degree temperatures of a Cincinnati mid-August, Jay struck out nine batters and had a shutout going for the first six innings. In fact, until Carrol Hardy tripled in the first Houston run in the seventh, Jay had only allowed two hits, and only one runner had reached third base. Then Bob Aspromonte (11) hit a home run off Jay in the ninth. Robinson hit his homer in the third, which sent Houston starter Ken Johnson (8–13) to the showers, and it proved to be the winning margin as the Reds took a 4–0 lead.

Following the Sunday game at home with the Colts, the Reds were bound for San Francisco to open a three-game series on Tuesday night. Acting manager Dick Sisler had some growing concern about the Reds' hitting of late and ordered extra batting practice for several of his players preceding the games on the West Coast.

With the boiling August afternoon temperatures in Cincinnati, Sisler had decided to delay the extra work in the batting cage until the club reached San Francisco. "We've got to score some runs," Sisler said. "We haven't been getting the clutch hit. Some of these guys have picked up some bad batting habits recently."[25]

One of the players targeted by Sisler for extra work in the batting cage was Pete Rose. Rose had gotten only two hits in his last 20 at bats. "There'll be some others," Sisler said.[26] However, he declined to identify just who the other players were targeted for extra batting practice until the Reds arrived in San Francisco.

However, on Saturday, August 15, Sisler had benched Pete Rose again so he could "think over the situation. I told him it was only temporary," said Sisler.[27]

The slump for Rose was not the first one that he had experienced in the 1964 season. Back in late June Pete had been stuck in the worst slump yet in his young career, with his batting average tumbling dangerously low, to below .200 even!

Rose told author Roger Kahn, "I couldn't understand what was happening. I was worried as hell. I was telling this to Walt Harmon, who I played ball with as a kid, and Walt didn't have a clue, either. But he had one good idea. He told me to talk to my Uncle Buddy. You know. The guy who got the Reds to sign me."[28]

According to Kahn, Buddy Bloebaum was sympathetic and professional. Rose was holding his hands too high. He was swinging defensively, as if afraid to strike out. "Lower your hands, Pete," Bloebaum said, "and attack the ball."[29]

Subsequently Rose got eight hits in the next two games. Now it was mid-August he was in need of additional batting practice, as the Reds headed to West Coast for a crucial series with the Giants.

At Los Angeles on Sunday, August 16, the Dodgers and Cardinals split a doubleheader before 38,072 fans at Dodger Stadium or, as L.A. writers sometimes referred to the pristine ball park in Chavez Ravine, the "Taj O'Malley."

In the first game Sandy Koufax (19–5) shut out the Cards, 3–0. Koufax allowed seven hits while striking out 13. It was his 19th victory of the season and his last. The next morning, Sandy Koufax was in excruciating pain.

According to author Gregg Scott, Koufax remarked that on the morning of August 17: "I had to drag my arm out of bed like a log. That's what it looked like…a waterlogged log. It was swollen all the way from the shoulder down to the wrist-inside, outside, everywhere. For an elbow, I had a knee. That's how thick it was."[30]

Adhesions in his pitching arm had broken loose, leading to traumatic arthritis. It was the beginning of a condition for Koufax that would lead to endless cortisone shots and would eventually end his career two years later.

Despite his early departure, Sandy Koufax had another great year in 1964, finishing with a record of 19–5 and a ERA of 1.74, with 223 strike outs in 223 innings pitched and seven shutouts. Also, he had pitched a no-hitter on June 4 against Philadelphia (the 3rd of his career).

Not knowing of the complications Koufax was suffering on the morning of August 17, *Los Angeles Times* staff writer Frank Finch wrote in his column that day: "Koufax notched his 19th victory, 3–0, with 13 strike-outs, and only global atomic warfare or perhaps housemaid's knee, can keep Koufax from entering the 25-game-winner circle again."

But unbeknown to Finch, Koufax was through and suddenly, without him for the rest of the season, the Dodgers' chances of repeating as World Champions in 1964 went from slim to none.

In the second game at L.A. the Cardinals turned the tables on the Dodgers, shutting them out, 4–0, behind the six-hit pitching of Curt Simmons (13–9).

Before striking out in the ninth inning of the second game, St. Louis center fielder Curt Flood had gotten eight consecutive hits in the doubleheader. If he had gotten a hit in the ninth, Flood would have become the first player in 70 years to get nine hits consecutively in a doubleheader.

The split of the doubleheader left the Cardinals nine games out of first place and the Dodgers 13½ games out.

Meanwhile, Dodger coach Leo Durocher was in potential hot water. Robert Hallsworth, 29, an engineer from Downey, had alleged that Leo Durocher had hit him in the jaw while in the parking lot at Dodger Stadium following Sunday's doubleheader with St. Louis. On Monday, August 17, Deputy City Attorney Robert O. Young ordered a full-scale hearing into a fracas involving Durocher to determine if a battery complaint should be issued for him.

Hallsworth said he was waiting in line with his stepdaughter to get Durocher to sign a Dodger phonograph record. Suddenly Durocher drove off, and someone said, "Durocher, you're a jerk!"[31]

"Durocher then backed up and demanded to know, who called him a jerk?"[32]

Hallsworth said that as a joke, he said, "Maybe I did."[33]

Then he said that Durocher got out of the car and hit him. Durocher, however, told newsmen that he acted in self defense, that Hallsworth raised his arm as if to hit him.

However, a spectator, George Quinones, 53, of Inglewood, told newsmen that Hallsworth did not raise his arm. "After Durocher hit Hallsworth," Quinones said, "another man walked over and bare-handed Durocher across the face."[34]

A security guard came up and Durocher drove away, Quinones said.

Winding up the action on Sunday, August 16, the Cubs and Pirates split a doubleheader at Wrigley Field in Chicago. The Cubs won the opener, 5–4, handing the Pirates' relief ace Al McBean (7–1), the fifth Bucs pitcher in the game, his first loss in ten games. With two out in the bottom of the ninth, Chicago pinch hitter Jimmy Stewart singled home the winning run. While McBean couldn't get through the ninth, previously he hadn't lost a game since July 27, 1963.

However, the Pirates rebounded in the nightcap to whip the Cubbies, 7–4, as Don Clendenon (7) and Bill Mazeroski (9) homered. Steve Blass (5–7) got the win for the Pirates, and Sterling Slaughter (2–4), pitching in his only Major League season, took the loss for the Cubs.

On Monday, August 17, St. Louis Cardinals general manager Bing Devine announced that he had resigned. Devine, 47 years old, had spent his entire 25-year career in baseball in the Cardinals organization, joining them right out of college in 1939. However, Gus Busch, the beer baron owner of the Cardinals, was getting antsy for a pennant. The Cards had last won a National League crown in 1946 and on August 16, the prospects of a Redbird pennant for 1964 didn't look very bright, as they were in fifth place, 9½ games behind the Phillies.

Devine said in a press release that he had met with Busch last Thursday and submitted his resignation. Devine also said that he would remain with the club "until or at least near the end of the season."[35] He made his decision, he said, because Cardinal president August A. Busch, Jr., had become frustrated over the team's inability to win a pennant.

Devine said, "I have no immediate plans for the future except to finish the season here and be of whatever assistance as might be desired by my successor. I'm open to ideas."[36]

Ironically, Devine had been named by the *Sporting News* as "Major League Baseball's Executive of the Year" for 1963, after the Cardinals had finished second the previous season.

Also departing with Devine would be Art Routzong, 52. Devine had brought up Routzong from the former Houston farm club to handle Cardinals business operations when he became General Manager in 1957. Bing Devine had succeeded Frank Lane when he left for the Cleveland GM job. Routzong's resignation would be effective immediately. His estimated salary was $17,500 a year. Devine's salary was $40,000 a year.

In the course of announcing his resignation Devine, also made a sincere attempt to absolve Cardinals manager Johnny Keane of any responsibility for the club's dismal record so far in the 1964 season.

"Naturally this move was made with a great deal of emotion and regret," Devine said. "But beyond the personal involvement, I would hope this might clear the air about Johnny Keane if indeed there is any need for it. I am certain it is generally known about my admiration for and loyalty to Keane as the manager.

"It is customary for any manager to be given the blame for the failure or disappointments of a club, but I have always felt and expressed my recognition of a necessity for sharing of this responsibility by the general manager. In one way my resignation is a specific demonstration of this view."[37]

Johnny Keane was contacted at his Houston home and had no comment. Subsequently, August A. Busch, Jr., had no immediate comment, either.

Likewise, there was no comment from Branch Rickey, who two years previously had been rehired by the Cardinals as a special consultant. However, it was well known in the Major League community in 1964 that Rickey was highly critical of Johnny Keane as a manager, as well as some of the Cardinals' front office executives, too.

On Monday, August 17, the Phillies increased their National League lead to five games as they defeated the Cubs, 8–1, while the second-place Giants were idle.

Chris Short (12–5) pitched a five-hitter in picking up his 12th win of the season, and Johnny Callison had a two-run triple in the five-run second that put the game out of reach. For Short, the victory enabled him reach a new milestone in his career, as it was the first time in his five years as a big league pitcher that he had won as many as 12 games, having achieved a season record of (11–9) in 1962.

Meanwhile at New York, the Mets whipped the Pirates, 5–0, as Dennis Ribant, acquired from the Braves in the deal for Frank Lary on August 8, pitched a four-hit shutout while Charley Smith hit two home runs. Smith, an infielder, was playing left field as Casey Stengel loaded his lineup with right-handed hitters against Pirates southpaw Bob Veale. The loss by the Pirates dropped them into fourth place behind the idle Reds.

In the only other game on August 17, the St. Louis Cardinals capitalized on two errors in the ninth to defeat the Houston Colts, 3–1.

On Tuesday, August 18, the Phillies would lose to the Cubs, 4–3, in a protracted 16-inning affair. The five-hour-and-23-minute game at Connie Mack Stadium in Philadelphia, that was interrupted once by rain, was the first game concluded after the 12:50 A.M. local time curfew that had recently been lifted by National League president Warren Giles.

The Cubs' Joe Amalfitano (4), who had homered earlier in the contest, would stroke a two-run double with two out in the top of the 16th inning, scoring Andre Rodgers and Dick Bertell to provide the Cubbies with what proved to be the winning runs.

However, the Phillies continued to hold their five-game lead as the Cincinnati Reds defeated the San Francisco Giants, 1–0, behind the four-hit pitching of left-hander Jim O'Toole (13–5). Bob Bolin took the loss (4–5). The deciding run in the game occurred when Chico Ruiz sped home from third on a disputed force play. Ruiz was playing second base as the Reds' acting manager continued to bench Pete Rose.

The victory moved the third-place Reds to within two games of the second-place Giants and seven games behind the Phillies.

When the reeling Pirates were again defeated by the Mets, 7–3, the Cardinals moved into fourth place as they defeated the Colts, 5–2. For St. Louis, Ray Sadecki won his 15th game of the season with some help from veteran reliever 38-year-old Barney Schultz in the eighth. Sadecki had helped his own cause by hitting a triple in the seventh and then scoring on a single by Lou Brock to break a 2–2 tie.

At Los Angeles, Don Drysdale (13–13) lost his fourth straight game as the Braves defeated the Dodgers, 3–1. Denny LeMaster (13–8) went the distance for the Braves pitching a four-hitter. The win left Milwaukee in 6th place, ten games behind league-leading Philadelphia.

With the Dodgers 13 games out of first place, general manager Buzzy Bavasi had become acutely aware of the Dodgers' anemic run production in the '64 season, and vowed that he would go all-out over the winter to obtain a .300 hitter who could knock in some runs.

In fact, at this point in the season not one player on the Dodgers was hitting over .300 against right-handers. Willie Davis led this department with a .297 average versus righties.

Dodgers manager Walter Alston was also feeling the frustration of going from World Champs to second division club. "It's been a frustrating year all round. A few of our players have had outstanding years, like John Roseboro and Willie Davis, but to win a pennant everybody has to have a good year."[38]

On Wednesday, August 19, the Phillies increased their lead to six games as they beat Chicago, 9–5, while the Reds downed the Giants again, 7–1.

In whipping the Cubs, the Phillies came from behind. Trailing 5–4 in the bottom of the eighth, the Phillies scored two runs on singles by Clay Dalrymple and Tony Taylor, followed by Wes Covington's double. Then three more runs crossed the plate before the inning ended.

For San Francisco, the loss on August 19 to the Reds was their fourth in a row. Suddenly the Giants found themselves not just falling further behind the first-place Phillies, but only one game ahead of third-place Cincinnati, and all at once fourth-place St. Louis trailed them by just three games.

Cincinnati acting manager Dick Sisler's mandate of extra batting practice for several members of the team apparently was paying off, as in the game Frank Robinson (23 & 24) had two home runs and Chico Ruiz had four hits while the Reds downed the Giants.

The following night on Thursday, August 20, the Reds capped their sweep of the series at San Francisco with a 10–7 victory, moving them into a second place with the Giants, who were suddenly reeling after having lost five in a row since August 16.

Pittsburgh also found itself spinning out of control as the Pirates on the morning of Friday, August 21, had slipped deep into 5th place, 11½ games behind the Phillies, following a five-game losing streak that included both ends of a twi-night doubleheader the previous night with the Phillies, 2–0 and 3–2. The twin bill was played at Connie Mack Stadium with 35,814 fans in attendance.

In the first game Art Mahaffey (11–6) pitched a two-hitter. The decisive blow in the game was a two-run home run by the Phillies' Frank Thomas (6) in the bottom of the 9th. Bob Friend (10–13) took the loss for the Bucs.

In the second game, Rick Wise (5–1) collared the Pirates with a little relief help from Ed Roebuck in the 9th. By winning the doubleheader, the Phillies had increased their league lead to 7½ games over the Giants and Reds.

The fact that Phillies were leading the league at this point in the season came as a surprise to Braves manager Bobby Bragan, who said, "I thought it would be Cincinnati or maybe the Giants."[39]

The Milwaukee Braves found themselves on the morning of August 21, after defeating the Dodgers, 8–2, locked in a 5th-place tie with the Pirates, 11½ games behind the Phillies. The nosedive of the Braves in the standings was being tied to the collapse of Warren Spahn and light hitting of Eddie Mathews at the plate. On August 21 Mathews was struggling to stay above a .230 batting average.

The idle St. Louis Cardinals, on the other hand, had pulled themselves into 4th place, ten games behind the Phillies, after winning two games and losing one with Houston during the week.

At the rear of the pack in the National League on August 21, Houston continued its tight hold on 9th place, 24 games behind the Phillies, while the not-so-amazing New York Mets seemed to have locked up 10th place for the 1964 season, 35½ games behind, despite being on a roll, as they had won their last three games in a row.

The Phillies maintained their 7½ game lead on Friday, August 21, by defeating the Pirates again, 2–0, while the Reds beat the Dodgers, 3–2. The Reds by virtue of their win moved into sole possession of second place as the Giants continued to reel, being beaten by the Cardinals, 6–5, to fall into third place, 8½ games behind the Phillies.

Meanwhile, the Cardinals now had sole possession of fourth place, but were 10 games behind the Phillies with 44 games to go in the season.

Unfortunately, in the Reds' 3–2 victory over the Dodgers on Friday night, they would lose the services of pitcher Jim Maloney's blazing fast ball for at least the next four days. Maloney suffered a sore muscle in his right arm during the game with the Dodgers and was pulled after the third inning and then flown back to Cincinnati to be examined by Reds team physician Dr. George Ballou.

Nonetheless, in the game Maloney had driven in the first two Cincinnati runs with a double and then scored the winning run on a bunt single by Chico Ruiz. In the ninth inning a great leaping catch by Marty Keough of a smash to right by Willie Davis would prevent the tying run from scoring.

The win would be their 13th in 16 games during the season with the Dodgers for the surging Reds. The loss would drop the seventh-place Dodgers to 15½ games behind the Phillies. However, with 27,918 fans on hand at Dodger Stadium, the Dodgers would send their 1964 season attendance soaring up to 1,764,734 for 55 home dates.

Over in the American League on Friday night, August 21, the Baltimore Orioles had moved into first place by one-half game over the Chicago White Sox. This prompted L.A. Times sports writer Al Wolf to raise the issue of how interesting it would be if the Phillies and Orioles faced each other in the 1964 World Series, as former Phillies great Robin Roberts was now pitching for Baltimore. When Gene Mauch took over as Philadelphia manager in 1960, one of his first unpopular acts was to run Roberts out of town following the 1961 season.

On Saturday, August 22, the Pirates snapped their losing streak at six as they scored five unearned runs in the seventh to down the Phillies, 9–4, causing the Philadelphia winning streak to end at four games. Roberto Clemente, leading the National League with a .347 average—"the Great One" as Pittsburgh broadcaster Bob Prince would ultimately dub him— had three doubles in leading the Pirates.

Likewise on August 22, San Francisco also snapped their losing streak at six with 4–2 victory over St. Louis. In the first inning the Giants hit four consecutive singles off Cardinals starter Roger Craig (6–6), including run-scoring hits by Jim Davenport and Tom Haller.

At New York, the Mets had their five-game winning streak halted by the Cubs, 3–2. Larry Jackson (15–10), who had never lost yet to the Mets at this point in his career, beat them for the 9th straight time. Jackson needed relief help from Lindy McDaniel in the ninth when Ron Hunt tripled and Joe Christopher singled to put the tying run on base. However, Ed Kranepool flied out, Jim Hickman singled Christopher to third, and then McDaniel got Charlie Smith on a line drive to shortstop and Chris Cannizzaro took a third strike.

Rookie Gary Kroll (0–1), making his first Major League start, took the loss. However, he struck out eight Cubs in the six innings he worked and left the game trailing 3–0.

Out at Los Angeles on Saturday night, August 22, it took the Reds 15 innings to defeat the Dodgers, 2–1. Reds pitcher Joey Jay had been seeking his sixth straight victory while pitching a five-hit, 1–0 shutout into the ninth. Hard-luck Don Drysdale had started for L.A. but was relieved in the eighth by Ron Perranoski.

Jay had retired 10 straight batters before he gave up his first walk to Tommy Davis in the seventh. Then in the bottom of the ninth Jim Gilliam led off with a single and then was moved over to second on a sacrifice. Jay then issued his second walk of the game to John Roseboro. Tommy Davis followed with a single to right, scoring Gilliam with the tying run, and Roseboro went to third on the play. On the play the relay throw by Chico Cardenas struck Roseboro in the back and he had to leave the game. Dick Tracewski was sent in to run for Roseboro.

Then with one out Wally Moon then lofted a fly to right that seemed deep enough to score Tracewski. He tagged up and headed for home, only to be cut down at the plate by a perfect throw from right fielder Marty Keough to catcher Johnny Edwards. The Reds eventually pushed a run across the plate in the top of the 15th to win their sixth straight game and pick up a full game on the Phillies, cutting their lead to 6½ games.

However, the Phillies sent their league lead back to 7½ games on

Sunday, August 23, with a turn-around 9–3 shellacking of the Pirates. For Philadelphia, Richie Allen led the offense, driving in four runs with two homers and a single. The starting pitcher for the Phillies was Jim Bunning, who won his 14th game of the season.

At Los Angeles, the Dodgers avoided a series sweep at home by putting an end to Cincinnati's six-game winning streak, defeating the Reds, 1–0, behind three-hit pitching of Phil Ortega (6–5). Jim O'Toole (11–6) was the losing pitcher.

At Candlestick Park the Giants moved back into a tie for second place with the Reds by slipping by the Cardinals, 3–2, in ten innings. The Giants scored the winning run in the bottom of the tenth on a single by Jesus Alou, a sacrifice, Tom Haller's long fly and an error by Dal Maxvill on a grounder by Harvey Kuenn.

The cellar-dwelling New York Mets were suddenly hot! After sweeping a doubleheader with the Chicago Cubs, 2–1 and 5–4, on August 23, the Mets had now won seven of their last eight games.

Down in Houston Don Larsen pitched his first complete game in five years, and a five-hitter to boot, as the Colts whipped the Braves for the third straight time, 7–1. The loss dropped Milwaukee to 13½ games behind Philadelphia.

On Monday, August 24, all the National League teams were scheduled with the exception of the New York Mets, who had an exhibition game scheduled with the New York Yankees, and the Cincinnati Reds, who were idle.

Subsequently, Milwaukee beat front-running Philadelphia, 12–9, reducing the Phillies' lead to 6½ games over the Giants.

The Braves' Rico Carty, who was challenging the Phillies' Dick Allen for "Rookie of the Year" honors, had five straight hits in the game, including a home run, three doubles and a single. His five hits in the game elevated his season batting average from .312 to .323 to go along with 13 home runs and 56 RBIs on the season.

Carty had been playing second fiddle to Dick Allen in the bid for the rookie award. Nonetheless, Allen's season stats were impressive too. Allen, who had played in 30 more games than Carty at that time, was hitting .314 with 23 home runs and 66 RBIs.

St. Louis beat fading Pittsburgh, 5–1. Houston shut out Chicago, 2–0, while San Francisco beat Los Angeles, 4–2.

The Giants wrapped up the game in the first inning with four runs, helped out by Tommy Davis's error on a liner by Willie Mays that scored one run and a grounder by Orlando Cepeda which drove in the second, before Jim Hart finished up the early scoring with a two-run homer.

The Dodgers scored their only run in the first, too, when Willie Davis tagged Giants starter Jim Duffalo for a homer. Then Duffalo shut out the Dodgers the rest of the way, pitching a complete game, his first since his first Major League start in 1961. Duffalo allowed six hits in the route-going job.

Finally on Monday, August 24, in New York City the twice-previously-delayed "Mayor's Trophy Game" was played between the Mets and Yankees.

Beginning in 1996, the Mets and Yankees have been meeting during the regular season in interleague games. As a matter of fact, the two teams even played a historic day-night doubleheader during the 2000 season, with an afternoon game being played in Queens at Shea Stadium and then moving the action over to the Bronx at Yankee Stadium for the nightcap.

But before these silly, fabricated and manufactured interleague rivalry games were implemented—mostly for the personal enjoyment of Commissioner Bud Selig and to squeeze a few extra bucks out of the fans— once upon a time in New York, the Mets and Yankees used to meet each year during the regular season in an exhibition game for charity.

And on the evening of Monday, August 24, 1964, a carnival-like atmosphere prevailed in Queens as a crowd of 55,396 went through the turnstiles at Shea Stadium to witness the latest edition of the Battle of the Boroughs.

It had been anticipated that perhaps as many as 8,000 youngsters might show up at the ball park with harmonicas in an attempt to mock the Yankees. Currently harmonicas were a very touchy subject for Yankee manager Yogi Berra, after he had recently slapped utility infielder Phil Linz with a $200 fine for playing one on the Yankees' team bus following a 5–0 loss by the Bronx Bombers to the Chicago White Sox on August 21.

This over-exaggerated event occurred when Linz aggravated Berra's fragile nerves following the team's fourth straight loss, coming at Comiskey Park the previous Thursday night. Berra went into a rage at Linz's rather casual attitude, blowing into the instrument while on the team bus en route to the Chicago airport following the loss that allowed the White Sox to move into first place, 4½ games ahead of the third-place Yankees.

Apparently Berra had yelled at Linz to stop the music and Linz did not hear the manager's order. Consequently, Berra went into a rage. Veteran Yankee coach Frank Crosetti had called the incident the worst that he had seen in 33 years with the Yankees.

However, for Linz, the object of Berra's verbal abuse and fine, harmonicas were not a touchy subject. In fact, since the highly publicized inci-

dent occurred Linz was receiving some rather attractive endorsement pro-
posals from harmonica manufacturers.

By the time of the exhibition game with the Mets on August 24, Berra
and Linz had met with Yankees general manager Ralph Houk and subsequently Linz had apologized for his bus concert.

"I left the matter entirely in Berra's hands," said Houk, who made a
hurried trip to Boston to look into the incident. "But I will say I don't approve
of playing a harmonica on the bus after we had lost a series like that one."[40]

Any fan wishing to read a more detailed account of this ridiculous
saga can find such in pitcher/author Jim Bouton's 1970 epic about his season with the Seattle Pilots, *Ball Four*.

As for the game, the Yankees bested the Mets, 6–4. The New York
Mets, however, gave the game away, allowing the Yankees to score two
runs in the top of the ninth when the Mets, ... well, became the Mets.

Joe Pepitone had hit a slow bouncer to first baseman Ed Kranepool
who muffed it. With Pepitone on first, Archie Moore then laid down a
bunt and Mets pitcher Willard Hunter's throw to second, attempting to
cut down Pepitone, was too late. Pedro Gonzalez then singled, driving in
a run, and Johnny Blanchard followed with a grounder that scored the
second run.

The first four Yankee runs came on home runs. Joe Pepitone connected with one on and Tom Tresh and Roger Maris hit solo shots. The
home run hit by Roger Maris was nostalgic, to say the least, as it came off
Jack Fisher. It was Fisher who had served up Number 60 to Maris in his
record-setting year of 1961, when he had hit 61 home runs.

Earlier in the game Yankee manager Yogi Berra had inserted himself
in the game as a pinch hitter and promptly hit into an inning-ending double play, wiping out a Yankees rally.

For the Mets, Bobby Klaus had two doubles and Ed Kranepool a single and two RBIs. The winning pitcher for the Yankees was Pete Milkkelsen
and the loser for the Mets was Willard Hunter.

National League Standings, August 25, 1964

Team	Won	Lost	Pct.	G.B.
Philadelphia	76	48	.613	—
San Francisco	70	55	.560	6½
Cincinnati	69	55	.557	7
St. Louis	66	58	.532	10
Pittsburgh	64	61	.512	12½
Milwaukee	63	60	.512	12½
Los Angeles	60	63	.488	15½
Chicago	57	68	.456	19½

Team	Won	Lost	Pct.	G.B.
Houston	55	71	.437	22
New York	42	83	.336	34½

On Tuesday, August 25, the Phillies lost to Milwaukee, 7–5. The Braves had built an early lead in the game on home runs by Eddie Mathews and Lee Maye, then hung in there to hold off a late-inning charge by the Phillies.

The loss allowed second-place Cincinnati to gain a full game on the Phillies as they beat New York, 7–2. For the Reds, Frank Robinson drove in two runs with a double and Deron Johnson drove in three.

The Reds, returning home from a successful West Coast road trip, seemed to be headed for a homecoming loss when the Mets' Ron Hunt touched Reds starter Bob Purkey for a two-run homer before there was one out in the game. However, Purkey then settled down, pitched a six-hitter and held the Mets scoreless the rest of the way.

Purkey's performance was reminiscent of an interview that had been conducted with the Phillies' Dennis Bennett. In the interview Bennett was asked if he preferred to be a starter or a reliever. "I prefer to be a starter," said Bennett. "That way you have a chance to overcome your mistakes in the game."[41]

Dick Sisler continued as interim manager of the Reds after manager Fred Hutchinson was granted a leave of absence on August 13. The following day Hutchinson, suffering from the effects of lung cancer, was admitted to Christ Hospital in Cincinnati, where he was being treated for back pains and also given further diagnostic tests. On August 25, Hutchinson remained hospitalized and it was not immediately known when he would be released. However, a hospital spokesperson reported that Hutch was in good spirits and doing well.

The Giants, continuing their visit to L.A., lost to the Dodgers, 3–1, to fall into third place, one-half game behind Cincinnati. The winning pitcher for the Dodgers was Howie Reed, who prior to August 25, 1964, had won his last and only game in the majors in 1958 with the Kansas City Athletics. Reed stopped the Giants on six hits with ninth-inning relief help from Ron Perranoski and Robert Miller.

Juan Marichal made his first appearance on the mound for the Giants since injuring his back on July 19. However, he lasted only five innings.

At St. Louis, the Cardinals' Lou Brock hit a home run in the bottom of the 13th inning to beat Pittsburgh, 7–6. Meanwhile Houston beat the Chicago Cubs, 5–4.

On the 26th of the month as the steamy dog days of August neared an end, the Philadelphia Phillies seemed as if they were becoming down-right stubborn about their league lead and rebounded from the previous night's loss to the Braves to hand them a 6–1 trouncing. Gus Triandos smacked two home runs for the Phillies, and Ruben Amaro and Tony Gonzalez both hit one each.

Chris Short (14–6) was the winning pitcher for the Phillies. With his latest effort Short had now lowered his league-leading ERA to 1.65.

The Philadelphia victory once again increased their league lead to seven games over second-place Cincinnati and to 7½ games over third-place San Francisco as both clubs took beatings.

The Reds lost to the Mets, 3–1, before a sparse crowd of 10,684 at Crosley Field as Tracy Stallard (8–16) pitched a five-hitter. Joey Jay (9–9) took the loss. The win for the Mets was their eighth in the last ten games.

In another close game at Dodger Stadium, the Giants were edged by Los Angeles, 2–1. A two-run bloop single by the Dodgers' Doug Camilli with two outs in the bottom of the ninth produced the winning run.

St. Louis got by Pittsburgh, 4–2, as rookie lefty Mike Cuellar pitched his first complete game in the majors. Ken Boyer drove in two runs and Lou Brock homered for the Cardinals. For the Pirates, Donn Clendenon and Gene Alley homered.

Finally on August 26 the Chicago Cubs got by Houston, 3–1, thereby stopping the Colts' winning streak at six. Larry Jackson (16–10) was the winning pitcher for the Cubs and Ernie Banks and Ron Santo homered.

Jim Bunning was to remark, in regard to the Milwaukee Braves of 1964, that they were dangerous because they still had a lot of guys on the team who could hit the ball hard. In the only National League game scheduled on Thursday, August 27, the Milwaukee Braves pounded the San Francisco Giants, 13–0.

The Braves scored six runs in the first inning as Rico Carty began the scoring when he hit his 14th home run of the season into the left-field bleachers. Hank Aaron also knocked in a run in the first with a double. Then Woody Woodward capped the scoring with a three-run double.

Carty went on to knock in three more runs with a triple in the fourth, and Aaron drove home another in the sixth with a single. Then Wood-ward drove home another run in the seventh with a single and big Lee Maye completed the Braves' 16-hit attack in the eighth with his 9th home run of the season.

Milwaukee starter Hank Fischer (10–8), who had been knocked out of the box in the first or second innings of his last four starts, pitched his fifth shutout of the season, while striking out four batters and issuing no walks.

The loss dropped the third-place Giants to eight games behind the Phillies and one game behind the second-place Reds.

On Friday, August 28, the Houston Colts were scheduled to play the Reds in a night game at Cincinnati.

Earlier in the day the Reds management had decided to decided part ways with coach Johnny Temple. Temple had originally been hired for the 1964 season as a player-coach at the insistence of manager Fred Hutchinson, who felt that he could serve several purposes on the club as a pinch hitter, spare infielder and mentor to Pete Rose. Also Hutch personally liked Temple and enjoyed hanging out with him on the road.

However, to the other Reds coaches Temple presented a problem. The other coaches, Dick Sisler, Reggie Ortero and Jim Turner, regarded Temple's position on the team as some sort of baseball patronage. They felt insecure with Temple around, they were suspicious and as a result acted coldly towards him.

On July 15 the Reds had pulled Temple off of the active roster and assigned him to coaching duties that did not require him to be in uniform for the games. Now in late August, with Fred Hutchinson in the hospital battling cancer and with Dick Sisler in charge of Reds field duties, Temple was cut loose altogether.

Reds assistant general manager Phil Seghi insisted that Temple had been given two choices when it was determined that he was not in condition to be of any serious help to the Reds in the final month of the season. The team was in second place, seven games behind the Phillies, and geared up for the stretch drive.

Seghi said, "We told Johnny that he could terminate his employment with the club, or he could continue special scouting assignments at the Major League level. In either case, he was to be paid for the remainder of the season."

"And John is being well paid for the work he had been doing," added Seghi."[42]

Reds president and general manager Bill DeWitt remarked, "Temple was taken on as a free agent last December at the insistence of manager Hutchinson. Hutch felt at the time that he could help us as both a player and adviser to Pete Rose. We signed him as a coach because we didn't have room on our playing roster at the time. But we wanted him chiefly as a player and we were disappointed when we learned he wasn't in condition to play."[43]

Well, none of this was satisfactory to the fierce competitor Temple, and he decided to walk and return to his home in Houston. Therefore, prior to the Friday evening game, Temple arrived at Crosley Field to clear out his locker in the Reds' clubhouse before heading home. Temple had a couple of drinks before arriving at Crosley Field.

Then, as he entered the Reds' clubhouse, Reggie Ortero was one of the first persons he encountered. Ortero was not aware of the fact that Temple had just been canned by the Reds' management; he slapped Temple on the back and asked him how he was doing.

Ortero's remark made Temple extremely angry and he took a swing at Ortero. Consequently, Ortero immediately swung back at Temple and landed a haymaker on him, cutting his face under the right eye. It turned out to be a four-punch fight, with three of the blows being thrown by Ortero.

Johnny Temple had played for 13 years in the Major Leagues with Cincinnati, Cleveland, Baltimore and Houston. He was leaving the game with a .284 lifetime batting average and 1,484 hits. His lifetime fielding average was .973.

During the middle 1950s, playing for the Reds, Temple had been an All-Star second baseman. He, along with shortstop Roy McMillan, had been one of the premier double play combinations in the Major Leagues.

Following his release by the Reds and the Ortero incident on August 28, 1964, Johnny Temple was never again offered a job in Major League Baseball. While the Reds were rained out, there were other games played on August 28.

At Pittsburgh, 15-year Major League veteran and former Phillie Smokey Burgess unloaded a three-run homer in the ninth inning that gave the Pirates a 4–2 victory over Philadelphia. The Phillies had been sailing along with a 2–0 lead going into the ninth behind the three-hit pitching of Jim Bunning, before the Pirates torpedoed them with a four-run rally to win the game. The loss shaved one-half game off of the Phillies' National League lead over second-place Cincinnati.

The game entered the eighth inning tied at 0–0, when Jim Bunning started a two-run Philadelphia rally with single off Pirate starter Joe Gibbon. He then took second on a single by Cookie Rojas and scored on a double by Johnny Callison. Rojas also scored when Callison became trapped in a rundown between second and third.

Ed Roebuck replaced Bunning in the ninth and Willie Stargell greeted him with a single off his first pitch to score a run. Then Burgess followed with his blast into the right-field stands at Forbes Field.

At County Stadium in Milwaukee, the Giants got by the Braves, 3–2, when Jim Davenport scored the winning run all the way from first base, as Lee Maye let a single skip past him in the outfield in the ninth inning.

St. Louis beat Los Angeles, 5–3, as Bill White's three-run homer made the difference.

Meanwhile, the Mets and Cubs hooked up in a wild game at Wrigley Field that saw the New Yorkers prevail, 12–10. A total of 11 pitchers for the two ball clubs allowed 33 hits, in a game that saw the Mets leading at one point, 5–0; then trailing, 6–5; then leading, 8–6; and again trailing, 10–8, before snapping a 10–10 tie in the eighth on a hit by Joe Christopher, his fourth of the game. The win for the Mets was their 9th in the last 11 games.

On Saturday, August 29, the Phillies survived another late-inning surge by the Pirates to escape with a 10–8 victory. Despite having been granted a 10–0 lead, Philadelphia starting pitcher Art Mahaffey (12–6) was unable to complete the game. Mahaffey was knocked out of the game in the eighth when the Pirates rallied for four runs. John Boozer came on in relief of Mahaffey but then ran into trouble himself in the ninth when the Pirates scored four more runs to cut the Phillies' lead to 10–8. Then Jack Baldshun came to the rescue for Philadelphia, with a runner on third and two out, to finish the game.

Rookie Richie Allen tripled and hit his 24th home run in the game while driving in four runs. Johnny Callison also singled and hit his 23rd home run for the Phillies while knocking in three runs. Bob Friend (10–15), the first of six Pittsburgh pitchers in the game, took the loss.

The second-place Reds had rescheduled their rained-out game from Friday as part of a doubleheader on Saturday.

Prior to the game—predictable as it was—players from both the Reds and Colts made light of the clubhouse donnybrook that had occurred on Friday between Johnny Temple and Reggie Ortero. Houston players shouted at Ortero from the bench, "How did Temple ever miss connecting with your big schnozzola?"[44]

Meanwhile former Reds shortstop Eddie Kasko, now playing for the Colts, was causing laughter in both dugouts as he came skipping out of the runway with a towel draped over his head and started to shadow box.

When Reds acting manager Dick Sisler was asked for a comment on the Temple-Ortero episode, he simply uttered, "It was a regrettable incident."[45]

It was Ladies Day at Crosley Field and a crowd of 12,965 watched as the Reds needed 11 innings to take the first game of the twin bill from the Colts, 2–1. The decisive blow in the game came when Steve Boros delivered a one-out bases-loaded single in the eleventh to hand Sammy Ellis (7–3) his seventh win. Ellis came on in relief of starter John Tsitouris. Hal Woodeshick (2–8) took the loss for Houston in relief of Don Larsen, who had ten strikeouts in the game, pitching 8⅓ innings.

Frank Robinson started the Cincinnati rally in the eleventh when he hit a line-drive double to center field. He then moved on to third via a wild pitch by Woodeschick. Deron Johnson then struck out for the fifth time in the game. Subsequently Jim Coker and Leo Cardenas were intentionally walked to load the bases and then Boros followed with a single to right.

The Reds completed the sweep of the doubleheader with an 8–7 win in the nightcap. Deron Johnson's 19th home run of the season, a long solo poke over the left-center-field fence near the score board in the bottom of the seventh, was the winning margin in the game. Acting manager Dick Sisler had benched Johnson for the second game after he fanned five straight times in the opener. However, he was inserted in the lineup in the top of the seventh as a defensive replacement for first baseman Gordy Coleman.

The Reds had built a six-run lead in the game through the first five innings but Reds starter Jim O'Toole and reliever Billy McCool (4–2) were unable to hold on, allowing the Colts to come back and tie the game, 7–7, in the seventh. Don Notterbat had started for the Colts and the third Houston reliever in the game, Danny Coombs (0–1), took the loss.

For the Reds, Frank Robinson drove in three runs in the second game with a single and a triple. The doubleheader sweep enabled the Reds to gain a half game on the Phillies who now had a six-game edge in the standings.

Acting manager Dick Sisler had Pete Rose ride the wood for the entire twin bill as he seemed to continue favoring Chico Ruiz at second base in the lineup recently.

Watching part of the doubleheader from the press box at Crosley Field was former All-Star third baseman Don Hoak. Hoak was currently touring the majors as a special assignment scout for the Phillies.

In other games played on August 29, the Giants beat the Braves, 7–2. In the first inning Willie Mays got the Giants' scoring going when he tripled off Braves starter Bob Sadowski to score Jesus Alou, and then scored on Willie McCovey's ground out.

Jim Hart, returning to the lineup for the first time after being beaned in Wednesday's game with the Dodgers, hit his 22nd home run of the season in the eighth off reliever Warren Spahn, and earlier had a double. In fact, Hart may have been robbed of a homer in the game when in the first inning a fan at County Stadium in Milwaukee reached out and interfered with Rico Carty's attempt to catch the ball. The ball went into the stands and umpire Doug Harvey ruled Hart out on fan interference.

For the Giants, Ron Herbel (9–8) pitched a seven-hitter.

At Bush Stadium in St. Louis, a crowd of 20,001 turned out to see

Bob Gibson (12–10) and the Cardinals defeat the Dodgers, 4–1, on a three-run pinch homer by Bob Skinner. Gibson had pitched a shutout until the ninth when Derrell Griffith (3) homered with one out. The Cardinals, who at this point were playing red-hot ball, enjoyed their 23rd win in the last 33 games.

At Wrigley Field, Ernie Banks (18) hit his third home run in the last three games to help Dick Ellsworth (13–14) beat the Mets, 4–3, in ten innings. The home run by Banks was his 371st of his career and moved him into the number seven place on the all-time list at that point in time.

Ellis Burton, who had just arrived in Chicago from the minors shortly before game time, delivered the decisive blow for the Cubs in the bottom of the 10th as he singled across the winning run. Galen Cisco (5–14) took the loss for the Mets, and Jim Hickman hit his 10th home run.

On Sunday, August 30, the National League pennant race tightened up a bit. Pittsburgh knocked off first-place Philadelphia, 10–2, as Phillies starter Chris Short got off to a very shaky start and Richie Allen made two errors, allowing the Pirates to score six runs in the first three innings.

Meanwhile at Cincinnati, the Reds and Colts, playing their second doubleheader in two days, split the games. The Colts won the opener, 8–5, as Joe Gaines led the way driving in four runs with a pair of triples. Then the Reds came back to bag the nightcap, 7–6, in the bottom of the ninth on a single by Vada Pinson and a double by Frank Robinson.

The twin bill wrapped up the season series between the Red and Colts with Cincinnati winning 12 of the games and Houston 6. The Reds' doubleheader split, coupled with the Phillies' loss, moved them to within 5½ games of the league lead.

The race tightened even more as San Francisco split a doubleheader with Milwaukee, winning the opener, 13–10. Then the Braves won the nightcap, 7–4, on a three-run home run by Hank Aaron in the eighth. The doubleheader split moved the third-place Giants to within 6½ games of the Phillies.

Also, the Cardinals moved to within a half game of the Giants by defeating the Dodgers, 5–1, behind the four-hit pitching of Curt Simmons and a three-run double by Mike Shannon.

Sandy Koufax had not pitched since August 16 but continued to travel with the Dodgers. Now as the inflammation in his left elbow saw no improvement, he left the team on Sunday, August 30, and flew home to Los Angeles for further treatment by Dr. Robert Kerlan, the Dodgers' team physician. If there had been any doubt that Koufax would not pitch again in the 1964 season, it was now certain as Dr. Kerlan indicated that he didn't think that Koufax would pitch again this season.

Dr. Kerlan, responding to questions about Koufax's future, stated, "It's going to be a gradual thing. I can't say how long it'll be before he is sound, but it probably won't be before the season is over."[46]

At Chicago, Larry Jackson (17–10) the Mets-killer upped his lifetime record against them to 10–0 as the Cubs beat the Mets, 7–3.

On the morning of the last day in August 1964, with the pennant stretch run lying dead ahead, the standings were the following.

National League Standings, August 31, 1964

Team	Won	Lost	Pct.	G.B.
Philadelphia	78	51	.605	—
Cincinnati	73	57	.562	5½
San Francisco	73	58	.557	6½
St. Louis	71	58	.550	7
Pittsburgh	66	64	.508	12½
Milwaukee	66	64	.508	12½
Los Angeles	62	66	.484	13½
Chicago	60	70	.462	15½
Houston	57	75	.432	22½
New York	44	86	.338	34½

On Monday, August 31, there was only one game scheduled in the National League, with Los Angeles playing a night game at St. Louis. The Dodgers beat the Cardinals, 12–3, snapping the Cards' six-game winning streak as light-hitting Maury Wills (2) and Wes Parker (1), who had hit a combined total of one home run between them so far in the 1964 season, both homered in the game.

Don Drysdale (15–13) went the distance for the Dodgers and had 12 strikeouts. The 12 strikeouts for Drysdale brought his season total to 201, second-highest on the team to the injured Sandy Koufax with 223, who had been advised by the team physician to not pitch again in the 1964 season.

Therefore with the end-of-August loss to L.A., the St. Louis Cardinals would enter the month of September 7½ games behind the league-leading Philadelphia Phillies with 34 games left to play in the 1964 season.

IX

September Collapse

Despite coming off a disastrous road trip in which the Philadelphia Phillies had lost four of six games, they still entered the month of September with a comfortable 5½ game lead over second-place Cincinnati with just 33 games left on the schedule. In fact, the Phillies had just concluded their best won-lost record in August since 1950. But before the month of September was concluded, the Phillies would blow it all in the end, when with a 6½ game lead with just 12 games left to play, they would lose 10 straight games.

As the Phillies' second baseman Tony Taylor would later remark, "When we went to spring training in 1964, everybody knew we were going to win a lot of games. We never thought something like that could happen to us. We played great, we had a lot of fun, and the team was a family."[1]

On Tuesday, September 1, the general feeling was that in order for the Phillies to win their first National League Pennant since 1950, they were going to have to win at least half their remaining games in September and early October to hold off the Cincinnati Reds, San Francisco Giants and suddenly charging St. Louis Cardinals.

However, the Phillies were confronted with another unique challenge, too, especially in the area of endurance, as the team would not have one day off in their September schedule.

While the Phillies were leading the National League in games won on September 1, the individual batting leader was the Pirates' Roberto Clemente with a .346 average. Following Clemente in the chase for the NL batting crown were three players in a tie for second—Billy Williams and Ron Santo of the Cubs and Hank Aaron of the Braves—all with a .326 average.

Hank Aaron had been particularly hot toward the end of August as he gained nine points with 14 hits in 29 at bats, hitting at a blistering .483 pace.

While Willie Mays had been nearly impossible for National League pitchers to get out in May, he had fallen off a bit in July and August. However, entering the month of September Mays was still hitting a respectable .306. While he was not in the top ten hitters for average in the league, he was the league leader in home runs with 39. As for the league leader in RBIs, on September 1 it was Ron Santo of the Cubs with 95. In fact, Santo had driven in five runs during the last week in August.

On September 1, as the National League teams prepared for the stretch drive, the San Francisco Giants were receiving some very good news. Juan Marichal, who had only pitched five innings since July 19, was given a clean bill of health by the Giants' team physician, Dr. Harrison McLoughlin, and was expected to be back in rotation by the weekend.

When Marichal injured his back while winning his 15th game at Philadelphia on July 19, the Giants were in a tie for first place with the Phillies. Now six weeks later, without Marichal's taking his place in the pitching rotation, they were in third place, 6½ games behind the Phillies.

On September 1 the Giants were in New York starting a three-game series with the Mets. It was expected that Marichal would start in the series with Philadelphia beginning on September 4.

Manager Alvin Dark said that he hadn't decided yet when to pitch Marichal. "It depends on how he feels. I don't want to do anything that might jeopardize his chances of complete recovery."[2]

That evening with 39,379 fans on hand at Shea Stadium, the third-place Giants lost to the Mets, 4–1, as Al Jackson (9–13) went all the way pitching a six-hitter for New York.

A history-making event occurred during the game when Al Dark inserted Masanori Murakami in the game to pitch relief in the eighth. Therefore Murakami, who had been pitching for the Giants' Fresno farm club, became the first Japanese national ever to play in a Major League game. He pitched a scoreless eighth for the Giants. In his final appearance for Fresno, Murakami had struck out 10 of the 12 batters he faced to protect a 6–5 lead over Reno.

Down at Philadelphia with 13,306 fans on hand, the front-running Phillies got by the Houston Colts, 4–3. In the seventh inning Johnny Callison and Wes Covington hit back-to-back home runs, and then one out later Frank Thomas homered for the Phillies, which in the end counteracted a three-run homer by the Colts' Joe Gaines off starter Jim Bunning (15–4) in the ninth. All three Philadelphia home runs in the seventh came off Houston starter and knuckleballer Hal (Skinny) Brown (2–14). Prior to Gaines' blast Bunning had been cruising toward his sixth shutout of the season.

However, Richie Allen's eighth-inning inside-the-park homer off Dick Ferrell was the clincher for the Phillies, giving Bunning his 15th win of the season. Allen's inside-the-park home run was the first in a Phillies game played either at home or away since June 9, 1963, when Pete Rose of the Reds had hit an inside-the-park job during the second game of a doubleheader with the Phillies.

Prior to the game the Phillies had reactivated reserve first baseman Danny Cater. Cater had sustained a broken arm in a game against Milwaukee on July 22. Meanwhile, the Phillies' Bobby Wine had to be sent home and placed in traction. Wine had hurt his back fielding a ground ball in Chicago two weeks prior to September 1.

As the month of September began, the Cincinnati Reds lost no ground in the pennant race and remained 5½ games behind the Phillies, after they slipped past the Cubs, 2–1, behind the dizzying pitching of big right-hander Jim Maloney (12–9), who gave up only three hits to the Cubs while fanning 13. Maloney was so overpowering that he struck out seven of the first nine Cubs he faced and did not give up a hit until the fourth.

Ernie Broglio (7–11), the Cubs' starter, had struck out the first two Reds he faced but gave up a single to Vada Pinson who then scored when Billy Williams fumbled a drive by Frank Robinson to right. The Cubs tied the score in the fourth when Jim Stewart led off with a double, then scored on a single by Williams. The deciding blow in the game came in the bottom of the fourth inning when, after Broglio had walked two batters, a single by Leo Cardenas drove in a run.

At St. Louis the Cardinals got back on the winning track, beating Milwaukee, 5–4, when former Milwaukee Brave and future Milwaukee Brewers broadcaster, comedian and actor, Bob Uecker, singled home Julian Javier in the bottom of the ninth with the winning run. Early in the game Uecker had hit his first and only home run of the year in 1964. Uecker finished the 1964 season playing in 40 games for St. Louis with a .198 batting average and would make an appearance in the 1964 World Series for the Cards.

During the game Stan "The Man" Musial, who was in attendance, collapsed of complete exhaustion and was taken to the hospital. Since retiring as an active player in September 1963 after 23 seasons with the Cardinals, Musial had kept an ambitious daily agenda serving as the nation's physical fitness director, under an appointment by President Lyndon Johnson on February 14, 1964, and Musial also served as a Vice President with the Cardinals.

Musial, it was reported, "became ill at the game with Milwaukee and was helped to the Cardinals clubhouse. There, he staggered and collapsed into the arms of former teammates. An ambulance, escorted by several police cars, sped him to Jewish Hospital in the city's mid-town medical complex on the edge of famous Forest Park. He was hospitalized, and a physician said he would remain at least a couple of days."[3]

"He was completely dehydrated by the time he reached the hospital," said Dr. I. C. Middleman, the Cardinals' and Musial's physician. "At times he was irrational."

Asked if Musial's condition was serious, Dr. Middleman said, "No, I don't think so—although it could become serious. His blood pressure is all right and he is rational now. The demands on Stan's time have been tremendous," said Middleman, "and this entered into his general condition."[4]

Each year on September 1, the rule that limits Major League rosters to 25 players is set aside to permit teams to bring up players from the minors so they can see their young prospects perform under big league conditions.

Subsequently, prior to the game with the Cardinals on September 1, the Milwaukee Braves, 12½ games out of first but still hopeful of challenging for the pennant, reactivated 22-year-old left-hander Dan Schneider and purchased the contract of right-hander Clay Carroll from Denver of the Pacific Coast League.

Rounding out the National League action on the first day of September, Willie Stargell's home run in the eighth started a three-run rally that carried Pittsburgh over Los Angeles, 5–2. Bob Friend (11–15) scattered seven hits for the Pirates.

On September 2, Juan Marichal unexpectedly returned to the San Francisco Giants' pitching rotation and took up right where he left off prior to his July 29 back injury.

Making only his second start since July 29, Marichal struck out nine while pitching a four-hit shutout against the Mets, beating them, 4–0. For Marichal, it was his 16th victory of the season.

Tragedy struck the Giants in the game, however, as right fielder Jesus Alou suffered a serious ankle wound when spiked in a rundown play and was now lost for the remainder of the 1964 season. Alou was hurt in an eighth-inning double-steal attempt when the Mets' Ron Hunt literally ran him down.

Following the incident he underwent exploratory surgery at New York's Roosevelt Hospital to determine the extent of the damage to his ankle. Seventy-five stitches had been required to close the cut on his ankle and a cast was then put on his leg. When discharged from the hospital, according to Dr. Peter LaMotte, the Mets team physician, Alou was expected to go directly to San Francisco rather than rejoin the Giants.

At Philadelphia the Beatles shared center stage with the Phillies, playing to a screaming mob of 13,000 teenagers at Convention Hall, while out at Connie Mack Stadium, Chris Short (15–7) struck out ten and also pitched a four-hitter, beating the Colts, 2–1. It was Short's third victory of the season over the Colts. Short had also lowered his ERA to 1.85, second-best in the NL.

Second baseman Tony Taylor drove home both Philadelphia runs with a fourth-inning single. The Phillies now enjoyed a 5½ game lead over the second-place Reds with 31 games to go in the season.

However, at Crosley Field with just 9,060 fans on hand, the Reds kept pace with the Phillies, beating the Cubs, 1–0, in 12 innings. In the bottom of the 12th Mel Queen singled to drive in pinch hitter Marty Keough from second base with the only run in the game. Southpaw Jim O'Toole (14–6) went the distance for the Reds, hurling a seven-hitter.

Bob Buhl had started for the Cubs, being relieved by Lindy McDaniel in the ninth and finally Don Elston (2–4) in the eleventh, who took the loss. The win kept the Reds 5½ games behind the Phillies with 31 games remaining to be played.

St. Louis remained "red hot," winning its eighth game in the last nine tries as they beat the Braves again, 6–2. For the Cards, Bob Gibson tossed a seven-hitter. It was Gibson's third straight complete-game victory and it kept the Cardinals in third place, one percentage point ahead of the Giants.

In another extra-inning affair at Pittsburgh, the Dodgers scored three runs in the top of the 12th to beat the Pirates, 8–5. Derrell Griffith supplied the big blow with a bases-loaded triple in the 12th. Earlier the Dodgers had tied the game at 5–5 in the 9th on a two-out pinch triple by Tommy Davis.

On September 3 the San Francisco Giants were still very much in the 1964 National League pennant race in fourth place, one percentage point behind the third-place St. Louis Cardinals and 7½ games behind the Philadelphia Phillies, with 28 games remaining to be played.

Yet the Giants seemed to be making plans for the 1965 season, rather than the 1964 stretch run. It was announced on September 3 by the Associated Press that the new manager of the Giants was scheduled to be Charley Fox, who was almost completely unknown outside of the organization. Fox was currently managing the Tacoma team in the Pacific Coast League, the top farm club of the Giants.

The AP article went on to say: "The Giants have shrouded the name of the man who will succeed Alvin Dark as manager of the Giants in complete secrecy. The Giants' front office has not officially announced that

Dark is through, and there probably will be no announcement until the Giants have lost all chance at the National League Pennant.

"Owner Horace Stoneham and Dark haven't been friendly for some time. Stoneham reportedly feels that Dark has not consulted him on team matters.

"Rumors have had Dark at Houston, with the New York Mets or at St. Louis next year. 'I don't know where I'll be in 1965,' was Dark's comment."[5]

Regardless of what the future held for Alvin Dark, he was still the San Francisco pilot and the Giants continued to challenge as they knocked off the Mets for the second night in a row, 3–1.

Gaylord Perry (9–9) went the distance for the Giants, pitching a five-hitter while striking out eight. Also Perry drove home two runs with a single in the fourth and a sacrifice fly in the sixth. Jack Fisher (9–16) took the loss for the Mets.

At Connie Mack Stadium with 12,908 fans in the stands, the Colts' Don Larsen (3–6) pitched his second complete game in the last 12 days as he shut out the Phillies, 6–0. It was the first shutout for Larsen in more than five years, as he hurled a four-hitter. Prior to blanking the Phillies on September 3, 1964, Larsen had last pitched a shutout on May 30, 1959, when he was with the New York Yankees.

For Houston it was sweet revenge as the Colts, who had won only four of the 15 games with Philadelphia in the season series, pounded out 16 hits and put the game away in the sixth on a two-run homer by Carroll Hardy. Ten of the Colts' hits came off Phillies starter Dennis Bennett. In all, the Colts scored five runs in the sixth, tying the largest outburst against Philadelphia pitching in the season, a feat previously accomplished by the Pirates (three times) and the Mets and Braves, one time each.

Despite the loss the Phillies didn't lose any ground to second-place Cincinnati, as the Reds were beaten by the Cubs, 3–0, as Lou Burdette (10–7) also tossed a four-hit shutout. For the Cubs, Billy Williams hit a two-run homer off Cincinnati starter John Tsitouris (7–11). The other Chicago run came on rookie Ron Campbell's first Major League hit following a walk and a steal in the second inning. Campbell played a total of 52 big league games in his career with the Chicago Cubs between 1964 and 1966, finishing with a lifetime batting average of .247.

Once again the attendance in Cincinnati was a sparse 5,403 despite the Reds' being in the thick of the pennant race.

In a third shutout in the National League on September 3, Milwaukee's Wade Blasingame hurled a seven-hitter in defeating St. Louis, 7–0, thereby dropping the Cards into fourth place, a full game behind the third-place Giants. Joe Torre broke the game open with a two-run triple in the seventh, then the Braves went on to score six runs in the inning.

Pittsburgh and Los Angeles were not scheduled.

On September 4 the Cincinnati Reds' Frank Robinson was named the National League's Player of the Month for August 1964 in a vote taken by 50 baseball writers and broadcasters. Robinson had swung a potent bat in the dog days of August while keeping the Reds in the pennant race. During the month of August, Robby hit an even .400 with 40 hits in 100 at bats. He hit eight home runs and drove in 24 runs in 27 games as the Reds won 17 and lost 10.

The award was the second for Robinson in his career; he had also been named Player of the Month in July 1961. Over his first nine years in a Cincinnati uniform, Robinson had done it all: National League Rookie of the Year, National League MVP, All-Star, led the league in slugging percentage and runs scored, was closing in on 300 career home runs, and in 1961 had led the Reds to their first pennant in 21 years with a .323 average, 37 home runs and 117 RBIs.

Yet for Reds owner and general manager Bill DeWitt, Sr., Frank Robinson could never accomplish enough. DeWitt let people know that he was the boss. He had limited racial tolerance and also had a personal dislike for what he perceived in Frank Robinson as an uppity, outspoken attitude by a black ballplayer.

When Robinson was arrested in Cincinnati early in the A.M. hours of February 9, 1961, on a concealed weapons charge, it only reinforced DeWitt's strong intolerant feelings. Robinson had been carrying an automatic pistol that he felt was needed for personal protection. Robinson had stopped in a White Castle hamburger joint at the corner of Reading and William Howard Taft Roads on his way home, and that is where the pistol was allegedly seen and reported to the Cincinnati Police.

Robinson said that he felt unsafe late at night in the parking lot of his apartment building in Avondale, a predominately black section of Cincinnati, because it was dark and he had to walk about 50 yards from his car to his apartment. He usually carried a lot of cash and felt the need for a gun to protect himself.

When the news of Robinson's arrest made page one news in Cincinnati, general manager Bill DeWitt acted both perturbed and pious about the predicament he found his star player in, and he refused to pay Robinson's $1,000 bail.

Following the 1965 season in which Robinson hit .296 with 33 home runs and 113 RBIs, a dispute developed between DeWitt and Robinson over the star's $60,000 a year salary, and without hesitation he was suddenly traded to the Baltimore Orioles for pitchers Milt Pappas, Jack Baldshun and outfielder Dick Simpson, in what is considered one of the worst baseball trades of all time. DeWitt rationalized the trade by calling Robinson "an old 30."

Old, indeed! In 1966, Frank Robinson's first year in a Baltimore Oriole uniform, he won the Triple Crown, leading the American League with a .316 batting average, 49 home runs and 122 RBIs, while leading the Orioles to the American League Pennant and a four-game sweep over the Los Angeles Dodgers in the World Series. Frank Robinson was also named the 1966 American League MVP, thereby becoming the only player to win the award in both the American and National Leagues.

For some time during his career Robinson had also been managing teams in the winter leagues, mostly in Puerto Rico. Gregg Scott, profiling Robinson's career in the booklet "Great Rookies," said of Robinson's managerial aspirations: "He was thinking about the future and he was learning how to transfer his skills and knowledge to another side of the game. He was also aware that there had never been a black manager in Major League Baseball. But if called, he wanted to be ready."[6]

Later he became the first Afro-American to manage a Major League team, taking over the helm of the Cleveland Indians as player-manager in 1975.

Robinson finished his 21-year big league career as a player in 1976, finishing with a lifetime batting average of .294 with 2,943 hits and 586 home runs. His career home run total of 586 is fourth on the all-time list.

In 1982 Robinson was voted in as a member of the National Baseball Hall of Fame in Cooperstown, New York. After he hung up his spikes, Robinson continued to manage in the big leagues, moving from the Cleveland job to managerial posts in San Francisco and Baltimore.

Meanwhile in St. Louis, the reports on Stan Musial, who was recuperating from a severe virus attack, were positive and "Stan the Man" was expected to resume his duties both as the nation's physical fitness director and as a Cardinal executive soon.

"I think I'll be here another day or two," said Musial from his bed in Jewish Hospital in St. Louis. "Of course, I'll have to take it easy. But the baseball season's almost over and I haven't many speaking engagements left."[7]

On Friday, September 4, the Giants went into pennant-crazed Philadelphia for a crucial five-game series. The advanced ticket sales for the big series indicated that there would be turnaway crowds at Connie Mack Stadium.

In the first game of the series the Phillies beat the Giants, 5–3, with manager Gene Mauch using a rather unorthodox strategy. Mauch dropped slugging right fielder Johnny Callison to seventh in the Phillies' batting order. The Giants were starting a rookie left-hander by the name of Dick Estelle and Mauch reasoned that Estelle would be shell-shocked by all the right-handed hitters in the lineup and that Callison would feel less pressure in the lower part of the batting order.

Well, the move paid off, as Callison delivered a key bloop single in the eighth that scored Gus Triandos with what proved to be the winning run. However, Dick Estelle was not the victim of Callison's hit, but rather veteran left-hander Billy O'Dell, who had replaced Estelle in the eighth.

Giants manager Alvin Dark replaced Estelle after he pinch hit for him in the seventh and it was expected that O'Dell could protect a two-run Giant lead. "That was the best man I had," said Dark. "If he can't hold it, we've got to lose it."[8]

In the fourth the Philadelphia crowd was treated to some classic Willie Mays fielding as he robbed Ruben Amaro of an extra-base hit, racing at top speed to deep right-center, while leaping against the scoreboard, bouncing off it and holding on to the ball.

In the sixth veteran Frank Thomas followed a lead-off single by Richie Allen by lining the first pitch to deep left. The ball hit the front of the roof and bounced back on the field for Thomas' ninth homer of the season and his sixth as a Phillie in less than a month.

The win increased the Phillies lead to 7½ games over the Giants and Cardinals.

Meanwhile at Cincinnati, the second-place Reds got shut out for the second game in a row as they were beaten by Milwaukee, 2–0. Tony Cloninger (15–12) tossed a three-hit shutout against the Reds, thereby moving the Phillies ahead by 6½ games. All the Braves' runs were provided by a two-run homer by Eddie Mathews. For the Reds, Joey Jay (9–10) took the loss.

Prior to the game the Braves brought up right-hander Jay Hook from Denver of the Pacific Coast League. Hook had been acquired on May 8 from the New York Mets and had a 5–4 record at Denver, where he was being used both as a starter and reliever.

Third-place St. Louis remained hot, defeating Chicago, 8–5, on Ken Boyer's three-run homer in the ninth.

Elsewhere in the National League on September 4, Pittsburgh defeated Houston, 10–2, and the Mets and Dodgers split a doubleheader in front of 45,065 fans at Shea Stadium. The Dodgers took the first game, 3–0, behind a three-hit shutout hurled by Don Drysdale (16–13). The Mets took the nightcap, 6–5.

Prior to the game the Dodgers had recalled Pete Richert from Spokane of the Pacific Coast League, where he had a 7–8 record with a 3.52 ERA, pitching five complete games in 24 starts.

On Saturday night, September 5 the Phillies toppled the Giants, 9–3, as Giants manager Alvin Dark's attempt to play head games with the Phillies failed miserably.

Prior to the game Dark had left-hander Bob Hendley warming up in front of the San Francisco dugout, and he was announced as the Giants' starting pitcher by PA announcer Pete Byron. Meanwhile, right-hander Bob Bolin was warming up in the Giants' bullpen. However, when Dark delivered his lineup card to home plate umpire Mel Steiner prior to the game he had right-hander Bob Bolin listed as the starting pitcher rather than Hendley.

The Phillies had listed three players in their lineup who would not ordinarily start against a right-hander—Cookie Rojas, Alex Johnson and Gus Triandos. Now if Dark's strategy was to stick Phillie manager Gene Mauch with a heavily laden right-handed-hitting lineup, it didn't work.

In the first inning right-handed-hitting Frank Thomas hit a two-run homer off Bolin that capped a four-run surge. Then in the fifth inning right-handed-hitting Gus Triandos hit a grand slam home run, capping off a five-run Phillies outburst.

Following the game, Phillies manager Gene Mauch downplayed Dark's subterfuge strategy. "You're not trying to outsmart anybody when you're managing," said Mauch, blinking his eyes innocently. "You're just trying to do what's best for your club. I'll bet you Dark says he didn't pitch Hendley because something happened to him warming up, not because he was trying to fool anybody."[9]

Jim Bunning, the Phillies' starting pitcher, won his 16th game of the season against only four defeats. For Bunning it was his seventh victory in a row.

With 31,482 fans on hand for the Saturday evening game, the Phillies' season attendance had soared to 1,176,234, second-best in the club's history. Furthermore, before the current home stand would end the following Thursday, it was expected that the 1950 record for home attendance would be broken.

Prior to the game the Phillies had announced that they had released Bob Oldis as a coach and signed him as a catcher for the remainder of the season.

Then on Sunday, September 6, San Francisco rebounded and beat Philadelphia, 4–3. Juan Marichal started for the Giants and struck out 13. The Giants scored what proved to be the winning run in the eighth when

Willie Mays walked and then scored following two wild throws by reliever Jack Baldshun.

The Cincinnati Reds on Saturday, September 5, beat the Milwaukee Braves, 5–1, and then whipped them again, 6–3, on Sunday, September 6.

As for the Cardinals, they were beaten by the Cubs, 8–5, on Saturday, September 5, as Larry Jackson (18–10) won his 18th victory of the season with a little relief help from Lindy McDaniel. Ernie Banks (19) had the big stick for Chicago, belting a home run that ignited an eight-run outburst by the Cubs in the second inning, that drove Cardinal starter Mike Cuellar to the showers early. Later in the same inning Banks doubled home two more runs.

On Sunday, September 6, the Cardinals outlasted the Cubs, 5–4, in 11 innings. In the bottom of the 11th a bad-hop single by Lou Brock with two out scored Tim McCarver with the winning run. McCarver had opened the 11th with a single and moved to third on a sacrifice and an infield out before Brock's hit bounced over Chicago shortstop Andre Rodgers' head.

So the 1964 National League pennant race arrived at Labor Day with the Phillies enjoying a 5½ game lead over the second-place Reds and a 7½ game lead over both the Cardinals and Giants. The four front-running teams had the following games remaining on the schedule.

Phillies: at home (12) Los Angeles 3; St. Louis 2; Cincinnati 3; Milwaukee 4.
on the road (15) San Francisco 3; Houston 3; Los Angeles 4; St. Louis 3; Cincinnati 2.

Reds: at home (8) St. Louis 3; Pittsburgh 3; Phillies 2.
on the road (18) St. Louis 2; Pittsburgh 2; Milwaukee 3; Chicago 3; Philadelphia 3; New York 5.

Giants: at home (16) Los Angeles 2; Philadelphia 3; New York 2; Pittsburgh 3; Houston 3; Chicago 3.
on the road (8) Pittsburgh 2; Houston 3; Chicago 3.

Cardinals: at home (8) Cincinnati 2; Philadelphia 3; New York 3.
on the road (18) Philadelphia 2; Chicago 3; Milwaukee 3; Cincinnati 3; New York 2; Pittsburgh 5.

The four front-running teams all played doubleheaders on Labor Day, Monday, September 7, 1964.

At Connie Mack Stadium the Phillies hosted the Dodgers and split a twin bill, the Phillies winning the opener, 5–1, and the Dodgers taking the nightcap, 3–1.

In the opener Philadelphia's Dennis Bennett snapped a seven-game losing streak, defeating L.A. with his 10th win of the season. It was the left-hander's first complete game pitched since May 19.

In the second game the Dodgers' Pete Richert, who had just been called up from Spokane of the Pacific Coast League, won his first game of the year. Nonetheless, the Phillies were encouraged by the fact veteran lefty Bobby Shantz, purchased from the Cubs on August 15, pitched seven strong innings in relief, allowing just three singles. One of the hits came in the first inning after he had replaced 18-year-old rookie starter Rick Wise, who had control problems.

With a crowd of 26,390 on hand at Connie Mack Stadium for the Labor Day twin bill, the Philadelphia Phillies' home attendance for the 1964 season soared to 1,224,172 and thereby shattered their previous all-time season home attendance record of 1,217,025 set in the 1950 pennant-winning season.

On the downside of things for the high-flying Phillies, it was revealed that catcher Clay Dalrymple had hurt his knee worse than anybody had believed while running the bases the previous week in the seventh inning of last Thursday's game with Houston. Dalrymple had been on first base when Colts second baseman Bob Lillis made a great catch of a looper hit by Frank Thomas, forcing Clay to get back to the bag in a hurry.

Dalrymple, remarking on his playing status, said, "I can catch if I'm needed. But it [the knee] won't be right all year. I jammed the knee getting back. I don't know whether it's a torn ligament or a bad pull. All I know is it hurts."[10]

St. Louis moved into Cincinnati for a holiday twin bill and swept the Reds by duplicate scores, 3–2 and 3–2. The Cardinals scored the winning margin in both games on singles in the ninth inning. In the first game a single by Tim McCarver in the ninth drove across the deciding run, and in the second game it was Curt Flood who singled home the deciding run.

San Francisco meanwhile played its Labor Day doubleheader at Pittsburgh and won both ends, 6–4 and 9–6. Willie Mays hit his 40th home run of the season in the opening game and then connected for his 41st in the nightcap, a three-run pinch-hit homer.

The results of the Labor Day action set up a virtual three-way tie for second place between the Reds, Cardinals and Giants, with the three deadlocked teams trailing the front-running Phillies by 6½ games.

National League Standings, September 8, 1964

Team	Won	Lost	Pct.	G.B.
Philadelphia	83	54	.606	—

Team	Won	Lost	Pct.	G.B.
Cincinnati	77	61	.558	6½
St. Louis	77	61	.558	6½
San Francisco	78	62	.557	6½
Pittsburgh	70	67	.511	13
Milwaukee	70	68	.507	13½
Los Angeles	68	69	.496	15
Chicago	62	76	.449	21½
Houston	58	82	.414	26½
New York	48	91	.345	36

On September 8, the New York Mets announced that they had signed 18-year-old right-hander Bill Denehy. The 6'3", 205-pound Denehy had just graduated in June from Woodrow Wilson High School in Middletown, Connecticut.

After he posted a 10–1 record in his senior year, striking out 151 batters in 81 innings, while leading his team to the Connecticut State championship by winning three games in the tournament, Denehy was sought by just about every Major League team.

However, Bill Denehy never established himself as a Major League pitcher. After playing in the minors for a couple of years he joined the Mets in 1967 and posted a 1–7 record, pitching in 15 games with an ERA of 4.70.

Nonetheless, Bill Denehy has a place in baseball folklore as on November 27, 1967, he was traded by the Mets along with a $100,000 cash payment to the Washington Senators. In exchange for Denehy, the Mets received the rights to Gil Hodges. Hodges, of course, then became the legendary manager of the 1969 World Champion "Miracle" or if you prefer "Amazing" Mets.

Bill Denehy continued to bounce back and forth between the minors and majors through 1971, when he finished his big league carrier with the Detroit Tigers, having pitched in a total of 49 big league games with a career record of 1–10 and ERA of 4.56.

The only game scheduled in the National League on Tuesday, September 8, saw Philadelphia hosting Los Angeles in an afternoon game. It was a make-up game between the two teams and played in the afternoon to allow the Dodgers more time to fly home.

Art Mahaffey (12–6), who had a 1–9 lifetime record against Dodgers, and Jim Brewer, a 26-year-old left-hander who in 20 starts had never completed a Major League game, were scheduled to be the starting pitchers.

Dodgers manager Walter Alston had elevated Brewer to a starting role to fill the void in his rotation left by the injuries to Sandy Koufax and

Joe Moeller. Subsequently Brewer, with relief help from Ron Perranoski, won his 5th big-league game and his first as a starter since beating Pittsburgh on August 27, 1961, as the Dodgers downed the Phillies, 3–2.

Los Angeles scored all three of their runs in the first inning that saw Maury Wills lead off against Mahaffey with a single, then race to second base with his 46th stolen base of the season. He then scored when Jim Gilliam doubled. Willie Davis followed with a single sending Gilliam to third, then John Roseboro doubled, scoring the two runners. For the Phillies, it was the second game in a row in which their starting pitcher could not get through the first inning.

In the fourth inning, shabby baserunning by the Phillies cost them opportunities to score. Allen led off with a triple off the scoreboard, then broke for home when Frank Thomas hit a chopper back to the mound. Allen apparently thought that the ball was going to bounce over Brewer's head. It didn't, though, Brewer fielded the ball and Allen was caught in a rundown between third and home.

On the play Thomas had reached second base before Allen was tagged out. Moments later Alex Johnson hit a grounder towards Maury Wills at shortstop; Thomas had broken from second and was tagged out by Wills as he attempted to slide back into second. Wills then threw to first to complete the double play on Johnson.

In the sixth the Phillies faltered on the base paths again. With one out Johnny Callison tripled off the right-field wall. With the Dodgers' infield pulled back, Richie Allen then hit a grounder to Wills at shortstop. However Callison hesitated before breaking from third for home. When Wills fielded Allen's grounder, he noticed that Callison was only halfway down the baseline and easily threw him out at the plate.

Following the game Maury Wills, who now had a lifetime batting average of .332 at Connie Mack Stadium, made the following comments about the Phillies and their baserunning: "The Phillies have been hustling all season. They've been playing good ball, forcing the opposition into mistakes with aggressiveness. They can't stop now. They can't get scared and start playing safety-first baseball.

"Look at the rundown," said Wills, referring to the play on which Allen was tagged. "We could have hit him in the back. And I could have booted the ball with Callison on third, too. I have admiration for that ball club [Phillies]. I'd like to see them win the pennant. They deserve it."[11]

The loss left the Phillies six games out in front of the Reds, Giants and Cardinals. However, the loss was more costly to the Phillies than just in the won-lost column, as they lost the services of Frank Thomas, who broke his right thumb in the game. A spokesman for the Phillies said a small cast had been placed over Thomas' right thumb, which will enable him to pinch hit and possibly see some limited action.[12]

Suddenly the Phillies, who with the exception of the injury to Danny Cater had been relatively injury-free all season, were losing starting players, with Thomas and Clay Dalrymple out of action.

On September 9, the St. Louis Cardinals arrived at Connie Mack Stadium for a two-game set with the Phillies.

Since the June 15 trade that sent Lou Brock from the Cubs to the Cardinals, it seemed as if Brock had suddenly became a different ballplayer. Coming into Philadelphia Brock was hitting .304, 40 points higher than he had ever hit in the majors before. In addition Brock had suddenly become a stolen base threat anytime he reached base and was in fact second only to Maury Wills in stolen bases in the National League.

In the first of the two games the Cardinals beat the Phillies, 10–5, in 11 innings as Bill White's two-run double in broke a tie in the top of the 11th. In the game Lou Brock had a home run and four singles, the last in the five-run 11th inning. Curt Flood led off the 11th with a single, then Brock followed with one and they both were driven in by White's ties breaking double.

For the Cardinals it was their 13th win in the last 16 games. The win shaved a full game off the Phillies' lead to five and gave the cards sole possession of second place.

To fill the void left by the loss of Frank Thomas, the Phillies purchased veteran first baseman Vic Power from the Los Angeles Angels for the $20,000 waiver price, along with a player to be named on or before October 4. At the time of the acquisition Power was hitting .247 for the Angels.

Cincinnati opened a series in Pittsburgh and remained six games behind in a third-place tie after being beaten by the Pirates, 4–1. San Francisco also remained six games behind, tied with Reds, after being beaten by the Dodgers, 8–1.

In the Pirates' victory over the Reds, Bob Veale won his 10th game of the season and became the first Pittsburgh pitcher in the history of the franchise to reach the 200-strikeout level for a season. All four Pirate runs came off Cincinnati starter Joey Jay in the 4th inning.

In the San Francisco game, the Dodgers rather than the Giants put on a power display as Willie Davis connected for a grand slam and then another homer with the bases empty, while Frank Howard also hit a three-run homer.

The following day on Thursday, September 10, the Phillies and Cardinals played a make-up game of a rained-out date on May 13. The Phillies once again expanded their lead to six games as Chris Short beat the Cardinals, 5–1, while striking out 12 and walking only one. Short also helped his own cause with two hits, including a key triple and a single.

Short came to the plate in the second inning with runners on first and third with one out. He promptly smashed a triple into the right-field bullpen, scoring Tony Taylor and Ruben Amaro with the first two Philadelphia runs in a five-run inning. Short won his 16th game of the season, tying him with Jim Bunning for the club lead in victories.

The victory was important to the Phillies, in that if they had lost the Cardinals would have moved to within four games of the lead, as they now prepared to head out to the West Coast for an important three-game series with the Giants. Since August 15, no team had been within four games of the Phillies.

Meanwhile, among the other top contenders, Cincinnati shut out the Pirates, 3–0, and San Francisco bested the Dodgers, 5–1, to permit both teams to remain in a three-way tie for second with the Cardinals, six games off the mark.

With the end of the season nearing, on September 10 Baseball Commissioner Ford Frick met with the front-running clubs in both the National (Phillies, Cardinals, Reds, Giants) and American (White Sox, Yankees, Orioles) Leagues and announced that there would be no travel day if only Eastern or only Midwestern teams are playing in the World Series. It was Frick's opinion that the travel day had only been added as a convenience for television to assure that the network got a Sunday televised game.

Therefore, if the World Series were between the Philadelphia Phillies and the Baltimore Orioles or New York Yankees, the Series would start on Wednesday, October 7, in the Phillies' ball park for two games and then move immediately to the American League park for the next three games.

If the Series were between the Chicago White Sox and the Cincinnati Reds or St. Louis Cardinals, there also would be no travel day.

Therefore, if one of these teams would sweep the Series in four games, there would be no Sunday game.

The following rules were also fixed for the Series:

"The 1964 World Series will open October 7 in the National League park, with three games to follow in the American League park, then if needed the final two in the National League park. Ticket prices will be $12 per game for box seats, $8 for reserved, $4 for unreserved and $2 for bleachers and standing room, in all cases tax included. All games will start at 1 p.m. local time."

There would only be a travel day if the conditions listed above did not apply. If playoffs were needed or a round robin series in the American League to determine the winner of either league, then the Series would start on October 12.

Frick concluded the meeting by authorizing the Phillies, Yankees, White Sox and Orioles to print tickets, which is an expensive process. Subsequently the Commissioner's office is responsible for the cost of all tickets printed by clubs that don't make the Series. In the 1963 season that cost was between $35,000 and $40,000.

On Friday, September 11, the Phillies opened their three-game series at San Francisco with a 1–0 victory as Dennis Bennett (11–12) shut out the Giants, yielding only six hits. It was second victory in a row for Bennett following a seven-game losing streak.

Bennett's performance was reassuring to Phillies manager Gene Mauch. With Art Mahaffey continuing to struggle, Mauch now seemed to have three strong starters in Bennett, Bunning and Short for the stretch run. While critics might call Dennis Bennett's 1964 performance to date mediocre, it had to be considered that Bennett wasn't even supposed to pitch again following an automobile accident that had shattered his left leg 18 months previously.

The loss dropped the Giants into a third-place tie, seven games behind the Phillies.

At Milwaukee a pitchers' duel ensued between Denny Lemaster and Jim Maloney. The Braves triumphed over the Reds, 1–0, with Lemaster (14–11) pitching a one-hitter and Maloney (13–10) pitching a two-hitter in a losing effort. Both Lemaster and Maloney had no-hitters going through the first five innings. Then Leo Cardenas led off the Reds' sixth with a hit. Maloney carried his no-hitter into the seventh when Joe Torre singled. The loss dropped the Reds seven games behind the Phillies.

Meanwhile, the controversy of whether or not the Braves would remain in Milwaukee continued. Braves officials were saying that no clear-cut decision could be made on the matter until the season was concluded. In 1963 the Braves had a season attendance mark of 773,018. Following the 1963 season the Braves launched an intensive ticket drive with massive support from Milwaukee officials and civic leaders. The results were that so far in the 1964 season, with 15 home dates remaining, the Braves had drawn 829,720 fans through the turnstiles and would only need to average 11,352 fans per game for the remainder of the home schedule to top the one million mark in attendance for the 1964 season.

To sweeten the pot in an attempt to prevent the Braves from leaving town, Robert A. Ulhlein, Jr., president of the Schlitz Brewing Company, said that his company "is willing to boost the TV-Radio guarantee to the

Braves by $375,000 for the three-year period in order to underscore our most strong and sincere desire to keep the team in Milwaukee."[13]

In 1964 the Braves had received $400,000 from Schlitz for the television-radio package. Therefore, the Braves were looking at a TV-radio package from Schlitz that would bring them $2,325,000 in revenue over the next three years.

However, it was becoming apparent to all concerned that the Braves' management was through milking Milwaukee for all it could get. It was no longer a question of if they were moving to Atlanta, but when.

At Chicago on September 11, the Cardinals' Bob Gibson (15–10) allowed only two hits as St. Louis beat the Cubs, 5–0, to remain six games behind the Phillies. Gibson had given up a lead-off single to Jimmy Stewart, then didn't give up another hit until the seventh. In the first inning Ken Boyer (22) had a two-run homer, staking Gibson to an early lead.

On Saturday, September 12, the San Francisco Giants turned on their awesome power and pounded the league-leading Philadelphia Phillies, 9–1. Orlando Cepeda (29 & 30) led the Giants' power surge by blasting two home runs, including a grand slam. Jim Ray Hart (28) also added a two-run shot. Phillies starter Art Mahaffey (12–8) got off to a shaky start, walking three, and it was Hart's homer in the first with Willie Mays on base that put the Giants out ahead to stay.

Cepeda's 380-foot grand slam over the right-center-field fence came in the third off Phillies reliever John Boozer and came with two outs after Boozer had hit two batters and walked another. Later Cepeda hit a two-run homer following a walk to Jose Cardenal.

For the Giants, starter Gaylord Perry (11–9) went all the way.

The Phillies, however, lost no ground in their league lead as the Cardinals lost to the Chicago Cubs, 3–2. In the first inning the Cardinals jumped out to 2–0 lead when Curt Flood singled and Lou Brock followed with his 11th home run of year into the catwalk in right field. However, in the sixth Billy Williams singled to open the inning off the Cards' Roger Craig. Ron Santo then flied out and Ernie Banks followed with his 20th home run of the season. Later the Cubs scored again to give Bob Buhl his 13th win, snapping a six-game losing streak for the Cubs' right-hander.

Likewise, Cincinnati failed to gain any ground as they were mauled by Milwaukee, 8–2. Hank Fischer (11–9) pitched a six-hitter for the Braves while tying the National League season high of six straight victories. Fischer, after giving up a run to the Reds in the first on a single by Vada Pinson following a walk, sacrifice and wild pitch, settled down to go all the way.

For the Braves, Dennis Menke hit an inside-the-park homer in the second inning when Deron Johnson, playing in left field for the Reds, failed to make a shoestring catch, allowing the ball to bounce off the wall. Later Gene Oliver drove in three runs for the Braves with his 20th home run of the season. Rico Carty also contributed two RBIs with a triple in the sixth and a single in the seventh.

As pennant fever tightened its hold on the city of Philadelphia, Eileen Foley, a *Philadelphia Bulletin* writer, talked with Nina Lee Mauch, the brunette wife of Phillies manager Gene Mauch, about the gathering hysteria surrounding the Phillies. Nina Lee confided, "He [Gene Mauch] never mentions the pennant. He only talks about today's ball game, and winning that."[14]

Nina Lee had recently returned to their California home with the Mauch's daughter, and in regards to plans for the World Series scheduled to open on October 7, she had the following to say:

"Gene didn't buy us round-trip tickets. We hate to leave Gene at any time and especially now. But as it is, we're cutting the time close, to get Leanne into ninth grade on Monday. Neither one of them expresses much excitement. Oh, Gene gets mad on the ball field sometimes, but he's very even-tempered at home. The only way I can tell if the team has lost is that he's quieter than usual.

"Of course, we're not superstitious [as she knocked on wood]. But wouldn't it be terrific if we did win the pennant."[15]

On Sunday, September 13, Philadelphia maintained its six-game lead by defeating San Francisco, 4–1, in ten innings. In the top of the tenth Johnny Callison stroked a run-producing single that broke a 1–1 deadlock, then Richie Allen followed with his 26th home run of the season. Jim Bunning (17–4) went the distance for the Phillies, scattering seven hits to get the win.

At Wrigley Field in Chicago the Cardinals ripped the Cubs, 15–2. In the game the Cards scored at least one run in all nine innings, thus becoming only the second team in modern Major League history to accomplish the feat.

Lt. Grover Edward McCarver, 53, father of Cardinals catcher Tim McCarver, had just retired from the Memphis Police Department and prior to beginning his own private detective agency was planning a vacation to St. Louis to watch the Cardinals and son Tim play ball down the stretch.

"After I'm in business for myself, I'll be able to take off and go to a ball game when I feel like it," said the elder McCarver.[16]

At Milwaukee, Warren Spahn returned to his spot in the starting rotation and was chased from the mound by Cincinnati in the third inning, as the Reds defeated the Braves, 6–2. The loss halted Milwaukee's six-game winning streak.

Also, at Los Angeles, Don Drysdale (18–13) won his 18th game of the year. The Dodgers defeated the Mets, 5–4, when Ed Kranepool committed a bases-loaded error in the ninth, allowing Jim Gilliam to scamper across the plate with the winning run.

Dennis Ribant (1–4) took the loss for the Mets. For the Dodgers, Frank Howard hit his 23rd home run of the season and for the Mets, Charley Smith hit his 18th.

On Monday, September 14, the Phillies increased their league lead to 6½ games as they defeated the Houston Colts, 4–1. Chris Short (17–7) threw a four-hitter against Houston and Johnny Callison had a big night, stroking three hits, including his 27th home run, a double and single, while driving in two runs and scoring two.

Short, who once again was tied with Jim Bunning for the club lead in games won, lost his bid for a shutout in the eighth when Houston's Bob Lillis doubled and came around to score on two infield outs. However, for Chris Short his 17th win on September 14 would be a harbinger of things to come for the Phillies, as this win would be the last one for him in the 1964 season.

In the only other game scheduled in the National League on September 14, the Pittsburgh Pirates defeated the Los Angeles Dodgers, 7–2.

National League Standings, September 15, 1964

Team	Won	Lost	Pct.	G.B.
Philadelphia	87	57	.604	—
St. Louis	80	63	.559	6½
Cincinnati	79	64	.552	7½
San Francisco	80	65	.552	7½
Milwaukee	74	69	.517	12½
Pittsburgh	74	69	.517	12½
Los Angeles	72	72	.500	15
Chicago	65	78	.455	21½
Houston	59	87	.404	29
New York	49	95	.340	38

Although the New York Mets on September 15 found themselves 38 games behind the Phillies, they still were a huge draw when playing at home in Shea Stadium. For 43 home dates the Mets had attracted 1,136,269 fans through the Shea turnstiles. However, on the road the Mets had drawn only 560,481 fans.

Meanwhile, the Philadelphia Phillies with a 6½ game lead announced that they would begin to accept World Series ticket applications beginning at 12:01 A.M. on September 23. Connie Mack Stadium had a seating capacity of 34,000. Therefore, the Phillies' management limited the sale of tickets to sets of two each.

The general feeling by the Phillies in limiting the number of seats that a fan could buy was that it would enable more fans to see at least one game and possibly two if the World Series happened to go six or seven games.

Cost of the tickets was announced as, for one set: $25.00 for box seats, $17.00 for reserved seats and $9.00 for bleacher seats. For two sets, the discounted cost was accordingly $49.00 box, $33.00 reserved and $17.00 for bleachers.

On September 15 the Phillies' Dennis Bennett (12–12) and Jack Baldshun teamed up to blank the Colts, 1–0. For Houston, Ken Johnson (10–16) was the loser, going five innings then being relieved by Hal Woodechick and Jim Owens. Once again Johnny Callison was the batting star for the Phillies, driving in Richie Allen from second with the only run of the game with a hit in the sixth inning.

However, Philadelphia's lead was cut by one-half game as the St. Louis Cardinals swept a twi-night doubleheader from Milwaukee, 11–6 and 3–1. Nonetheless, Philadelphia now had a six-game lead over second-place St. Louis with just 17 games left on the schedule to play.

At Chicago in a day game Larry Jackson became the 1964 season's first 20-game winner as he pitched the Cubs to a 6–1 victory over the Cincinnati Reds. The loss dropped the Reds into fourth place, 8½ games behind the Phillies.

At Candlestick Park the Giants defeated the Mets, 3–1, behind the four-hit pitching of Juan Marichal (18–7) to take sole possession of third place. Tom Haller (10) homered for the Giants in the game to keep them in contention for the first- or second-place money, 7½ games behind. For the Mets, Galen Cisco (5–17) took the loss.

In Los Angeles on September 15 the Dodgers had beaten the Pirates, 5–3, and there was speculation that Dodger ace Sandy Koufax might be able to pitch again soon. The Associated Press was reporting that Koufax (19–5) with an ERA of 1.74 might be able to pitch for the Dodgers on their next road trip. Koufax had worked out at Dodger Stadium the previous night and said later he was very pleased. He said he felt a slight stiffness in his shoulder but expected that.

Dr. Robert Kerlan said that Koufax definitely would be able to go on the road with the Dodgers next week and might get a start during the trip. However, it was all a Dodger pipe dream; Koufax would not make another start in the 1964 season.

On Wednesday, September 16, Houston defeated Philadelphia, 6–5. All six Colt runs were given up by Phillies ace Jim Bunning (17–5), who lasted just 4⅓ innings. Hal Brown (3–15), an American League cast-off, got the win in relief for Houston.

Phillies manager Gene Mauch took the loss at Houston particularly hard: "I don't expect those people to score on us. Get 11 runs [combined] in a game and the Phillies are supposed to win. How do we let those blankety blanks beat us?"[17]

When Mauch was suddenly interrupted by a reporter, reminding him that the Phillies had won the season series with Houston, 13–5, he replied testily. "Thirteen to five," repeats Mauch, spitting out the numbers. "That doesn't sound bad—until you say 14–4."[18]

The Phillies' lead over second-place St. Louis remained at six games as the Cardinals lost, 3–2, at Milwaukee. However, it was only the 7th defeat for St. Louis in the last 23 games.

For the Braves left-hander Denny Lemaster picked up his 15th win with relief help from Bob Tiefenauer. In the second inning Dennis Menke hit a three-run homer, his 18th of the year off Ron Taylor. Taylor, ordinarily a reliever, was making his second start of the season for the Cards after being pressed into service due to manager Johnny Kean's lining up his rotation for the crucial three-game series that was coming up on the weekend, with the Reds at Cincinnati. In the Cincinnati series, Keane intended to throw his big three, Simmons, Gibson and Sadecki, at the Reds.

Following the defeat at Milwaukee, Johnny Kean was unrelenting in his pursuit of the league-leading Philadelphia Phillies as he spoke to the Associated Press.

"We're not shooting for anything but first," said Keane. "Sure every loss hurts, especially with Philadelphia continuing to win, but we're in this thing right down to the end. Our chances? Just look at the standings. We know the Phillies have to lose."[19]

At the same time that Kean was rallying his Cardinals in the stretch run, rumors were beginning to circulate with the press, and would be published in such papers as the *Philadelphia Inquirer* in early October, that St. Louis Cardinals president August A. Bush, Jr., had offered Dodger coach Leo Durocher the Cards' manager job if Johnny Kean failed to deliver the 1964 pennant.

In Chicago the third-place Reds defeated the Cubs, 5–3, to remain 7½ games behind the Phillies and just 1½ games behind the Cardinals.

Rounding out the action on September 16 of the top four competing teams for the pennant, the Giants were shut out by the Mets, 4–0. Tracy

Stallard (10–18) held the Giants to just five hits while he struck out 10 in posting his 10th victory of the season. Gaylord Perry (11–10) took the loss for San Francisco.

However, in the game the Mets' Charlie Smith was hit in the back of the neck with the ball as he beat out an infield hit. As Smith reached the first base bag he was plunked in the neck by a throw to the base by pitcher Gaylord Perry. Subsequently, Smith was carried from the field on a stretcher and taken to a local hospital for X-rays, which showed no serious injury.

On Thursday, September 17, there were only two games scheduled in the National League. In a day game at Wrigley Field, the Cincinnati Reds refused to be counted out in the pennant race as they defeated the Cubs, 7–5.

Out on the West Coast in a night game at Dodger Stadium before 21,175 fans, Philadelphia defeated Los Angeles, 4–3, scoring the winning tally in the top of the ninth. Bobby Shantz (2–4) got his first win for Philadelphia, coming in to relieve Rick Wise with one out in the first inning. Shantz then went on to pitch 7⅔ innings, allowing just one run and three hits, until being replaced for pinch hitter John Briggs in the 9th. For Shantz it was the longest he had pitched in a game since April 1962.

Don Drysdale (18–14) took the loss for the Dodgers. However, all four Philadelphia runs scored off him were unearned. Drysdale used to have the Phillies' number when he pitched against them, having won 13 games in a row versus the Phillies between 1958 and June 1, 1962. However, since then he had now lost seven games in a row to the Phillies.

The win reduced the Phillies' magic number to 10 with 15 games remaining on the schedule. Therefore, in order for the Phillies to win their first National League title since 1959, from that point on any combination of wins by the Phillies and losses by the Cardinals that totaled ten would do the trick.

Also, the loss by the 1963 World Champion Dodgers dropped them 16 games behind the Phillies and mathematically eliminated them from the 1964 pennant race.

Prior to the game Philadelphia left-hander Dennis Bennett threw along the sidelines. Bennnett, who had won his last three games, giving up only one run in the last 24 innings that he pitched, had suddenly developed a sore shoulder. Gene Mauch had tentatively scheduled Bennett to pitch the Saturday night game against Los Angeles.

"I'm going to try," Bennett insisted, but judging from the way the shoulder felt during the pregame workout Thursday night, the chances seemed slim. Feeling a sharp pain in his shoulder when he threw, Bennett said: "It makes it so you want to hold back because you know it's going to hurt."[20]

At Los Angeles on Friday, September 18, with two outs in the bottom of the ninth inning, Dodger rookie Bart Shirley lined a single to center to drive home the winning run as L.A. defeated the Phillies, 4–3.

With the score tied, 3–3, Tommy Davis led off the bottom of the ninth with a walk off reliever Jack Baldschun. Baldshun then struck Frank Howard, who in the seventh had hit his 24th home run of the season off starter Chris Short. Baldshun then got John Roseboro to pop up for the second out. Ron Fairly then came to bat and with the count 3–1, Davis took off for second base. The throw from catcher Clay Dalrymple seemed to be in time and second base umpire Chris Pelekoudas even called Davis out. However, shortstop Ruben Amaro could not hold onto the ball and he let it roll behind him, allowing Davis to be safe at second. With the count now 3–2, Baldshun walked Fairly on the next pitch. That brought Bart Shirley to the plate, and he lined a clean single to center, scoring Davis with the winning run.

For Shirley, his game-winning hit would be one of just 33 hits that he would get in his four-year Major League career between 1964 and 1968, playing parts of seasons with the Dodgers, Mets and Dodgers again.

Prior to the game the Phillies had called left-hander Morrie Stevens up from San Diego. Stevens had been scheduled to start the fourth game of the Pacific Coast League playoffs at Arkansas, but instead found himself at Dodger Stadium.

With 14 games to go in the season, the Phillies still enjoyed a six-game lead as the Cardinals saw a 4–0 lead over the Reds go down the drain when their game at Cincinnati was called due to rain after four innings played. Also the Giants remained in fourth place, eight games behind after they had lost to Pittsburgh, 4–3.

Back in Philadelphia on Saturday, September 19, news was breaking in the *Philadelphia Inquirer* that Mayor James H. J. Tate and the City Council had proposed a $25-million loan to build a new stadium in South Philly. The issue was now going to the voters on the November ballot and if approved the stadium could be operational for Phillies baseball games beginning in the 1967 season.

Meanwhile, back on the West Coast Saturday night, the Phillies again lost to the Dodgers in the ninth inning. However, on Sunday they defeated the Dodgers, 3–2, behind the pitching of Jim Bunning (18–5), who won his 18th game of the season.

Once again the Dodgers had placed the potential tying run on base in the ninth inning with two out. However, Bunning struck out John Roseboro to end the game.

On Saturday night in Cincinnati, the Cardinals and Reds split a doubleheader, making up the rained-out game of Friday night. Then on Sunday the Reds beat the Cardinals, 9–6, with the help of two St. Louis errors committed by reliever Barney Schultz and center fielder Curt Flood.

St. Louis had gotten off to a fast start with a 2–0 lead on consecutive homers by Lou Brock and Dick Groat in the first. However, the Reds battled back from a 6–0 deficit to tie the game at 6–6 in the sixth. Cincinnati then scored three unearned runs in the eighth to take the game, as Barney Schultz couldn't hold onto a bunt by pitcher Sammy Ellis that allowed the Reds to load the bases with one out. Then Pete Rose followed with a fly ball to center that Curt Flood muffed, allowing the ball to drop, scoring Marty Keough and Johnny Edwards with the tie-breaking runs. Chico Ruiz followed with a fly ball to center that brought Ellis home.

At Pittsburgh on Saturday, the Giants clobbered the Pirates, 13–4, as Willie Mays earned every dime of his $110,000 annual salary, scoring five times. Mays also batted in his 101st run of the year with his 44th home run. Prior to his home run Mays had reached base on two walks, a single and a fielder's choice, scoring each time. Juan Marichal (19–7), the Giants' starting pitcher, won his 19th game of the year.

On Sunday the Giants beat the Pirates, 4–3, in 11 innings.

With the Giants seven games behind the Phillies, controversy continued to dog manager Alvin Dark in the press. It was now being widely reported that Dark's troubles began with the Giants the first day he took over the club. He called the Latin players together that day and issued a decree that "no Spanish be spoken on the field."[21]

On Monday morning, September 21, at 12:30 A.M. the Phillies arrived home from Los Angeles at Philadelphia International Airport aboard an American Airlines 707 Astro Jet, leading the National League by 6½ games over the Cardinals and Reds with 12 games remaining in the season.

The Mayor of Philadelphia and 2,000 fans were at the airport to greet the team. As the Phillies deplaned, the assembled crowd in the second-floor concourse went wild.

The *Philadelphia Inquirer* reported that "The packed crowd which had been waiting since late Saturday night, feverously wiped the fogged-up plate glass windows with handkerchiefs and coat sleeves to better see their 'boys.' School children who had been industriously working on their homework threw their books down and cheered lustily as Manager Gene Mauch led the team off the ramp."[22]

For the Philadelphia Phillies, after 150 games they had arrived at their high-water mark of the 1964 season. However, there would be no National League flag that would fly high above Connie Mack Stadium, as the Phillies would immediately begin a ten-game losing streak. Ultimately they would lose 10 out of their final 12 games in the season and blow the pennant.

National League Standings, September 21, 1964

Team	Won	Lost	Pct.	G.B.
Philadelphia	90	60	.600	—
St. Louis	83	66	.557	6½
Cincinnati	83	66	.557	6½
San Francisco	83	67	.553	7
Milwaukee	77	72	.517	12½
Pittsburgh	76	72	.514	13
Los Angeles	75	75	.500	15
Chicago	67	82	.450	22½
Houston	63	88	.417	27½
New York	50	99	.336	39½

Gene Mauch was later to remark, "In those first 150 games of the 1964 season, we played as perfectly as I have ever seen a team play. I have never seen a team that had as many guys who knew exactly how the game was supposed to be played and enjoyed playing it the right way. My only regret is that they were never rewarded for playing such astute baseball as they did for the first 150 games."[23]

On Monday, September 21, the Phillies opened a three-game series at Connie Mack Stadium with the Reds with 20,067 fans on hand. Cincinnati won the first game of the series, 1–0, as John Tsitouris (8–11) blanked the Phillies on six hits.

The only run of the game occurred in the sixth inning when Chico Ruiz stole home. Ruiz singled off Phillies starter Art Mahaffey (12–9) with one out in the sixth and then reached third on a single by Vada Pinson, who was then thrown out attempting to reach second. With two outs and Frank Robinson at bat, Ruiz liberally moved off third base and stretched his lead down the third base line. Then suddenly he broke for home! Mahaffey, caught off guard, fired the ball to catcher Clay Dalrymple but it sailed past home plate. Ruiz, however, had already crossed the plate.

The Reds' win reduced the Phillies' lead to 5½ games with 11 to play.

In the only other game played in the National League on September 21, Ken Johnson of the Colts pitched a four-hitter, beating the Giants, 3–1. The win was the Colts' fifth straight victory, all by one run, and third under new manager Luman "Lum" Harris, who had taken over from Harry Craft just a few days ago. The only Giants run had come on Jim Hart's 24th home run of the year.

As the Cardinals, now in third place by one-half game behind the

Reds, were about to open a series with the Mets, speculation about the Cardinals' hiring Leo Durocher as their manager for 1965 continued. Jack Herman of the *St. Louis Globe-Democrat* was quoted by an unnamed source as saying, "Leo is open for a managership. He's making a strong pitch for the Cardinal job."[24]

August A. Bush, Jr., Cardinals president, said he had not talked to Durocher, "but I've known him for many years before we got into baseball. I'm a great admirer of his. Nothing has been done on the managerial situation one way or another."[25]

New Cardinal general manager Bob Howsam, who had taken over from the departed Bing Devine, said, "The Cardinals will make no decision on [Johnny] Keane's status until the end of the season."

On Tuesday, September 22, the Reds once again whipped the Phillies, this time by a score of 9–2, thereby cutting their lead to 4½ games.

Following the game, *Philadelphia Inquirer* staff writer Frank Dolson spoke with the Reds' Pete Rose about the possibility of Cincinnati's pulling out the pennant.

"Pennant?" said Rose. "How could we have been thinking of winning the pennant? We've been battling for fourth. I don't think anybody in Cincinnati has been thinking pennant, judging from the crowds we've had.

"We've got the steam up now. Listen. You can tell. This is a pretty lively clubhouse, right?" Rose continued. "I think we've got the best club in the league—I really do. It would be real nice for Hutch [ailing Reds manager Fred Hutchinson] if we win. It would help him out a lot."[26]

"Hutch?" acting manager Dick Sisler had said a few minutes earlier. "Yeah. That has something to do with the way we've come back. They're thinking of Hutch and they're thinking of themselves. They smell that money now."[27]

At New York, St. Louis kept up with the pennant crunch, defeating the Mets, 2–1, while the Giants defeated the Colts, 7–1.

On Wednesday, September 23, the Reds completed the three-game sweep of the reeling Phillies, defeating them, 6–4, to move within 3½ games of the league leaders.

The Phillies got off to 1–0 lead in the second inning when Reds starter Billy McCool walked Bobby Wine and Clay Dalrymple tripled. However, the Reds were led by the power hitting of Chico Ruiz and Vada Pinson. In the fourth inning Ruiz hit his second Major League home run to tie the score at 1–1. Ruiz' blast was a 400-foot-plus shot off Phillies starter Dennis Bennett. Then in the sixth inning Vada Pinson (22) led off by hitting his first home run of the night to give the Reds a 2–1 lead.

The Phillies regained the lead in the bottom of the sixth when Alex Johnson homered with Johnny Callison on base to make the score 3–2. Then in the seventh the Reds knocked Bennett out of the game, rallying for four runs. Johnny Edwards began the rally with a single to left off Bennett. Then he moved to second when Leo Cardenas followed with a single. At that point Gene Mauch replaced Bennett on the mound with right-hander Ed Roebuck. Reds interim manager Dick Sisler then sent Marty Keough up to pinch hit. He promptly forced Cardenas at second, but on the play Johnny Edwards took third, putting Reds base runners on first and third. Pete Rose then lined Roebuck's first pitch into center for a single, scoring Edwards and tying the game at 3–3. One out later Vada Pinson (23) smacked Roebuck's second pitch over the right-field fence near the scoreboard for his 2nd home run of the night, giving the Reds a 6–3 lead.

In the eighth the Phillies cut the lead to 6–4. Billy McCool (6–3) got his first win as a starter in the game with relief help from Sammy Ellis.

For the crumbling Phillies, the home run by Alex Johnson in the game was the first hit by a Phillie in 10 games. Furthermore, the four runs scored by the Phillies in the game were the most in their last six games.

Following the Reds' 6–4 victory over the Phillies, completing the three-game sweep, there was sheer pandemonium in the Reds' clubhouse, as Chico Ruiz was dancing about waving a news clipping from a Philadelphia newspaper that read, "Phils unworried by Red surge."

"Take it over to Gene Mauch," shouted Joe Nuxhall decisively, "and ask the Little General what he has to do now."[28]

In fact, Gene Mauch was in the Philadelphia clubhouse contemplating what he had to do to stop the Phillies' collapse. His decision was, with the Braves now coming into Connie Mack Stadium for a four-game series, that he would revise his pitching rotation and have Jim Bunning and Chris Short both pitch with two days' rest, rather than the usual three.

Rounding the action of the four top teams on Wednesday night, September 23, both the Cardinals and Giants won again. The Cardinals defeated the Mets, 2–1, and the Giants defeated the Colts, 7–1.

Suddenly with nine games left to play in the season, the Phillies had let the Reds, Cardinals and Giants back in the race. Consequently, the National League standings on Thursday morning, September 24, all at once looked very different from the those on the first of the month, when the Phillies had been the only National League team authorized by the Commissioner's office to begin printing World Series tickets.

National League Standings, September 24, 1964

Team	Won	Lost	Pct.	G.B.
Philadelphia	90	63	.588	—
Cincinnati	86	66	.566	3½
St. Louis	84	67	.556	5
San Francisco	85	68	.556	5
Milwaukee	78	73	.517	11
Pittsburgh	77	73	.517	11½
Los Angeles	75	77	.493	14½
Chicago	69	82	.457	20
Houston	64	90	.416	26½
New York	51	100	.338	38

On Thursday, September 24, the Phillies lost their fourth straight game, being beaten by the Milwaukee Braves, 5–3. It was also their sixth loss in the last seven games.

With the Phillies continuing to swoon, the Associated Press reported, "The Philadelphia Phillies are so anxious to win the National League Pennant, they may run themselves right out of it."

Jim Bunning (18–6) took the loss for Philadelphia in game that featured some controversial baserunning by his teammates.

Braves starter Wade Blasingame (7–5) had been cruising along with a 3–0 lead and had only allowed one hit through the first six innings when Richie Allen singled with one out in the seventh. Alex Johnson then hit a ground ball back to Blasingame, who then made a wide throw to second, pulling shortstop Sandy Alomar off the bag. However, Allen running from first overslid second base and Alomar quickly tagged him out.

With Alex Johnson on first, Vic Power then hit a slow grounder toward third. Johnson sped towards second and rounded the base only to be immediately cut down by Eddie Mathews' throw to Denis Menke, thereby wiping out the Phillies threat.

The shoddy baserunning by the Phillies became more important to the outcome of the game when the Braves scored two more runs in the top of the eighth and then the Phillies rallied for three in the bottom half of the inning. Following the game, Phillies manager Gene Mauch actually defended the baserunning of Allen and Johnson.

"Allen slides aggressively into second trying to break up the double play and doesn't even know the umpire has called him safe. He overslides the bag and is out. There is no way he could know he was safe, he was so intent on taking out the relay man.

"And Johnson has no way to know that Eddie Mathews won't throw to first on the dribbler. He rounded second figuring to take third and maybe score if Mathews makes a bad throw on a tough play."[29]

The loss reduced Philadelphia's lead over second-place Cincinnati to three games. The Reds, who had just been authorized to print World Series tickets, were idle waiting to begin a five-game series with the Mets over the weekend that would include two doubleheaders. The Phillies had just eight games left to play, while the Reds had ten.

However, St. Louis was now in the thick of the running for the pennant after taking a doubleheader from Pittsburgh on September 24, 4–2 and 4–0. With the Cards' sweep of the doubleheader, they were now just 3½ games behind the Phillies with nine games left to play. Also, idle fourth-place San Francisco moved to within 4½ games of the Phillies.

On Friday night, September 25, with a packed house of 30,447 on hand at Connie Mack Stadium, the Phillies lost to the Braves, 7–5, in a very exciting game.

It was their fifth straight loss, seventh in the last eight games, and it suddenly threw the pennant race up for grabs. Second-place Cincinnati had swept a doubleheader at New York, 3–0 and 4–1, to move within 1½ games of the Phillies. And for the second straight night, third-place St. Louis had beaten Pittsburgh, this time by the score of 5–3, to move within 2½ games of the Phillies. Meanwhile, fourth-place San Francisco defeated Chicago, 3–1, to move within 3½ games of the league lead.

With the Phillies leading the game, 1–0, the Braves' first two runs came as a result of an interference call on Phillies catcher Clay Dalyrmple in the seventh. With one out Denis Menke was awarded first base when Dalrymple tipped his bat on a foul strike.

Menke then moved to third on a double by Mike de la Holz and scored when Lee Maye flied out. On the play de la Holz took third and then scored on a single by Felipe Alou. The Braves then took a 3–1 lead in the top of the seventh.

However, the Phillies put up a never-say-die struggle in their loss to the Braves, twice coming from behind to force the game into extra innings. In the 8th Johnny Callison hit a two-run homer to tie the score at 3–3. Then in the top of the 10th Joe Torre had hit a two-run homer to give the Braves a 5–3 lead, but in the bottom of the 10th Richie Allen socked a two-run homer to tie the score at 5–5.

However, it was all for naught as the Braves scored the tie-breaking and winning runs in the 12th. The Braves' rally in the 12th started when Gene Kolb got on base with an infield single. One out later Gene Oliver walked. Then Eddie Mathews singled off Frank Thomas' glove at first base and Kolb dashed for home with the tie-breaking run. Oliver moved to third on the play. Then Mathews attempted to steal second and Oliver broke for home with the second Braves run of the inning. However, Mathews was called safe when Clay Dalrymple's throw was dropped by Tony Taylor.

Chris Short had started for the Phillies with two days rest, but John Boozer (3–4), the fourth Philadelphia reliever in the game, took the loss. For the Braves, Hank Fischer had started the game but rookie Clay Carroll (1–0), the third Milwaukee reliever, got the win.

At New York the Cincinnati pitchers held the Mets to just four hits in a doubleheader sweep. In the first game Jim Maloney pitched a one-hitter, Joe Christopher's second-inning single being the only hit that Maloney allowed while he struck out eight and walked two. For the Mets, Al Jackson (10–16) took the loss.

The Reds came into Shea Stadium all business and touched Jackson for two runs immediately in the first inning. Pete Rose led off against Jackson and hit a loop single into center. Rose then took second on a bunt by Chico Ruiz and scored when Vada Pinson singled between first and second. Frank Robinson followed with a single to left-center, scoring Pinson.

In the second game Bob Purkey and Sammy Ellis combined to pitch a three-hitter. The Mets had actually taken a 1–0 lead in the fourth after Purkey had thrown a knuckle ball into the dirt that catcher Johnny Edwards let get by, that scored Bobby Klaus from third.

However, the Reds wiped out the Mets' lead in the sixth when Chico Ruiz singled and Frank Robinson hit a 3-and-2 pitch over the 358-foot marker on the left-field fence.

Jack Fisher (10–18) had started the game for the Mets and was the losing pitcher.

As soon as the second game ended, the Reds dashed to the clubhouse to get reports on the extra-inning game taking place down in Philadelphia.

As there was no cable TV, ESPN or FOX sports network in 1964, interim manager Dick Sisler, in order to get the score from Philadelphia, had called the sports department of United Press International on the telephone and subsequently was getting reports on the extra-inning game coming out of Connie Mack Stadium. Sisler then announced to the gathered players hanging on his every comment.

"The Braves scored two in the top of the 12th. The Phils have two on and two out in the bottom of the 12th." Then shouted Sisler, "Braves win!"[30]

There was an immediate spontaneous universal roar of approval in the Cincinnati clubhouse. "We're not worried. Those will be Gene Mauch's famous last words," declared pitcher Bob Purkey.[31]

About 350 Reds fans had accompanied the team to New York and according to the *New York Times* received the Queens version of the Bronx cheer when they unfurled a banner in the upper stands that advised the Mets fans not to worry—"We'll take care of the Yankees."[32]

Prior to the game Cincinnati had brought up several farm hands for the final week of the season, who included former Yankee pitcher Jim Coats, second baseman Gus Gil, left-handed pitcher Ted Davidson, shortstop Tommy Helms, right-handed pitcher Dan Neville, and once again first baseman Tony Perez rejoined the club.

The third-place Cardinals beat the Pirates by capitalizing on an error by Gene Alley in the first inning that led to their scoring three runs. While the Pirates outhit the Cards, 8–4, in the game, the St. Louis pitching of Gordon Richardson (4–2), Ron Taylor and Barney Schultz shut down Pirate threats in the fifth and eighth. Don Cardwell (1–1) took the loss.

The Giants downed the Cubs, led by Tom Haller's home run and a double by Gaylord Perry that drove in two runs.

On Saturday, September 26, the Phillies were beaten again by the Braves for their sixth straight loss and ninth in the last eleven games. It was Knothole Day at Connie Mack Stadium and there were 26,381 screaming Philly fanatics in the stands.

The Phillies were leading, 4–0, after the second inning that featured a triple by Richie Allen and a home run by Alex Johnson. The Phillies carried the 4–0 lead into the fifth inning when Milwaukee scored two runs, then scored another in the eighth to send the game into the ninth inning with Phillies leading, 4–3.

However, Rico Carty tripled off Bobby Shantz with the bases loaded with Braves in the ninth to beat Philadelphia, 6–3. Hank Aaron and Eddie Mathews opened the inning against Shantz with singles. Then pinch-hitter Frank Bolling grounded to Ruben Amaro, whose throw to second was dropped by Tony Taylor, loading the bases.

Oddly enough, with bases loaded and the right-handed-hitting Carty coming up, Gene Mauch did no go to the bullpen, where he had right-hander Ed Roebuck warming up.

Following the game Rico Carty said, "I'll tell you. I was happy. The last time I faced Shantz in Chicago or St. Louis, he got me out easy. But still I'd rather hit a left-hander than a right-hander."[33]

Up at Shea Stadium in New York before 14,265 fans, Cincinnati remained "Red" hot as they defeated the Mets, 6–1, for their 7th straight victory and 10th in the last 11 games. John Tsitouris started the game for

Cincinnati and went 6⅓ innings. Then Billy McCool was every bit of his namesake, coming into the game in relief to snuff out a New York rally and striking out five of the eight batters that faced him. The win put the Reds just one-half game behind the faltering Phillies.

For the Mets, Ed Kranepool got his 100th hit of the season in the game.

Third-place St. Louis defeated Pittsburgh again, 6–3, and moved to within 1½ games of the lead.

While fourth-place San Francisco had their game at Chicago postponed due to rain, they picked up a half game in the standings to move within only three games of the Phillies.

On the morning of September 27, the *Philadelphia Inquirer* threw in the towel in publishing the Phillies "Magic Number." Consequently, space dedicated to the recent practice in the paper now read:

"The magic number has, at least temporarily, lost its significance in the National League pennant race. The Phillies held a one-half game lead on Sunday over the second place Cincinnati Reds with six games to play, all but one against other contenders. Thus the Phillies must beat the contenders to win their first pennant since 1950."[34]

On Sunday, September 27, the Milwaukee Braves completed the four-game sweep of the series in Philadelphia and dropped the Phillies out of first place for first time since July 16, as Cincinnati completed a five-game sweep of the Mets, winning their second doubleheader in three days.

In what was referred to as the "blackest seven days in Philadelphia baseball history" by the *Philadelphia Inquirer*, the Phillies had squandered a 6½ game lead in a week, losing seven straight games. Playing at home, no less.

In the series final Milwaukee pounded Jim Bunning (18–7) and the Phillies, 14–8, getting 22 hits in the game. Even an ultra-heroic effort by Johnny Callison, who hit three home runs in the game, was not enough to overcome the monumental slump the Phillies found themselves in.

The Braves were leading in the game, 12–3, when Callison (29) came to bat in the sixth inning. In his previous two at-bats against Tony Cloninger he had been hitless. However, this time he slammed a home run over the right-field fence.

Callison remarked after the game, "Just before I went up I started chewing tobacco. I got it from Bob Oldis. I told him, I might as well try that. I've tried everything else."[35]

In the eighth inning Callison (30) connected for his second home run of the day off reliever Chi Chi Olivo. Then in the ninth with Richie Allen on second base, Callison (31) connected for his third home run of the game, driving the ball high into the right-field light tower.

Following the game manager Gene Mauch simply said, "We've got
to do in five days what Cincinnati took 5½ months to do. There's a good
chance we're better going after something than holding onto something."[36]

Milwaukee's catcher Joe Torre who in the Sunday slaughter had two
singles and a home run, and in all had 11 hits and seven RBIs in the four-
game series, said after the game:

"You've got to feel sorry for them. They'd come up to the plate speaking slowly, groping for the right words, and—well, usually you talk to hitters. You kid around with them a little bit. But these guys...I didn't know
what to say to them. I mean it's hard to believe what happened to them.
I can't believe it myself. I guess that's what makes this blankety-blank
game so great."[37]

The Cincinnati Reds, by virtue of winning their doubleheader on
Sunday from the New York Mets by scores of 4–3 and 3–1, had moved
into the National League lead by one game over the Philadelphia Phillies.
Just a week ago Cincinnati had been trailing Philadelphia by 6½ games.
The Reds had now extended their winning streak to nine games as they
moved into first place for the first time since the first week of the season.

In the first game's 4–3 victory, Frank Robinson led the Reds attack.
In the fourth inning Robinson singled, stole second, went to third on a
wild throw by Mets starter Tracy Stallard, and scored on a sacrifice fly by
Deron Johnson. Then in the eighth he hit a two-run double.

Jim O'Toole (17–7) with relief help from Sammy Ellis in the ninth
got the win. Tracy Stallard (10–20) lost his 20th game of the year for New
York.

It was Fan Appreciation Day at Shea Stadium. Besides every fan in
attendance receiving a memento from the Mets' management to say thanks
for 1.7 million attendance during the 1964 season, in between games they
were treated to a field day event with players from both the Mets and Reds
participating. The field events included such nonsense as a milking contest, a relay throwing contest, a wheelbarrow race and an egg-throwing
tournament.

When the silly carnival-like atmosphere subsided and the second game
began, the Reds became all business again and took the nightcap, 3–1. This
time Vada Pinson took over the leadership and in the first inning he smashed
a two-run triple that proved to be the winning margin in the game.

Joey Jay (11–11) got the win, going all the way for the Reds, while
Galen Cisco (6–18) took the loss for the Mets.

In the clubhouse following the Reds' twin victories, a hoarse and joy-
filled interim manager Dick Sisler made a telephone call to ailing Reds
manager Fred Hutchinson.

He told Hutch, "I'm not saying for sure yet we're going to win, but I'll guarantee you this club won't choke."[38]

Outside Sisler's room the photographers were entreating the Cincinnati players to show more animation by whooping it up a little more. "Cool it," snapped third baseman Steve Boros. "Just remember that's what the Phillies were doing only a week ago."[39]

Nonetheless, reminiscent of the greeting that the battered Phillies had enjoyed only seven days ago, that evening when the Reds' chartered United Airlines plane set down at Greater Cincinnati Airport, thousands of fans packed the facility and pressed their way onto the ramp, making it impossible for the team to deplane.

With the crowd almost out of control, a second ramp was placed at the cabin door on the opposite side of the plane and the team departed. With unsafe conditions prevailing, the "welcome home" speech that was to be delivered by Cincinnati Mayor Walton Bachrach was cancelled.

With all the hoopla surrounding the Reds' sudden ascent to the top of the heap in the National League, the reality of the pennant race was that the St. Louis Cardinals were hot, too, and breathing down the necks of both the Reds and Phillies.

After defeating the Pirates, 5–0, on Sunday for their fifth straight win, all against the Pirates, the Cardinals were now in third place, just a half game behind the Phillies and only 1½ games behind the Reds. Furthermore, the Cardinals were now about to begin a three-game series with the Phillies on Monday evening.

In the St. Louis victory over the Pirates on Sunday, Roger Craig (7–9) and Barney Schultz combined for a six-hit shutout. Vernon Law (12–11) took the loss.

While the Reds and Cardinals reveled in their Sunday victories, things for the San Francisco Giants suddenly looked very grim. In Chicago the Giants had dumped a doubleheader to the Cubs, 4–1 and 4–2, dropping them 4½ games behind the Reds with only six games to go and subsequently putting them on the edge of elimination.

In the first game Larry Jackson held the Giants to three hits while notching his 23rd victory of the season. In the second game a grand slam by Ernie Banks provided all the runs the Cubs needed to down the Giants.

National League Standings, September 27, 1964

Team	Won	Lost	Pct.	G.B.
Cincinnati	91	66	.580	—
Philadelphia	90	67	.573	1

Team	Won	Lost	Pct.	G.B.
St. Louis	89	67	.571	1½
San Francisco	86	70	.551	4½
Milwaukee	82	73	.529	8
Pittsburgh	77	78	.497	13
Los Angeles	76	79	.490	14
Chicago	72	83	.465	18
Houston	65	91	.417	25½
New York	51	105	.327	39½

With the final week of the 1964 season about to begin, the remaining games on the schedules of the top four contending teams were the following.

Cincinnati	at home 5 games
	Pittsburgh 3 and Philadelphia 2
Philadelphia	away 5 games
	at St. Louis 3 and at Cincinnati 2
St. Louis	at home 6 games
	Philadelphia 3 and New York 3
San Francisco	at home 6 games
	Houston 3 and Chicago 3

On Monday, September 28, the Philadelphia Phillies continued their free fall in the standings as they suffered their eighth straight defeat, this time at the hands of the St. Louis Cardinals, 5–1.

The *Philadelphia Inquirer* stated in its next day edition, "The fighting Phillies have become the fading Phillies, and they're on the verge of fading right out of the National League pennant race."[40]

The win was the sixth straight for the rampaging Cardinals, and it catapulted them into second just place one game behind Cincinnati and one-half game ahead of the third-place Phillies.

Bob Gibson (18–11) started for the Cards and held the Phillies to two hits in the first three innings, both by Tony Gonzalez, before retiring the next 13 batters in a row. In the seventh the Phillies finally touched Gibson for a lone run. Gibson went on to win his 18th game of the year with relief help from Barney Schultz in the ninth.

The Cardinal attack was led by Ken Boyer with two doubles, Bill White with three singles and Mike Shannon, who drove in three runs with a single and a sacrifice fly.

Chris Short (17–9) was the starter for Philadelphia. Short, who up until now had found pitching against the Cardinals a marginal task, allowing only two runs in the last three games he faced them, got into trouble early in the second inning. Regardless it was Short's fourth start in eleven days and his second in a row with only two days' rest.

With one out Bill White stroked Short's first pitch into right field for a single. Julian Javier then also hit the first pitch for a single and White went all the way around to third. Then Mike Shannon hit a sacrifice fly scoring White, giving the Cards a 1–0 lead.

The Cardinals got to Short again in the fourth as Ken Boyer doubled to left then took third on Bill White's second straight single. Julian Javier then hit a bouncer to second, but Boyer took off for home and slid safely across the plate ahead of the throw from Tony Taylor. The Cardinals now led, 2–0.

The Cardinals added their third run in the sixth when Ken Boyer hit his second double of the game and then scored on Bill White's third consecutive single. The Cardinals added their final two runs in the eighth.

Philadelphia scored its only run in the eighth on a walk, a fielder's choice that put Johnny Callison on base and Richie Allen's single.

In the Philadelphia clubhouse, however, the spirit to win was still alive. Left-hander Dennis Bennett stood there with a large black and blue spot on his left shoulder, but he intended to pitch against the Cardinals on Tuesday night.

"It's internal bleeding," said Bennett. "They're a little concerned about it. No sweat. I'll beat 'em tomorrow. (Jim) Bunning will beat 'em the next night. We're a long way from [censored] dead."[41]

According to popular sportswriter Red Smith, several weeks ago realistic innkeepers in Cincinnati took a look at the National League standings and started to book rooms for as many conventions as possible for the second week in October. Consequently as fans were now attempting to make World Series reservations in Cincinnati, they were informed, "Sorry, sold out and closed."[42]

On Tuesday, September 29, as the Cincinnati Reds prepared to open a three-game series with the Pittsburgh Pirates, they were ready to put their nine-game winning streak and National League lead on the line in the hands of 20-year-old rookie southpaw Billy McCool.

Despite the fantastic ball that the Reds had been playing, advance ticket sales for the game were only 10,000. However, the Reds' management was hopeful that a large rush on the Crosley Field ticket windows prior to the game would hike the attendance to 20,000. The swell of fans never happened, though, as 10,858 in attendance saw the Reds' winning streak snapped at nine and their league lead suddenly taken away, as they went down to defeat at the hands of the Pirates, 2–0.

At St. Louis the Cardinals had beaten the Phillies, 4–2, to send the

National League pennant race into a deadlock between the Cards and Reds, with each team having four games left to play.

At Cincinnati the Reds' Billy McCool (6–4) and veteran Pirates pitcher Bob Friend (13–18) had been locked in scoreless duel through eight innings. McCool hadn't even allowed a base runner until one out in the fifth when Donn Clendenon singled. Furthermore, the young left-hander had worked out of trouble in the sixth when singles by Gene Alley and Jerry May and a wild pitch had loaded the bases with none out.

But in the ninth inning Bob Bailey singled. It was only the fourth hit off McCool. He then struck out Bill Virdon. The next batter was Roberto Clemente, who doubled off the center-field wall, sending Bailey to third. Gene Freese was then intentionally walked, loading the bases. However, Donn Clendenon followed by fouling out. Two outs, and Bill Mazeroski came to the plate and promptly singled to center, scoring Bailey and Clemente.

Bob Friend had been in trouble all night and gave up 11 hits in the game, but he struggled through it all and made it, pitching a compete game and shutout. The Reds came back to threaten in the ninth when Marty Keouh and Pete Rose both singled. However, Friend then got Chico Ruiz to hit a taper to second base ending the game.

Cincinnati's undisputed stay at the top of the heap had lasted only 48 hours.

At Bush Stadium in St. Louis before 27,433 paying customers, the Cardinals extended the Phillies' losing streak to nine, defeating them, 4–2. For the Cards it was their seventh win in a row. For St. Louis, Ray Sadecki (20–10) won his 20th game of the season going 6⅔ innings, allowing two runs and seven hits before giving way to Barney Schultz who hurled the last 2⅓ innings without giving up a hit.

Ailing left-hander Dennis Bennett started for the Phillies and lasted only 1⅓ innings. The Cardinals went right after Bennett in the first inning as Curt Flood led off with a single, then Lou Brock sacrificed, sending Flood to second. Dick Groat followed with a double into the right-field alley, scoring Flood. In the second inning Bennett yielded three straight hits as Julian Javier doubled down the left-field line, Mike Shannon singled to right and Tim McCarver singled past second, making the score 3–0 Cardinals. Ray Sadecki then bunted his way on first and Bennett was relieved by Ed Roebuck.

The Phillies fought hard to stay in the game, using 17 players. Frank Thomas, who had broken his thumb three weeks ago, appeared in the game as a pinch hitter wearing a cast on his hand; and Johnny Callison, suffering from a virus infection, was sent into the game in the seventh and even singled.

Ray Sadecki had not yielded a run to the Phillies in the last 20 innings that he had pitched against them. However, the Phillies scored two runs off him in the fourth, when he walked Richie Allen, Adolpho Phillips and Ruben Amaro. Gus Triandos then followed with a pinch-hit single to center, scoring two runs and making the score 3–2 Cardinals.

The Cardinals scored their final run in the sixth when Bill White (19) homered high off the top of the right-field screen. Following that, 38-year-old Barney Schultz shut down the Phillies the rest of the way.

The ninth straight loss for Philadelphia was their longest losing streak since 1961, when they lost 23 straight games.

Technically, the San Francisco Giants were not eliminated from the race and on September 29 they beat the Houston Colts in 11 innings, 5–4. Matty Alou had hit his first home run in two years to provide the run needed to give the Giants' pitcher from Japan, Masanori Murakami, his first Major League victory. Murakami had pitched masterful one-hit ball over the last three innings.

With four games to go in the season for the Reds and Cardinals, three for the Phillies and five for the Giants, the standings for the top four teams still in contention were the following.

National League Standings
(top four teams), September 30, 1964

Team	Won	Lost	Pct.	G.B.
Cincinnati	91	67	.576	—
St. Louis	91	67	.576	—
Philadelphia	90	69	.566	1
San Francisco	87	70	.554	3

As Cincinnati, St. Louis, Philadelphia and San Francisco took the battle for the 1964 National League Pennant down to the final hours of the season, some of the other clubs were now turning their attention to the 1965 campaign.

In Los Angeles, the Dodgers announced that they had rehired Walter Alston as manager for the 1965 season. The 1963 World Champions had a disaster of a season in 1964 and on September 30 they were in 7th place with a record below .500 (77–80), 13 games out of first place.

The Dodgers had an unwritten policy of only offering managers a one-year contract. Therefore Alston signed a one-year contract to become manager for the 12th consecutive season. Alston's salary was reported to be $50,000.

General manager E. J. (Buzzie) Bavasi said in announcing the rehiring of Alston, "We certainly don't blame Alston for the terrible job the team did this year. He's still our man and will continue to be until told differently."[43]

The 52-year-old Alston also had the confidence of Dodger owner Walter O'Malley. The reality of the Dodgers' collapse was tied to such factors as having two of their best pitchers, Sandy Koufax and Johnny Podres, injured and out for more than month each. Also, 1963 National League batting champion Tommy Davis was hitting 50 points below his league-leading pace of a year ago. In addition, Frank Howard and Jim Gilliam had experienced monumental slumps along the way in the season.

In a news conference at New York, the Mets ended speculation that Casey Stengel's days as the manager were numbered by rehiring him for the 1965 season and giving him a pay raise to boot. M. Donald Grant, chairman of the board, said that decision to return or not to return as manager of the Mets had always been Stengel's alone.

"Casey isn't back with us, because he never left. He's been with us all the time. He's been our boy and he's still our boy. No other available person was spoken to, but we did discuss matters with others if Casey did retire. He told us yesterday he wanted to manage again, and that was that."[44]

Stengel said that he had discussed the future with Mets president George Weiss on Monday. "I wanted to get it all straightened out then, because of my going on the road at the end of the season, and why wouldn't you want it settled so you wouldn't have to come back? I have a one year contract, as I've always had with the Mets, and an increase in pay which makes me very happy that they would want to give it to me. It's a very splendid raise. I believe that I can use it—this suit's a little old, I might get a new wardrobe."[45]

The 74-year-old Stengel's Mets salary was reported to be in the range of $80,000 a year, and in the off season he served as the director of the Valley National Bank in Glendale, California.

One could surmise that M. Donald Grant, George Weiss and other members of the Met's brass came to the conclusion on rehiring Stengel, that with the team having another 100-plus-loss season and lacking excitement, that perhaps the charisma of Stengel had something to do with brining those 1,732,597 fans through the turnstiles at Shea Stadium during the 1964 season.

Also, during the September 29th news conference, the Mets also announced some restructuring in their front office. Vaughan P. (Bing) Devine, who had been forced out as general manager of the St. Louis Cardinals in August, had been hired as an assistant to George Weiss.

Also, former Brooklyn Dodger and New York Giant second baseman Eddie Stankey, who had resigned the previous week as director of player development for the Cardinals, had been appointed to a similar position with the Mets. Finally, two Mets executives had been promoted to the level of vice president: Johnny Murphy, who had been serving as an assistant to Weiss, and Jim Thomson, who had been the business manager for the Mets since their inception in 1962.

On Wednesday, September 30, the St. Louis Cardinals took over sole possession of first place in the National League when they beat Philadelphia for the third consecutive night, while Cincinnati lost again to Pittsburgh.

At St. Louis, before an excited crowd of 29,920 fans, Curt Simmons (18–9) beat his former Philadelphia teammates, 8–5, to elevate the Cardinals to a one-game lead over Cincinnati. For 6⅔ innings the 35-year-old Simmons had a no-hitter going. Then with the Cardinals leading, 8–0, in the seventh, the Phillies scored twice. Simmons yielded a two-out single to Richie Allen, then Alex Johnson (4) hit a 415-foot home run into dead center field to make the score, 8–2.

The Phillies finally sent Simmons to the showers in the eighth as they scored another run, then two in the ninth to narrow the Cards' lead to 8–5. However, Simmons was then relieved by Ron Taylor and Gordon Richardson who finished up the game, as the Cardinals won their 8th straight game, while handing the Phillies their 10th straight defeat.

Jim Bunning (18–8), starting again on two days' rest for Philadelphia, got through the first inning then was shelled by Cardinal batters for two runs in the second, two more in the third and then departed with one out in the fourth and Cardinals leading, 8–0.

In the second inning Dick Groat singled off Bunning, then Tim McCarver (9) followed with a 350-foot home run into the right-field screen.

Then in the fourth the Cards went back to work on Bunning, as eight Cardinals came to the plate and four got hits. Curt Flood started the rally with a double, then took third when Lou Brock laid down a bunt which Tony Taylor couldn't handle. Bill White followed with a double, scoring Flood, and Ken Boyer smashed a single on a ball too hot to handle by Richie Allen at third. Subsequently Dick Groat singled, then Julian Javier was safe on an error by Allen, scoring Brock to make the score 4–0.

Bunning was finally knocked out the game in the fourth, when the Cards scored four more runs with five hits in a row and a throwing error on Johnny Callison to make the score 8–0. Bobby Locke, Rick Wise and Morrie Steevens finished up the game for Philadelphia in relief.

Jim Bunning, working on two days' rest, had failed to win for the third straight time. In a postgame interview the Cardinals' Curt Flood made the following remarks in regards to Bunning's mound appearance: "He's pitched better games. He wasn't ripping that ball in. He wasn't real strong."[46]

However, Bunning gave no excuses about his lackluster performance. "I felt very good. No excuses at all."[47]

In the Philadelphia locker room, manager Gene Mauch had kept the door closed for 30 minutes after the game, then he stood by himself in a corner sipping a beer. When the press approached him all he would say was, "We worked hard. We've just got to work harder, that's all [referring to next season]."[48]

Curt Simmons had spent 13 seasons with the Philadelphia Phillies and been a member of the 1950 pennant-winning team that was dubbed "the Whiz Kids." Asked if he wanted to beat the Phillies for some special reason, he replied:

"I don't want to beat them more than I do the other clubs. That story is five years old now. I just wanted to win, that's all. I feel sorry for them a little bit, but in this game you say I'm sorry, but I'm gonna beat you. But I've said that if we don't win, I'd like to see them win."[49]

Prior to the game a fit and tanned Stan Musial, three weeks after collapsing at Bush Stadium after suffering a virus attack, visited the Cardinals' dugout. Musial said he "felt good" and gave Cardinals manager Johnny Keane a vigorous handshake.

When Musial was asked what conclusion he drew from the fact that, in the first year after he retired from playing for the Cardinals they had became contenders, he laughed and replied, "Now we've got guys who can run. For seven years with this club I didn't miss a game. And after seven months with the [Government's] physical fitness program, I get sick."[50]

Now with a one-game lead over the Reds, with Philadelphia just hanging on 2½ games behind and the Giants eliminated, the Cardinals were about to begin a three-game series with the last-place New York Mets to wind up the season.

Regardless of the fact that the Cardinals had an edge in the season series with the Mets, 10–5, Cardinal manager Johnny Keane was guarded in his prediction on the outcome of the upcoming series. "I don't take the Mets lightly. We beat them two out of three here and two out of three there. That's no run-away."[51]

Following their 8–5 victory over the Phillies, the Cardinals rushed into the clubhouse to listen to the Cincinnati-Pittsburgh game on the radio that had gone into extra innings. Jim Maloney and Bob Veale had been locked in a scoreless duel through 11 innings at Crosley Field, and the anxious Cardinals now hung on every pitch as they waited to see if they had taken over first place.

"I'd rather play anytime than watch or listen," said Ken Boyer. I'm more nervous now than I was on the field."[52]

After the game had gone beyond the 12th inning still scoreless, Boyer decided that the suspense was too anxiety-provoking, so he dressed and left. Nonetheless other Cardinal players remained and hung on every pitch. Still in his uniform, Dick Groat said, "I'm in no hurry to leave until the game's over."[53]

However, Cardinals manager Johnny Keane didn't linger in the clubhouse following the Cardinals' win over the Phillies. He immediately dressed and with his wife drove to downtown St. Louis for dinner. But Keane couldn't avoid the broadcast of the Reds and Pirates marathon taking place at Crosley Field, for when he and his wife entered the restaurant, the game was blaring out of a radio in the establishment loud and clear.

Over the last few weeks pennant fever had swept its way across St. Louis. A large button on Bill White's locker proclaimed, "WE TRY HARDER."

On Wednesday night both before and after the Cardinals' win over the Phillies, hundreds of fans had lined up at the Main Post Office at Seventeenth and Market Streets to mail World Series ticket requests, which according to the rules issued by the Commissioner's office would not be accepted if postmarked before October 1. A constant line, two abreast, shuffled into the post office lobby. A special detail of policemen directed rush-hour-like traffic.[54]

All over St. Louis on the night of September 30, while the Cardinals were playing the Phillies, radios were turned on and the voices of announcers Harry Caray and Jack Buck filled the air from one end of the city to the other. In a 16-story dormitory at St. Louis University the game was broadcast into the lobby and lounges over the loudspeaker system.

As all of St. Louis waited for the final score to come in from Cincinnati, the Reds and Pirates continued to battle in the scoreless duel that lasted 16 innings and was not completed until 12:30 A.M.

Jim Maloney had started for the Reds and gone 11 innings, giving up no runs and just three hits while striking out 13 batters. Maloney left for a pinch hitter in the bottom of the 11th and was replaced by Sammy Ellis.

For the Pirates, Bob Veale had started the game and gone 12⅓ innings without giving up a run, limiting the Reds to seven hits, while striking out 16. Veale was relieved with one out in the 13th by Al McBean.

In all there would 36 strikeouts in the game, establishing a record for two teams in an extra-inning game (Maloney 13, Ellis 4, Tsitouris 2, Veale 16, McBean 1).

In the top of the 16th, with the score tied, 0–0, and John Tsitouris pitching in relief for the Reds, Donn Clendenon doubled off the scoreboard for the first extra-base hit of the game and only the fourth hit by the Pirates. Bill Mazeroski then sacrificed Clendenon to third. Then rookie Jerry May laid down a squeeze bunt along the third base line and beat it out for a single, scoring Clendenon from third with the only run of the game that would give the Pirates a 1–0 victory.

From the eighth inning until Clendenon's double in the 16th, three Cincinnati pitchers (Maloney, Sammy Ellis and Tsitouris) had retired 17 consecutive batters.

In the game the Reds had stranded 18 base runners, including three in the 11th, 13th and 14th innings and two on in the 6th, 9th and 10th. Consequently, the Reds had now failed to put a run on the scoreboard for a total of 32 consecutive innings.

Future "All-time Hit King" Pete Rose, who would go on to get a total of 4,256 hits in his 24-year big league career, was 0-for-7 in the game. Roberto Clemente who would achieve 3,000 hits in his in his 18-year big league career, did not play, sitting out the entire game.

If the loss for the Reds was not heart-wrenching enough by itself, the ghostly figure of manager Fred Hutchinson, who was suffering from the late stages of cancer and was in uniform for the game, was felt as well. Although Hutchinson had formally given up the reins of field-leadership to interim manager Dick Sisler on August 14, he was at Crosley Field on September 30 to lend his support and work closely with Sisler.

However, Sisler was clearly in control of the club. "Hutch hasn't second guessed me once," remarked Sisler.[55]

But probably the biggest disappointment to the team and management was that only a sparse crowd of 8,188 turned out to witness the game at Crosley Field, despite the fact that the Reds had begun the game tied for first place and were playing some exciting ball. *New York Journal-American* writer Jimmy Cannon had been covering the Reds and Pirates at Crosley Field on Wednesday night and the sparse attendance prompted him to write in his column for the next day:

"They talk about it in the taverns. But they get the ball games on the radio as they drink their beer. Seldom has a ball club demeaned [behaved itself] with such disinterest. This town [Cincinnati] doesn't deserve a big league team.

"There were 5,000 at the airport to meet them [the Reds] when they

Crosley Field, Cincinnati. (National Baseball Hall of Fame Library, Cooperstown, N.Y.)

came home as winners. You don't have to pay to get into airports. And they gave away tickets for [Barry] Goldwater's rally [1964 GOP presidential candidate]. Maybe that's the reason there were so many empty seats in Crosley Field. This has to be a city of freeloaders.

"All of this is reminiscent of the time former manager Bill Terry of the New York Giants asked the question that stirred up controversy for years: 'Is Brooklyn still in the league?'"[56]

Controversy had been growing for some time about the Reds' decline in attendance and pressure was now being applied by Reds president and general manager Bill DeWitt, Sr., on the city fathers to build a new stadium. On the same day that Jimmy Cannon's scathing denunciation of the Cincinnati fans appeared in the *Cincinnati Enquirer*, the paper's sports editor Lou Smith ran a letter from a reader by the name of Ted Connally who had the following to say.

"Soon the Reds will move on to a more deserving city. Eulogies will be spoken and black headlines will stream across the front page of *The Enquirer* announcing the sad event. Dwindling attendance will be the official scapegoat.

"Cincinnatians will then be notified that double and triple the crowds are now viewing the Reds in their new city. Why not? Major League Baseball is a major attraction and the fans in the new city will be seeing the Reds in a first-class stadium. Of this you can be sure. Nothing less will be settled for. Why then should we in the Queen City [Cincinnati] settle for anything less."[57]

Also on Wednesday night, September 30, the San Francisco Giants edged the Houston Astros, 2–1, in 11 innings. Mathematically, the Giants still had a slim chance to win the pennant.

The Giants won the game played at Candlestick Park in the 11th when with two outs the Astros made two critical errors. Tom Haller walked and moved to second on a single by Orlando Cepeda. Duke Snider was then sent up to pinch hit and was safe on an error. Jim Davenport followed by hitting a ground ball to Eddie Kasko at third. However, Kasko fumbled the ball, allowing Haller to score the winning run.

National League Standings
(top four teams), October 1, 1964

Team	Won	Lost	Pct.	G.B.	Games Remaining
St. Louis	92	67	.578	—	3
Cincinnati	91	68	.573	1	3
Philadelphia	90	70	.563	2½	2
San Francisco	88	70	.557	3½	4

In fact, with just four days remaining in the season, a four-way tie for the 1964 National League Pennant was possible. What would have to happen is that St. Louis would have to lose their final three games with New York. Cincinnati would have to beat Pittsburgh on Thursday and then lose both games with Philadelphia. Finally, San Francisco would have to win its four remaining games, one with Houston and three with Chicago. If this scenario occurred, all four teams would wind up with identical final records of 92–70. However, National League president Warren Giles was only making plans for a three-team playoff schedule. On the afternoon of October 1 in the National League office in the Carew Tower in Cincinnati, Giles would conduct a three-team drawing to determine the schedule.

Invited to participate were representatives from the Cardinals, Reds and Phillies. Each team would draw a number and then the number would correspond to the pre-developed schedule that follows.

Team 1 plays team 2 on the home grounds of team 1.

Team 2 plays 3 on the home grounds of team 1.

Team 3 plays 1 on the home grounds of team 3.

If all three, at that point have won one game and lost one, lots again are drawn to designate the teams by numbers and the same schedule is resumed until two teams have lost two games.

If after the first three games any team is eliminated, lots shall be drawn to determine the site of the first game between the remaining teams. If a fifth game is required, the visiting team in game 4 will select the site for game 5, the final game.

Giles stated that in the event that a four team playoff still remained a possibility on Friday, October 2, then a procedure for that playoff would be determined then.

If this all sounds bizarre, it does not hold a candle to the scheme cooked up by Giants official Al Rosen and sold to the other clubs in 1981. The season was shortened by a 50-day strike from June 12 through August 10 by the Major League Players Association. Therefore, the owners were looking for a way to salvage the season and stimulate revenues. So Rosen became the chief architect of a cheesy method to provide a format for the Major League Divisional Championship Series games.

In that scenario the season was divided into two halves, with each team that was in first place in their division when the strike occurred (June 12) being declared the divisional champion for the first half of the season. Subsequently, when the season resumed after the strike was settled (August 10), all won-lost records would begin again at zero-zero and the team that was in first place at the end of the second half of the season would be declared the winner for that period. This provided an extra tier of playoff games where the two teams from the same division played a five-game series to determine the Division Champion.

According to later analysts, "The extra tier of playoffs proved disastrous for the Reds, who finished the first half with a 35–21 record, one-half game behind Los Angeles, and ended the second half with a 31–21 record, 1½ games behind Houston. While the Dodgers (63–47) and the Astros (61–49) would up battling for the Western Division crown and a berth in the National League Championship Series, the Reds sat at home—despite compiling the majors' top overall mark in '81, 66–42."[58]

The St. Louis Cardinals were idle on Thursday, October 1, as they waited to begin their three-game, do-or-die series with the New York Mets at Busch Stadium. However, in order to keep Cardinal fans totally up-to-date on the tight pennant race, radio station KMOX announced that Harry Caray and Jack Buck would travel to Cincinnati and broadcast the Reds-Pirates game live back to St. Louis.

Earlier in the day, Danny Murtaugh had announced he was resigning as manager of the Pittsburgh Pirates "because of health reasons, effective at the end of the 1964 season." The popular Murtaugh had been manager of the Pirates since 1957 and had guided the team in 1960 to its first National League Pennant in 33 years (since 1927) and first World Championship since 1925. However, it was announced by Pirates general manager Joe E. Brown that Murtaugh would remain with the Pirates' organization in an administrative capacity, doing scouting work and work for the club's minor league farm teams.

On Thursday night, October 1, the Cincinnati Reds redeemed themselves by finally scoring a run after 34 scoreless innings and then going on to post a stunning victory over the Pittsburgh Pirates, 5–4. The Cincinnati fans, however, found no redemption in their lack of support for the Reds. Even after being chastised in the press earlier in the day, a pitiful showing of only 7,081 fans were on hand at Crosley Field to witness the team's climb back to within one-half game of the league lead with just two games remaining.

Leading the Reds to their 5–4 triumph was reserve catcher Jim Coker with three hits. Coker was starting in place of injured catcher Johnny Edwards. In the second inning Coker singled off Pirates starting pitcher Joe Gibbon to end the Reds' 34-inning runless streak. The second run came in on a wild pitch by Gibbon. Then in the fourth inning Coker doubled off the left-field screen and scored, to put the Reds ahead 3–1. Finally in the sixth he hit a towering home run off Pirate reliever Steve Blass that broke a 3–3 deadlock, putting the Reds ahead, 4–3.

However, the Pirates kept scrapping for the lead. Dick Schofield drove the Pirates' first run home with a double in third to make the score 2–1 Reds. In the fifth Roberto Clemente drove in two runs with a single to knot the score at 3–3. Finally Bill Virdon drove home a run in the seventh to make the score 5–4 Reds.

The final Reds run had come in the seventh when Vada Pinson tripled off Richie Sisk and Frank Robinson then drove him in with a double. Bob Purkey had started for the Reds and gave up in the fourth to Joe Nuxhall (9–8), and Sammy Ellis finished up the final two innings for the Reds. Steve Blass (5–8), the second of four Pittsburgh pitchers(Gibbon, Blass, Sisk, Face), took the loss for the Pirates.

Jim Coker, the star of the game, was playing in his 10th game with the Reds since joining the team in late August, after having previously played during 1964 with St. Louis, Milwaukee and Denver.

On the morning of October 2, 1964, the *New York Times* summarized the previous night's game in Cincinnati with the following comments:

"In a short but sloppy game before 7,081 fans at ugly little Crosley Field, the Reds snapped a 34-inning scoreless streak and put themselves back in the pennant race.

"The statistical drama of teams coming down to the wire in the traditional run for the flag is further complicated here at Crosley Field by human drama.

"Fred Hutchinson, the Reds manager is gravely ill, sitting on the sidelines. Danny Murtaugh, the Pittsburgh manager, announced his retirement Wednesday night because of ill health.

"But hardly anybody comes to the ball park.

"An hour before game time there were only a few hundred fans scattered on the Red lower-deck seats and the green upper-deck seats. There were 12 persons in the bleachers. The crack of fungo bats was drowned out by the roar of traffic along Route 75 directly behind center-field fence.

"It is not a pretty ball park, with its dirty-white facade like some unpleasant public building and the weak but glaring lights pick up the scuffs and patches on a blotchy green field.

"The Reds management has ordered a rush supply of a chemical spray to turn the scorched earth green should the Reds win the pennant and their World Series games be televised in color."[59]

The Reds' win on Thursday night moved them back to within one-half game of the league-leading Cardinals.

In the game witnessed by only 3,350 fans at Candlestick Park, the Giants beat the Colts, 6–3, as Juan Marichal (21–8) won his 21st game of the year, going the distance in a shaky but effective start. For the Giants, Willie Mays, Willie McCovey and Tom Haller each drove in two runs, handing Chris Zachary (0–1) his first loss of the season.

However, it was not yet curtains for the San Francisco Giants. After they had defeated Houston Thursday night, they still had a remote chance to tie for the pennant, with three games remaining with the Cubs.

National League Standings
(top four teams), October 2, 1964

Team	Won	Lost	Pct.	G.B.	games to play
St. Louis	92	67	.579	—	3
Cincinnati	92	68	.575	½	2
Philadelphia	90	70	.563	2½	2
San Francisco	89	70	.560	3	3

On October 1 in Cincinnati, National League president Warren Giles flipped the same coin used to decide the playoff site between the 1962 Dodgers and Giants to determine the parings in the event of a 1964 playoff. There were six playoff possibilities—two 2-team playoffs, three 3-team playoffs, and one 4-team playoffs.

Cincinnati Reds president and general manager Bill DeWitt won the first flip of the coin. DeWitt chose to open the playoffs against the St. Louis Cardinals in Cincinnati, should these two teams prevail. Giles had represented the Cards in the coin toss.

The Philadelphia Phillies' general manager John Quinn won the second coin toss for a two-team playoff scenario and also chose to open at home if the Phillies wound up in a tie with the Cardinals.

The two-team playoffs would be decided by a best-two-out-of-three-game series.

Then the three-way playoffs pairings were determined by drawing sticks. As an example of this scenario, the Cardinals, Phillies and Giants figure in one. In the second scenario, the Cardinals, Reds and Phillies in another; yet in a third one, the Cardinals, Reds and Giants.

To demonstrate how the three-team playoffs would have worked, in the first scenario the Cardinals would have played the Phillies at Philadelphia. Then the Cardinals would host the Giants. The Giants in turn would host Philadelphia. Then if one of the teams had not lost twice at the end of the round, lots would be drawn to determine where the round-robin would resume, and then play would continue until a team was eliminated with two loses.

If a four-way playoff were necessary, San Francisco would play at Cincinnati and St. Louis at Philadelphia in a two-out-of-three-game series. The winners of those series would draw lots for the site of the final series.

Also, NBC announced that if there were a two-way playoff between the Cardinals and Reds, the network would televise it.

Finally on October 1, the Los Angeles Dodgers announced that they had released coach Leo Durocher at his own request.

"Dodgers general manager B.J. "Buzzie" Bavasi said that Durocher had come to him some weeks ago and asked permission to negotiate for a managerial spot. Bavasi said he got the impression that St. Louis was involved in the picture."[60]

"I can't say with whom I'm talking," Durocher commented. "It's still in the talking stage. There might be something more definite within the next two days."[61]

Durocher, who had managed in Brooklyn and New York, winning a World Championship with the Giants in 1954, was brought back into baseball by the Dodgers in 1961 after he had publicly charged that there was a conspiracy to keep him out.

While the Dodgers were giving Durocher his release, they decided to clean house and fired all their other 1964 coaches, including Peter Rieser, who had a heart attack early in the 1964 season, Joe Becker and Gregg

Mulleavy. Replacing the above would be Jim Gilliam, Danny Ozark, Preston Gomez and Harold "Lefty" Phillips.

Gilliam, after playing for 11 years in Brooklyn and Los Angeles, would become the Dodgers' first African American coach. Subsequently Gilliam would become the third Negro coach in the history of Major League Baseball, following Gene Baker for the Pittsburgh Pirates and Buck O'Neil for the Chicago Cubs.

Danny Ozark had managed the Dodgers' farm club in Spokane during the 1964 season, Preston Gomez had managed at Richmond, and Lefty Phillips had been a Dodger scout.

X

The Final Weekend

After handing the Philadelphia Phillies their 10th straight defeat on Wednesday night, Johnny Keane gave the Cardinals a day off to rest on Thursday as they waited for the New York Mets to arrive from Milwaukee to begin the final series of the regular season.

When the Mets did arrive in St. Louis late on Thursday night, they arrived without four regular players, Ron Hunt, Chris Cannizzaro, Larry Bearnarth and Tracy Stallard. All four players were back in New York with injuries.

Although the Mets had already lost 108 games in the 1964 season, including the last eight in a row, while the Cardinals had won 92, including the last 8 games in a row and the Cards were ahead in the season series with the Mets, 10 to 5, Johnny Keane declared that he was taking absolutely nothing for granted.

"We walk out there even," said Keane. "It doesn't make any difference what's written on their uniforms—Milwaukee, Cincinnati, New York."[1]

"Yes, we're confident—but not over-confident. And I wouldn't mind carrying an 11–game streak into the [World] Series if we get there."[2]

Keane's pitching rotation for the crucial series was exactly what he had hoped for. In the opening game on Friday night he would send fastballing, 18–game winner Bob Gibson to the mound, then on Saturday he would follow with Ray Sadecki and wrap up the season on Sunday with Curt Simmons.

On Friday night, October 2, a crowd of 19,019 fans turned out at Bush Stadium to see if the Cardinals could come a step closer to clinching the pennant. However, the outcome of the 1964 pennant race was kept further in doubt as Casey Stengel sent left-hander Al Jackson (11–16) out to oppose Bob Gibson (18–12) and he got the job done in magnificent style, throwing a five-hit shutout against the Red Birds and beating them, 1–0.

The victory for the Mets was their 52nd of the season and set a new franchise record. New York scored the only run of the game in the third when George Altman singled off Gibson, sole second base and went on to third on an infield hit. Ed Kranepool then followed with a single and Altman came across the plate with the only run that the Mets needed.

Al Jackson was in command most of the way and only allowed two hits through the first seven innings. Things did get tense, though, in the bottom of the 8th with two outs, when Johnny Keane sent Ed Spiezio up to pinch hit for Bob Gibson and he singled. At that point Dale Maxvill was sent in to run for Spiezio. Curt Flood followed with a liner to right field and Maxvill chugging full steam rounded second, ignored a stop signal from third-base coach Vern Benson and slid safely into third. Flood held at first.

Then Lou Brock hit a hard grounder directly to Roy McMillan at shortstop that in almost all cases would have been the third out. However, umpire Ed Vargo had taken up his position between the pitcher's mound and second base and the ball bounded off him, despite a quick lunge to avoid it, and rolled into short left field.

As the ball struck Vargo, Maxvill crossed the plate. However, he was ordered back to third. The regulation covering the play was that had the ball struck the umpire beyond the infield it would have been considered in play. However, since the ball struck Vargo before McMillan had a chance to make a play on the ball, it was ruled dead. Nonetheless, Brock was awarded a single and took first base, Flood was now on second and Maxvill was on third again with two outs.

Dick Groat then came up to bat and Joe Christopher, playing in right field, moved over closer to the line. Subsequently Groat lined the ball to right and Christopher made a running catch to end the Cardinals' threat.

While the Cardinals suffered a defeat in the first game of the series with the Mets, they maintained their one-half game lead over Cincinnati as the Reds lost to the Phillies, 4–3.

At Crosley Field on Friday, October 2, the Reds fans finally showed up, 25,228 of them in all, and they were witness to a wild and memorable game that saw the home team lose, but also a game that remains widely controversial with baseball historians to this very day. The starting pitchers were Chris Short (17–9) for the Phillies and Jim O'Toole (17–7) for the Reds.

In the bottom of the first inning the Reds started quickly on Short. Pete Rose led off with a walk, then was sacrificed to second by Chico Ruiz and then to third by Vada Pinson. Frank Robinson then doubled down the right-field line, scoring Rose to make the score 1–0 Reds.

In the Reds' half of the fourth with Vada Pinson on second and Frank

Robinson on first, Deron Johnson came to the plate. Johnson then lined the ball to deep left field. Both Pinson and Robinson believed that it was impossible for the ball to be caught and took off running. However, the Phillies' rookie left-fielder Alex Johnson was off at the crack of the bat, raced up the terrace and caught up with the ball, making a spectacular over-the-shoulder catch. As Pinson and Robinson attempted a hasty retreat to second and first, Johnson wheeled around and threw a bullet to the relay man, shortstop Bobby Wine, who in turn tossed it to Tony Taylor, doubling-up Pinson at second. Robinson had not yet gotten back to first and Taylor threw to Vic Power at first, completing the triple play.

The fact that Pinson and Robinson had taken off when Deron Johnson smashed the ball to left was not a hit-and-run play, or a sudden impulse on the part of the base runners. Their action was in fact based on a scouting report the Reds had gotten on Alex Johnson, which according Reds interim manager Dick Sisler stated, "that he's not a good outfielder, that he didn't have good hands."[3]

Alex Johnson was, however, a bit more confident in his ability. "I was pretty sure I'd get it after I got up the hill [left field terrace]," said Alex. "I kept track of it pretty good."[4]

Short and O'Toole continued their mound duel into the bottom of the 6th with the score 1–0 Reds. Then the Reds scored two more runs as a result of a double steal by Chico Ruiz and Vada Pinson that was aided with two errors on the play by Richie Allen and Bobby Wine, to make the score 3–0 Reds.

With one out in the bottom of the seventh, controversy entered the game when Phillies starter Chris Short hit the Reds' Leo Cardenas between the shoulders with a curve ball. Immediately the outraged Cardenas started toward the mound with his bat in hand. Clay Dalrymple, the Philadelphia catcher, quickly restrained Cardenas as Jim Coker and Frank Robinson disarmed Cardenas, taking the bat away, while the umpires blocked off Short from accepting the challenge. All at once both benches emptied and Phillies and Reds players began to mingle on the field, although no punches were thrown.

Soon order was restored and Short was relieved by Ed Roebuck, who quickly got Jim Coker to hit into an inning-ending double play.

Entering the top of the eighth with a 3–0 lead, Jim O'Toole had only allowed three hits. Then Frank Thomas was sent up to pinch hit and looped a single into short center field. According to *Cincinnati Post* sportswriter Earl Lawson, "a still pouting Cardenas made only a half-hearted attempt to catch the ball."[5]

John Briggs was sent in to run for Thomas and O'Toole then walked

Cookie Rojas. With runners on first and second, Tony Taylor singled to center, scoring Briggs to make the score 3–1 Reds. Dick Sisler then replaced O'Toole with Billy McCool. McCool quickly fanned Johnny Callison for the second out, but Richie Allen followed with triple to right, scoring Rojas and Taylor to tie the score at 3–3. Alex Johnson then put the Phillies ahead when he lined a single over second, scoring Allen to make the score 4–3, Phillies.

Jack Baldshun came on to pitch the 8th and 9th for the Philadelphia and shut the Reds down. Philadelphia had finally ended its losing streak at 10 games.

Ed Roebuck (5–3) was credited with the win although he faced just one batter, and Billy McCool (6–5) was the losing pitcher.

The defeat was costly for the Reds and came suddenly after they seemed to have the game in the bag. Instead of being in first place by one-half game with one game to go, they were still one-half game behind the Cardinals with one game to go. Furthermore, on the verge of eliminating the Phillies, they had permitted them to remain alive in the pennant race.

Throughout the ensuing decades the debate has continued on how much effect the irrational behavior of Leo Cardenas had on suddenly arousing the Phillies from the monumental ten-game sleep. Also, the controversy continues on what was the extent of the impact of Cardenas' alleged loafing on the ball hit to short center by Frank Thomas in the 8th?

In the Reds' clubhouse following the game, tempers flared. Sisler, upon entering his office, took a swift kick at a chair. Reporters in the hall could hear violent arguing and a lot of commotion.

Reds starter Jim O'Toole felt that the actions of Leo Cardenas had aroused the Phillies and cost the Reds the game.

"An infuriated O'Toole went berserk, grabbing Cardenas in the club-house and flinging him across the room. Cardenas then grabbed an ice pick and went after O'Toole before being restrained by 6–4, 220–pound Joey Jay. 'If there's gonna be any fighting,' Jay said, 'it's not going to be with an ice pick.'"[6]

The clubhouse door had been locked during the fireworks and shortly it was open and interim manager Dick Sisler emerged to downplay the clubhouse frustrations with the press.

"Of course they took it tough. Tempers go up a little. Guys blame each other. So I had to go in and cool them off. Although, I didn't leave any orders to lock the door."[7]

"It was nothing. Just forget it," continued Sisler. "In the heat of a pennant race like this, players say things before they think. It is a thing that has happened before elsewhere and will happen again. I went out and quieted the boys. We're a happy team, and I think we still can win."[8]

Still Sisler was uncertain that Cardenas' behavior might have motivated the Phillies, as he told reporters, referring to the Phillies' ten-game losing streak, "you don't wake up a sleeping dog."[9]

Over in the Philadelphia clubhouse the players were also discussing the Cardenas incident. When Cardenas came up to bat Gene Mauch had trotted out to the mound to talk with Phillie pitcher Chris Short. "He told me not to give him a good pitch," recalled Short.[10]

Immediately following the conference on the mound, Short plunked Cardenas in the back with a curve and for a brief period nothing happened. "I guess he made up his mind he was mad," said Phillies catcher Clay Dalrymple.[11]

"I heard him say to Chris, 'You so-and-so. I'm going to hit you with a bat.' So I turned around and grabbed him and said, 'You're not gonna hit anybody.' Then two other guys grab him [Reds catcher Jim Coker and outfielder Frank Robinson] and took his bat."[12]

The Reds and Phillies were now idle until the final game of the season on Sunday. Meanwhile, with both the Cardinals and Reds losing on Friday night, October 2, the San Francisco Giants seized the opportunity and kept themselves mathematically alive with a 9–0 win over Chicago.

Dick Ellsworth (14–18) started for the Cubs and took the loss, while Bob Bolin (6–9) went the distance for the Giants, pitching a three-hitter. Willie Mays and Hal Lanier both had four hits in the game and Tom Haller (16) homered.

National League Standings
(top four teams), October 3, 1964

Team	Won	Lost	Pct.	G.B.	games to play
St. Louis	92	68	.575	—	2
Cincinnati	92	69	.571	½	1
Philadelphia	91	70	.565	1½	1
San Francisco	90	70	.563	2	2

On Friday night prior to the Cardinals' 1–0 loss to the Mets, manager Johnny Keane had been offered a new one-year contract with a substantial increase in salary. However, a Cardinal spokesman said, "Keane said he had so many things on his mind that he preferred to wait until the season was over, and Mr. Busch [Cardinal president August A. Busch, Jr.] agreed."[13]

One of the things that Keane undoubtedly had on his mind was the

pennant. On Saturday, October 3, at Busch Stadium, the Mets pounded
the Cardinals, 15–5. Consequently, once again the Reds were tied for first
with the Cardinals and the National League pennant race was in a dead
heat going into the final day of season.

The Cardinals' second defeat in less than 24 hours at the hands of
the cellar-dwelling Mets came quickly, as by the bottom of the sixth
inning they found themselves attempting to overcome a 15–4 deficit. The
Mets pounded eight Cardinal pitchers for 17 hits including five home
runs in the game. Ray Sadecki (20–11) started and took the loss for the
Cards, lasting only one inning and giving up five runs (four earned) on
five hits.

In the first inning Bobby Klaus, leading off for the Mets, hit a pop
foul that Cardinal catcher Tim McCarver dropped for an error. Then
Klaus hit a liner into left field that Lou Brock couldn't handle and Klaus
wound up on second by virtue of a two-base error.

New York then went on to load the bases against Sadecki and Jim
Hickman drove two in with a single. One out later Bob "Hawk" Taylor
drove in two more with a single off Sadecki to give the Mets a 4–0 lead in
the first.

However, the Cardinals came back immediately in their half of the
first. Mets starter Jack Fisher got by lead-off hitter Curt Flood, but then
followed with a walk to Lou Brock. Next up was Bill White (20) who hit
a long home run on the roof of the right-field pavilion. The Ken Boyer
(24) followed with a home run to make the score Mets 4, Cardinals 3.

In the 2nd the Mets' home run barrage began as George Altman (9)
led off with a homer into the right-field seats, to make the score 5–3 Mets.
Once again the Cardinals came back to score a run in the 2nd when Bill
White drove home another run with a single to make the score 5–4 Mets.

In the Mets' half of the 3rd Roger Craig, who relieved Sadecki in the
second, gave up the next home run to Ed Kranepool (10) who connected
with two on to make the score 8–3 New York. In the 5th Charlie Smith
(19) hit a solo homer off the fifth Cardinal pitcher in the game, Ron Taylor, to make the score 9–4 Mets.

The Mets' home run barrage was completed in the 6th when Bobby
Klaus (4) connected with two runners on and Joe Christopher (16) hit a
solo shot into the left-field bleachers. In all the Mets scored 6 runs in the
sixth to take a 15–4 lead.

The Cardinals did score again in the 8th when Charley James singled,
went to third on a single by Curt Flood and scored on a sacrifice fly by
Lou Brock to make the score 15–5 New York. The winning pitcher in the
game was Tom Parsons (1–2), the third Mets pitcher who had taken over

for Dennis Ribant in the fourth and proceeded to work the final 5⅓ innings in the game.

Following the game Johnny Keane kept the doors to the St. Louis clubhouse closed for a brief time, then opened them and talked with reporters.

"The situation is still in our hands," said Keane. "We've bounced back from shellackings all year. Baseball is a game of bounces. The clubs that didn't or couldn't bounce are not in the position we are. We have no excuses, we just got bombed. We changed pitchers. That's all you can do when you get hit hard."[14]

Asked if Bob Gibson might be in the bullpen Sunday, Keane replied, "He might."[15]

Over in the New York locker room a delighted Casey Stengel was also holding court with reporters. "We got fellows who can hit home runs, too. It's tough to catch those balls in the bleachers. We couldn't catch them in the first inning ourselves."

Casey was then asked if he thought St. Louis was choking up.

"No," said Stengel. "The third baseman doesn't choke up. The first baseman doesn't choke up. The shortstop doesn't choke up. The Cardinals just had a bad day. It looked like we had a whammy on them from Friday night."[16]

Casey Stengel also had a visitor to the Mets' clubhouse prior to the game, Heine Mueller who played in the Major Leagues for 11 years between 1920 and 1935 with the Giants, Cardinals and Braves and also played in the minors with Stengel at Toledo in 1927. "Any chance of getting a ball?" he asked Casey.

"Well, I'll tell you," Stengel said, "Baseballs are pretty scarce around here. Like we haven't hit one all year."[17]

Bing Devine, who had been forced out as Cardinals general manager on August 17 and was now a front office executive with the Mets, announced that he planned to be in attendance for Sunday's finale at Bush Stadium and be rooting for St. Louis. "You can't wipe out 35 or 40 years of rooting for your club just like that—before switching allegiance."[18]

Also on Saturday, October 3, it was curtains for the pennant hopes of the San Francisco Giants as they lost to the Chicago Cubs, 10–7. A small but loyal crowd of 10,417 turned out at Candlestick Park to witness the Giants' pennant hopes become shattered in the wake of a pair of three-run homers by the Cubs' Doug Clemens (3) in the 4th and Billy Williams (33) in the 8th.

The Giants had taken an early lead, scoring a run in the first inning, then advancing the lead to 2–0 in the third inning on Willie Mays' 45th home run of the season. However, led by Clemens' blast in the 4th, the Cubs scored five runs to jump out ahead 5–2 and they never looked back.

In the bottom of the ninth Willie Mays (46) attempted to keep the Giants alive as he homered for the second time in the game with Duke Snider on base off reliever Lindy McDaniel. However, McDaniel prevailed and closed out the game, dashing the Giants' pennant hopes. Willie Mays' two home runs in the game established a new National League record for that point in time as it was his 50th multiple home run game in his career, eclipsing the old mark of 49 set by Mel Ott.

Bob Buhl (15–14) started for the Cubs and got the win. For the Giants, Dick Estelle (1–2) started and took the loss. Estelle would only start one more game in his Major League career, winding up his two years in the majors the following year with a lifetime record of 1–2. Ironically, Doug Clemens, who hit the three-run homer that started the five-run Chicago rally in the 4th, had come to the Cubs on June 15 in the trade that sent Lou Brock to the Cardinals.

Although the Reds and Phillies were idle on Saturday, October 4, acting manager Dick Sisler—faced with a Reds team that had lost the last three out of four games, while scoring just eight runs in the last 43 innings, and that was not only slumping, but also feuding—ordered a midday one-hour-and-15-minute workout at Crosley Field.

Following the workout, Sisler made the shocking disclosure that he had selected John Tsitouris (9–12) to be his starting pitcher on Sunday against the Phillies. "If you remember," said Sisler, "he's the guy who started us off."[19]

Sisler was referring to Tsitouris' six-hit shutout that he pitched against the Phillies on September 21, which was the second victory in a string of nine the Reds tied together during their surge to the top of the standings.

When Sisler was asked why he had selected Tsitouris to pitch on Sunday, instead of Jim Maloney, he remarked, "Jim Maloney requires extra rest after pitching 11 innings Wednesday night."[20] Maloney was reported to have come down with a chronic, but not serious, problem with a shoulder muscle.

In addition, Sisler stated that he did not feel that Friday night's clubhouse incident would have any effect on the performance of the team on Sunday. "We got that all squared away at a meeting this morning. It was unfortunate, but that can happen in as hectic a race as this. No hard feelings. They know they've got a job to do."[21]

The Philadelphia Phillies took the day off, waiting for the Sunday finale. However, it was obvious that various players were already mentally packing their bags to go home. The remarks of shortstop Bobby Wine were typical as the Phillies ruminated about the passing season on Saturday:

"We would have breezed in with just a couple of wins in that stretch [10–game losing streak]. The way these other clubs are playing, we might have won even though losing our last five games out here, if we'd have taken a couple at home.

"The tough part about it is that our key guys may not put together years like this at the same time again. I'm talking about [John] Callison and [Richie] Allen and [Chris] Short and [Jim] Bunning. Now all their good work has been wasted. It's just a crime."[22]

Gene Mauch announced on Saturday that his starting pitcher for tomorrow's game would be Jim Bunning (18–8). Bunning would be starting with three days' rest for the first time since September 20.

After five months and 19 days, each team had played 161 games in the 1964 season and the pennant race was down to ground zero. The whole affair would be decided on the last day of the season.

National League Standings
(of top three teams), October 4, 1964

Team	Won	Lost	Pct.	G.B.
Cincinnati	92	69	.571	—
St. Louis	92	69	.571	—
Philadelphia	91	70	.565	1

Prior to the last day of the season, the batting and pitching leaders in the National League were the following.

Batting Average		Home Runs		RBIs		Pitching	
Clemente, Pitt.	.339	Mays, S.F.	46	Boyer, St.L.	118	Koufax, L.A.	19–5
Carty, Mil.	.329	Williams, Chi.	33	Santo, Chi.	114	Marichal, S.F.	21–8
Aaron, Mil	.328	Callison, Phil.	31	Mays, S.F.	110	O'Toole, Cin.	17–7
Torre, Mil	.322	Cepeda, S.F.	31	Torre, Mil.	107	Bunning, Phil.	18–8
Allen, Phil.	.314	Hart. S.F.	31	Callison, Phil.	104	Jackson, Chi.	23–11
Brock, St.L.	.314						

On Saturday, October 3, the American League pennant race came to a conclusion as the New York Yankees defeated the Cleveland Indians, 8–3, and won their 29th pennant and 5th straight under three managers dating back to 1960. This time it was rookie manager Yogi Berra who had piloted the Yankees home with a record of 99–61 going into the final game of the season.

Mayo Smith, a former manager for the Philadelphia Phillies and Cincinnati Reds, had been scouting the St. Louis Cardinals for the Yankees and was of the opinion that the Cards, if they prevailed in the National League, could keep the Bronx Bombers plenty busy in the World Series.

"The Dodgers had better pitching a year ago than the Cards," said Smith, who performed the same cloak-and-dagger function on Los Angeles prior to the '63 Series. "But otherwise the Cardinals have the better team in every department."

"I would say that it would be a good series," Smith went on, "because the Cards are moving. They have momentum. The Yankees have nobody in their bullpen to match [Barney] Schultz's consistency. He's done a helluva job for them. He could be the difference."[23]

On Sunday, October 4, the St. Louis Cardinals' pennant hopes hung on the left arm of 35-year-old pitcher Curt Simmons, whom Johnny Keane had selected to start the final game of the season.

In 1962 on the last day of the season Simmons, pitching for the Cardinals, had beaten the Los Angeles Dodgers, 1–0, on a home run by Gene Oliver to force the Dodgers into a playoff with the San Francisco Giants. Now two years later he was going to attempt to keep the Cardinals out of a playoff for the pennant.

The irony is that a few weeks ago, Simmons was not sure that he would get the chance to see the World Series, much less be playing in it. "A month ago I was trying to get Phillies' World Series tickets," recalled Simmons. "A month ago? Heck, I was still trying to get them a week ago."[24]

Asked to reflect on his feelings about the collapse of the Phillies during the 1964 season in light of the fact that when Gene Mauch took over as manager of the team in 1960, Simmons, who had played 13 years in Philadelphia, was considered expendable and released, he remarked:

"I was very upset. I was out of a job. When you're released, you're at the end of the line. I'd just turned 31—in fact, I was 30 when they dumped me. Probably they wanted to get rid of old guys. Probably they wanted to get rid of Robbie [pitcher Robin Roberts] too, but [Phillies owner Robert] Carpenter stopped them.

"My arm feels good. Heck, when they released me I knew I had a good arm. It was just a matter of selling somebody else on the idea. You know, I feel for them [the Phillies' collapse] a little bit. I just hope it never happens to us like that. It would stay with you all your life."[25]

On Sunday, October 4, both the Philadelphia vs. Cincinnati game and the New York vs. St. Louis game were scheduled to begin at 1:30 P.M. However, Cincinnati was in the Eastern Standard time zone and St. Louis in the Central Standard time zone, so the Reds began their game at Crosley Field one hour before the Cardinals at Busch Stadium.

The large crowd of 28,535 were all in their seats well before the first pitch. John Tsitouris started for the Reds and Jim Bunning for the Phillies. For the first two innings the pitchers went head-to-head in a scoreless duel and the large partisan Reds crowd cheered every pitch Tsitouris made. Then with one out in the third, Tsitouris started coming in high with his pitches. That was the beginning of the end for the Reds.

Tsitouris walked Tony Gonzalez and Richie Allen followed with a double off the center-field wall. Acting manager Dick Sisler went to the mound, being cheered wildly by the crowd, and then ordered an intentional walk be issued to Johnny Callison.

With one out, one run in and two runners on base, that brought Wes Covington to the plate to face Tsitouris. Sisler's strategy immediately backfired as Covington drove a single into right field, making the score Phillies 2, Reds 0.

Sisler then yanked Tsitouris and replaced him with left-hander Joe Nuxhall and he fanned Vic Power for the second out. However, Tony Taylor then touched Nuxhall for a single, making the score 3–0 Phillies, before Nuxhall got the final out.

Billy McCool took over the mound duties for the Reds in the fourth and retired the Phillies in order. However, in the fifth he gave a lead-off home run to Richie Allen (28) high off the center-field fence, making the score 4–0 Phillies.

With one out in the fifth Joe Jay, the fourth Cincinnati pitcher, replaced McCool. McCool was so upset about being knocked out of the game that when he stormed into the Reds' dugout, he slammed the water cooler so hard that a pipe burst and a repairman had to be summoned to fix it.

Joey Jay finished up the fifth all right, but in the sixth he could not get anyone out. He capped his relief appearance by giving up a three-run homer to Richie Allen (29). For Allen it was his second of the game and landed high in the right-field bleachers. In all Jay had given up five hits and five runs in pitching two-thirds of an inning. Bill Henry, the fifth Cincinnati pitcher, came on to replace Jay and stifle the Philadelphia rally that had elevated the score to 9–0 Phillies. Meanwhile, Jim Bunning was on cruise control. Bunning had handcuffed the Reds' batters, permitting just three base runners through the first six innings.

In the seventh Bob Purkey became the sixth Reds pitcher. The Phillies clipped him for another run, making the score 10–0 Phillies as Tony Taylor hit a ground-rule double down the right-field line and came around to score on sacrifice flies by Clay Dalrymple and Bobby Wine.

By the end of the seventh, a large portion of the disappointed sell-out crowd at Crosley Field began quietly to leave the park. Purkey then pitched the eighth without any problems, then gave way to Sammy Ellis in the ninth, the seventh Reds pitcher.

Bunning (19–8) faced 12 batters in the final three innings without any trouble as he pitched a six-hitter (all singles). The win allowed Bunning to have at least one victory over every club in the National League during 1964. John Tsitouris (9–13) took the loss.

For the Phillies, their 10 runs in the game was the most they had scored since August and their most lopsided victory since April.

In the Reds' clubhouse a radio was tuned in to the St. Louis Cardinals game at Busch Stadium, and the game was down to the final innings. Cincinnati now needed a miracle in the presence of a three-game sweep of the Cardinals by the Mets.

At Busch Stadium 30,146 fans were hand as the Cardinals scored first in the game, taking a 1–0 lead after two innings. Going into the top of the fifth the score was 2–1 Cardinals. Then in the fifth the Mets scored two runs to take the lead, 3–2, and force Cardinal manager Johnny Keane, who was smelling victory, to relieve starter Curt Simmons with Bob Gibson.

Gibson, making his fourth relief appearance of the season, came on with one out and one man on. He proceeded to get Joe Christopher to fly out to Mike Shannon in right and then retired Jim Hickman on a tap in front of the plate to wipe out the Mets' rally.

The Cardinals then roared back, scoring three runs in their half of the fifth. Lou Brock led off with a walk from Mets starter Galen Cisco, and Bill White followed with a single. Ken Boyer then hit a double down the left-field line, scoring Brock to tie the score at 3–3. For Boyer it was his league-leading 119th RBI of the season.

At that point Casey Stengel relieved Cisco with Bill Wakefield. Bill White then scored the second run of the inning as he raced home on a ground-out by Dick Groat, making the score 4–3 St. Louis. Boyer held at second on the play and then scored on a single by Dal Maxvill, making the score 5–3 St. Louis. Jack Fisher came on to pitch for New York and got the final out.

In the sixth the Mets came back and got a run off Gibson to make the score 5–4 St. Louis. The Mets had actually loaded the base with a single by Hawk Taylor with one out, a walk to Ed Kranepool, followed by an intentional walk to Jesse Gonder after an infield out had advanced Taylor to third and Kranepool to second. Then Gibson followed with a walk to Bobby Klaus on a 3–2 count, forcing in the Mets' fourth run.

However, Gibson then got Roy McMillan to hit into a force play to end the inning.

In the bottom half of the sixth Willard Hunter became the fourth Mets pitcher, and the Cardinals exploded again for three more runs. With one out in the sixth Lou Brock doubled and scored on a home run by Bill White (21) over the right-field pavilion roof to make the score 7–4 Cardinals. For Brock, it was his 200th hit of the season. For White, it gave him 102 RBIs for the season. Ken Boyer then walked and scored on a double by Tim McCarver to make the score 8–4 Cardinals.

At about this time the fans at Busch Stadium saw on the scoreboard that the Phillies had beaten the Reds, and the crowd let out a thunderous roar, then littered the field with paper confetti.

In the eighth, with the Mets' Dennis Ribant on the mound, the Cardinals scored three runs again. Curt Flood (5) led off with a home run to make the score 9–4 St. Louis. Then Ken Boyer drew another walk and went to third on a double by Dick Groat. Then Tim McCarver doubled, scoring both Boyer and Groat to make the score 11–4 Cardinals.

In the top of the ninth with one out, Gibson, probably tiring from the four innings' work following his 1–0 loss to the Mets on Friday night, suffered some wildness and quickly walked Roy McMillan and Jim Hickman. Johnny Keane then summoned Barney Schultz from the bullpen to replace Gibson. He proceeded to strike out Charlie Smith, but the runners advanced on a passed ball. Rod Kanehl then singled in McMillan to make the score 11–5 Cardinals.

Cardinal president August A. Busch, Jr., was excited and screaming from his box, "Come on—let's go—get him out!"[26]

Then Ed Kranepool hit a pop foul off the third-base line and Tim McCarver raced out and made the catch for the final out, then raced toward Schultz and embraced him in a bear hug as the rest of the Cardinals team streamed out of the dugout to join in the celebration, while sheer pandemonium broke out at Busch Stadium at 4:37 P.M.

At that moment KMOX announcer Harry Caray began yelling on the air, "The Cardinals win the pennant, the Cardinals win the pennant," mimicking the famous victory chant of Russ Hodges on WMCA following Bobby Thomson's infamous home run in the 1951 National League playoffs between the New York Giants and Brooklyn Dodgers.[27]

Bob Gibson (19–12) got the win and Galen Cisco (6–19) took the loss.

Suddenly the Cardinals, who had not even been in first place the entire season until last Tuesday, September 29, had won the National League Pennant! For the Cards, it was their 10th pennant in the history of the franchise and first since 1946.

Johnny Keane shook Schultz's hand, then headed for the screen back of home plate, where he tossed a smooch to his wife Leia. Then he headed to the box of Cardinals president August A. Busch, Jr., for a handshake, then into the clubhouse for the celebration.

In the box, Busch was shaking hands with St. Louis Mayor Raymond R. Tucker while Mrs. Tucker joined in the crowd hysteria. Said Busch, "I'm whipped, but extremely happy."[28]

The *St. Louis Globe Democrat,* describing the excitement in the Cardinals' clubhouse, stated that it was like New Year's Eve had erupted early in St. Louis. Champagne was being poured over Bob Gibson and Roger Craig by jubilant rookie Dave Dowling, Carl Warwick was pouring the stuff over coach Red Schoendienst and Bob Uecker, while Julian Javier poured the bubbly over other teammates.

In the midst of the celebrating, former general manager Bing Devine visited the Cardinals' clubhouse to offer his congratulations to what many felt was the team that he had built into a champion. "It's been a series of conflict of emotions," said Devine. Asked if the Cardinals were going to pay him a bonus, he replied, "I got a bonus in thrills."[29]

Ken Boyer, the team captain, held a glass high with sparkling champagne. Boyer had been targeted for trading by former Cardinal general manager Frank Lane, when Devine took over in 1957.

"The big thing," he said, "I was looking up at the scoreboard and seeing that the Phillies were clobbering the Reds. That took the pressure off us. Our guys swung at good pitches and weren't overly anxious. And Lou Brock helped take off the pressure, too, with that great catch and his baserunning."

"Yes," Boyer continued, "this will be the first time I've played against my brother [Clete Boyer of the Yankees] in a World Series."[30]

Shortly thereafter, Stan Musial showed up in the clubhouse and gave Johnny Keane a hug.

For hours after the game, traffic was tied up outside of Busch Stadium with long lines of automobiles with fans honking horns. Then within an hour long, lines of fans began to form outside the stadium who planned to wait all night to buy World Series tickets when the ticket office opened at 9:00 A.M. Monday.

Back in Cincinnati there was a silenced and solemn air to the Reds' clubhouse.

"Sure, I'm disappointed and so are the players," said interim manager Dick Sisler. "But I told the players they have nothing of which to be ashamed. They can walk out of this clubhouse with their heads held high."[31]

Over in the corner of the Reds' clubhouse sat Reds manager Fred

Hutchinson, who was slowly losing his courageous battle with cancer. Sisler, nodding in Hutch's direction, said, "I just wish that we could have won the pennant for that gentleman over there."[32]

"I just wish," replied Hutchinson, "that the players could have won the pennant for themselves."[33]

Sisler continued his postgame news conference as Hutchinson began to circulate through Reds' clubhouse, shaking the hands of depressed-looking players. He wanted to say goodbye before he departed for his home in Anna Maria Island, Florida.

Bill Ford, a *Cincinnati Enquirer* staff writer, was witness to the players' saying their goodbyes to Hutchinson and remarked in his column the next day, "More than a tear slid down a face as the skipper's hand was clasped."

The press now began to grill Sisler on his reason for starting John Tsitouris rather than Jim Maloney in the game. Sisler said that Maloney had pitched 11 innings against the Pirates on Wednesday night. "He gives his arm a terrific pounding. We've learned that he needs more than three days' rest. The records will prove we are right. I conferred with Hutch and my pitching coach Jim Turner, and they agreed with me that Tsitouris was the pitcher I should use. But, the final decision was mine."[34]

Sisler, going to great pains in explaining why he didn't start Maloney, continued, "We were going to use him in extreme emergency only. After all, we did have to look to Monday in case of a playoff.[35]

Jim Maloney had a record of (9–2) from July 11 through the end of the 1964 season. The reluctance by Sisler to use Maloney in the crucial final game has continued to be debated by baseball historians for nearly four decades now. In the end analysis, Sisler's decision not to start Maloney is a classic case of putting the cart before the horse. Sisler may have blown the pennant worrying about who he would start in a possible playoff game the following day with the Cardinals, rather than concentrating on the task at hand.

Pete Rose attempted to sum up the Reds' disappointment. "Sure it's tougher this way," said Rose. "We lost two games we shouldn't have lost [Wednesday night's 1–0, 16–inning loss to the Pirates, and Friday night's 4–3 loss to the Phillies]. It was ours, I thought we were going to win it when we got into first place. I think we all got pennant fever. I think the fellas tried too hard. I wish we could have had another week on the road."[36]

The Philadelphia Phillies had wound up the season tied for second place with Cincinnati. A mood similar to that of the Reds' clubhouse prevailed in the Phillies' clubhouse, too.

Gene Mauch left the field and walked into the Phillies' clubhouse looking straight ahead. He sat down in front of his locker, lit a cigarette and began to address the press. "All I can say is, I wish that I did as well as the players did. They did a great job. That's all I've got to say."[37]

Mauch then got up and walked away from the reporters.

Later, when he was asked if his earlier words implied that he had done something wrong, he replied, "If I knew how it was going to come out, I might have done a couple of things different. When you manage the way I want to manage, you don't miss something by a game or two."[38]

Wes Covington then picked up the interview where Mauch left off. The clubhouse radio was broadcasting the game from St. Louis as he spoke. "It's not how much we lost by. It's the way we lost. You can't ask for a miracle."[39]

Like everyone else in the Phillies' clubhouse, Covington didn't have much faith in the Mets' beating the Cardinals for the third game in a row. The team dressed quickly and headed for home for Philly.

At San Francisco on Sunday, October 4, the Giants wound up the season in fourth place after being thrashed, 9–2, by the Chicago Cubs. In the game Willie Mays hit his 47th home run of the year for the Giants and Jimmy Stewart hit his third for the Cubs. Larry Jackson (24–11) went all the way to get the win. Gaylord Perry (12–11) took the loss.

In the sixth inning of the game, owner Horace Stoneham went to the Giants' clubhouse personally to tell manager Alvin Dark that he had been fired. In addition, Stoneham fired the entire Giants coaching staff.

In a press conference 30 minutes after the game, Stoneham remarked, "I believe that we can do a better job as far as the club's standing goes. We felt as early as June this year that we could do better. Then after our last road trip to Houston and Chicago, I decided to make a change."[40]

Herman Franks, 50, was named to replace Dark. He was offered a one-year contract at a salary of $35,000. Previously Franks had been a coach with the Giants and managed the Giants for three games in the 1958 season when Bill Rigney became ill.

Also following the game in San Francisco, veteran left-hander Billy Pierce announced his retirement from baseball after 17 seasons. Pierce said that he was now going to enter into an automobile dealer partnership in Illinois and Wisconsin. His record for the 1964 season was (3–0) and his lifetime record (211–152). He had pitched in the World Series with the White Sox in 1959 and with the Giants in 1962.

On the last day of the 1964 season in Los Angeles, a crowd of 13,824 fans at Dodger Stadium saw the Dodgers whip Houston, 11–1. Rookie John Purdin (2–0) got the win for L.A. with a little relief help from Ron Perranoski and Robert Miller.

Rookie Don Bradey (0–2) took the loss for the Colts. It was Bradey's 30th birthday and the only start of his one-year Major League career. In his 15 minutes of fame, Bradey lasted only two-thirds of an inning, giving up four hits and five runs; he walked two and struck out none.

Although the Dodgers had slipped in 1964 from defending World Champions to a 6th-place tie with Pittsburgh, the club still achieved a season home attendance mark of 2,228,754—although still 300,000 below the 1963 mark.

At Milwaukee the Braves beat the Pirates, 6–0. There were 10,079 fans at County Stadium and they saw Bob Sadowski (9–10) pitch eight innings of scoreless ball before Warren Spahn came on in relief to pitch the ninth inning and preserve the shutout.

Roberto Clemente did not play in the game. However, he was the 1964 National League batting champion with an avenge of .339, getting 211 hits for 622 at bats. It was Clemente's second batting championship, having previously won in 1961 with an average of .351.

At 8:30 P.M. the Phillies' chartered plane touched down at Philadelphia International Airport. Some 7,000 cheering fans were on hand to greet them. Some were carrying signs that read, "Welcome Home Phillies—You Played Like The Champs You Will Be in 65."

"We Love You Phillies," proclaimed another.

The first to deplane was manager Gene Mauch. "You know how I feel," said Mauch. "I feel like we should've won it. This is the only thing in my life that I thought I had a chance for that I didn't win."

Airport officials stated that general manager John Quinn had telephoned them ahead of the Phillies' flight arrival, requesting that any signs brought to the airport by fans that may have had a negative or derogatory message be banned.

Final National League Standings, 1964

Team	Won	Lost	Pct.	G.B.	1963 NL finish
St. Louis	93	69	.574	—	2
Cincinnati	92	70	.568	1	5
Philadelphia	92	70	.568	1	4
San Francisco	90	72	.556	3	3
Milwaukee	88	74	.543	5	6
Los Angeles	80	82	.494	13	1
Pittsburgh	80	82	.494	13	8
Chicago	76	86	.469	17	7
Houston	66	96	.407	27	9
New York	53	109	.327	40	10

1964 National League
Batting and Pitching Leaders

Batting Average		Home Runs		RBIs	
Clemente, Pitt.	.339	Mays, S.F.	47	Boyer, St.L.	119
Aaron, Mil.	.328	Williams, Chi.	33	Santo, Chi.	114
Torre, Mil.	.321	Cepeda, S.F.	31	Mays, S.F.	111
Allen, Phil.	.318	Hart, S.F.	31	Torre, Mil.	109
Brock, Chi./St.L.	.315	Callison, Phil.	31	Callison, Phil.	104
Santo, Chi.	.313	Santo, Chi.	30	White, St.L.	102
Williams, Chi.	.312	Allen, Phil.	29	Williams, Chi.	98
Flood, St.L.	.311	Robinson, Cin.	29	Cepeda, S.F.	97
Robinson, Cin.	.306	2 tied with	24	Robinson, Cin.	96

Wins		Wining Percentage		Earned Run Average	
Jackson, Chi.	24	Koufax, L.A.	.792	Koufax, L.A.	1.74
Marichal, S.F.	21	Marichal, S.F.	.724	Drysdale, L.A.	2.18
Sadecki, St.L.	20	O'Toole, Cin.	.708	Short, Phil.	2.20
Bunning, Phil.	19	Bunning, Phil.	.704	Marchial, S.F.	2.48
Cloninger, Mil.	19	Jackson, Chi.	.686	Bunning, Phil.	2.63
Gibson, St.L.	19	Simmons, St.L.	.666	O'Toole, Cin.	2.66
Koufax, L.A.	19	Short, Phil.	.653	Maloney, Cin.	2.71

The day after the season ended on Monday, October 5, the Philadelphia Phillies' team ticket sales office began returning fans' ticket requests for the World Series from the more than 30 bags of mail that had arrived at the Connie Mack Stadium office.

At the same time Robert R.M. Carpenter, Phillies president, and John Quinn, general manager, expressed their confidence in manager Gene Mauch's leadership, absolved him from any blame for the collapse of the ball club in the pennant race, and offered him a new contract with a substantial increase over the $40,000 salary he received for 1964.

Quinn, announcing the re-signing of Mauch to a new two-year contract, said, "Both Bob and myself think Gene's done a terrific job and we wanted him to know we felt that way. Bob said to me, 'I'd like to renew Gene's contract through 1966' this morning. I said fine, and we called Gene in and we tore up the old contract and Gene signed a new one."[41]

Gene Mauch had personally taken the responsibility for the Phillies' collapse and told everyone to "blame me."[42] With a new contract and vote of confidence from the Phillies' front office, Mauch expressed his gratitude and immediately left for St. Louis to attend the World Series.

In fact, the Philadelphia press was already blaming Mauch for the Phillies' collapse. The most notable criticism of Mauch as a manager surrounded his decision to pitch Jim Bunning and Chris Short the last couple weeks of the season with only two days' rest. Furthermore, that critique of Mauch's decision-making continues to be the most widely accepted reason for the Phillies' collapse to this very day.

In a retrospective interview in 1994, 30 years after the 1964 season, former Cardinals star Lou Brock put the blame squarely on Gene Mauch for the Phillies' collapse: "When you pitch two pitchers during the stretch every two days, .200 hitters become .400 hitters."[43]

Mauch, however, has never wavered from his defense of his pitching rotation strategy in the final two weeks. "I wouldn't do a thing differently. Not with that club. I don't think people really realize what our options were. Dennis Bennett was down. Ray Culp was down. Jack Baldshun was down. I knew I was going to manage the team again, and I was perfectly willing to take full responsibility."[44]

As for Reds acting manager Dick Sisler's questionable decision to pitch John Tsitouris in the final game of the season against the Phillies and withhold Jim Maloney for tomorrow in the event of a playoff game with the Cardinals, perhaps someone should have reminded him of the wisdom of Leo Durocher, who said about such circumstances, "You don't save a pitcher for tomorrow. Tomorrow it may rain."[45]

On Wednesday, October 7, the 1964 World Series began in St. Louis. The Cardinals defeated the New York Yankees, 4 games to 3.

Following the World Series, Yogi Berra was fired as manager of the New York Yankees and was replaced by his series rival, Johnny Keane.

With the departure of Keane, Red Schoendienst became manager of the Cardinals. Yogi Berra was hired as a coach by the New York Mets and reunited with his old boss and biggest fan, Casey Stengel.

On Monday, October 19, Fred Hutchinson formally resigned as manager of the Cincinnati Reds. Less than a month later, Hutch died on November 12 in Bradenton, Florida.

Notes

Chapter I

1. "I don't believe in calisthenics for baseball players…" From a monthly feature, "Talk to the Stars," published in *Sport* magazine, June, 1967, VOL. 43, NO 6.

2. "We're down only six weeks and that isn't long enough…" From an article by sports editor Lou Smith, published in the *Cincinnati Enquirer*, April 6, 1964.

3. "Sandy is concentrating on conditioning…" From an article by Neal Russo published in the *St. Louis Post-Dispatch*, April 14, 1964.

4. Ibid.

5. "Everyone knows that our club is short on power…" From an article by sports editor Lou Smith published in the *Cincinnati Enquirer*, April 6, 1964.

6. Ibid.

7. "I think we can win again because we've got the pitching…" From an AP article by Joe Reichler published in the *Daily Home News*, April 7, 1964.

8. "Chico has wider range in covering either side…" From an article by sports editor Lou Smith published in the *Cincinnati Enquirer*, April 11, 1964.

9. "That fellow deserves a lot of credit the way he battled…" From an article by Earl Lawson, published in the *Cincinnati Post*, April 10, 1964.

10. "He can get down to first base faster than anyone…" From *Hustle— The Myth, Life, and Lies of Pete Rose*, by Michael Y. Sokolove, Fireside, 1992.

11. "Don't send him to the minors, send him to a doctor." From an article by John Devaney published in *Sport* magazine, June 1967, VOL 43, NO 6.

12. "Mr. Bragan, you talk too much about Alou and Bailey…" From an article published in the *Cincinnati Post*, April 9, 1964.

13. Ibid.

14. Ibid.

15. "When we went to spring training in 1964…" From *50 Phabulous Phillies* by Skip Clayton and Jeff Moeller, Sports Publishing, Inc., 2000.

16. "Unless you can make a trade that can help you…" From an article by Joe Reichler published in the *Daily Home News*, April 7, 1964.

17. "As a final tribute to the passing of the Polo Grounds…" Extracted from an article by Arthur Daley published in the *New York Times*, April 15, 1964.

Chapter II

1. "There was a little extra reason for this one…" From a wire service article published in the *St. Louis Post-Dispatch*, April 14, 1964.

2. "I'm hoping to rejoin the team in time for the…" From an article by Earl Lawson published in the *Cincinnati Post*, April 13, 1964.

3. "His homer came on one of Spahn's screwballs…" From an article published in the *St. Louis Post-Dispatch*, April 15, 1964.

4. "Just the opportunity to play with a contender again…" From an Associated Press article published in the *Daily Home News*, April 15, 1964.

5. "I have been with a contender all my life except…" From a United Press International article published in the *St. Louis Post-Dispatch*, April 14, 1964.

6. "Maybe he'll be more content on the coast and will..." From a special to the *New York Times*, published April 15, 1964.

7. "It was the most eeriest feeling in my life to look down..." From *The Boys of Summer, the Video*, VidAmerica, Inc. #8020, 1987.

8. "The Mets called me three or four times. They cried that..." From an Associated Press article published in the *St. Louis Post-Dispatch*, April 15, 1964.

9. "The saddest day of my life was when I was sold to..." From *The Boys of Summer, the Video*, VidAmerica, Inc. #8020, 1987.

10. "You could manage a club sitting here..." From an Associated Press article by Jack Hand published in the *Daily Home News*, April 18, 1964.

11. "We have no curfew on this club..." From an Associated Press article published in the *Daily Home News*, April 21, 1964.

12. Ibid.

13. "He hadn't bothered to report it..." From an Associated Press article published in the *Daily Home News*, April 23, 1964.

14. "How's a guy supposed to feel, Notty?" From an Associated Press article published in the *Daily Home News*, April 24, 1964.

15. "So I made history..." From an Associated Press article published in the *Daily Home News*, April 24, 1964.

16. Ibid.

17. Ibid.

18. Ibid.

19. "There have been only two geniuses in the world..." From *Baseball Wit and Wisdom*, Running Press, 1992.

20. "Willie is just too brilliant an all-round player..." From an Associated Press article published in the *Daily Home News*, April 30, 1964.

21. Ibid.

22. "The injuries have hurt us..." From an Associated Press article published in the *Daily Home News*, April 28, 1964.

Chapter III

1. "The Giants have too many outfielders..." From a *Post-Dispatch* wire service article published in the *St. Louis Post-Dispatch*, April 15, 1964.

2. "I'll marry him." From *Great Sluggers* by Bill Gutman, Mallard Press, 1989.

3. "You better talk to your boy..."

From an article by Harry Jupiter published in *Sport*, June, 1967, Vol. 43, No. 6.

4. Ibid.

5. Ibid.

6. Ibid.

7. "Well, I suppose most of the club owners will be..." From an Associated Press article published in the *Daily Home News*, May 27, 1964.

8. "It is the position of the association that we have been..." From an Associated Press article published in the *Daily Home News*, May 27, 1964.

9. Ibid.

10. Ibid.

Chapter IV

1. "Gilliam's one man on our club who doesn't get..." From an article by staff writer Frank Finch published in the *Los Angeles Times*, June 4, 1964.

2. Ibid.

3. "I am only playing because Tony got a bad start..." From an Associated Press article published in the *Daily Home News*, June 4, 1964.

4. Ibid.

5. "Batting against Drysdale rates just behind..." From an article by John Patrick published in *Pro Sports*, November, 1965.

6. "Absolutely none. It's up to Walter Alston whether..." From an article by Sid Ziff published in the *Los Angeles Times*, June 5, 1964.

7. "I have been studying pictures in magazines of my..." From an Associated Press article published in the *Los Angeles Times*, June 5, 1964.

8. Ibid.

9. Ibid.

10. "Why, the way this guy is going he has..." From an Associated Press article published in the *Daily Home News*, June 5, 1964.

11. Ibid.

12. Ibid.

13. Ibid.

14. "Did he win it?" From an Associated Press article published in the *Los Angeles Times*, June 6, 1964.

15. "I didn't even know he could pitch..." From an article by John Bach published in University of Cincinnati *Horizons*, May, 2000.

16. Ibid.

17. "I've often thought back to the first

time I saw Sandy..." From an Associated Press article by Charles Maher, published in the *Daily Home News*, July 15, 1964.

18. "No human being ever threw harder than Koufax..." From an article by Maury Allen published in *Sport*, June 1967, Vol. 43, No.6.

19. "Sandy is a perfectionist..." From an Associated Press article by Charles Maher published in the *Daily Home News*, July 15, 1964.

20. Ibid.

21. Ibid.

22. Ibid.

23. "I asked him how things were going..." From an article by John Bach published in University of Cincinnati *Horizons*, May 2000.

24. "It was designed by Emil Praeger, who conceived..." From an article by staff writer Frank Finch published in the *Los Angeles Times*, June 6, 1964.

25. "We need outfield help and some hitting..." From an article by staff writer Neal Russo published in the *St. Louis Post-Dispatch*, June 15, 1964.

26. Ibid.

27. "My defense was pretty good, but that was playing..." From an article by Mike Eisenbath of the *St. Louis Post-Dispatch* published in *Baseball Digest*, December 1994, Vol. 53, No. 12.

28. Ibid.

29. Ibid.

30. Ibid.

31. "The Ernie Broglio-Brock trade is expected to be X-rayed..." From an article by staff writer Neal Russo published in the *St. Louis Post-Dispatch*, June 16, 1964.

32. "The worst mistake." From an Associated Press article published in the *Daily Home News*, April 7, 1964.

33. Ibid.

34. Ibid.

35. "We love you Burkhart." From an article by Gordon S. White Jr. published in the *New York Times*, June 21, 1964.

36. "I felt that Bunning himself sensed it early..." From an article published in the *New York Times*, June 22, 1964.

37. "We want Bunning, we want Bunning!" From an article published in the *New York Times*, June 22, 1964.

38. "I was aware I was pitching a perfect game..." From an article published in the *New York Times*, June 22, 1964.

39. Ibid.

40. "Oh, I'm happy," he said... "From an Associated Press article published in the *Daily Home News*, June 22, 1964.

41. Ibid.

42. "I was so excited I lost my sunglasses twice..." From an article published in the *New York Times*, June 22, 1964.

43. "No no-hitter is easy though..." From an Associated Press article published in the *Daily Home News*, June 22, 1964.

44. "However, I couldn't think of any..." From the wire services of *Philadelphia Inquirer*, June 22, 1964.

Chapter V

1. "I can see how he won twenty-five games..." From *Great Pitchers* by Gregg Scott, Mallard Press, 1989.

2. "During the past few days the Braves have..." From an article in the *New York Times*, July 5, 1964.

3. Ibid.

4. "At this rate no team will be able to match..." From an article by Arthur Daley published in the *New York Times*, July 12, 1964.

5. Ibid.

6. Ibid.

Chapter VI

1. "It's the damndest lineup card that's ever..." From an article by Arthur Daley published in the *New York Times*, August 8, 1964.

2. "Mine was a slider..." From an article by the *St. Louis Post-Dispatch* wire services, published in the *St. Louis Post-Dispatch*, August 8, 1964.

3. "I felt good out there, but I could feel this in..." From a Special to the *Inquirer*, published in the *Philadelphia Inquirer*, July 8, 1964.

4. "He beat us enough. I figured he owed us something." From an article by Associated Press sports writer Joe Reichler, published in the *Daily Home News*, July 8, 1964.

5. Ibid.

6. Ibid.

7. "This looks like the Phillies' year..." From a special to the *Inquirer*, published in the *Philadelphia Inquirer*, July 8, 1964.

8. "We're even." From an article by Joseph Durso published in the *New York Times*, July 8, 1964.

9. "The star of stars." From an article by Leonard Koppett published in the *New York Times*, July 8, 1964.

10. "I tell you I was just lucky..." From an Associated Press article published in the *Daily Home News*, July 8, 1964.

11. "Go get Callison, go get Callison, I'm no hero." From an Associated Press article published in the *St. Louis Globe-Democrat*, July 8,1964.

12. "Johnny Callison of the Phils put the issue out of..." From an article by Arthur Daley published in the *New York Times*, July 8, 1964.

Chapter VII

1. "We'll have the best defensive outfield..." From an article by sportswriter Jack Herman published in the *St. Louis Globe-Democrat*, July 9, 1964.

2. "I came down here with my intentions of..." From an interview recorded on "Hank Aaron—The Life of a Legend," narrated by Curt Gowdy, Fleetwood Records FCLPP3081, 1974.

3. "I don't want to be anything special or..." From *Great Sluggers* by Bill Gutman, Mallard Press, 1989.

4. "I'm not dodging the question, but I really don't..." From an article by sports editor Lou Smith published in the *Cincinnati Enquirer*, July 21, 1964.

5. "Unbelievable. I read about all the beating the Mets..." From an article by sports editor Lou Smith published in the *Cincinnati Enquirer*, July 22, 1964.

6. "He merely grazed me..." From an article by sports editor Lou Smith published in the *Cincinnati Enquirer*, July 23, 1964.

7. "I don't relish the idea of going to the bullpen..." From an article by sports editor Lou Smith published in the *Cincinnati Enquirer*, July 29, 1964.

8. "You never know about this game." From an Associated Press article published in the *Daily Home News*, August 30, 1964.

Chapter VIII

1. "There's nothing definite about his release..." From an Associated Press article published in the *St. Louis Globe-Democrat*, August 1, 1964.

2. "Between you'n me, hounding Fred Hutchinson about..." From an article by Murray Oderman published in the *Daily Home News*, August 16, 1964.

3. "We saw Hutch go from 220 pounds to 140 pounds..." From *Pete Rose: My Story*, by Pete Rose and Roger Kahn, Macmillan Publishing Co., 1989.

4. "We have a ball club that has a will to win..." From the recording "Go! Phillies Go!," narrator Ron Sherwood, American Record Guild 8801, 1964.

5. Ibid.

6. Ibid.

7. Ibid.

8. "We have trouble because we have so many Negro and..." From an Associated Press article by Joe Reichler published in the *Daily Home News*, August 5, 1964.

9. Ibid.

10. Ibid.

11. "Who's a little Howard Hughes-ish in his habits..." From an article by Murray Olderman published in the *Daily Home News*, August 16, 1964.

12. "Alvin Dark, a no-nonesense player who became,..." From *The Giants—Memories and Memorabilia from a Century of Baseball*, by Bruce Chadwick and David M. Spindel, Abbeville Press, 1993.

13. "I shouldn't be playing..." From an Associated Press article published in the *Daily Home News*, August 6, 1964.

14. "The AP is not running my life and Reichler is..." From an Associated Press article published in the *Daily Home News*, August 6, 1964.

15. Ibid.

16. "I'm probably the only guy who worked for Stengel..." From *The Greatest Baseball Players—from McGraw to Mantle*, by Bert Randolph Sugar, Dover Publications, Inc., 1997.

17. "Joe Torre is the hottest property in baseball today..." From an article by sports editor Lou Smith in the *Cincinnati Enquirer*, August 7, 1964.

18. Stoneham called the story "exaggerated and distorted..." From an Associated Press article published in the *Daily Home News*, August 7, 1964.

19. Ibid.

20. Ibid.

21. "Damnit, Earl, I'm so skinny it hurts just sitting down." From *Cincinnati Seasons—My 34 Years with the Reds*, by Earl Lawson, Diamond Communications, Inc., 1987.

22. "No one intentionally lets a ball go through..." From the recording "Go!"

Phillies Go!, narrator Ron Sherwood, American Records Guild 8801, 1964.

23. "The grass will be rolled up in Wharton like a carpet…" From an Associated Press article published in the *Daily Home News*, August 18, 1964.

24. "He didn't know; he'd never smoked it…" *From Baseball—An Illustrated History*, by Geoffrey C. Ward and Ken Burns, Alfred A. Knopf, Inc., 1994.

25. "We've got to score some runs…" From an article by Bill Ford published in the *Cincinnati Enquirer*, August 17, 1964.

26. Ibid.

27. "Think over the situation…" From an article by Bill Ford published in the *Cincinnati Enquirer*, August 16, 1964.

28. " I couldn't understand what was happening…" From *Pete Rose: My Story*, by Pete Rose and Roger Kahn, Macmillan Publishing Co., 1989.

29. Ibid.

30. "I had to drag my arm out of bed like a log…" From *Great Pitchers* by Greg Scott, Mallard Press, 1989.

31. "Durocher, you're a jerk…" From an Associated Press article published in the *Daily Home News*, August 18, 1964.

32. Ibid.

33. Ibid.

34. "After Durocher hit Hallsworth, another man walked…" From an article published in the *Los Angeles Times*, August 18, 1964.

35. "Until or at least near the end of the season." From an Associated Press article by Tom Pendergast, published in the *Daily Home News*, August 18 1964.

36. Ibid.

37. Ibid.

38. "It's been a frustrating year all round…" From an article by Sid Ziff published in the *Los Angeles Times*, August 20, 1964.

39. Ibid.

40. "I left the matter entirely in Berra's hands…" From an Associated Press article published in the *Daily Home News*, August 22, 1964.

41. "I prefer to be a starter…" From the recording "Go! Phillies Go!," narrator Ron Sherwood, American Records Guild 8801, 1964.

42. "We told Johnny that he could terminate his…" From an article by sports editor Lou Smith published in the *Cincinnati Enquirer*, August 30, 1964.

43. Ibid.

44. "How did Temple ever miss connecting with…" From an article by sports editor Lou Smith published in the *Cincinnati Enquirer*, August 30, 1964.

45. Ibid.

46. "It's going to be a gradual thing…" From an Associated Press article published in the *Daily Home News*, August 31, 1964.

Chapter IX

1. "When we went to spring training in 1964…" From *50 Phabulous Phillies*, by Skip Clayton and Jeff Moeller, Sports Publishing, Inc., 2000.

2. "It depends on how he feels…" From an Associated Press article published in the *Daily Home News*, September 1, 1964.

3. "Became ill at the game with Milwaukee and was helped…" From an Associated Press article published in the *Daily Home News*, September 2, 1964.

4. Ibid.

5. "The Giants have shrouded the name of the man who…" From an Associated Press article published in the *Daily Home News*, September 4, 1964.

6. "He was thinking about the future and he was learning…" From *Great Rookies* by Greg Scott, Mallard Press, Tarrytown, New York, 1989.

7. "I think I'll be here another day or two," From an Associated Press article published in the *Philadelphia Inquirer*, September 4, 1964.

8. "That was the best man I had," From an article by Frank Dolson published in the *Philadelphia Inquirer*, September 5, 1964.

9. "You're not trying to outsmart anybody…" From an article by Frank Dolson published in the *Philadelphia Inquirer*, September 7, 1964.

10. "I can catch if needed…" From an article published in the *Philadelphia Inquirer*, September 8, 1964.

11. "The Phillies have been hustling all season…" From an article by Allen Lewis, published in the *Philadelphia Inquirer*, September 9, 1964.

12. "A spokesman for the Phillies said a small cast…" From an Associated Press article published in the *Daily Home News*, September 10, 1964.

13. "Is willing to boost the TV-radio guarantee to the Braves…" From an arti-

cle published in the *Daily Home News*, September 12, 1964.

14. "He never mentions the pennant." From an article by Eileen Foley, *Philadelphia Bulletin* writer, Published by UPI in *Daily Home News*, September 13, 1964.

15. Ibid.

16. "After I'm in business for myself…" From an Associated Press article published in the *Daily Home News*, September 13, 1964.

17. "I don't expect those people to score on us,…" From an article by Frank Dolson published in the *Philadelphia Inquirer*, September 18, 1964.

18. Ibid.

19. "We're not shooting for anything but first…" From an Associated Press article published in the *Daily Home News*, September 17, 1964.

20. "I'm going to try…" From an article by Frank Dolson published in the *Philadelphia Inquirer*, September 18, 1964.

21. "No Spanish be spoken on the field." From an article published in the *Daily Home News*, September 20, 1964.

22. "The packed crowd which had been waiting since late…" From an article by staff writer Dennis M. Higgins published in the *Philadelphia Inquirer*, September 21, 1964.

23. "In those first 150 games of the 1964 season…" From *50 Phabulous Phillies*, by Skip Clayton and Jeff Moeller, Sports Publishing Inc., 2000.

24. "Leo is open for a managership…" From an Associated Press article published in the *Daily Home News*, September 22, 1964.

25. Ibid.

26. "Pennant?" said Rose. "How could we have been…" From an article by Frank Dolson published in the *Philadelphia Inquirer*, September 24, 1964.

27. Ibid.

28. "Take it over to Gene Mauch…" From an article by Earl Lawson published in the *Cincinnati Post*, September 23, 1964.

29. "Allen slides aggressively into second trying…" From an Associated Press article published in the *Daily Home News*, September 25, 1964.

30. "The Braves scored two in the top of…" From an article by Earl Lawson, published in the *Cincinnati Post,* September 26, 1964

31. Ibid.

32. "We'll take care of the Yankees." From the *New York Times*, September 26, 1964.

33. "I'll tell you. I was happy…" From the *Philadelphia Inquirer*, September 27, 1964.

34. "The magic number has at least temporarily…" From the *Philadelphia Inquirer*, September 27, 1964.

35. "Just before I went up , I started chewing tobacco…" From an article by Frank Dolson published in the *Philadelphia Inquirer*, September 28, 1964.

36. "We've got to do in five days what took Cincinnati…" From an article by Frank Dolson published in the *Philadelphia Inquirer*, September 28, 1964.

37. "You've got to feel sorry for them…" Ibid.

38. "I'm not saying for sure yet we're going to win…" From an article by UPI correspondent Milton Richman, published in the *Cincinnati Post*, September 28, 1964.

39. Ibid.

40. "The fighting Phillies have become the fading Phillies…" From an article by staff writer Allen Lewis published in the *Philadelphia Inquirer*, September 29, 1964.

41. "It's internal bleeding,"… From an article by staff writer Frank Dolson published in the *Philadelphia Inquirer*, September 29, 1964.

42. "Sorry sold out and closed." From an article by Red Smith published in the *Philadelphia Inquirer*, September 29, 1964.

43. "We certainly don't blame Alston for the terrible job…" From a United Press International article published in the *New York Times*, September 30, 1964.

44. "Casey isn't back with us…" From an article by Leonard Koppett published in the *New York Times*, September 30, 1964.

45. Ibid.

46. "He's pitched better games…" From an article by staff writer Frank Dolson published in the *Philadelphia Inquirer*, October 1, 1964.

47. Ibid.

48. Ibid.

49. "I don't want to beat them more than I do other clubs…" From an article by Neal Russo, published in the *St. Louis Post-Dispatch*, October 1, 1964.

50. "Now we've got guys who can run…" From an article published in the *New York Times*, October 1, 1964.

51. Ibid.

52. "I'd rather play anytime than watch

or listen..." From an Associated Press article published in the *Daily Home News*, October 1, 1964.

53. Ibid.

54. "Lined up in front of the Main Post Office at Seventeenth and..." From an article published in the *St. Louis Globe-Democrat*, October 1, 1964.

55. "Hutch hasn't second guessed me once." From the *St. Louis Globe-Democrat*, October 1, 1964.

56. "They talk about it in taverns. But they get the ball games..." From an article by Jimmy Cannon of the *New York Journal-American*, published in the *Cincinnati Enquirer*, October 1, 1964.

57. "Soon the Reds will move on to a more deserving city..." From a letter by Ted Connally published in the *Cincinnati Enquirer*, October 1, 1964.

58. "The extra tier of playoffs proved disastrous for the Reds..." From *"Baseball—A Doubleheader Collection of Facts, Feats & Firsts,"* by the Editors of the *Sporting News*, Galahad Books, 1992.

59. "In a short but sloppy game before 7,081 fans..." From an article by Robert Lipsyte published in the *New York Times*, October 2, 1964.

60. "Bavasi said Durocher had come to him some weeks ago..." From a UPI article published in the *St. Louis Post-Dispatch*, October 1, 1964.

61. Ibid.

Chapter X

1. "We walk out there even..." From an article by Joseph Durso published in the *New York Times*, October 2, 1964.

2. "Yes, we're confident—but not..." From an article by Jack Herman published in the *St. Louis Globe-Democrat*, October 2, 1964.

3. "That he's not a good outfielder..." From an article by staff writer Frank Dolson published in the *Philadelphia Inquirer*, October 3, 1964.

4. Ibid.

5. "A still pouting Cardenas made only a half-hearted attempt..." From *Cincinnati Seasons*, by Earl Lawson, Diamond Communications, Inc., 1987.

6. Ibid.

7. "Of course they took it tough..." From an article by staff writer Frank Dolson published in the *Philadelphia Inquirer*, October 3, 1964.

8. "It was nothing. Just forget it..." From a UPI article published in the *St. Louis Post-Dispatch*, October 3, 1964.

9. "You don't wake up a sleeping dog." From an article by staff writer Frank Dolson published in the *Philadelphia Inquirer*, October 4, 1964.

10. Ibid.

11. Ibid.

12. Ibid.

13. "Keane said he had so many things on his mind..." From an article in the *St. Louis Post-Dispatch*, October 4, 1964.

14. "The situation is still in our hands..." From an article by Neal Russo published in the *St. Louis Post-Dispatch*, October 4, 1964.

15. Ibid.

16. Ibid.

17. "Any chance of getting a ball..." From an article by Rick Koster published in the *St. Louis Globe Democrat*, October 4, 1964.

18. "You can't wipe out 35 or 40 years of rooting..." From an article in the *St. Louis Globe Democrat*, October 4, 1964.

19. "'If you remember,' said Sisler..." From an article by staff writer Bill Ford published in the *Cincinnati Enquirer*, October 4, 1964.

20. Ibid.

21. Ibid.

22. "We would have breezed in with just a couple of wins..." From an article by staff writer Allen Lewis, published in the *Philadelphia Inquirer*, October 4, 1964.

23. "The Dodgers had better pitching a year ago..." From an article by Rick Koster published in the *St. Louis Globe Democrat*, October 4, 1964.

24. "A month ago I was trying to get Phillies' World Series tickets..." From an article by staff writer Frank Dolson published in the *Philadelphia Inquirer*, October 2, 1964.

25. Ibid.

26. "Come on—let's go—get him out." From *Baseball's Greatest Pennant Races*, Major League Baseball Productions, Major League Baseball Home Video, 1994.

27. Ibid.

28. "I'm whipped, but extremely happy." From an article by Jack Herman published in the *St. Louis Globe Democrat*, October 5, 1964.

29. Ibid.

30. Ibid.

31. "Sure, I'm disappointed and so are the players..." From an article by Earl Lawson published in the *Cincinnati Post*, October 5, 1964.

32. Ibid.

33. Ibid.

34. Ibid.

35. "We were going to use him in extreme emergency only..." From an article by staff writer Bill Ford published in the *Cincinnati Enquirer*, October 5, 1964.

36. "Sure it was tougher, this way." From an article by staff writer Frank Dolson published in the *Philadelphia Inquirer*, October 5, 1964.

37. "All I can say is I wish I did as well as..." From an article by staff writer Frank Dolson published in the *Philadelphia Inquirer*, October 5, 1964.

38. Ibid.

39. Ibid.

40. "I believe that we can do a better job..." From a UPI article published in the *St. Louis Post-Dispatch*, October 5, 1964.

41. "Bob said to me, 'I'd to like to renew Gene's contract...'" From an article by staff writer John Dell, published in the *Philadelphia Inquirer*, October 6, 1964.

42. Ibid.

43. "When you pitch two pitchers during the stretch..." From *Baseball's Greatest Pennant Races*, Major League Baseball Productions, Major League Baseball Home Video, 1994.

44. "I wouldn't do a thing differently..." From *50 Phabulous Phillies*, by Skip Clayton and Jeff Moeller, Sports Publishing, Inc. 2000.

45. "You don't save a pitcher for tomorrow..." From *Baseball Wit and Wisdom*, Running Press, 1992.

Bibliography

Aaron, Hank, and Lonnie Wheeler, *I Had a Hammer: The Hank Aaron Story*, New York: 1992.

Chadwick, Bruce, and David M. Spindel, *The Dodgers: Memories and Memorabilia from Brooklyn to LA*, New York: 1993.

_____ and _____, *The Giants: Memories and Memorabilia from a Century of Baseball*, New York: 1993.

Clayton, Skip, and Jeff Moeller, *50 Phabulous PHILLIES*, Sports Publishing, 2000.

Lawson, Earl, *Cincinnati Seasons: My 34 Years with the Reds*, South Bend, Ind.: 1987.

Microsoft, *Complete Baseball—The Ultimate Multimedia Reference for Every Baseball Fan*, Microsoft Corporation, 1994.

Rose, Pete, and Roger Kahn, *Pete Rose: My Story*, New York: 1989.

Scott, Greg, *Great Pitchers*, Tarrytown, N.Y.: Mallard Press, 1989.

Sokolove, Michael Y., *Hustle—The Myth, Life, and Lies of Pete Rose*, New York: Fireside Books, 1992.

Sugar, Bert Randolph, *The Great Baseball Players*, Mineola, N.Y.: 1997.

Ward, Geoffrey C., and Ken Burns, *Baseball: An Illustrated History*, New York: Alfred A. Knopf, 1994.

Wolff, Rick, ed., *The Baseball Encyclopedia*, 8th edition, New York: Macmillan, 1990.

Index

Pepitone, Joe 186
Perez, Tony 9, 68, 144, 226
Perranowski, Ron 2, 7, 43, 66, 67, 90, 133, 138, 149, 183, 187, 208, 261
Perry, Gaylord 14, 54, 62, 63, 101, 108, 140, 171, 175, 200, 212, 217, 226, 261
Peterson, Cap 63, 85,
Philadelphia 1, 25, 27, 29, 37, 52, 55, 98, 147, 159, 162, 169, 180, 196, 199, 202, 218, 225, 244, 261
Philadelphia Athletics 21, 20, 66, 61, 111, 162
Philadelphia Bulletin 213
Philadelphia Eagles 54, 161
Philadelphia Inquirer 216, 219, 221, 227, 230
Philadelphia International Airport 219, 262
Philadelphia Phillies 3, 4, 5, 6, 10, 14, 15, 16, 25, 26, 29, 31, 35, 36, 37, 38, 41, 42, 44, 45, 46, 47, 48, 49, 51, 52, 53, 54, 55, 57, 58, 59, 63, 65, 66, 67, 68, 69, 70, 76, 77, 78, 79, 80, 81, 85, 86, 87, 88, 91, 92, 93, 97, 98, 99, 100, 101, 102, 103, 105, 106, 107, 108, 109, 115, 117, 119, 121, 127, 129, 130, 131, 132, 134, 135, 136, 137, 138, 139, 140, 141, 142, 143, 144, 145, 146, 147, 148, 150, 151, 152, 155, 156, 157, 158, 163, 165, 166, 167, 168, 169, 171, 172, 173, 174, 175, 177, 178, 179, 180, 181, 182, 183, 184, 187, 188, 189, 190, 192, 193, 194, 195, 196, 197, 199, 200, 203, 204, 205, 206, 207, 208, 209, 210, 211, 212, 213, 214, 215, 216, 217, 218, 219, 220, 221, 222, 223, 224, 225, 226, 227, 228, 229, 230, 231, 232, 233, 235, 236, 237, 240, 244, 246, 247, 248, 249, 250, 253, 254, 255, 256, 257, 258, 259, 260, 261, 262, 263, 264
Philips, Adolpho 233
Phillips, Harold "Lefty" 245
Pierce, Billy 153, 261
Pinson, Vada 9, 11, 23, 30, 31, 38, 39, 83, 90, 99, 105, 106, 131, 139, 141, 151, 164, 166, 172, 193, 197, 212, 220, 221, 222, 225, 228, 242, 247, 248
Pioneer League 85
Pittsburgh 1, 37, 53, 117
Pittsburgh Pirates 5, 10, 13, 15, 17, 21, 26, 33, 34, 41, 49, 53, 54, 55, 57, 58, 66, 68, 69, 74, 76, 77, 78, 79, 80, 81, 84, 86, 87, 88, 90, 97, 100, 103, 105, 106, 109, 110, 119, 127, 128, 131, 135, 136, 138, 139, 142, 145, 148, 151, 152, 153, 155, 157, 164,

167, 170, 172, 178, 179, 180, 181, 183, 184, 188, 190, 191, 193, 195, 198, 199, 200, 201, 203, 205, 206, 208, 209, 210, 214, 215, 219, 224, 226, 227, 229, 230, 231, 237, 238, 240, 241, 242, 243, 245, 260, 262
Pizzaro, Juan 137
Podres, Johnny 2, 7, 43, 44, 234
Pollet, Howie 37
Polo Grounds 3, 18, 19, 27, 32, 51, 52, 80, 111, 131, 168
Pompano Beach 5
Poulson, Norris 111
Power, Vic 209, 223, 248, 256
Powers, Dave 23
Powers, Johnny 167
Prager, Emil 77
Prince, Bob 183
Providence 91
Pryor, Paul 166
Puerto Rico 202
Purdin, John 261
Purkey, Bob 9, 10, 36, 56, 66, 99, 105, 140, 141, 157, 171, 187, 225, 226, 256, 257

Queen, Mel 23, 153, 154, 155, 199
Queen, Mel, Sr. 153
Queens (Flushing Meadow) 3, 18, 32, 33, 113, 150, 185, 226
Quinn, John 151, 173, 244, 262, 263
Quinones, George 178

Radatz, Dick 117, 120, 121, 123
Radovich, Bob 8
Ranew, Merritt 135
Rapp, Col. Barney (Reds Rooters Band) 22
Raynolds, John J. 56
Reading Road 201
Reed, Howie 187
Reese, Pee Wee 66, 161, 163
Reichler, Joe 164
Rhodes, James A. 22
Ribant, Dennis 175, 179, 214, 252, 258
Richardson, Bobby 119, 120
Richardson, Gordon 226, 235
Richert, Pete 204, 206
Richmond 245
Richmond, John Lee 91
Rickey, Branch 11, 74, 84, 136, 179
Rieser, Pete 244
Rigney, Bill 162, 261
Rixey, Eppa 127